HENRY CLAY ADDRESSING THE SENATE

GREAT DEBATES IN AMERICAN HISTORY

*From the Debates in the British Parliament on the
Colonial Stamp Act (1764–1765) to the Debates
in Congress at the Close of the Taft
Administration (1912–1913)*

EDITED BY

MARION MILLS MILLER, Litt.D. (Princeton)

Editor of "The Life and Works of Abraham Lincoln," etc.

IN FOURTEEN VOLUMES

EACH DEALING WITH A SPECIFIC SUBJECT, AND CONTAINING A SPECIAL INTRODUC-
TION BY A DISTINGUISHED AMERICAN STATESMAN OR PUBLICIST

VOLUME TWELVE

REVENUE: THE TARIFF AND TAXATION

With an Introduction by IDA M. TARBELL, L.H.D.
Associate Editor of the *American Magazine*

CURRENT LITERATURE PUBLISHING COMPANY
NEW YORK

CONTENTS OF VOLUME TWELVE

ILLUSTRATIONS IN VOLUME TWELVE

INTRODUCTION

SOME MORAL ASPECTS OF TARIFF-MAKING[1]

DIFFICULT as it would be for one to realize it who took up for the first time the present tariffs of the United States, they rest on a formula which, as it always has been understood by the majority of the people of the country, is not especially intricate or confusing. Put yourself back a hundred years or so, when the country was busy with agriculture and commerce and mining. We had an enormous advantage in these pursuits. We were at a disadvantage in manufacturing. To be sure, from the start we did a little. In the nature of things we would gradually do more, and what we did would be on a solid basis. But, obviously, only the born ironmaster, potter, weaver, was going to practice his trade in the new country with the foreigner importing goods cheaper than he as a rule could make them. And so we decided to encourage manufacturing by taxing ourselves.

The amount of the tax decided on was to be only enough to put our would-be manufacturers on an even basis with the foreigner. This meant what? By general consent it meant giving our people enough to cover the difference in the cost of labor. Plainly, Americans were not going to work for the same wages that Europeans did. There were too many ways in which they could earn more. The country was new and men could have land of their own on easy terms. Commerce called them, for, having

---

[1] Adapted from the author's book, "The Tariff in Our Times," published by the Macmillan Company, New York, 1911.

1

land, we were raising foods, and Europe and the Orient, worn and old and privilege-ridden, were crying for food. They could make everything we wanted, and far cheaper. They were eager to exchange. If we were to do our own manufacturing we were obliged to devise a scheme which would make the wages of operatives approximately equal to those which could be earned in our natural occupations. *Thus protection was not adopted for the sake of producing generous wages for labor. It was adopted because the rewards to labor in the new country were already generous and promised to be more so.*

There is another equally important point to remember, and that is that it was expressly understood that the duty was never to be prohibitive. It was to be one that would permit the man at home to compete with the man from abroad; no more. Sensible people have always agreed that we would injure ourselves if we allowed prohibitive duties, since they would *cut us off from the stimulus of competition and also from models.*

The old countries had been for centuries making the goods we wanted. *They knew how to do it. We needed constantly before us in our markets the educational effect of their work.*

There were few, if any, at the start to deny that this taxing of ourselves to establish industries was dangerous business, undemocratic, of course—probably unconstitutional—and an obvious bait to the greedy; but they comforted themselves with the gains which they believed would speedily result. The list was tempting:

1. We were to build up industries which would supply our own needs.

2. The laborers attracted into these industries were to make a larger home market.

3. We were soon to out-rival the foreigner in cost of production, giving the people in return for the tax they had borne cheaper goods than ever the Old World could give.

4. We were to outstrip the Old World in quality and variety—another reward for taxation patiently borne.

5. We were to over-produce and with our surplus enter the markets of the world.

Nobody pretended to deny that if it was found on fair experiment that these results were impossible in a particular industry the protection must be withdrawn. Otherwise it amounted to supporting an industry at public expense—an unbusinesslike, unfair, and certainly undemocratic performance.

But what has happened when the formula has not worked? Take the failure after decades of costly experiments to grow all the wool we use, to make woolens of as high a quality and at a price equal to those of the English. Fully sixty per cent. of the raw wool used in the United States is brought from other lands, and a tax of 11 or 12 cents is collected on every pound of it. Our high grade woolens cost on an average twice what they do in Europe. The fact is, the protective dogma has not, and probably never can, make good in wools and woolens. It is one of those cases where we can use land, time, labor, and money to better advantage. The doctrine of protection as well as common humanity and common sense orders the gradual but steady wiping out of all duties on everything necessary to the health and comfort of the people, unless in a reasonable time these duties can supply us better and cheaper goods than we can buy in the world market. That time was passed at least twenty years ago in wool, but Schedule K still stands. It is supported by an interpretation of the formula of protection, which, as one picks it out to-day, from the explanations and practices of the wool growers and wool manufacturers, is only a battered wreck of its old self. It ignores utterly the time limit, the "reasonable" period in which an industry was to make good. It ignores the condition that the duty should not destroy fair competition. Moreover, it stretches the function of the duty from that of temporarily protecting the cost of production to one of permanently insuring profits. The chief appeal of those who employ this distorted notion is not to reason at all, but to sympathy—sympathy for the American working-man. Call their attention to the inequalities of the duties on raw wool, and they will tell you of the difference in the labor cost of dress goods here and in England. Tell them the quality of our goods is deteriorating, and they will draw you a picture of the blessings of the American working-man. Tell them that the wool schedule has taken blankets and woolen garments from the sufferers from tuberculosis, who certainly need them, and they will tell you that "the American people are better clothed than any other people in the world and their clothes are better made."

Any one who has observed the life of the working-man on both sides of the Atlantic knows that wages, conditions, opportunities are vastly superior as a whole in the United States. It is a New World, with a New World's hopes. But it is only the blind and deaf who do not realize that the same forces of allied greed and privilege which have made life so hard for so many in the Old World are at work, seeking to repeat here what they have done there. The favorite device of those who are engaged in this attempt is picturing the contrast between the most favored labor of the United States and the least favored of Europe. It is a device which "Pig Iron" Kelley used throughout his career with utter disregard of facts. Mr. McKinley followed him. In the course of his defence of the tinplate duty he read, with that incredible satisfaction which the prohibitive protectionist takes in the thought that his policy may cripple the industry of another nation, an English view of the effect the proposed duty would have in Wales. "The great obstacle to tinplate making on a large scale in the States," said the article, "is the entire absence of cheap female labor." Mr. McKinley paused and said impressively, "We do not have cheap female labor here under the protective system, I thank God for that." And yet at that moment in the textile mills of New England, of New York, and of Pennsylvania, not only were thousands of women working ten, eleven, and more hours a day, because their labor was cheap, but thousands of *children* under twelve years of age were doing the same.

The average weekly earnings for 58 hours in cotton factories in 1907, a "boom" year in the industry, were: For the carding room, $7.80; for mule spinners, $12.92; for speeders, $10.62; for weavers, $10.38. In the woolen industry the picker received $8.00; the woman spinner,

$7.25; the man spinner, $12.91, and the weaver, $15.34.

If a man could make these wages for fifty-two weeks a year throughout his working life, if he had a thrifty wife and healthy children, his lot, if not altogether rosy, would be far from hopeless; he might even be able to realize the dream of a little home and garden of his own which lurks in the mind of every normal man, and which, in the case of the textile operative, is almost imperative if he is to have a decent and independent old age. For this man, however husky he may be at the start, however skilful a laborer, has always a short working life. There are few old men and women in textile factories. By 55 they are unfit for the labor. The terrible strain on brain and nerve and muscle has so destroyed the agility and power of attention necessary that they must give up the factory, where, indeed, for several years their output has probably been gradually decreasing. As almost all textile operatives are paid by the piece the wage will gradually fall off as dexterity declines. By 55, then, if not earlier, he drops out, picking up thereafter any odd job he may.

It is this short working life of the father, with the declining wage for years before it actually ends, that makes woman and child labor an essential factor in the solving of the problem of the textile family.

The protectionist who answers every criticism of his rates by conjuring a picture of "pauper labor" is equally conscienceless in his attitude toward the relation of protection to the two most disquieting industrial phenomena of our day, the increase in the cost of living and the multiplicity of corporations which aim to become and often are monopolies.

In recent years the problems of the operative have been complicated by the soaring cost of living. Almost everything he buys is higher in price, or, if he insists on a standard price, the article is poorer in quality. Take the very protected articles from which a manufacturing State such as Rhode Island draws its wealth. All of the 68,000 textile workers in that State must have clothes. Now the price of women's all-wool dress goods increased in Providence, the center of the industry, over 33 per cent. between 1891 and 1907. There was an increase in virtually all the cotton-warp goods, varying from 4 to 40 per cent. Underwear in which there was any mixture of wool cost a fourth more in 1907 than sixteen years before. Bleached muslin used for shirtings was 34 per cent. dearer. That is, their own industries are taking out of the textile operatives the increase in wages which this same period has seen!

No evil concealed in the doctrine of protection was ever more thoroughly advertised than monopoly. At every stage since Hamilton's time we have been warned that it waited us just around the turn. For the last twenty-five years, especially, we have seen it pour down upon us—an army whose ranks yearly grew thicker, stronger, and more cruel. This is the very army against which we have been cautioned for decades as waiting in ambush. There was a counter force provided, of course, for this waiting enemy—domestic competition. Now, we know what has happened to domestic competition in the last thirty years in this country. Freed from foreign competition—something which the doctrine never intended should happen—the home manufacturers have by a succession of guerilla campaigns, often as ruthless and lawless as those of wild Indians or Spanish freebooters, corralled industry after industry so completely that they could control its output and at once cheapen the quality and increase the price.

One of the most serious results of this distortion of the protective system is the kind of man it encourages: a man unwilling to take his chances in a free world-struggle; a man whose sense of propriety and loyalty has been so perverted that he is willing to treat the Congress of the United States as an adjunct to his business; one who regards freedom of speech as a menace, and the quality of his product of less importance than the quantity; one whose whole duty toward his working-man is covered by a pay envelope. This man at every point is a contradiction to the democratic ideal of manhood. The sturdy self-reliance, the quick response to the ideals of free self-government, the unwillingness to restrain the other man, to hamper his opportunity or sap his resources, all of these fine things have gone out of him. He is an unsound democratic product, a very good type of the creature that privilege has always produced.

But this man would be impossible were it not that he has the backing of politicians and law-makers. Behind and allied with every successful high-tariff group is a political group. That is, under our operation of the protective doctrine we have developed a politician who encourages the most dangerous kind of citizenship a democracy can know—the panicky, grasping, idealless kind. Moreover, we have developed a politician whose principal method of getting things done is by barter.

Let us admit that reasonable people must not expect in a popular government to arrive at results save by a series of compromises. No reasonable person can expect the protective system to be handled without compromises, backsets, and errors of judgment, but *he can expect it to be handled as a principle and not as a commodity*. The shock and disgust come in the discovery that our tariffs are not good and bad applications of the principles of protection, but that they are good or bad bargains. Dip into the story of the tariff at any point since the Civil War and you will find wholesale proofs of bargaining in duties; rates fixed with no more relation to the doctrine of protection than they have to the law of precision of the equinoxes. The actual work of carrying out these bargains is of a nature that would revolt any legislator whose sensitiveness to the moral quality of his acts had not been blunted—who had not entirely eliminated ethical considerations from the business of fixing duties. And this is what the high protectionist lawgiver has come to—a complete repudiation of the idea that right and wrong are involved in tariff bills. There is no man more dangerous in a position of power than he who refuses to accept as a working truth the idea that all a man does should make for righteousness and soundness, that even fixing a tariff rate must be moral. But this is the man the doctrine of protection, as we know it, produces, and therein lies the final case against it—men are worse, not better, for its practice.

Ida M. Tarbell

CHAPTER I

DIRECT VS. INDIRECT TAXATION

Tariff Acts of 1789—Alexander Hamilton, Secretary of the Treasury, Advocates Protection in His "Report on Manufactures"—Internal Duties Are Laid on Spirits—Debate in the House on the Excise: in Favor, James Madison [Va.], Samuel Livermore [N. H.], Theodore Sedgwick [Mass.], William B. Giles [Va.]; Opposed, James Jackson [Ga.], Jonathan Parker [Va.], John Steele [N. C.], William L. Smith [S. C.]—Revenue Act of 1794—Debate in the House on Direct *vs.* Indirect Taxation: in Favor of Direct Taxation, John Smilie [Pa.], Mr. Madison, William Findley [Pa.], Samuel Smith [Md.], John Nicholas [Va.]; in Favor of Indirect Taxation, Uriah Tracy [Ct.], Mr. Sedgwick, Fisher Ames [Mass.], William L. Smith [S. C.]—Debate on the Land Tax: in Favor, Thomas Scott [Pa.], Mr. Sedgwick; Opposed, William Lyman [Mass.], Samuel Dexter [Mass.]; It Is Negatived.

BEFORE the Confederation the tariff had never been a leading American issue. But during the period in which this plan of union was in operation it was the tariff question, together with that of internal revenue, as we have seen in Vol. I, which brought to light the underlying weakness of the existing system of government, and subsequently led to the adoption of the Constitution.

The first tariff act was passed on July 4, 1789. By this act Congress laid specific duties on many articles, and *ad valorem* duties, varying from 7½ to 15 per cent., on others. There was also a large free list, for the act was only a slight beginning of the protective system. The preamble to this act declared:

It is necessary for the support of the Government, for the discharge of the debts of the United States, and the encouragement and protection of manufacturers that duties be laid.

On July 20, to provide additional revenue, an act laying a tonnage duty was passed. This act discriminated in favor of American shipping, higher duties being imposed on foreign than on American bottoms. This system of protection was defended and explained by the Secretary of the Treasury, Alexander Hamilton, in his "Report on Manufactures" (1791), in which he gave the arguments for protection which have been used and elaborated by various writers since his time.

In 1790, the customs receipts having proved inadequate for the purposes of the tariff acts, Hamilton outlined a system of internal revenue. Though this plan was not adopted until four years later, an act was passed in 1791 by which alcoholic beverages were subjected to a moderate tax. This act was extremely unpopular, and in 1794 caused an uprising in western Pennsylvania known as the "Whisky Insurrection."

In the debate on this measure in the House of Representatives the leading speakers in favor of excise were James Madison [Va.], Samuel Livermore [N. H.], Theodore Sedgwick [Mass.], and William B. Giles [Va.], while among the most important of those opposed to this system of taxation were James Jackson [Ga.], Jonathan Parker [Va.], John Steele [N. C.], and William L. Smith [S. C.].

Duties on Spirits

House of Representatives, January 5-25, 1791

Mr. Jackson said this mode of taxation was odious, unequal, unpopular, and oppressive, more particularly in the Southern States; in which he observed its unequal operation would be most sensibly felt, as the citizens of those States have no alternative to adopt by which they can diminish the weight of the tax—no breweries or orchards to furnish a substitute for spirituous liquors; hence they become a necessary article. He contended that they were not only necessary, but salutary in the Southern regions.

Mr. Jackson then gave a short sketch of the history of excises in England. He said they always had been considered by the people of that country as an odious tax from the time of Oliver Cromwell to the present day; even Blackstone, a high prerogative lawyer, has reprobated them. He said he hoped this country would take warning by the experience of the people of Great Britain, and not sacrifice their liberties by wantonly contracting debts which would render it necessary to burden the people by such taxes as would swallow up their privileges. We are, said he, too much in the habit of imitating that country, and I plainly perceive that the time will come when a shirt shall not be washed without an excise.

MR. PARKER touched on the mode of collecting the tax. It will, he said, convulse the Government; it will let loose a swarm of harpies, who, under the denomination of revenue officers, will range through the country, prying into every man's house and affairs, and like a Macedonian phalanx bear down all before them.

MR. MADISON felt the force of the objections which had been urged against the bill. He was in general principled against excises, but, of all excises, that on ardent spirits he considered the least exceptionable. The question now to be determined, he conceived, was this: is an addition to the present amount of the revenue necessary? It had appeared that an addition is necessary; for his own part, he should prefer direct taxation to any excises whatever, but he conceived this would be contrary to the sentiments of the majority of the people of the United States, and he was fully convinced that it was contrary to the opinion of a great majority of the House.

MR. JACKSON doubted not other resources of revenue might be explored which would be more palatable; he instanced a tax on salaries, pensions, and lawyers, and in these particulars he wished that the example of Great Britain might be followed.

He then dilated on the practice of smuggling, which he contended would be promoted by this bill; also the difficulties and opposition which were justly to be expected, by which the dignity of the Government would be insulted. Can this Government, said he, protect its officers from the resentment of any one State in the Union? He reprobated the idea of placing the Government in such a situation.

MR. STEELE said such was the present state of the public mind in various parts of the Union that he should dread taking any measures which might serve to increase the fermentation which the people were in. An excise he considered of this nature; it would in its operation produce the worst consequences. A more exceptionable mode of taxation, he conceived, could not be devised. A direct or poll tax, he supposed, would not be so odious; and though, for his own part, he should prefer an excise to either of the former taxes, yet such was the aversion of the people to it that he should prefer almost any other alternative. He thought other objects might be found from which the necessary revenue could be raised. He instanced duties on inland navigation, law proceedings, legal conveyances, etc.

He then adverted to the operation of an excise, especially in the State of North Carolina, and said that the consumption of ardent spirits in that State was so great that the duty would amount perhaps to ten times as much as in the State of Connecticut. On the whole, he hoped, if the section is not struck out, that the excise will be reduced.

MR. LIVERMORE was in favor of the bill. He considered it an equal and just mode of taxation, and as such one that would be agreeable to the people; they would consider it as drinking down the national debt. He then obviated the objections to the bill, which, he conceived, arose principally from the word excise. He thought the term very improperly applied on the present occasion, for the duty cannot be said to be an excise. He then gave a description of what had been considered in times past as an excise, which, to be sure, is a very unequal tax, inasmuch as it fell on the poor only, who were obliged to purchase in small quantities, while the rich, by storing their cellars, escaped the duty. But this bill provides that the duty shall fall equally on the rich and poor. It is to be paid, or secured, by the importer of foreign spirits, and on the still-head on domestic spirits. This will equalize the burthen, and leave no room for complaint. He then adverted to direct taxation, and, by a variety of particulars, showed that it was utterly impossible to lay a direct tax that would not prove unjust, unequal, and grievously oppressive.

MR. SEDGWICK was unhappy to hear that discontents prevailed in any part of the United States. He could assure gentlemen that he did not contemplate the execution of the laws by military force. In framing the present bill, great attention had been paid to prevent its being attended with those qualities which, in other countries, rendered taxation by excise justly obnoxious to popular resentment. He believed that of all the subjects of revenue which were within the power of Congress, none was so proper as the duty on ardent spirits, contemplated by the bill. The several species of taxation may be divided into the four following: by impost; a tax on internal negotiations; direct taxes; and that now under consideration, excise.

The impost duties had been extended as far as was, in the opinion of any gentleman, dictated by sound policy. The tax on internal negotiations, which could not be carried on to any considerable extent without the intervention of stamps, was subject to the objection brought against the present bill, and that in a degree incomparably beyond it, of being opposed by public opinion. Direct taxes are still more objectionable on that account, at least in every part of the country to which his knowledge extended. They are of all taxes the most unequal, and in this country would be found the most oppressive. They are unequal, because, with whatever exactness they may be apportioned upon capital or income, the only two principles on which an apportionment can be made, they may, and will, be very unequal as to the burden imposed; because a man's ability to pay taxes is not in proportion either to his capital, his property, or his income, but to that part of his income which is over and above his necessary expenses, according to the usual manner of living for persons of his degree in the community. They will be oppressive in this country, because in many of the States the plentiful circulation of money, and the facility of obtaining it, does not extend to the interior parts, nor could it be obtained by many of our citizens without a great sacrifice of property. It may be added that, from the extent of our settlements compared with the number of our citizens, the expense of collection would be immense.

In regard to excises, Mr. Sedgwick said that in all insensible modes of taxation it should be observed that a much greater sum would be obtained from an individual than by any mode of direct imposition; this, without entering into a discussion of the reasons upon which it is founded, is demonstrated by fact. He instanced the porters of London, from whom, in the single article of beer, were drawn ten times as much as could be procured by the most rigorous mode of direct taxation. With regard to the proposed duties, though the well-meant consideration of morality which had been urged by some gentlemen weighed but little with him, because he doubted whether it was well founded, yet, if the consumption, which at present amounts to an enormous quantity, should be lessened, he did not believe that it would be attended with any sensible inconvenience.

Mr. Smith said the present bill was not so exceptionable on account of its violating private property as the collection law.

He instanced, in a particular clause of that law, the power of entering houses by warrant from a justice of the peace—

trial by jury is secured by this bill, and other provisions friendly to personal rights are added.

MR. GILES stated certain principles on which taxation should be formed. Taxes should be necessary, and raised on a plan consistent with the principles of liberty. The expediency of the present mode, he argued, from the impost's being carried to the utmost; from the approbation of this mode by a majority of the people, and, though uneasiness might prevail in some of the Southern States, he considered them as originating altogether from the want of due information.

When, in June, 1794, Hamilton's plan was carried into effect, and duties were laid on carriages, sales at auction, snuff, sugar, and tobacco, the measure encountered vigorous opposition. The duty on carriages was declared by many to be unconstitutional, and in Virginia the collection of this tax was disputed until the Supreme Court of the United States declared in favor if it.

In the debate on this bill the relative merits of direct and indirect taxation formed the chief issue.

Those speakers who argued in favor of direct taxation were John Smilie [Pa.], James Madison [Va.], William Findley [Pa.], Samuel Smith [Md.], and John Nicholas [Va.]; the speakers in favor of indirect taxation were Uriah Tracy [Conn.], Theodore Sedgwick [Mass.], Fisher Ames [Mass.], and William L. Smith [S. C.].

DIRECT VS. INDIRECT TAXATION

HOUSE OF REPRESENTATIVES, MAY 1-4, 1794

MR. SMILIE.—Taxes which are paid imperceptibly are more dangerous than others, because by their invisibility the people are seduced from thinking to what purposes their money went.

MR. TRACY could not believe that the member was serious in advancing such a doctrine, for the sum of it is that when taxes are to be raised Government is in duty bound to give the people who pay these taxes *as much trouble as possible!* There was nothing but this alternative—a tax on tobacco, or a land tax—which was equivalent to a tax upon necessaries.

MR. MADISON had always opposed every tax of this nature,

and he should upon all occasions persist in opposing them. If we look into the state of those nations who are harnessed in taxes, we shall universally find that, in a moral, political, and commercial point of view, excise is the most destructive of all resources. Much of the collection of this tax on tobacco would depend on the oath of the manufacturer, and this was but another term for the multiplication of perjuries. The tax would therefore injure the morals of the people.

MR. FINDLEY.—Ruin and depravity have always attended excise. It has been one of the principal sources of the corruption of Britain. The same effects must follow in America. He objected to the mode of taxation; and, besides, the tax is partial. It falls on the poor in cities. In the country nobody will pay it.

MR. SEDGWICK would vote against the tax if he thought it was contagious for public morality. But human nature has always been very corrupted without the aid of excise laws. The State which he represents has been excised for two generations, and yet no bad consequence has arisen to the morals of the people. As to the corruption of Britain, described by the member who spoke last, he admitted that the account was just, but this was not to be traced to excise laws. They had been the subject of much clamor, but what, in fact, was their history? A profligate opposition rail at all the measures of a minister, whether they be good or bad, and an excise act is often one of them. In the course of political changes these men get into place. But they do not attempt to take off the taxes against which they declaimed. In the meantime the new ex-minister harangues against the very taxes of which he was the author. As to this law being a source of perjury, oaths are necessary in imposts of all sorts. Why, then, object to them in this particular instance? Is an excise oath worse than a custom-house oath? There is often no other method of getting at truth. If we desert this way of raising revenue, what are we to do? Taxes cannot be imposed on personal income with any sort of justice, because the actual degree of a person's wealth does not depend on the nominal amount of his income. One man has a thousand dollars a year, but such may be his situation that the taxing him in so small a sum as ten dollars may be distressing. Others, again, with only five hundred dollars per annum, are, perhaps, in much more easy circumstances than the former, upon whom the tax of personal revenue would press with superior weight. Direct taxes Mr. Sedgwick regarded as of an improper nature. But, with regard to snuff and tobacco, nobody can ever feel the burden of a trifling tax upon them.

MR. SMILIE considered this measure as pregnant with serious consequences. He was opposed to every system of excise, because such systems had always produced mischief. If this were a despotic country, he could see a good reason for an excise system of revenue, because it was proper, in that case, to debase, by every possible expedient, the minds of the people, that their feelings might sink to a level with the meanness of their condition. But in a republic taxes should be of a different nature and operate with a different tendency.

MR. AMES had a better opinion of government than the gentleman who spoke last. He did not think excise a mark of despotism. He did not think the people stocks and stones, or their rulers knaves and fools. The member had spoken of the citizens of this country, as if to rouse their attention it was requisite to keep a flapper, like that of Gulliver, at their ears.

As to the resolution upon the table, is there any comparison between a snuff tax and a land tax? Land is the great *substratum* of American prosperity. Difficulties had been started as to the *collection* of excise; an oppressive law was a bad thing, but resistance was worse. Can any man think that a land tax does not open a much greater door to imposition than a tax on tobacco? In what way is a land tax to be laid that can avoid inequality and injustice? Are we to tax the public funds, that last and most desperate resource of national distress, and then to be told that we dare not impose a duty on snuff and tobacco?

MR. S. SMITH considered the observations of the member who had just sat down as amusing and ingenious, but they were not satisfactory. To him it seemed a very odd scheme to crush American manufactures in the bud. Men of capital and enterprise advanced large sums of money in erecting snuff mills. After long exertions they began to reap the reward of their expenses and their labor. At that critical moment the Government souses down upon them with an excise, which ends not in revenue, but extirpation.

MR. NICHOLAS.—We are going on exactly in the steps of Britain, of which this excise is one instance. That country once had a revolutionary spirit. How sunk are they now? Not one-tenth part of them dare to say that they are against the war with France, which is sweeping them with velocity over the precipice of ruin. What has degraded and annihilated the spirit of Britain? Public debts, taxes, and officers of excise. One-half of the nation has been loaded with the plunder of the rest. It is too much the American character to bear as right what does not immediately hurt. It is a duty to keep the citizens alive to the operations of Government. It is somewhat strange to blame this attempt when there is such an alarming indifference on the subject. As to this tax, it will put an end to the consumption of manufactured tobacco. Planters will make it ready for themselves. They can do so with very great ease by a method in the process of curing it. Mr. Nicholas was therefore against the resolution.

MR. MADISON.—Tobacco excise was a burden the *most unequal*. It fell upon the poor, upon sailors, day-laborers, and other people of these classes, while the rich will often escape it. Much had been said about the taxing of luxury. The pleasures of life consisted in a series of innocent gratifications, and he felt no satisfaction in the prospect of their being squeezed. Sumptuary laws had never, he believed, answered any good purpose. Something had been said about the difference between direct personal taxes and those raised by indirect means, such as excise and customs. He quoted an author of respectable character in England, who estimated the expense of uplifting [collecting] *direct* taxes in that country, such as the land tax, at 3 per cent., and that of uplifting *indirect* taxes, such as those of excise and customs, upon the whole, at 30 per cent.

Excise had at first been resorted to upon a few manufactures. The dealers indemnify themselves at the expense of their customers. At the same time they endeavored to evade the duties, and thus there commences a struggle which has many bad effects, both upon industry and public morals. In Europe, when tobacco is excised, the Government forbids it from being planted. [Some years ago the British farmers were obliged, by an act of Parliament, to pull up and burn their tobacco before it was full grown.] No such measure, he hoped, would be adopted here, but it was hard to say where the subject might, one day, end. Statesmen, in general, do not study the liberty, the virtue, or the comforts of the people, but merely to collect as much revenue as they can. Taxes are not, for the most part, the work of patriotism. An excise established in America would discourage the emigrations from Europe that might, at this time, be so much expected. He was determined to vote against the resolution.

MR. SMILIE.—An excise, in its very outset, is a violation of the rights of freemen, independent of the extent to which it might or might not be carried and, whether it oppressed the manufacturer, or did not oppress him, by making his house liable to be searched at all hours it violated the natural sanctuary of domestic life. It creates a number of artificial crimes; an additional code of laws must be invented in order to punish them, and this punishment cannot be inflicted without the ruin of American citizens, or neglected without the ruin of American excise revenues. What mischiefs have not excise laws produced in England? It has been found necessary to form a new set of laws in which the British subjects have lost the protection of a trial by jury.

Mr. W. L. Smith observed that, if objections were to be made to every tax, and every sum of duty was to be left blank, what was the occasion for appointing a select Committee of Ways and Means? One gentleman insisted upon striking out this resolution; another on striking out that resolution till in short they would leave nothing at all. This proceeding reminded him of a story in the fables of Phœdrus. A man whose head was covered with black and gray hairs had two female friends. One of them, who desired that he should have a youthful appearance, carefully pulled out some of his gray hairs as often as he paid her a visit. The other lady, who wanted him to look like an old man, was industrious in pulling out the black hairs. Between their joint endeavors he became bald. Thus, by the time that every gentleman has done with plucking, we shall have nothing of the report left.

The original bill contemplated a direct tax of $750,000 apportioned among the States by population. Leading supporters of this measure were Thomas Scott and Theodore Sedgwick, and leading opponents were William Lyman and Samuel Dexter. It was negatived.

Direct Taxation [Land Tax]

House of Representatives, May 5-9, 1794

Mr. Lyman moved to strike out the resolution because it contemplated a *land tax*. Owing to the variation of the tenure of lands in the different States, in some States the lands were pretty well distributed, and held in small parcels by those who cultivated them, and in other States they were held in larger quantities and cultivated in a different way. A tax on them,

XII—2

therefore, which, in the one case might be considered unacceptable, would probably be less so in the other. However, speculative opinions in questions of this sort were but a feeble opposition to fact and experiment. In this country some of the States at least have made the experiment. It had proved oppressive, excited discontents, and even convulsed the Government. The experience of other countries did not furnish much more favorable arguments. In the Republic of Rome they never had a land tax. It had its odious origin under the tyranny of the emperors. In France they have no land tax. This, in that country, he was sensible, was complained of, but it must have been because the lands were held by the nobility, to whom it proved an exemption from the burdens of society, and from that cause the exemption was disagreeable to the people; but, had the lands been of a different tenure, there would have been no such complaint. How stood the case in England, a country where every species of taxation was carried to its utmost stretch? Their land tax was a mere trifle compared with their other impositions, and, trifling as it was, they embraced every occasion, when not pressed by particular exigencies, requiring the utmost exertions, to lessen it from an apprehension of exciting uneasiness and tumult. Indeed he did not know but it might there be deemed a modified relic of their former slavish tenures. Under these impressions, and the consideration of the expense of collecting a tax of this sort, he hoped it would not now be resorted to.

MR. SCOTT was firmly persuaded that, in the exigencies of a nation, all sorts of property should be taxed because all sorts of property required to be defended. He was quite satisfied that all property should defend itself—that is, should pay for its own defence. He would cheerfully submit his own property to a general tax, were it even to half its value, if such an impost were necessary for the independence of America.

MR. SEDGWICK, after commenting on the opinion of certain political economists, who held that all taxes ultimately fell upon land, and, therefore, that those which were imposed on it were direct, and all those imposed on any other subject indirect, proceeded to state his own opinion.

He said that, in forming a Constitution for a National Government, to which were intrusted the preservation of that Government and the existence of society itself, it was reasonable to suppose that every means necessary to those important ends should be granted. This was, in fact, the case in the Constitution of the United States. To Congress it was expressly granted to impose taxes, duties, imposts, and excises. It had been universally concluded, and never, to his knowledge, denied, but that the legislature, by those comprehensive words, had authority to impose taxes on every subject of revenue. If this position be just, a construction which limited their operation of this power (in its nature and by the Constitution illimitable) could not be the just construction.

He observed that, to obviate certain mischiefs, the Constitution had provided that capitation and other direct taxes should be apportioned according to the ratio prescribed in it. If, then, the legislature be authorized to impose a tax on every subject of revenue (and surely pleasure carriages, as objects of luxury, and, in general, owned by those to whom contributions would not be inconvenient, were fair and proper subjects of taxation), and a tax on them could not be apportioned· by the constitutional ratio, it would follow irresistibly that such a tax, in this sense of the Constitution, is not "direct." On this idea he enlarged his reasoning, and showed that such a tax was incapable of apportionment.

He said that, so far as he had been able to form an opinion, there had been a general concurrence in a belief that the ultimate sources of public contributions were labor, and the subjects and effects of labor. That taxes, being permanent, had a tendency to equalize and to diffuse themselves through a community. According to these opinions, a capitation tax and taxes on land, and on property and income generally, were direct charges, as well in the immediate as ultimate sources of contribution. He had considered those, and those only, as direct taxes in their operation and effects. On the other hand, a tax imposed on a specific article of personal property, and particularly if objects of luxury, as in the case under consideration, he had never supposed had been considered a direct tax, within the meaning of the Constitution. The exaction was indeed directly of the owner, but, by the equalizing operation, of which all taxes more or less partook, it created an indirect charge on others besides the owners.

He said it would astonish the people of America to be informed that they had made a Constitution by which pleasure carriages and other objects of luxury were excepted from contributing to the public exigencies, which was undoubtedly the case if the reasoning of gentlemen who opposed the resolution was well founded. If the imposition of a duty on pleasure carriages was a direct tax, it must then be apportioned, but, as several of the States had few or no carriages, no such apportionment could be made, and the duty of course could not be imposed. Such a construction was inadmissible, because it would exempt, in times of the greatest distress, the fairest objects of contribution from the imposition of any burden. If there was doubt, we certainly ought not to incline to that side which, at the same time it might compel the legislature to impose grievous burdens on the poorest and most laborious part of the community, shall exempt the affluent from contributing for their objects of distinguishing enjoyments. This seemed not to carry into effect that doctrine of equality of which gentlemen said so much.

Mr. Dexter said a land tax was a tax on the laborious poor. If every acre is to pay the same tax, it must prove very unequal, as poor men generally live on the poorest lands, and must pay oppressive taxes. If the lands are to be valued, the delay and expense must be enormous. Lands increase in value very unequally in different places, and the proportion will be forever altering. He had been told that two thousand persons had once been concerned in apportioning and collecting the land tax of Pennsylvania. He thought that, if any mode of taxation be permanent, it will soon be equal. The most unequal imposition will, like a fluid, soon diffuse itself equally through all the proper and natural subjects of taxation. Mr. Dexter thought, also, that direct taxation ought not to be pursued by the general Government, except in time of war, because it is the only source of revenue for the support of State governments and payment of State debts.

The revenue act was repealed in 1801, owing to the advent to power of the Democratic party, whose principles were opposed to all forms of internal taxation. But, during the War of 1812 the urgent need of additional revenue made it necessary to resume the former system.

CHAPTER II

THE TARIFF OF 1816

[PROTECTION OR REVENUE?]

Revenue Measures at the Close of the War of 1812—Protective Tariff Bill Is Introduced in the House—Debate: in Favor, John C. Calhoun [S. C.], Henry Clay [Ky.], Thomas R. Gold [N. Y.]; Opposed, John Ross [Pa.], Robert Wright [Md.], Thomas Telfair [Ga.], John Randolph [Va.]; Daniel Webster [N. H.] Compromising—Bill Passes Both Houses and Is Approved by the President.

A T the close of the War of 1812 the finances of the country were in such a deplorable condition that it was found necessary to continue several of the special taxes which had been laid during the war and were about to expire.

On April 19, 1816, President James Madison approved an act replacing the existing excise duties with licenses on stills and their output, which method still forms the basis of the system of collecting internal revenue.

The revenue bill which created the most discussion was a new tariff laid on manufactures of almost every description, with *ad valorem* duties on some articles and specific duties on others. This bill was proposed as the result of a report of the Congressional Committee on Trade and Manufactures. In this report, which was drafted by John C. Calhoun [S. C.], a protective tariff was strongly advocated. It is interesting to note that Calhoun, who was later to oppose protection to the verge of leading his State out of the Union, was at this time not only a protectionist but an ardent Unionist. The committee, in its report, said as follows:

21

PROTECTION AND UNION

JOHN C. CALHOUN, M. C.

The inducements to industry in a free government are numerous and inviting. Effects are always in unison with their causes. The inducements consist in the certainty and security which every citizen enjoys of exercising exclusive dominion over the creations of his genius, and the products of his labor; in procuring from his native soil, at all times, with facility, the raw materials that are required, and in the liberal encouragement that will be accorded by agriculturists to those who, by their labor, keep up a constant and increasing demand for the produce of agriculture.

Every State will participate in those advantages. The resources of each will be explored, opened, and enlarged. Different sections of the nation will, according to their position, the climate, the population, the habits of the people, and the nature of the soil, strike into that line of industry which is best adapted to their interest and the good of the whole; an active and free intercourse, promoted and facilitated by roads and canals, will ensue; prejudices, which are generated by distance, and the want of inducements to approach each other and reciprocate benefits, will be removed; information will be extended; the Union will acquire strength and solidity, and the Constitution of the United States, and that of each State, will be regarded as fountains from which flow numerous streams of public and private prosperity.

Our wants being supplied by our own ingenuity and industry, exportation of specie, to pay for foreign manufactures, will cease. The value of American produce, at this time exported, will not enable the importers to pay for the foreign manufacture imported. Whenever the two accounts shall be fairly stated, the balance against the United States will be found many millions of dollars. Such is the state of things that the change must be to the advantage of the United States. The precious metals will be attracted to them; the diffusion of which, in a regular and uniform current, through the great arteries and veins of the body politic, will give to each member health and vigor.

In proportion as the commerce of the United States depends on agriculture and manufactures as a common basis, will it increase and become independent of those revolutions and fluctuations, which the ambition and jealousy of foreign governments are too apt to produce. Our navigation will be quickened, and, supported as it will be by internal resources never before at the command of any nation, will advance to the extent of those resources.

The manufacturers of cotton, in making application to the National Government for encouragement, have been induced to do so for many reasons. They know that their establishments are new and in their infancy, and that they have to encounter a competition with foreign establishments, that have arrived at maturity, that are supported by a large capital, and that have from the Government every protection that can be required. The foreign manufacturers and merchants will put in requisition all the powers of ingenuity; will practice whatever art can devise, and capital can accomplish, to prevent the American manufacturing establishments from taking root and flourishing in their rich and native soil. By the allowance of bounties and drawbacks, the foreign manufacturers and merchants will be furnished with additional means of carrying on the conflict, and of insuring success.

Should the National Government not afford the American manufacturers protection, the dangers which invest and threaten them will destroy all their hopes, and will close their prospects of utility to their country. A reasonable encouragement will sustain and keep them erect, but if they fall, they fall never to rise again, since their mouldering piles—the visible ruins of a legislative breath—will warn all who shall tread in the same footsteps of the doom, the inevitable destiny, of their establishments.

But, should the National Government, pursuing an enlightened and liberal policy, sustain and foster the manufacturing establishments, a few years would place them in a condition to bid defiance to foreign competition, and would enable them to increase the industry, wealth, and prosperity of the nation; and to afford to the Government, in times of difficulty and distress, whatever it may require to support public credit, while maintaining the rights of the nation.

The bill was laid before the House of Representatives by Albert Gallatin [Pa.], Secretary of the Treasury, on February 13, 1816, and referred to the Committee on Ways and Means. On March 23 Mr. Calhoun, of the committee, laid the bill before the House. It was debated until April 8, when it was passed by a vote of 88 to 54.

The schedules that were chiefly objected to were the woolen and cotton manufactures, upon which a duty of twenty-five per cent. *ad valorem* was laid. It was the evident design in these schedules, and, indeed, though in a minor degree, in all the schedules, to "protect" domestic manufacturing industries that had arisen during the war, and which, upon its cessation, had been forced to reduce their prices by competing with foreign industries, chiefly English (including East Indian manufactures of cotton).

Leading speakers in favor of the principle of protection in the bill were Mr. Calhoun, Henry Clay [Ky.], and Thomas R. Gold [N. Y.]. Those speakers who were in favor of a tariff mainly for revenue were John Ross [Pa.], Robert Wright [Md.], Thomas Telfair [Ga.], and John Randolph [Va.]. Daniel Webster [N. H.] supported the protective principle under the special circumstances of the case. He did not vote on the final passage of the bill.

The bill passed the Senate on April 19 by a vote of 25 to 7, and was approved by the President on April 27.

PROTECTION OR REVENUE?

HOUSE OF REPRESENTATIVES, MARCH 23-APRIL 8, 1816

MR. WEBSTER proposed a stated graduated reduction upon the duties. He said that he was not prepared to say that the Government was bound to adopt a permanent protection, or one which would exclude those goods already in the country. From the course pursued by the Government for some years back, the community had a right to expect relief from the danger to which the sudden change of circumstances exposed our manufactures, but Government had a right to say whether that relief should be permanent or not, and to reduce the protecting duties if it thought proper.

MR. CALHOUN hoped the amendment proposed by Mr. Webster would not prevail. He believed the policy of the country required protection to our manufacturing establishments.

MR. CLAY said the object of protecting manufactures was that we might eventually get articles of necessity made as cheap at home as they could be imported, and thereby to produce an independence of foreign countries. In three years, he said, we could judge of the ability of our establishments to furnish those articles as cheap as they were obtained from abroad, and could then legislate with the lights of experience. He believed that three years would be sufficient to place our manufacturers on this desirable footing, and others would not hesitate to enter into the business, because they would look to that liberal and enlarged policy which they might anticipate from the Government at a future period.

Mr. Ross desired the independence of the people as well as national independence, and wished not to see one class of the community enslaved by another. If the extravagant duties proposed were not necessary for revenue, he could see no strong necessity for them. The failure of certain manufacturers was no reason for them, because some individuals of all professions were unfortunate in the best times, and no sympathy was felt for the merchants who failed. Adverting to a remark that some manufactories were worked in Kentucky by slaves, Mr. Ross said all manufactories were conducted with slaves, because the occupation had a tendency to degrade and debase the human mind. It was, he argued, a vain attempt to carry manufactures to such extent in this country, while there were so many inducements to seek an independent support by agriculture, and other beneficial pursuits. The only kind of manufactures he wished to see flourish were those conducted in families; any other would prove destructive to the liberties of this Republic, by combinations effecting a revolution in this House and in the Government.

Mr. Webster's amendment was agreed to by a large majority.

When the schedules of cotton and woolen goods were reached Mr. Wright moved to exclude from voting all members concerned in their manufacture, but, upon the earnest protest of his colleague, Mr. Smith, withdrew the motion.

MR. TELFAIR spoke as follows: On the subject of impost I hold it a sound general rule that no other or higher duties should be laid than are both necessary and proper for the purposes of revenue. To attempt more necessarily increases the inducements to smuggling; and if the encouragement of manufactures be the object, it is, in effect, to plunge on the wide ocean of uncertainty, guided by factitious lights, emanating from the selfishness alone of those who tender them, and which never can be relied upon for the purposes of wise legislation.

I will not deny but that, in the imposition of duties for the purposes of revenue, it is wise so to select your objects that, while the original intent is secured, the interest of the manufacturer may be regarded as an incidental consideration. But what is the character of the measure before you? Instead of contemplating the protection and encouragement of manufactures as secondary or collateral, it refers to them as the primary and essential cause of legislation; instead of the benefits flowing to them being considered merely as some alleviation of burdens, made necessary by the wants of the Government, their encouragement has, in the whole course of the discussion, been placed in the foreground, and admitted to be the principal object for which so enormous a tax is laid upon the people of this country—a tax, the proceeds of which, so far as it means protection, are never to enter the coffers of the nation, but, by a species of magic, are to be transferred from the hands of the consumer into those of the manufacturer—paid by the people indeed, but not for the purposes of Government.

The support of this bill rests upon two considerations. First, it is urged that the course of measures pursued by Government for some time previous to, as well as during, the war had the tendency of a pledge of support. To what an infinite order of pledges would such a system give rise? A change from peace to war necessarily injures the immediate interests of commerce and agriculture; a return of peace alike injures those institutions which grow up amid the circumstances of war. Is the nation, after all these changes and effects, to hold itself as bound to compensate the losses of those who may have suffered? I presume this will not be urged. But I may be told that the manufacturing class constitutes so small a portion of the community that, while public policy requires it, they may be sustained by less injury to the others and less expense to the Government, and therefore they should be upheld. Sir, I deem it unsafe to legislate for particular interests. Did not the interest of the merchant and the planter suffer under those very causes which cherished the manufacturer? While the latter was accumulating wealth, were not the former consuming their capital? And, because they now begin to derive a profit, is it wise and just in us to rob them of it by increasing the expenses of articles of consumption, merely to contribute such a bounty to the manufacturer as will enable him to derive something like his accustomed profits?

In your munificence, you are about to allow, by way of bounty, five per cent. more than is required for revenue upon cottons and woolens, which is as much as the duties during the war, and one hundred per cent. more than those prior to the war. In words you are called upon for protection, but what are the ideas involved in this phrase? Why, that the planter of this country, who consumes the article manufactured, shall be made to pay the difference between the wages of labor in the factory and field, together with the difference of profit which superior skill in the foreign manufacturer gives over the manufacturer of this country. In one word, all articles are made dear to the consumer, whether of foreign or domestic fabrication, merely that the manufacturer may derive a profit upon his capital.

The second consideration, and that which is most relied on, arises from the policy of other nations, and promises a more permanent security to the independence of this people. Imposing, indeed, is such a ground of argument; and, if the independence of this nation either required or could be guaranteed by this bill, abhorrent indeed would be all opposition to it; but, believing, as I do, that the liberties of this people, and the independence of this Government, rest on a basis too firmly laid in their very genius and nature to require such protection, for one I will not consent to adopt the measure proposed. After having advanced in prosperity and improvement far beyond the march of any other nation on the globe, in the same period of time, you are now called upon to reject the admonitions of experience, and adopt a part of the very policy which, with reference to the people of Europe, is congenial, because it denotes the absence of all ideas of self-government. You are about to abjure that principle which was peculiarly your own, and the offspring of freedom, of leaving industry free to its own pursuit and regulation, and to assume to yourself the capacity and right of judging and dictating that labor which is wisest and best for the people of this country. The extent of territory, the exuberance of our soil, the genius of our people, the principles of our political institutions, have in their combination decreed, as by a law of nature, that, for years to come, the citizens of America shall obtain their subsistence by agriculture and commerce. And we, in our wisdom, would fain issue a counter order, to withdraw industry from its natural and accustomed channels, and by our laws, force into a state of prematurity the manufacturing enterprise of this country. But we are told it would be idle, weak, and absurd in us, while all the powers of Europe are devising plans for the encouragement of manufactures, to let them stagnate for want of national aid. To this I answer that, such are the profits and enjoyments flowing from labor in the ordinary pursuits of life with us, you cannot draw off the citizen and tempt him to a new and less active pursuit, without robbing from the national wealth a considerable portion which is thrown in to make up his profits. Is not, then, the productive labor of the country thereby diminished? Has not a great portion of it been thrown away, unless some great benefit is derived from this new direction of industry? And is the policy of other governments to be urged as sufficient justification? It must be borne in mind that the circumstances of our country are totally different from those of Europe; there, a crowded population causes it to be an object of real national importance to discover means of employment for the many hands which would otherwise encumber society. With us, however, the case is widely different. Here, every hand would find ample employment in tilling the earth; and the calls of society are sufficient, without bounty, to give occupation to such as prefer other employments to those of agriculture. And every occupation which requires the aid of bounty contains within itself a proof that it is not productive of national wealth, though it may be of national glory. I must protest against the habit of resorting to the regulations of other governments, as rules by which to quadrate our own. Because the governments of the Old World have resorted to this mode of facilitating the collection of taxes by creating protuberances upon the body politic, are we to be influenced by their examples? Because monopolies have for ages become familiarized to them, are we to disregard the evidence in favor of an unshackled pursuit of our own interest, and, in despite of the warning voice of these very nations, which attests the ruinous effects of such a policy upon every principle held sacred by the friends of freedom, are we to give aid to a favorite class of the community by a tax upon the rest? Like the State banks, sir, these manufactures grew up while a state of war gave a feverish heat to our political atmosphere, because the temporary wants of the people and the Government, and the sluggish state of trade, required them. The return of peace has diminished the demand for the paper of the one and the fabrics of the other; they may both be said to have depreciated in their relative value. The depreciation of bank paper, it is to be hoped, will be arrested in its progress, the combination of these moneyed monopolists broken as to all capacity for harm by the establishment of a bank, governed in part by ourselves, and by other ulterior measures in contemplation. But, when the different manufacturing States may have deemed it wise to follow the example of Great Britain, and incorporate the different manufacturing establishments, grant them exclusive privileges, prop them by by-laws, and regard them as favorites, how, I ask, are you to control the mighty combination to which such a policy would give rise, for they can concert as well as the State banks? Will you, in such event, open the flood-gates and let in the ocean of foreign goods threatening to overwhelm them? Certainly not, and yet this would be the only corrective left you.

Sir, while these establishments grow as other branches of industry have done, I shall feel for them no hostility; on the contrary, my preference would be given to articles manufactured by them, but their interest once identified with that of the Government, and I do fear them.

It has been remarked that the arts flourish in the society of each other; not so, however, in their infancy, while both are attempted to be encouraged at the same time, do the manufactures and the navy spring up. For all the protection given to the former is a deduction from the support of the latter.

Mr. Gold.—It is not, Mr. Speaker, a distinct class of manufacturers who have petitioned Congress for relief, but almost all classes, and principally the farmers, have embarked in the manufacture of woolen and cotton, and now pray at your hands the protection of their interests, put in so great jeopardy. It is proper, I should state, after the example of some who have preceded me in debate, that I too have a concern in those manufactures.

Arkwright's machinery has produced a revolution in the manufacture of cotton; the invention is so excellent, the effect in saving labor so immense, that five or six men are sufficient for the management of a factory of two thousand spindles, spinning one hundred thousand pounds of twist or yarn yearly; the other hands are mere children, whose labor is of little use in any other branch of industry. The nation which does not avail itself of this machinery, and pays another nation for fabrics produced by it, sacrifices the entire value of the labor saved by the machinery. It is a maxim of political economy, laid down by Sir James Stewart, that "a nation ought to restrain, by duty on importation, that which may be produced at home, and to manufacture as much as possible of the raw material."

The same writer says that a *new manufacture* cannot be established without encouragement, without restraint on importation; old establishments in possession of the ground, in possession of capital (a most important consideration), in possession of extended machinery, with all the fruits of experience in skill and economy, actuated by a *jealousy* against rival establishments, rising into competition, which never sleeps, never did cease, in any age or country, to exert their undivided force upon these rival establishments, and for a time to make sacrifices in the sale of their goods. The Government itself not unfrequently lends itself, by bounties on exports, to such unhallowed designs upon the manufactures of other nations; where these nations have, as is the case of the United States, been long the great customers and consumers of the fabrics of such government.

Now agriculture is certainly the great and favorite theater of industry in the United States, and, so long as our surplus products can find a good foreign market, it should be the first object. But, how is this fact? With the exception of a period of war, no such market is found, and the grain of our country raised beyond consumption must rot in the granary. Lord Sheffield, in his "American Commerce," states that there never was a good market for American flour and wheat for more than three or four years. Though Europe is not recovered from the shock of war, yet Great Britain is now giving a bounty on the export of grain. Where can the United States now look for a market for her grain equal to that at home?

No friend of his country can look at the enormous importation of goods into the United States, the past year, without concern. The British accounts give thirty millions sterling (above one hundred and thirty millions of dollars) as the amount of her export of goods to the United States, while our whole export to Great Britain is twenty-one millions only. Is it possible to see such a course of trade in any other light than as most ruinous to the country? "If the balance of trade be against a nation, it is her interest to put a stop to it," is the language of Sir James Stewart.

It is further objected that our manufacturers will extort extravagant prices, and the prices during the last year are referred to in support of the objection. Is this charge against manufacturers just? Does not every member of this committee know that the charge applies equally against all classes during the late war? Instead of concert to raise prices, competition and the spirit of underselling prevail to such an extent that sales are often made without a profit.

Justice to different portions of the Union, and the harmony of the whole, require the encouragement of manufactures.

While the South has, from the export of her cotton and tobacco alone, received about thirty millions the last year, the Northern and Middle States, having no such great staples, must of necessity turn their attention to manufacturing, or become greatly impoverished, to the injury of the whole. The relinquishment of the port duties by the Northern and Middle States, to the amount of nearly three-fourths of the customs, by the adoption of the Constitution, creates an equitable claim to such an adjustment of the duties as shall favor and protect the interests of those States.

MR. RANDOLPH made some general remarks on the inconsistency of the proposed policy with that formerly pursued on the subject of commerce. He declared his unwillingness to sacrifice the *bona fide* American merchants to what he called the mushroom interest which had sprung into favor; and argued, at some length, and with some invective, against the object of the bill, which he characterized as a scheme of public robbery.

MR. CALHOUN.—Neither agriculture, manufactures, nor commerce, taken separately, is the cause of wealth; it flows from the three combined, and cannot exist without each. The wealth of any single nation, or any individual, it is true, may not immediately depend on the three, but such wealth always presupposes their existence. Without commerce, industry would have no stimulus; without manufactures, it would be without the means of production; and without agriculture neither of the others can subsist. When separated entirely and permanently, they perish. War in this country produces, to a great extent, that effect; and hence the great embarrassments which follow in its train. The failure of the wealth and resources of the nation necessarily involved the ruin of its finances and its currency. It is admitted, by the most strenuous advocates on the other side that no country ought to be dependent on another for its means of defence; that, at least, our musket and bayonet, our cannon and ball, ought to be of domestic manufacture. But what, he asked, is more necessary to the defence of a country than its currency and finance? Circumstanced as our country is, can these stand the shock of war? Behold the effect of the late war on them! When our manufactures are grown to a certain perfection, as they soon will under the fostering care of Government, we will no longer experience these evils. The farmer will find a ready market for his surplus produce, and, what is almost of equal consequence, a certain and cheap supply of all his wants. His prosperity will diffuse itself to every class in the community, and, instead of that languor of industry, and individual distress now incident to a state of war, and suspended commerce, the wealth and vigor of the community will not be materially impaired. The arm of Government will be nerved, and taxes in the hour of danger, when essential to the independence of the nation, may be greatly increased; loans, so uncertain and hazardous, may be less relied on; thus situated, the storm may beat without, but within all will be quiet and safe. There are two ways by which the people can be placed beyond the power of a foreign war materially to impair.

It is certainly a great political evil, incident to the character of the industry of this country, that, however prosperous our situation when at peace, with uninterrupted commerce, and nothing then could exceed it, the moment that we were involved in war the whole is reversed. When resources are most needed; when indispensable to maintain the honor, yes, the very existence of the nation, then they desert us. Our currency is also sure to experience the shock, and becomes so deranged as to prevent us from calling out fairly whatever of means is left to the country. The result of a war in the present state of our naval power is the blockade of our seacoast, and consequent destruction of our trade. The wants and habits of the country, founded on the use of foreign articles, must be gratified; importation to a certain extent continues, through the policy of the enemy, or unlawful traffic; the exportation of our bulky articles is prevented, too; the specie of the country is drawn to pay the balance perpetually accumulating against us; and the final result is a total derangement of our currency.

To this distressing state of things there are two remedies, and only two; one in our power immediately, the other requiring much time and exertion, but both constituting the essential policy of this country; he meant the navy, and domestic manufactures. By the former, we could open the way to our markets; by the latter, we bring them from beyond the ocean, and naturalize them. Had we the means of attaining an immediate naval ascendency, he acknowledged that the policy recommended by this bill would be very questionable, but as this is not the fact—as it is a period remote, with any exertion, and will be probably more so, from that relaxation of exertion, so natural in peace, when necessity is not felt, it became the duty of this House to resort, to a considerable extent, at least as far as is proposed, to the only remaining remedy. But to this it has been objected that the country is not prepared, and that the result of our premature exertion would be to bring distress on it, without effecting the intended object. Were it so, however urgent the reasons in its favor, we ought to desist, as it is folly to oppose the laws of necessity. But he could not for a moment yield to the assertion; on the contrary, he firmly believed that the country is prepared, even to maturity, for the introduction of manufactures. We have abundance of resources, and things naturally tend at this moment in that direction. A prosperous commerce has poured an immense amount of commercial capital into this country. This capital has, until lately, found occupation in commerce, but that state of the world which transferred it to this country, and gave it active employment, has passed away, never to return. Where shall we now find full employment for our prodigious amount of tonnage; where markets for the numerous and abundant products of our country? This great body of active capital, which for the moment has found sufficient employment in supplying our markets, exhausted by the war, and measures preceding it, must find a new direction; it will not be idle. What channel can it take but that of manufactures? This, if things continue as they are, will be its direction. It will introduce a new era in our affairs, in many respects highly advantageous, and ought to be countenanced by the Government. Besides, we have already surmounted the greatest difficulty that has ever been found in undertakings of this kind. The cotton and woolen manufactures are not to be introduced—they are already introduced to a great extent; freeing us entirely from the hazards, and, in a great measure, the sacrifices, experienced in giving the capital of the country a new direction. The restrictive measures and the war, though not intended for that purpose, have, by the necessary operation of things, turned a large amount of capital to this new branch of industry. He had often heard it said, both in and out of Congress, that this effect alone would indemnify the country for all of its losses. But it will no doubt be said, if they are so far established, and if the situation of the country is so favorable to their growth, where is the necessity of affording them protection? It is to put them beyond the reach of contingency. Besides, capital is not yet, and cannot, for some time, be, adjusted to the new state of things. There is, in fact, from the operation of temporary causes, a great pressure on these establishments. They had extended so rapidly during the late war that many, he feared, were without the requisite surplus capital or skill to meet the present crisis. Should such prove to be the fact, it would give a back set, and might, to a great extent, endanger their ultimate success. Should the present owners be ruined, and the workmen dispersed and turn to other pursuits, the country would sustain a great loss. Such would, no doubt, be the fact to a considerable extent, if not protected. Besides, circumstances, if we act with wisdom, are favorable to attract to our country much skill and industry. The country in Europe having the most skilful workmen is broken up. It is to us, if wisely used, more valuable than the repeal of the Edict of Nantz was to England. She had the prudence to profit by it; let us not discover less political sagacity. Afford to ingenuity and industry immediate and ample protection, and they will not fail to give a preference to this free and happy country.

It has been objected to this bill that it will injure our marine, and consequently impair our naval strength. How far it is fairly liable to this charge he was not prepared to say. He hoped and believed it would not, at least to any alarming extent, have that effect immediately, and he firmly believed that its lasting operation would be highly beneficial to our commerce. The trade to the East Indies would certainly be much affected, but it was stated in debate that the whole of that trade employed but six hundred sailors. But whatever might be the loss in this, or other branches of our foreign commerce, he trusted it would be amply compensated in our coasting trade—a branch of navigation wholly in our own hands. It has at all times employed a great amount of tonnage, something more, he believed, than one-third of the whole.

An objection had been made that capital employed in manufacturing produced a greater dependence on the part of the employed than in commerce, navigation, or agriculture. It is certainly an evil, and to be regretted, but he did not think it a decisive objection to the system, especially when it had incidental political advantages which, in his opinion, more than counterpoised it. It produced an interest strictly American, as much so as agriculture, in which it had the decided advantage of commerce or navigation. The country will from this derive much advantage. Again, it is calculated to bind together more closely our widely spread Republic. It will greatly increase our mutual dependence and intercourse, and will, as a necessary consequence, excite an increased attention to internal improvement—a subject every way so intimately connected with the ultimate attainment of national strength and the perfection of our political institutions. He regarded the fact that it would make the parts adhere more closely; that it would form a new and most powerful cement, as far outweighing any political objections that might be urged against the system. In his opinion the liberty and the union of the country were inseparably united. That as the destruction of the latter would most certainly involve the former, so its maintenance will with equal certainty preserve it. He did not speak lightly. He had often and long revolved it in his mind, and he had critically examined into the causes that destroyed the liberty of other states. There are none that apply to us, or apply with a force to alarm. The basis of our Republic is too broad, and its structure too strong to be shaken by them. Its extension and organization will be found to afford effectual security against their operation, but let it be deeply impressed on the heart of this House and country that, while they guarded against the old, they exposed us to a new and terrible danger—disunion. This single word comprehended almost the sum of our political dangers, and against it we ought to be perpetually guarded.

CHAPTER III

THE TARIFF OF 1824
[THE AMERICAN SYSTEM]

Protective Tariff Bill Is Introduced in the House—Debate: **in Favor**, Henry Clay [Ky.]; Opposed, Daniel Webster [Mass.].

THE financial depression in the country continued, and early in 1824 Henry Clay, who had in the meantime formulated a comprehensive policy by joining his favorite projects of a protective tariff and internal improvements—which policy he presumptuously christened the ''American System''—instigated the introduction of a bill in the House of Representatives which increased the duties on imports to a point where the former policy of the country to lay a ''tariff for revenue with incidental protection'' threatened to become the reverse—''a tariff for protection with incidental revenue.'' Indeed, the average rate of duties under the bill was 37 per cent., whereas, in the tariff of 1816, 25 per cent. had been considered a most liberal protective rate, and had been laid on only a few commodities such as cotton, the home manufacture of which was thought especially desirable.

The measure was debated in the House from February 14 until April 14, 1824, when it was passed by a vote of 105 to 102. In the Senate it commanded a majority of four votes.

From the alignment for and against this bill it was apparent that sectional interests were coming more and more to replace economic theories as a cause for upholding or opposing the protective system. Thus the Senators and Representatives from the importing and agricultural South, with notable exceptions, such as Senator

36

Andrew Jackson [Tenn.], voted generally against the bill, along with a majority of men from New England, where commercial interest still overbalanced manufacturing; and, on the other hand, most of the Senators and Representatives of the manufacturing Middle States were in favor of the measure, as well as a majority of the men of the growing West, who had visions of great manufacturing development in the region, and to whom the bill offered further inducements in the form of heavy duties on their sectional products, such as wool and hemp.

Indeed, this tariff bill was the first in which a design was apparent to secure votes by an appeal to local interests, and in framing which "log-rolling" or bargaining between the sections began to play a part.

The chief of the many speakers upon the bill were Henry Clay [Ky.] and Daniel Webster [Mass.],[1] who discussed in the House of Representatives the general principles of a tariff primarily for protection *versus* a tariff primarily for revenue, Clay advocating the former and Webster the latter, and each claiming that he was presenting the policy for which America by nature and institutions was peculiarly adapted.

THE AMERICAN SYSTEM

HOUSE OF REPRESENTATIVES, MARCH 31-APRIL 2, 1824

MR. CLAY.—Two classes of politicians divide the people of the United States. According to the system of one, the produce of foreign industry should be subjected to no other impost than such as may be necessary to provide a public revenue, and the produce of American industry should be left to sustain itself, if it can, with no other than that incidental protection, in its competition, at home as well as abroad, with rival foreign articles. According to the system of the other class, while they agree that the imposts should be mainly, and may, under any modifications, be safely, relied on as a fit and convenient

---

[1] In August, 1816, Webster removed from Portsmouth, N. H., to Boston, Mass., and on the expiration of his second term in Congress [March 4, 1817], devoted himself to the practice of law. In 1822 he was returned to Congress from Boston.

source of public revenue, they would so adjust and arrange the duties on foreign fabrics as to afford a gradual but adequate protection to American industry, and lessen our dependence on foreign nations, by securing a certain and, ultimately, a cheaper and better supply of our own wants from our own abundant resources. Both classes are equally sincere in their respective opinions, equally honest, equally patriotic, and desirous of advancing the prosperity of the country. In the discussion and consideration of these opposite opinions, for the purpose of ascertaining which has the support of truth and reason, we should, therefore, exercise every indulgence, and the greatest spirit of mutual moderation and forbearance. And, in our deliberations on this great question, we should look fearlessly and truly at the actual condition of the country, retrace the causes which have brought us into it, and snatch, if possible, a view of the future. We should, above all, consult experience—the experience of other nations as well as our own, as our truest and most unerring guide.

In casting our eyes around us, the most prominent circumstance which fixes our attention, and challenges our deepest regret, is the general distress which pervades the whole country. It is forced upon us by numerous facts of the most incontestable character. It is indicated by the diminished exports of native produce, by the depressed and reduced state of our foreign navigation, by our diminished commerce, by successive unthreshed crops of grain, perishing in our barns and barn-yards for the want of a market, by the alarming diminution of the circulating medium, by the numerous bankruptcies, not limited to the trading classes, but extending to all orders of society, by a universal complaint of the want of employment, and a consequent reduction of the wages of labor, by the ravenous pursuit after public situations, not for the sake of their honors, and the performance of their public duties, but as a means of private subsistence, by the reluctant resort to the perilous use of paper money, by the intervention of legislation in the delicate relation between debtor and creditor, and, above all, by the low and depressed state of the value of almost every description of the whole mass of the property of the nation, which has, on an average, sunk not less than about fifty per cent. within a few years. This distress pervades every part of the Union, every class of society; all feel it, though it may be felt, at different places, in different degrees. It is like the atmosphere which surrounds us—all must inhale it, and none can escape it—and in some places it has burst upon our people without a single mitigating circumstance to temper its severity.

What is the *cause* of this wide-spreading distress, of this deep depression, which we behold stamped on the public countenance? We are the same people. We have the same country. We cannot arraign the bounty of Providence. The shadows still fall in the same grateful abundance. The sun still casts his genial and vivifying influence upon the land, and the land, fertile and diversified in its soils as ever, yields to the industrious cultivator, in boundless profusion, its accustomed fruits, its richest treasures. Our vigor is unimpaired. Our industry is not relaxed.

The causes, then, of our present affliction, whatever they may be, are human causes, and human causes not chargeable upon the people, in their private and individual relations. They are to be found in the fact that, during almost the whole existence of this Government, we have shaped our industry, our navigation, and our commerce in reference to an extraordinary war in Europe, and to foreign markets, which no longer exist; in the fact that we have depended too much upon foreign sources of supply, and excited too little the native; in the fact that, while we have cultivated with assiduous care our foreign resources, we have suffered those at home to wither, in a state of neglect and abandonment. The consequence of the termination of the war of Europe has been the resumption of European commerce, European navigation, and the extension of European agriculture and European industry in all its branches. Europe, therefore, has no longer occasion to any thing like the same extent as that which she had during her wars for American commerce, American navigation, the produce of American industry. Europe in commotion, and convulsed throughout all her members, is to America no longer the same Europe as she is now, tranquil, and watching with the most vigilant attention all her own peculiar interests, without regard to the operation of her policy upon us. The effect of this altered state of Europe upon us has been to circumscribe the employment of our marine, and greatly to reduce the value of the produce of our territorial labor. The further effect of this two-fold reduction has been to decrease the value of all property, whether on the land or on the ocean, which loss I suppose to be about fifty per cent. And the still further effect has been to diminish the amount of our circulating medium, in a proportion not less by its transmission abroad, or its withdrawal by the banking institutions, from a necessity which they could not control. The quantity of money, in whatever form it may

be, which a nation wants is in proportion to the total mass of
its wealth, and to the activity of that wealth. A nation that
has but little wealth has but a limited want of money. In
stating the fact, therefore, that the total wealth of the country
has diminished, within a few years, in a ratio of about fifty per
cent., we shall at once fully comprehend the inevitable reduction which must have ensued in the total quantity of the circulating medium of the country. A nation is most prosperous when
there is a gradual and untempting addition to the aggregate
of its circulating medium. It is in a condition the most adverse when there are a rapid diminution in the quantity of the
circulating medium and a consequent depression in the value
of property. In the former case the wealth of individuals
insensibly increases and income keeps ahead of expenditure.
But, in the latter instance, debts have been contracted, engagements made, and habits of expense established, in reference to
the existing state of wealth and of its representative. When
these come to be greatly reduced, individuals find their debts
still existing, their engagements unexecuted, and their habits
inveterate. They see themselves in the possession of the same
property on which, in good faith, they had bound themselves.
But that property, without their fault, possesses no longer the
same value, and, hence, discontent, impoverishment, and ruin
arise.

The greatest want of civilized society is a market for the
sale and exchange of the surplus of the produce of the labor
of its members. This market may exist at home or abroad, or
both, but it must exist somewhere, if society prospers, and wherever it does exist it should be competent to the absorption of
the entire surplus of production. It is most desirable that
there should be both a home and a foreign market. But with
respect to their relative superiority I cannot entertain a doubt.
The home market is first in order, and paramount in importance. The object of the bill under consideration is to
create this home market, and to lay the foundations of a
genuine American policy.

Mr. Chairman, our Confederacy comprehends within its
vast limits great diversity of interests—agricultural, planting,
farming, commercial, navigating, fishing, manufacturing. No
one of these interests is felt in the same degree, and cherished
with the same solicitude, through all parts of the Union. Some
of them are peculiar to particular sections of our common
country. But all these great interests are confided to the
protection of one government—to the fate of one ship, and a

most gallant ship it is, with a noble crew. If we prosper, and are happy, protection must be extended to all—it is due to all. It is the great principle on which obedience is demanded from all. If our essential interests cannot find protection from our own Government against the policy of foreign powers, where are they to get it?

Need I remind the committee of the great advantages of a steady and unfailing source of supply, unaffected alike in war and in peace? Its importance, in reference to the stability of our Union, that paramount and greatest of all our interests, cannot fail warmly to recommend it, or at least to conciliate the forbearance of every patriot bosom. Now our people present the spectacle of a vast assemblage of jealous rivals, all eagerly rushing to the seaboard, jostling each other in their way, to hurry off to glutted foreign markets the perishable produce of their labor. The tendency of that policy, in conformity with which this bill is prepared, is to transform these competitors into friends and mutual customers, and, by the reciprocal exchanges of their respective productions, to place the Confederacy upon the most solid of all foundations, the basis of common interest. And is not the Government called upon, by every stimulating motive, to adapt its policy to the actual condition and extended growth of our great Republic? Our policy should be modified so as to comprehend all and sacrifice none. And are we not encouraged by the success of past experience in respect to the only article [cotton] which has been adequately protected? Already have the predictions of the friends of the *American system*, in even a shorter time than their most sanguine hopes could have anticipated, been completely realized in regard to that article, and the consumption is now better and cheaper supplied with coarse cottons than it was under the prevalence of the foreign system.

The benefits of the policy are two-fold, direct and collateral, and in the one shape or the other they will diffuse themselves throughout the Union. All parts of the Union will participate, more or less, in both. As to the direct benefits, it is probable that the North and the East will enjoy the largest share. But the West and the South will also participate in them. And where the direct benefit does not accrue, that will be enjoyed of supplying the raw material and provisions for the consumption of artisans. Is it not most desirable to put at rest and prevent the annual recurrence of this unpleasant subject so well fitted by the various interests to which it appeals to excite irritation and to produce discontent? Can that be effected by its rejection? Behold the mass of petitions which lie on our table, earnestly and anxiously entreating the protecting interposition of Congress against the ruinous policy which we are pursuing. Will these petitioners, comprehending all orders of society, entire States and communities, public companies, and private individuals, spontaneously assembling, cease in their humble prayers, by your lending a deaf ear? Will you delay the passage of this bill while these petitioners, and others in countless numbers, contemplate their substance gradually withdrawn to foreign countries, their ruin as inevitable as death itself?

Our convictions, mutually honest, are equally strong. What then is to be done? I invoke that saving spirit of mutual concession under which our blessed Constitution was formed, and under which alone it can be happily administered. I appeal to the South—to the high-minded, generous, and patriotic South—with which I have so often coöperated in attempting to sustain the honor and to vindicate the rights of our country. Should it not offer, upon the altar of the public good, some sacrifice of its peculiar opinions? Of what does it complain? A possible temporary enhancement in the objects of consumption. Of what do we complain? A total incapacity, produced by the foreign policy, to purchase, at any price, necessary foreign objects of consumption. In such an alternative, inconvenient only to it, ruinous to us, can we expect too much from Southern magnanimity? The just and confident expectation of the passage of this bill has flooded the country with recent importations of foreign fabrics. If it should not pass, they will complete the work of destruction of our domestic industry. If it should pass, they will prevent any considerable rise in the price of foreign commodities, until our own industry shall be able to supply competent substitutes.

This bill may be postponed, thwarted, defeated. But the cause is the cause of the country, and it must and will prevail. It is founded in the interests and affections of the people. It is as native as the granite deeply embosomed in our mountains. And, in conclusion, I would pray God, in His infinite mercy, to avert from our country the evils which are impending over it, and, by enlightening our councils, to conduct us into that path which leads to riches, to greatness, to glory.

Mr. WEBSTER.—Being intrusted with the interests of a district highly commercial, and deeply interested in manufactures also, I wish to state my opinions on the present measure, not as on a whole, for it has no entire and homogeneous character,

but as on a collection of different enactments, some of which
meet my approbation, and some of which do not.

And allow me, sir, in the first place, to state my regret,
if, indeed, I ought not to express a warmer sentiment, at the
names, or designations, which Mr. Speaker has seen fit to adopt
for the purpose of describing the advocates and the opposers
of the present bill. It is a question, he says, between the
friends of an "American policy" and those of a "foreign
policy." This, sir, is an assumption which I take the liberty
most directly to deny. Mr. Speaker certainly intended nothing
invidious or derogatory to any part of the House by this mode
of denominating friends and enemies. But there is power in
names, and this manner of distinguishing those who favor and
those who oppose particular measures may lead to inferences
to which no member of the House can submit. It may imply
that there is a more exclusive and peculiar regard to American
interests in one class of opinions than in another. Such an
implication is to be resisted and repelled. Every member has
a right to the presumption that he pursues what he believes
to be the interest of his country with as sincere a zeal as any
other member. I claim this in my own case, and, while I
shall not, for any purpose of description, or convenient arrangement, use terms which may imply any disrespect to other men's
opinions, much less any imputation of other men's motives, it
is my duty to take care that the use of such terms by others
be not, against the will of those who adopt them, made to
produce a false impression. Indeed, sir, it is a little astonishing,
if it seemed convenient to Mr. Speaker, for the purposes of
distinction, to make use of the terms "American policy" and
"foreign policy," that he should not have applied them in a
manner precisely the reverse of that in which he has in fact
used them. If names are thought necessary, it would be well
enough, one would think, that the name should be, in some
measure, descriptive of the thing, and since Mr. Speaker de-
nominates the policy which he recommends "a new policy in
this country"; since he speaks of the present measure as a
new era in our legislation; since he professes to invite us to
depart from our accustomed course, to instruct ourselves by the
wisdom of others, and to adopt the policy of the most distinguished foreign states, one is a little curious to know with
what propriety of speech this imitation of other nations is de-
nominated an "American policy," while, on the contrary, a
preference for our own established system, as it now actually
exists, and always has existed, is called a "foreign policy."

This favorite American policy is what America has never tried, and this odious foreign policy is what, as we are told, foreign states have never pursued. Sir, that is the truest American policy which shall most usefully employ American capital and American labor, and best sustain the whole population. With me it is a fundamental axiom, it is interwoven with all my opinions, that the great interests of the country are united and inseparable; that agriculture, commerce, and manufactures will prosper together, or languish together, and that all legislation is dangerous which proposes to benefit one of these without looking to the consequences which may fall on the others.

Passing from this, sir, I am bound to say I dissent entirely from the justice of that picture of distress which Mr. Speaker has drawn. I have not seen the reality, and know not where it exists. Within my observation there is no cause for so gloomy and terrifying a representation. It is not, indeed, a time for great profits and sudden acquisition; not a day of extraordinary activity and successful speculation. There is, no doubt, a considerable depression of prices, and, in some degree, a stagnation of business. But the case presented by Mr. Speaker was not one of depression, but of distress; of universal, pervading, intense distress, limited to no class, and to no place. We are represented as on the very verge and brink of national ruin. So far from acquiescing in these opinions, I believe there has been no period in which the general prosperity was better secured or rested on a more solid foundation. A country enjoying a profound peace, a perfect civil liberty, with the means of subsistence cheap and abundant, with the reward of labor sure, and its wages higher than anywhere else, cannot be represented in gloom, melancholy, and distress but by the effort of extraordinary powers of tragedy.

I will now proceed, sir, to state some objections which I feel, of a more general nature, to the course of Mr. Speaker's observations.

He seems to me to argue the question as if all domestic industry were confined to the production of manufactured articles; as if the employment of our own capital, and our own labor, in the occupations of commerce and navigation, were not as emphatically domestic industry as any other occupation Some other gentlemen, in the course of the debate, have spoken of the price paid for every foreign manufactured article as so much given for the encouragement of foreign labor, to the prejudice of our own. But is not every such article the product of our own labor as truly as if we had manufactured it ourselves? Our labor has earned it, and paid the price for it. It is so much added to the stock of national wealth. If the commodity were dollars, nobody would doubt the truth of this remark; and it is precisely as correct in its application to any other commodity as to silver. One man makes a yard of cloth at home; another raises agricultural products, and buys a yard of imported cloth. Both these are equally the earnings of domestic industry, and the only questions that arise in the case are two: the first is, which is the best mode, under all the circumstances, of obtaining the article; the second is, how far this first question is proper to be decided by government, and how far it is proper to be left to individual discretion. There is no foundation for the distinction which attributes to certain employments the peculiar appellation of American industry; and it is, in my judgment, extremely unwise to attempt such discriminations. We are asked what nations have ever attained eminent prosperity without encouraging manufactures? I may ask what nation ever reached the like prosperity without promoting foreign trade? I regard these interests as closely connected, and am of opinion that it should be our aim to cause them to flourish together. I know it would be very easy to promote manufactures, at least for a time, but probably only for a short time, if we might act in disregard of other interests. We could cause a sudden transfer of capital and a violent change in the pursuits of men. We could exceedingly benefit some classes by these means. But what, then, becomes of the interests of others? The power of collecting revenue by duties on imports, and the habit of the Government of collecting almost its whole revenue in that mode, will enable us, without exceeding the bounds of moderation, to give great advantages to those classes of manufactures which we may think most useful to promote at home. What I object to is the immoderate use of the power—exclusions and prohibitions; all of which, as I think, not only interrupt the pursuits of individuals, with great injury to themselves, and little or no benefit to the country, but also often divert our own labor, or, as it may very properly be called, our own domestic industry, from those occupations in which it is well employed, and well paid, to others, in which it will be worse employed, and worse paid. For my part, I see very little relief to those who are likely to be deprived of their employments, or who find the prices of the commodities which they need raised, in any of the alternatives which Mr. Speaker has presented. It is nothing to say that they may, if they choose, continue to buy the foreign article; the answer is, the price is augmented; nor that they may use the domestic article; the price of that also is increased. Nor can they supply themselves by the substitution of their own fabric. How can the agriculturist make his own iron? How can the ship owner grow his own hemp?

But I have yet a stronger objection to the course of Mr. Speaker's reasoning; I can hardly express the surprise I feel that he should fall into the common modes of expression used elsewhere, and ask if we will give our manufactures no protection. Sir, look to the history of our laws; look to the present state of our laws. Consider that our whole revenue, with a trifling exception, is collected at the custom house, and always has been; and then say what propriety there is in calling on the Government for protection, as if no protection had heretofore been afforded. The real question before us, in regard to all the important clauses of the bill, is not whether we will *lay* duties, but whether we will *augment* duties. The demand is for something more than exists, and yet it is pressed as if nothing existed. We hear of the fatal policy of the tariff of 1816; and yet the law of 1816 was passed avowedly for the benefit of manufacturers, and, with very few exceptions, imposed on imported articles very great additions of tax; in some important instances, indeed, amounting to a prohibition.

On the general question, sir, allow me to ask if the doctrine of prohibition, as a general doctrine, be not preposterous? Suppose all nations to act upon it; they would be prosperous, then, according to the argument, precisely in the proportion in which they abolished intercourse with one another. The less of mutual commerce the better, upon this hypothesis. Protection and encouragement may be, and are, doubtless, sometimes, wise and beneficial, if kept within proper limits; but when carried to an extravagant height, or the point of prohibition, the absurd character of the system manifests itself.

Let me now ask, sir, what relief this bill proposes to some of those great and essential interests of the country, the condition of which has been referred to as proof of national distress; and which condition, although I do not think it makes out a case of distress, yet does indicate depression.

And first, as to our foreign trade. The Speaker has stated that there has been a considerable falling off in the tonnage employed in that trade. This is true, lamentably true. But what do we propose to do for it? Why, simply to burden and to tax it. The shipping interest pays, annually, more than half a million of dollars in duties on articles used in the construction

of ships. We propose to add nearly, or quite, fifty per cent.
to this amount, at the very moment that we bring forth the
languishing state of this interest as a proof of national distress.
Let it be remembered that our shipping employed in foreign
commerce has at this moment not the shadow of government
protection. It goes abroad upon the wide sea to make its own
way, and earn its own bread, in a professed competition with
the whole world. This right arm of the nation's safety strength-
ens its own muscle by its own efforts, and by unwearied exertion in its own defence becomes strong for the defence of the
country. We have left this interest hitherto to maintain itself
or perish; to swim if it can, and to sink if it cannot. But, at
this moment of its apparent struggle, can we, as men, can we,
as patriots, add another stone to the weight that threatens to
carry it down? Sir, there is a limit to human power and to
human effort. Some things are impossible to be done; and some
burdens may be impossible to be borne; and, as it was the last
ounce that broke the back of the camel, so the last tax, although
it were even a small one, may be decisive as to the power of our
marine to sustain the conflict in which it is now engaged with
all the commercial nations on the globe.

It has been often said, sir, that our manufactures have to
contend not only against the natural advantages of those who
produce similar articles in foreign countries, but also against
the action of foreign governments, who have great political interest in aiding their own manufactures to suppress ours. But
have not these governments as great an interest to cripple our
marine by preventing the growth of our commerce and navigation? What is it that makes us the object of the highest respect or the most suspicious jealousy to foreign states? I need
not say that this results, more than from anything else, from
that quantity of military power which we can cause to be water
borne, and of that extent of commerce which we are able to
maintain throughout the world.

Mr. Chairman, the best apology for laws of prohibition and
laws of monopoly will be found in that state of society, not only
unenlightened, but sluggish, in which they are most generally
established. Private industry in those days required strong
provocatives, which governments were seeking to administer by
these means. Something was wanted to actuate and stimulate
men, and the prospects of such profits as would, in our times,
excite unbounded competition would hardly move the sloth of
former ages. In some instances, no doubt, these laws produced
an effect which, in that period, would not have taken place

without them. But our age is wholly of a different character, and its legislation takes another turn. Society is full of excitement; competition comes in place of monopoly; and intelligence and industry ask only for fair play and an open field. Profits, indeed, in such a state of things, will be small, but they will be extensively diffused; prices will be low, and the great body of the people prosperous and happy. It is worthy of remark that, from the operation of these causes, commercial wealth, while it is increased beyond calculation in its general aggregate, is, at the same time, broken and diminished in its subdivisions. Commercial prosperity should be judged of, therefore, rather from the extent of trade than from the magnitude of its apparent profits. When the diminution of profits arises from the extent of competition it indicates rather a salutary than an injurious change.

Labor is the great producer of wealth; it moves all other causes. If it call machinery to its aid, it is still employed, not only in using the machinery, but in making it. I cannot find that we have those idle hands of which the chairman of the committee speaks. The price of labor is a conclusive and unanswerable refutation of that idea; it is known to be higher with us than in any other civilized state, and this is the greatest of all proofs of general happiness. Labor in this country is independent and proud. It has not to ask the patronage of capital, but capital solicits the aid of labor.

CHAPTER IV

THE TARIFF OF 1828

[PROTECTION AND POLITICS]

Silas Wright [N. Y.] Introduces in the House a Tariff Bill "For the
Working up of Domestic Raw Materials"—Debate in the House:
Denunciation of Bill by Nathaniel H. Claiborne [Va.], George McDuffie
[S. C.], James Hamilton [S. C.], Daniel Turner [Va.], John Randolph
[Va.]—Bill Is Passed.

AS had been prophesied by the opponents of the protective features of the tariff of 1824, the manufacturing interests were not satisfied with the duties levied upon the products of their foreign competitors, and soon demanded that they be raised still higher. Thus, in 1826, a petition came to Congress from Boston, praying that the duties on woolen goods be increased, and in 1827 a bill to this effect passed the House but failed to become a law. In July, 1827, a convention of wool growers and woolen manufacturers was held at Harrisburg, Pa. Other interests asked to be admitted, and their request was granted. The convention thus unified all the interests demanding a high tariff, and focused the attention of the country upon the question.

During the congressional session of 1827-28, Silas Wright [N. Y.] introduced a tariff bill, which, as he said, was "intended to turn the manufacturing capital of the country to the working up of domestic raw material, and not foreign raw material." However, its scope was soon broadened far beyond this purpose by the many amendments made to it by the various political, no less than industrial, interests.

After a protracted debate the bill passed in the House by a vote of 105 to 94, and in the Senate by a vote of 26 to 21.

The speakers in advocacy of the bill, almost without exception, confined themselves to discussing specific schedules, and hence their speeches are of little interest. The opposition, however, was rich in oratorical denunciation of the principle of the bill and its political animus, terming it a "bill of abominations." Among the brilliant speakers from the South who opposed the measure as an act of tyranny toward their section were Nathaniel H. Claiborne [Va.], George McDuffie [S. C.], James Hamilton [S. C.], Daniel Turner [Va.], and John Randolph [Va.].

THE TARIFF BILL

HOUSE OF REPRESENTATIVES, MARCH 5-APRIL 18, 1828

MR. CLAIBORNE dwelt particularly upon the great masses who had abandoned the cultivation of the earth. This occupation, he said, is the primitive and favorite pursuit of man.

When the population has advanced to a point where the soil will not maintain it, the eagle-eyed sagacity of the citizen will open to him the road to such employments as will best maintain him. There is no necessity for the Government to resort to a hot-bed system of legislation, to force into premature existence a number of sickly manufacturing establishments that will want constant aid from the Government. When the population advances to that point, Government has only to afford protection to all, secure to every man, by an even-handed justice, the fruits of his labor, whether that labor is devoted to the cultivation of the earth, the navigation of the seas, or the labors of the loom, anvil, or hammer. Need I go further than our own country for a happy illustration of the results flowing from a system of government founded on the mild and philosophical principle I here advocate? Under their influence we have, from small beginnings, grown up into a great people—worthy the respect of the world. Sir, we must become a great agricultural people— we have a sufficiency of arable land for the accommodation of the people of the present day. Nay, more, for the accommodation of our probable population for five hundred years to come.

If eventually we must become a manufacturing people, let it be by a slow process.

How long did Great Britain exist as a nation before she

soared to unrivaled excellence in commerce and manufactures? I answer, until her population advanced to that point that the soil could not maintain it; then her manufactures and commerce flourished. Do we expect to maintain, in a moment, that which in older countries has been more than equal to the labor of ages? If manufactures are necessary to our independence, they will grow under existing circumstances.

The history of the tariff in this country deserves some notice. There have been four revisals, and they have invariably been effected by compromise. To break in so frequently on the system, and extend the duties, produces jealousy, dissatisfaction, and strife. It keeps the price of labor and property constantly fluctuating. It unhinges the confidence of the people in your laws, and it disorders the circulating medium of the country. This incessant advance in duties entices people to embark in manufacturing establishments with an impression that the Government will sustain them at all events, and make their labor productive. The course pursued by Congress in 1824 has let to this effort to increase the duties. It will be remembered that that enterprising State, now the most extensively engaged in the woolen manufactures, was then opposed to increased duties on foreign woolens. That State, I am told, is now at the opposite point, and for greater increase. Sir, your legislation seduces your citizens to invest time and money in those establishments; and, unless you take a firm stand, you must end in the Chinese system of exclusion. In 1824 the vote of the Massachusetts delegation encouraged a belief that the manufactures there were then prosperous; the increased duties laid that year seduced very many to invest their capital in woolen manufactures. Many entered into the business, no doubt, with borrowed capital. What followed? That which was to be apprehended: competition was encountered at home and from abroad. The profits, at first large, are reduced and now comes the application for further protection; and no doubt, in my mind, it will be continued until it works a total exclusion.

This system of exclusion I can never agree to; a mutual exchange of commodities, or free commerce, makes the most distant people friends, and converts the universe into a community of brothers.

MR. McDUFFIE.—Mr. Speaker, it is distressing to witness the kind of aristocratic influence by which measures of this sort are obviously controlled. I have witnessed, with astonishment and regret, as a strong proof of the aristocratic tendency of every system of government, the melancholy fact that intelligent and honorable men upon this floor, in whose congressional districts there is perhaps a single manufactory of iron, owned by perhaps the very wealthiest man in the country, will give their votes, without the least compunction, to impose an odious and oppressive tax upon the remaining thousands of their poor constituents, to increase the profits of one wealthy nabob.

And yet, sir, we talk about a democratic government and the responsibility of the Representative to the people! I speak not the language of a demagogue, but the grave and solemn language of historical and philosophical truth, when I say that it is the very genius of this system, as exhibited in this and every other country, to tax the many and the poor for the benefit of the few and the wealthy. Take up the articles embraced in the scheme of protection, one by one, and I defy any man to point out a single one of them that does not specifically prove and illustrate the proposition I have laid down. Salt, for example, is an article of first necessity, equally consumed by the poor and the rich. The people of the United States now pay about one hundred per cent. on every bushel of salt they consume, amounting in the aggregate to a tax of at least a million and a half dollars, paid by all classes, for the exclusive benefit of the owners of some one or two hundred salt works at the utmost. The same remark is strictly applicable to the duty on iron. It imposes a universal tax, both heavy and permanent, for the benefit of not more than one or two hundred iron masters in the United States. And I appeal to the members from Pennsylvania, Maryland, and Western Virginia, to state whether these men have not accumulated princely fortunes by the very business which we are taxing the people still higher to sustain? I was myself informed by one of those iron masters that the establishment in which he was concerned yielded an annual income of, I think it was, $15,000 or $20,000, and that he could afford to sell iron at ten dollars a ton less than the present prices and do a profitable business. And yet, sir, with all the republican simplicity imaginable, we are imposing a heavy tax upon the whole democracy of the country, to increase the already overgrown fortunes of this single branch of the aristocracy! The high duty on imported sugar is another illustration of the view I am attempting to impress upon the House; and I am induced to notice it the more particularly because it has been urged as a reason why the Southern States generally ought to submit to the proposed imposition of high duties on other articles. Sir, what sort of logic is that which urges the justice of imposing a tax upon South Carolina for the benefit

of Massachusetts, because a tax has already been imposed upon
both South Carolina and Massachusetts for the benefit of Louisiana? I do not understand this system of sectional combination—I am sure it is not founded upon the principles of the
Constitution—by which South Carolina is to be made responsible
to Massachusetts for the duty on sugar, any more than she is
responsible to Louisiana for the duty on woolens. By all the
ties which consecrate this Union, my State stands in as near a
relation to Massachusetts as to Louisiana, and he does not consult either the spirit of the Constitution or the harmony of the
Union who deduces such an argument as that which I am considering from geographical juxtaposition merely. I, sir, complain of the duty upon sugar as much as any other member of
this House. It is obnoxious, in a peculiar manner, to the objection I have urged against the duties on salt and iron; it is a tax
on the great body of the people for the benefit of some two or
three hundred sugar planters who are men of immense wealth;
for the fact is notorious that the business is almost conclusively
confined to large capitalists. Every family in the United States
that consumes 33 1-3 pounds of sugar pays a tax of one dollar
to these wealthy monopolists; and I know a single individual—
he is a personal friend—worth between two and three millions
of dollars, who receives annually about $30,000 as his dividend
of this national bounty.

Can there be a more striking proof of the injustice, and im-
policy, and anti-republican tendency of this system? It imposes a tax of at least four millions five hundred thousand dollars upon the mass of the people in every State in the Union,
for the sole and exclusive benefit of the iron masters, sugar
planters, and owners of salt works, not amounting, in the whole
Union, to more than from five hundred to one thousand persons; and, if we add all the owners of cotton and woolen manufactories in the United States, it would not swell the number
to two thousand. Sir, the foundation of an aristocracy of wealth
was never more distinctly laid in the legislation of any country
on earth; nor was the democracy of any other country ever
subjected to such an enormous tax to sustain a privileged order.
There is nothing in the legislation of England, not excepting
the oppressive system of the corn laws, more justly obnoxious to
condemnation.

But, sir, the manufacturers, with an art common to all those
who, by the various devices of human cunning, have made sub-
servient to their purposes the credulity of the multitude, allege
that the great body of farmers, constituting, perhaps, three-

fourths of our population, are interested in the establishment
of manufactures as a means of obtaining a market for their
wool. Conceding, as I readily do, that the establishment of
manufactories, when not forced by artificial means, is beneficial
to such farmers as live within their vicinity and have capital
sufficient to embark in the business of wool-growing, yet I confidently appeal to every member from the wool-growing portions
of the Union to say whether the business of growing wool for
the manufacturing establishments is not confined to a very
small portion of farmers, consisting of those who have the
largest capital? Yes, sir, I have been assured by members on
this floor, engaged in the business of wool-growing, that the
small farmers do not even raise wool for their own consumption, but actually buy it from those of the more wealthy class.
I may venture to assert that, taking the average even of the
wool-growing States, there is not one in fifty of the farmers who
raises wool for sale; and that the whole number of wool growers in the United States who would be at all benefited by the
duty upon raw wool and woolens would not exceed ninety thousand persons. Thus it is, sir, that this bill maintains a consistent character throughout all its provisions, and the great democratic farming interest, represented as constituting nine millions of our population, dwindles into an aristocracy of ninety
thousand of the most wealthy farmers. It is to provide a small
bounty for those wool growers and a very large one for the still
smaller number of woolen and cotton manufacturers, iron masters, sugar planters, and owners of salt works, that the other
classes of the people, including more than eight millions nine
hundred thousand of the people of the farming States, are
compelled to pay an annual tax of about fifteen millions of
dollars. Such, sir, is the operation, and such the political
tendency of this system. I shall be probably asked how it happens that the capitalists of the South, the wealthy cotton planters, are arrayed on the side of the great mass of the people in
this contest between capital and labor? Sir, such is our position in this contest that our interest throws us into a natural
alliance with the great body of the people in the farming States.
The wealthy cotton planter of the South fights by the side of
the small farmer, the mechanic, the merchant, and the laborer,
in New York and Pennsylvania, because they all have a similar
interest in opposing a system of which the burden falls upon
them and the benefit on others. And this accounts for the fact
—notorious in our political history—that what some are pleased
to call the aristocracy of the Southern States has always been

found on the same side with the democracy of the Northern States in the political controversies by which the country has been divided. It is a natural alliance. The Southern States, depending on free trade for their prosperity, must always be opposed to any attempts on the part of this Government to build up, by commercial prohibitions, an aristocracy of favored monopolists. Sir, this is not a contest, as some are anxious to represent it, between the Southern and Northern States. It is a contest of less than one hundred thousand manufacturers and farmers against all the other farmers and manufacturers in the Union, and against the whole population in the Southern States.

Mr. Speaker, such are the disguise and delusion incident to this sort of legislation that baseness and treachery are not unlikely to receive the reward appropriate to disinterested patriotism.

Indeed, sir, when I contemplate the extraordinary infatuation which a combination of capitalists and politicians have had the singular art to diffuse over more than one-half of this Union—when I see the very victims who are about to be offered up to satiate the voracious appetite of this devouring Moloch paying their ardent and sincere devotions at his bloody shrine, I confess I have been tempted to doubt whether mankind was not doomed, even in its most enlightened state, to be the dupe of some species of imposture and the victim of some form of tyranny. For, sir, in casting my eye over the history of human idolatry, I can find nothing, even in the darkest ages of ignorance and superstition, which surpasses the infatuation by which a confederated priesthood of politicians and manufacturers have bound the great body of the people in the farming States of this Union, as if by a spell, to this mighty scheme of fraud and delusion.

MR. HAMILTON.—Sir, one of the great masters of human knowledge, who with a ken little short of the spirit of prophecy, perceived some of the causes of the success of our revolution in the very turn of thinking of our people on the subject of taxation, has told us that "Liberty inheres in some sensible objects; every nation has formed for itself some favorite point, which, by way of eminence, becomes the criterion of their happiness. It happened that the great contests for freedom, in this country, were, from the earliest times, chiefly upon the question of taxing. It is not easy to make a monopoly of theorems and corollaries. The colonies draw from you, as with their life blood, these ideas and principles. Their love of liberty is fixed, and attached, on this specific point of taxing." And so, sir, it has continued, down to the present day, in our transit from colonial dependence to sovereign States. This habitual sensibility, which belongs to a free people, you have aroused, by observing no sort of moderation in your objects, until you have fixed the conviction in the public mind that the difference between "taxation without representation" and taxation with representation, in violation of the spirit if not the letter of the constitution, is too idle, in the abstract, to mitigate the evils which, in practice, are common to both; and depend upon it that it will require a more ingenious and talented casuist than even such a man as the pensioned author of "Taxation no Tyranny" to satisfy our people that you are not doing the same thing, in a different form, with the superadded burden of an amount of impost, which never arose even in the imaginations of Grenville and of North, to stimulate their cormorant appetites for American revenue; aggravated, as all this is, by the irrepressible sentiment that you are breaking the faith of that equal compact by which this Union can alone hope to live—"the fountain from which its current runs, or bears no life."

But I trust, sir, that this cup may pass from us; that in our firmness and enlightened patience—not base submission—and in your returning sense of justice, we shall find our remedy and relief; that the spirit of concord and affection may again be breathed into this Union, animating it with the durability of eternal life. But, if an adverse destiny should be ours—if we are doomed to drink "the waters of bitterness," in their utmost woe—if we are doomed under a tyrannous legislation to be reduced in effect again to a condition of colonial vassalage, by your compelling us to purchase, in one quarter of this Union, all that we may consume, and of selling all that we may procure by the sweat of our brow to the same favored portion, you may rely at least on one thing—that, in a juncture so full of difficulty, South Carolina will be found on the side of those principles, standing firmly on the very ground which is canonized by that revolution which has made us what we are, which has imbued us with the spirit of a free and sovereign people.

Mr. Turner.—This Government was formed for great and noble purposes; it was formed upon the principle that the people should be able to control their rulers; it was formed for the benefit of the whole; it was not formed for a majority to promote their own views, as their private interest may direct.

And, sir, these political schemes, which I conceive to be entirely hostile to our institutions, are doing more to weaken the Union of these States than any plan that could be devised. Instead of leaving the people to manage their own affairs in their own way, we must administer our medicine most profusely; and God grant that we may not inscribe on the tomb of our patient the old Spanish epitaph: "I was well, would be better, here I am." It is but too evident that both in our general and State governments we have too much legislation. Let us pass only those laws that are absolutely necessary, and no more; leave the rest to the people—let nature take its course; this is the correct policy of this Government. For all these fine-spun political schemes, which appear so well in theory, when reduced to practice, nine times in ten bring misery and oppression upon some one portion of the community. Something is left out of the calculation which was not foreseen—it produces too artificial a state of authority; and the machine ultimately becomes so complicated that no political juggler, however expert he may be, will be competent to its management. It is upon these principles that I am opposed to all those political measures which, in a country so extensive as this, where the interest of the people is so diversified, must have a tendency to build up one portion of the community at the expense of the other. For the justice of these remarks I would instance England, that glorious but unfortunate country, where political legerdemain has been exercised, until their tricks can no longer conceal that they have brought their country to the brink of national bankruptcy.

It appears, sir, that we, too, like England, must have our schemes; and to render them the more palatable great names are given—the American system. But gentlemen differ widely as to what is the American system. Just as the supposed interests of particular portions of country, which gentlemen happen to represent, require, so they speak. Sir, we all know and feel the influence and magic of a name; but the veriest minnow, to whom this bait is thrown, will, I hope, discover too much sagacity to be deceived. The American system! Sir, we disclaim the name; and denominate it a system to use this Government to promote the views of particular sections of country. The true American system consists in the Government not interfering in matters which are calculated alone to promote the interest of comparatively few individuals, and those confined to particular sections of country, at the expense, nay, sir, the ruin, of other portions of the Union.

After the bill was passed a Representative moved to amend its title by adding the words "for the encouragement of domestic manufactures."

MR. RANDOLPH opposed the motion, insisting that domestic manufactures meant those which were carried on in the families of farmers, in the fabrication of what used to be called Virginia cloth; and that the bill, if it had its true name, should be called a bill to rob and plunder nearly one-half of the Union, for the benefit of the residue, etc. Let the friends of the bill christen their own child; he would not stand godfather to it. The title was merely *ad captandum vulgus*;[1] like the words of the continental money ridiculed in Swift's verses:

> "*Libertas et natale solum*,"[2]
> Fine words indeed! I wonder where you stole 'em."

The bill referred to manufactures of no sort or kind, but the manufacture of a President of the United States.

[1] "For taking (in) the common folk."
[2] "Liberty and native land."

CHAPTER V

THE TARIFF OF 1832

[PROTECTIVE PRINCIPLE]

Revision of the Tariff in Further Interest of Manufacturers—Debate in the Senate: in Favor, Henry Clay [Ky.]; Opposed, John Tyler [Va.]—Debate in the House: in Favor, Rufus Choate [Mass.]; Opposed, Thomas Clayton [Ga.], Dixon H. Lewis [Ala.].

IN 1831 the issue between free trade and protection had been squarely drawn for the first time in American history, the free traders meeting in convention in Philadelphia, and the protectionists in New York, and both assemblies sending memorials to Congress.

In the protracted congressional session of 1831-32 a number of tariff bills were prepared, the result of which was the passage, on July 14, 1832, of a composite act in which the protective features of the existing tariff were maintained, and a number of revenue taxes reduced, and duties abolished on some raw materials, such as varieties of wool—a measure, as will be inferred, in further interest of the manufacturer and against that of the agriculturist. The Southern Congressmen were greatly indignant at the imposition of additional burdens where relief from present ones had been expected by them, and, indeed, promised in the beginning of the session by their opponents—Henry Clay [Ky.] himself introducing in the Senate a resolution in favor of "reduction of duties."

In the debate in the Senate Clay was a leading speaker in favor of the principle of protection, and John Tyler [Va.] was prominent among those in opposition.

THE SOUTH'S COMPLAINT AGAINST THE TARIFF

SENATE, FEBRUARY 2-13, 1832

SENATOR CLAY.—Eight years ago it was my painful duty to present to the House of Congress an unexaggerated picture of the general distress pervading the whole land. If 1 were to select any term of seven years since the adoption of the present Constitution which exhibited a scene of the most widespread dismay and desolation, it would be exactly that term of seven years which immediately preceded the establishment of the tariff of 1824.

I have now to perform the more pleasing task of exhibiting an imperfect sketch of the existing state of the unparalleled prosperity of the country. On a general survey, we behold cultivation extended, the arts flourishing, the face of the country improved, our people fully and profitably employed, and the public countenance exhibiting tranquillity, contentment, and happiness. And, if we descend into particulars, we have the agreeable contemplation of a people out of debt; land rising slowly in value, but in a secure and salutary degree; a ready, though not extravagant, market for all the surplus productions of our industry; innumerable flocks and herds browsing and gamboling on ten thousand hills and plains, covered with rich and verdant grasses; our cities expanded, and whole villages springing up, as it were, by enchantment; our exports and imports increased and increasing; our tonnage, foreign and coastwise, swelling and fully occupied; the rivers of our interior animated by the perpetual thunder and lightning of countless steamboats; the currency sound and abundant; the public debt of two wars nearly redeemed; and, to crown all, the public treasury overflowing, embarrassing Congress, not to find subjects of taxation, but to select the objects which shall be liberated from the impost. If the term of seven years were to be selected of the greatest prosperity which this people have enjoyed since the establishment of their present Constitution, it would be exactly that period of seven years which immediately followed the passage of the tariff of 1824.

This transformation of the condition of the country from gloom and distress to brightness and prosperity has been mainly the work of American legislation, fostering American industry, instead of allowing it to be controlled by foreign legislation, cherishing foreign industry.

It is now proposed to abolish the system to which we owe so much of the public prosperity, and it is urged that the arrival of the period of the redemption of the public debt has been confidently looked to as presenting a suitable occasion to rid the country of the evils with which the system is alleged to be fraught. But the people of the United States have not coupled the payment of *their* public debt with the destruction of the protection of *their* industry against foreign laws and foreign industry. They have been accustomed to regard the extinction of the public debt as relief from a burden, and not as the infliction of a curse. If it is to be attended or followed by the subversion of the American system, and the exposure of our establishments and our productions to the unguarded consequences of the selfish policy of foreign powers, the payment of the public debt will be the bitterest of curses. Its fruit will be like the fruit

> "Of that forbidden tree, whose mortal taste
> Brought death into the world, and all our wo,
> With loss of Eden."

MR. TYLER.—The honorable Senator from Kentucky [Mr. Clay] has drawn a glowing picture of the condition of the country. He has spoken of this as the golden age of these confederated States. By the magic of his eloquence he has transported us to what, with classical taste, he was pleased to call La Belle Rivière, and, sailing down its stream, he pointed out to us a smiling, animated scene—villages rising up in endless succession on its banks, while the arts were gaily meeting us at every step. From thence he led us into the interior of his own State, and there again all was beautiful and enticing: widely extended lawns—animated groves—and hills covered with numberless flocks. All was gay—all was beautiful—all enchanting. He then translated us to the North, and again we stood in fairyland. Here flourished the arts, and the buzz of industry arose from numberless villages. And, finally, to touch off with still deeper tint the glowing scene, he pointed to us that great mart of commerce, the city of New York—the modern Tyre. But the honorable Senator here stopped—his pencil fell from his hands, when he turned to the South, and she was not found upon his canvas. Where were her rising towns? Where her lawns, her animated groves, and living hills? I said she was not on his canvas—I mistake—she was there, but she was enveloped in gloom. She had ventured to utter complaints—to put forth her grievances respectfully, but strongly— and she was scowled upon—reprehended as uttering unfounded complaints, entertaining unwise opinions, and as advocating a system which would recolonize America. If the Senate could see nothing in all this to justify complaint, then are we indeed fairly subject to reproach. What, sir! could not that fervid and glowing fancy create one animated spot—find one oasis in the wilderness of gloom on which to rest? How comes this, Mr. President? Is there anything in soil, in climate, in position, to explain it? Do we sow and not reap? Has the earth suddenly refused to yield to us her harvests? I beg leave to give you an anecdote which is said to have occurred at the table of General Washington shortly after the adoption of the Federal Constitution. The party consisted of several Southern gentlemen and one gentleman from the North. That great and good man was dwelling on the benefits which would arise from the adoption of the Constitution; he portrayed the countless blessings which it would bring to the South—dwelt on its rich productions, and the profitable interchange which it would carry on with all parts of the world. At length, turning to his Northern friend, he inquired, "But what will the North do?" The brief and laconic answer was, "We will live by our wits." And well has this reply been realized. By their wits they have acquired much of the wealth which properly appertains to a more genial climate and richer soil. Their ingenuity has brought forth useful inventions for the benefit of mankind: hardy, industrious, enterprising, they have, in the pursuit of fortune, roamed over distant lands and braved the terrors of the mighty deep. The compliment paid them by Edmund Burke, on the floor of the British Parliament, was every way deserved.[1] Every Southern man rejoiced in their prosperity, so long as it was the result of their own indefatigable industry. Even their wooden nutmegs excited but a smile, and nothing more. They may, for me, make trade and profit of all their notions, except their tariff notions. Against that I do protest with all my strength. But let me return to the course of my inquiry. How comes it now about that, while the South is impoverished, the North has suddenly become so rich?

The honorable Senator, in his effort to find out causes of Southern depression, has seen proper to remark that we were "too poor to live—too proud to work—too high-minded and honorable to resort to ignoble means of acquisition—brave, daring, chivalrous." That we are too poor to live as did those who, but a short time ago, preceded us, is most true—and, sir, it is our misfortune to be growing poorer and poorer: the cause of this I shall attempt presently to explain. But that we are indolent or idle I utterly deny. There lives not a more industrious population under the sun, taken in the mass.

The honorable Senator, then, is mistaken as to the true cause

[1] See Volume I., pages 117, 118.

of our distress and impoverishment. I have looked carefully into the matter; and my inference is that it results, to a great extent, from the simple fact that we sell cheap and purchase dear. Other causes may conjoin with this, but this is the great controlling cause, and amply sufficient in itself to account for the condition of the South.

The home market has been represented to us as of vast importance, more especially in reference to breadstuffs. This delusion has now been kept up for fifteen years. An increase of duties has never, at any time, been proposed, but we have had representations made of the great importance of the home market, produced by the encouragement of domestic manufactures. And yet, sir, no man has ever known produce so low as it has been during the last seven years.

The foreign price regulates the domestic price; and the fluctuations which take place every fall in the wheat market here are ascribable to hopes excited by the slightest circumstance of an increased price abroad. If a cloud is over the face of the sun during the harvest time in England, prices advance; and, if accounts are brought of a fall of rain, the spirit of speculation immediately becomes more active, and the farmer pockets the benefit.

Simplify this American system, and what is it? Take for illustration four individuals: one shall represent the Southern producer, the second the English manufacturer, and the remaining two Northern manufacturers. The Southern farmer interchanges the valuable productions of the soil, at their minimum price of production, with the English manufacturer, for articles necessary for his consumption, at their minimum price of fabrication. The exchange thus made is equally beneficial to each, and neither, notwithstanding the great fall in price which has taken place in the fruits of their industry, experiences decline. The first obtains for his flour, his tobacco, his cotton, or rice, as great a quantity of the articles which constitute the mass of his consumption as he formerly did when he obtained much higher prices; and so does the latter. The means of living as abundantly as ever exist with both, and both are equally prosperous; but the two Northern capitalists suddenly interpose, and forbid this advantageous course of exchange. They shackle it with heavy restraints, imposing upon the farmer the necessity either of purchasing of them at a greatly augmented price or of encountering still greater exactions in the course of the foreign trade. They are enabled to legalize their purpose, if indeed injustice can ever be legalized, by the majority power which they wield. I submit it to honorable Senators to say if I have not drawn, by this example, the epitome of the American system; and I demand of all candid men to say whether the power thus exerted is not selfish, despotic, and unjust.

Since the main debates on the tariff in the House occurred at a time when popular feeling in the South was aroused to the last degree in opposition to the oppressive measures, the Southern Representatives proclaimed resistance by their States even to the point of secession from the Union.

Rufus Choate [Mass.] was the leading advocate of the tariff in the House, and Thomas Clayton [Ga.] and Dixon H. Lewis [Ala.] were its chief opponents.

"To Your Tents, O Israel!"

DEBATE ON THE TARIFF, HOUSE OF REPRESENTATIVES, JUNE 13-15, 1832

MR. CHOATE.—The question pending is the broad one: Shall the existing protective system be maintained, or shall it be overthrown, either by direct abolition, or by compromise?

I have heard only one plausible reason suggested for the abandonment of the protective system. That reason is that the system operates with a local and partial severity upon the planting States. It is true that other considerations are pressed in argument. Elsewhere, as well as in the South, there is hostility to the system. Elsewhere, as well as there, there are political economists and politicians who maintain that it rests upon an unsound theory of the wealth of nations; that it unduly depresses and unduly fosters individual interests; that it is aristocratical and anti-republican in its tendencies, and that it produces, in the long run, national loss and national immorality. Elsewhere, as well as there, there are pursuits on which some of its provisions do press with unquestionable severity. Elsewhere, as well as there, it produces some good and some evil, like all other contrivances of man; and it divides public opinion, to some extent, like every other subject which addresses itself to the reason and passions of man.

Now, as a matter of course, as fast as we could, we should reduce the revenue to the wants of government, but we should do this without so much as touching the principle of the protective portions of the tariff.

I repeat it, then, the only plausible ground of attack on this policy is this that it oppresses the States of the South; that it blights their harvests, blasts their fields, and causes the grass to grow on the wharves, and in the great thoroughfares of their commercial cities; that it enhances the prices of all they buy, and depresses the prices of all they sell.

To this argument of the South various answers may be given. I shall confine myself to one, and that a plain, practical, and intelligible answer. It is this: that the injury which the abandonment of this policy will do to the individuals, and to the interests and sections remotely or directly connected with, and dependent on, manufacturing and mechanical industry, and to the country, will outweigh, immeasurably, any rational estimate of the good which it will do to the South.

It is a question of expediency we are debating. "The greatest good of the greatest number" is the turning consideration, is it not? If the act to which gentlemen urge you so zealously will occasion more evil than good, in a large and comprehensive estimate of its consequences, will you be persuaded into it?

It is true, certainly, that a different doctrine has been insinuated, if not openly pressed, in this discussion. It has been argued that this is not a question of expediency, but of right, justice, and principle. It has been argued that, no matter how great may be the amount of the pecuniary, economical, individual and national sacrifice on the one side, occasioned by the subversion of the protective policy, or how trivial the compensation on the other, our Southern brethren may demand its subversion as a matter of clear right and justice.

Gentlemen assert a moral right, not a constitutional one, to have the protecting system forthwith abandoned without reference to consequences. *Fiat justitia, ruat cœlum*,[1] say they.

Now, the constitutional power to continue or withdraw protection is conceded to us. By what principle of political morality ought we to regulate the exercise of this power? For all legislation which is admitted to be authorized by the Constitution, the people of the United States are one people. The confederated character of the Government and the separate existence of the States, for all such legislation, are of no importance. The power of the majority, and the rule of political morality which should control its exercise, are precisely the same, for such legislation, as if the Government were consolidated. Local in-

[1] "Let justice be done though the heavens fall."

XII—5

terests, pursuits, and opinions there are, of course, different, conflicting, almost irreconcilable. The South, the North, the West have each their own. We are called to deliberate upon a policy which affects them all; some favorably, others unfavorably, or less favorably. What is the rule of our right and our duty? Sir, we ought, if we could do so, to adopt a policy which shall reconcile and harmonize all these interests, and promote the good of all, and of all equally. But that is impossible. What then are we to do? Consult the greatest good of the greatest number; regardless where or on whom the particular hardship which all general policy must produce shall fall, but regretting that it should fall on anybody, and lightening it as well as we may. The moral right of the minority is that the majority shall exercise a sound discretion in good faith. The moral duty of the minority is acquiescence. If they are subjected to loss and hardship, and it be direct, specific, measurable in money, or such as the customs of civil societies recognize as a fit subject of compensation, they must be compensated. If not so, it is what the gentleman from South Carolina calls *damnum absque injuria*.[1] Extreme cases provide for themselves, and are a law unto themselves.

All men admit, and free trade theorists as fully as any, that manufactures are indispensable to the higher attainments of national greatness, and consideration, and wealth, and enjoyment. What they contend for is that you shall not force manufactures upon our people by commercial regulation. They are a great good, only you may give too much for it. But they all admit that manufactures, however unphilosophically introduced and sustained, when established, are a perennial spring of resource and energy to a State. They all admit that it is the industry of England, helped forward perhaps by a hundred foolish laws of Edward or Elizabeth, which has placed her at the head of modern civilization, and put into her hands more than the scepter of the sea. Now you choose to begin by forcing this species of industry by a protecting tariff. Grant that you started wrong. It is better to go through than to go back. It is more economical to do so. Do you not see that the country has grown to your laws? Occupation, capital, hope, which is the life of the world, are they not rapidly accommodating themselves to this policy? The first bad effects, the disturbance and derangement which mark the moment of its introduction, are disappearing. Consumers of all classes feel the benefits of a full domestic competition. A great body of skill is generated, worth

[1] "Hurt without injustice."

more, in the contemplation of philosophical statesmanship, than a thousand mines of barbaric gold.

What is there, sir, so very terrible in the signs of these times? What is this great crisis upon which gentlemen are so eloquent? What if there be some excitement of feeling, some harsh words, and some lowering looks between the brethren of this wide household? All these things must needs be, and may very safely be. They are only part of the price! how inadequate the price!—which every nation pays for greatness and liberty. All signal and durable national fame and empire are reached, if they ever are reached, through such occasional and temporary tribulation as this. Instead, then, sir, of anticipating with the gentleman from Georgia the time when, in pursuance of the pathetic suggestion of the patriarch which he has just repeated, we shall divide our flocks and herds, and take each our several way, "that there be no more strife between us"; instead of looking with so much apprehension upon this diversity of pursuits and interests, let us adopt a more cheerful theory. Let us agree to see in it, as long as we can, "merely that combination and that opposition of interests, that action and that counteraction which, in the natural and the political world, from the reciprocal struggle of discordant powers, draws out the harmony of the universe." This is the language of one of the wisest men and most accomplished minds that ever lived. I hope our example may illustrate its truth.

MR. CLAYTON.—I could give you a most feeling account of a city in my own State, once the pride of the South, the busy mart of one of the greatest staples of the earth, the source of wealth, the seat then and now of hospitality, and every generous virtue; but what is the fate of Savannah? Let her withering commerce and her sinking dwellings tell the story; and, sir, to your American system will she point you for the cause of all her misfortunes.

The mere operation of human law, actuated by the selfishness of human nature, has done this foul deed of mischief; has drawn, secretly and insidiously, all the resources of the South to the Northern and Middle States. We have generally been instructed to believe that man alone, in his individual character, is disposed to be a despot, but a regulation of a whole community is sometimes as great a tyrant, and we are often deceived and lulled into security under the tame belief that it is intended to protect, and not to destroy, when it oftens happens that some combination of robbers or usurpers have artfully transferred their power into the form of law, and, in that way, as effectually accomplished the purposes of fraud and ambition as if achieved by the dagger or the fagot.

Mr. Chairman, this country was never perhaps, except in time of war, in a higher degree of excitement. We hear of meetings at the North; indeed, very large ones have lately been gotten up to dictate to the House the course it must pursue; we hear of legislatures pursuing the same course, and saying the protecting system shall not only not be repealed, but it shall not be relaxed; we hear of the presses saying that even the measures of compromise suggested, with the best intentions, by the Administration, for the sake of peace, will be resisted by ''a million of musket-bearing people.'' Now, sir, when the South acts or talks thus, it is treason! She must suffer, and, if she complains in a tone anything above the strain of supplication, she is rebuked for insolence, and charged with a design to dismember the Union.

Such a charge I fling back in the teeth of our accusers. What! the South disaffected to the Union! The South that suffered so much in the Revolutionary War from the common enemy, from savages on her frontier, and Tories, worse than savages, in her very heart! The South, that so gallantly opened her purse and shed her blood in the last war with the British and Indians, when in another quarter —— But I forbear. It cannot be believed that the South is disloyal. Who were the supporters of Jefferson, and Madison, and Monroe? And who, more than Jefferson, Madison, and Monroe, were the defenders of those republican principles which moved, directed, and consummated the Revolution of '76, and were happily laid at the foundation of the Federal Government? Did the South keep back when the North refused to give up a sacrifice rightfully necessary to support and defend the principles of the Constitution? No, sir; it is a slander to whisper the slightest suspicion of disloyalty against the South.

MR. LEWIS.—Mr. Chairman, the crisis has at length arrived when this question must be settled on a permanent basis. The Southern people have looked with delight to the payment of the public debt, as a period when they might expect some alleviation of their burdens. There is no longer an excuse or pretext for continuing the present rate of duties, except for the single purpose of making the South tributary to the North. We have borne, patiently, our unequal burdens in discharging a debt incurred in our common defence, and we now demand of you to lessen our taxes to the amount annually paid in the discharge of that debt. Partaking in the common feeling of our countrymen, in satisfaction at an event which has freed the Government from pecuniary obligation, we call upon you to adjust your revenue to the legitimate wants of the Government. Sir, do we ask too much in calling for a reduction of our taxes to the fiscal demands of the Government? The subjects of European despotism would have at least this claim on the humanity of their sovereign. Sir, I will state that nothing short of a practical abandonment of the principle of protection can or ought to satisfy the wounded feelings of the South. The repeal of the duties on the unprotected articles which forms the basis of the present bill will never be considered a fair adjustment of this question. It has been no part of our complaint that revenue duties should be levied on those articles which are not manufactured in this country. Such articles are mostly luxuries consumed by the rich, and are the most legitimate subjects of revenue, because the duties on them are borne equally by all who consume them. Our complaint has been that protecting duties have been levied on those articles which are manufactured in one portion of our country, for the purpose of raising the price of manufacturing labor; and that, while those duties operate as a tax on the South, they operate as a bounty on the North. This is the sum and substance of the whole controversy; and if you take the duties off of wines, silks, teas, spices, and such other luxuries, and throw the whole burden of the revenue on salt, iron, cotton, and woolen goods, and such other necessaries of life as are consumed by the South and manufactured by the North, you not only relieve that section from the whole burden of taxation, but you make the labor of the South tributary to the North.

Mr. Chairman, the Southern people will abandon the Union only in the last struggle for their rights; and when it is gone they will have no cause to upbraid themselves. They have not asked, nor will they ask, any favors, or bounties, or privileges at your hands; they claim but the right to enjoy the proceeds of their honest labor. In their name, I invoke you, by the blood of our common ancestors, by the independence which they struggled to achieve, by the emblems of liberty which surround us, by the stars and stripes of our national banner, suffer us to remain in the Union, not as slaves, but as freemen, paying no other tribute than that which we owe to our common country.

CHAPTER VI

THE TARIFF OF 1833

[HORIZONTAL REDUCTION]

Gulian C. Verplanck [N. Y.] Introduces Bill to Reduce the Tariff to the Act of 1816—The Clay Compromise Bill, Which Provides for Gradual Reduction Through Successive Years, Is Substituted—Debate in the Senate: in Favor, Henry Clay [Ky.], John C. Calhoun [S. C.]; Opposed, John Forsyth [Ga.], Daniel Webster [Mass.]—Bill Is Passed—Its Subsequent Expiration.

IN accordance with a suggestion of President Andrew Jackson in his message of December 4, 1832, to reduce the tariff substantially to the act of 1816, a bill was introduced in the House early in the session of 1832-33 by Gulian C. Verplanck [N. Y.]. Within a week of the close of this session Robert P. Letcher [Ky.] proposed as a substitute a bill offered in the Senate by Henry Clay [Ky.]. This was afterward designated a "horizontal reduction" bill. It provided for the gradual reduction of the tariff through successive years until 1842, after which the highest duty levied should not exceed 20 per cent. Senator Benton said of this bill, in his "Thirty Years' View":

It was offered in the House, without notice, without signal, without premonitory symptom, and just as the members were preparing to adjourn. The Northern Representatives from the great manufacturing States were astounded, and asked for delay, which, not being granted, Mr. John Davis [Mass.], one of their number, thus gave vent to his amazed feelings:

"THE SOUTH'S COMPLAINT DEEPER THAN THE TARIFF"

JOHN DAVIS, M. C.

I do not object to a reasonable adjustment of the controversies which exist. I am in favor of a gradual reduction on

70

protected articles; but it must be very gradual, so that no violence shall be done to business; for all reduction is necessarily full of hazard. But I do object to a compromise which destines the East for the altar. No victim, in my judgment, is required, none is necessary; and yet you propose to bind us, hand and foot, to pour out our blood upon the altar, and sacrifice us as a burnt offering, to appease the unnatural and unfounded discontent of the South; *a discontent, I fear, which has deeper root than the tariff, and will continue when that is forgotten.*

The substitute bill passed in the House by a vote of 105 to 71, and in the Senate by 29 to 16. The debate in the Senate on the bill which Clay had previously offered, afterward known as the "Compromise Bill," called forth speeches in its favor from Senator Clay and John C. Calhoun [S. C.], and in opposition from John Forsyth [Ga.] and Daniel Webster [Mass.].

THE COMPROMISE TARIFF

SENATE, FEBRUARY 12, 1833

SENATOR CLAY.—I believe the American system to be in the greatest danger; and I believe it can be placed on a better and safer foundation at this session than at the next. Put it off until the next session, and the alternative may, and probably then would be, a speedy and ruinous reduction of the tariff, or a civil war with the entire South.

It is well known that the majority of the dominant party is adverse to the tariff. Judging from the present appearance, we shall, at the next session, be in the minority. How, then, I ask, is the system to be sustained against numbers, against the whole weight of the Administration, against the united South, and against the impending danger of civil war?

I have been represented as the father of this system, and I am charged with an unnatural abandonment of my own offspring. I have never arrogated to myself any such intimate relation to it. I have, indeed, cherished it with parental fondness, and my affection is undiminished. But in what condition do I find this child? It is in the hands of the Philistines, who would strangle it. I fly to its rescue, to snatch it from their custody, and to place it on a bed of security and repose for nine years, where it may grow and strengthen, and become acceptable

to the whole people. I behold a torch about being applied to a
favorite edifice, and I would save it, if possible, before it was
wrapt in flames, or at least preserve the precious furniture
which it contains.

Senator Clay advanced another reason for his bill:
the desirability of separating the tariff from politics and
elections. This wish, says Senator Benton, being afterward interpreted by events, was supposed to be the basis
of the coalition with Mr. Calhoun, both of them having
tried the virtue of the tariff question in elections, and
found it unavailing either to friends or foes. Mr. Clay,
its champion, could not become President upon its support. Mr. Calhoun, its antagonist, could not become President upon its opposition. To both it was equally desirable, as an unavailable element in elections, and as a
stumbling-block to both in the future, that the tariff
should be withdrawn for some years from the political
arena; and Mr. Clay thus expressed himself in relation
to this withdrawal:

I wish to see the tariff separated from the politics of the
country, that business men may go to work in security, with
some prospect of stability in our laws, and without everything
being staked on the issue of elections, as it were on the hazards
of the die.

Senator Forsyth replied to Mr. Clay.

The avowed object of the bill would meet with universal
approbation. It was a project to harmonize the people, and it
could have come from no better source than from the gentleman
from Kentucky: for to no one were we more indebted than to
him for the discord and discontent which agitate us.

The Senator from Kentucky says the tariff is in danger; aye,
sir, it is at its last gasp. It has received the immedicable
wound; no hellebore can cure it. The confession of the gentleman is of immense importance. Yes, sir, the whole feeling of
the country is opposed to the high protective system. The wily
serpent that crept into our Eden has been touched by the spear
of Ithuriel. The Senator is anxious to prevent the ruin which
a sudden abolition of the system will produce. No one desires
to inflict ruin upon the manufacturers; but suppose the South-

WHIG APPEAL FOR AN EXCUSE

[Caricature of Clay and Frelinghuysen in Presidential Campaign of 1844]

From the collection of the New York Historical Society

73

ern people, having the power to control the subject, should totally and suddenly abolish the system; what right would those have to complain who had combined to oppress the South? What has the tariff led us to already? From one end of the country to the other, it has produced evils which are worse than a thousand tariffs. The necessity of appealing now to fraternal feeling shows that that feeling is not sleeping, but nearly extinguished.

SENATOR CALHOUN said: Entirely approving of the object for which this bill was introduced, he should give his vote in favor of the motion for leave to introduce. He who loved the Union must desire to see the agitating question brought to a termination. Until it should be terminated, we could not expect the restoration of peace or harmony, or a sound condition of things, throughout the country. The general principles of this bill received his approbation. He believed that, if the present difficulties were to be adjusted, they must be adjusted on the principles embraced in the bill, of fixing ad valorem duties, except in the few cases in the bill to which specific duties were assigned. He said that it had been his fate to occupy a position as hostile as anyone could, in reference to the protecting policy; but, if it depended on his will, he would not give his vote for the prostration of the manufacturing interest. A very large capital had been invested in manufactures, which had been of great service to the country; and he would never give his vote suddenly to withdraw all those duties by which that capital was sustained in the channel into which it had been directed. There were some of the provisions which had his entire approbation, and there were some to which he objected. But he looked upon these minor points of difference as points in the settlement of which no difficulty would occur, when gentlemen meet together in that spirit of mutual compromise which, he doubted not, would be brought into their deliberations, without at all yielding the constitutional question as to the right of protection.

SENATOR WEBSTER.—It is impossible that this proposition of the honorable member from Kentucky should not excite in the country a very strong sensation. If I understand the plan, the result of it will be a well-understood surrender of the power of discrimination, or a stipulation not to use that power, in the laying duties on imports, after the eight or nine years have expired. The honorable member admits that, though there will be no positive surrender of the power, there will be a stipulation not to exercise it; a treaty of peace and amity, as he says, which no American statesman can, hereafter, stand up to violate. For one, sir, I am not ready to enter into the treaty. I propose, so far as depends on me, to leave all our successors in Congress as free to act as we are ourselves.

The honorable member from Kentucky says the tariff is in imminent danger; that, if not destroyed this session, it cannot hope to survive the next. This may be so, sir. But, if it be so, it is because the American people will not sanction the tariff; and, if they will not, why, then, sir, it cannot be sustained at all. I am not quite so despairing as the honorable member seems to be. I know nothing which has happened, within the last six or eight months, changing so materially the prospects of the tariff. I do not despair of the success of an appeal to the American people, to take a just care of their own interest, and not to sacrifice those vast interests which have grown up under the laws of Congress.

Senator Webster then introduced the following resolutions, setting forth his tariff principles:

Resolved, That the annual revenues of the country ought not to be allowed to exceed a just estimate of the wants of the Government; and that, in making this reduction, just regard should be had to the various interests and opinions of different parts of the country, so as most effectually to preserve the integrity and harmony of the Union, and to provide for the common defence and promote the general welfare of the whole.

But, whereas it is certain that the diminution of the rates of duties on some articles would increase, instead of reducing, the aggregate amount of revenue on such articles; and whereas, in regard to such articles as it has been the policy of the country to protect, a slight reduction on one might produce essential injury, and even distress, to large classes of the community, while another might bear a larger reduction without any such consequences; and whereas, also, there are many articles, the duties on which might be reduced, or altogether abolished, without producing any other effect than the reduction of revenue: Therefore,

Resolved, That, in reducing the rates of duties imposed on imports, it is not wise or judicious to proceed by way of an equal reduction per centum on all articles; but that, as well the amount as the time of reduction ought to be fixed, in respect to the several articles, distinctly, having due regard, in each case, to the questions whether the proposed reduction will affect revenue alone, or how far it will operate injuriously on those domestic manufactures hitherto protected; especially such as are essential in time of war, and such, also, as have been established on the faith of existing laws; and, above all, how far such proposed reduction will affect the rates of wages and the earnings of American manual labor.

Resolved, That it is unwise and injudicious, in regulating imposts, to adopt a plan which shall, either immediately or prospectively, reject all discrimination on articles to be taxed, and which shall confine all duties to one equal rate per centum on all articles.

Resolved, That, since the people of the United States have deprived the State governments of all power of fostering manufactures, however indispensable in peace or in war, by commercial regulations, or by laying duties on imports, and have transferred the whole authority to make such regulations, and to lay such duties, to the Congress of the United States, Congress cannot surrender or abandon such power, compatibly with its constitutional duty; and, therefore,

Resolved, That no law ought to be passed on the subject of imposts, containing any stipulation, express or implied, or giving any pledge or assurance, direct or indirect, which shall tend to restrain Congress from the full exercise, at all times hereafter, of all its constitutional powers, in giving reasonable protection to American industry, countervailing the policy of foreign nations, and maintaining the substantial independence of the United States.

Although the Compromise Tariff was intended for perpetuity it failed to outlive even the first of its two parts—that which provided for the protection of manufactures for a term of nine years. It expired in 1841. During the following year a new tariff act was passed, by which the average rate of duty was raised to about 33 per cent.

CHAPTER VII

THE WALKER TARIFF
[ACTS OF 1846 AND 1857]

The Tariff Act of 1846 (Proposed by Robert J. Walker, Secretary of the Treasury)—Surplus in Treasury in 1857—Bill to Reduce Duties on Raw Materials Introduced in the House—Debate: in Favor, Nathaniel B. Durfee [R. I.], William W. Boyce [S. C.]; Opposed, Benjamin Stanton [O.], Justin S. Morrill [Vt.]—Bill Is Passed in the House—Robert M. T. Hunter [Va.] Proposes a Substitute in the Senate Embodying the Principle of Horizontal Reduction—Debate: Speakers of Varying Views, Sen. Hunter, Jacob Collamer [Vt.], George E. Pugh [O.], Henry Wilson [Mass.], William H. Seward [N. Y.], Robert Toombs [Ga.], Andrew P. Butler [S. C.]—Hunter's Substitute Is Adopted—Bill Is Passed in Both Houses and Approved by President Pierce.

D URING 1842 revenues had so decreased as to be insufficient for the support of the Government. From this period down to 1846 various remedial plans were advanced but none was adopted.

Robert J. Walker, Secretary of the Treasury under President Polk, soon after his advent in the Cabinet prepared an able and exhaustive report upon the tariff, laying down the following principles:

(1) That no more money should be collected than is necessary for the wants of the Government, economically administered; (2) That no duty be imposed on any article above the lowest rate which will yield the largest amount of revenue; (3) That below such rate discrimination may be made, descending in the scale of duties, or, for imperative reasons, the article may be placed in the list of those free from all duty; (4) That the maximum revenue duty should be imposed on luxuries; (5) That all minimums and all specific duties should be abolished, and *ad valorem* duties substituted in their place, care being taken to guard against fraudulent invoices and undervaluation, and to assess the duty upon the actual market value;

77

(6) That the duty should be so imposed as to operate as equally as possible throughout the Union, discriminating neither for nor against any class or section.

In accordance with these principles the tariff of 1846 was passed by Congress. This tariff approached nearer to a free trade policy than any in the history of this country. It was called "a revenue tariff with incidental protection," yet, according to Prof. William G. Sumner, of Yale, under it the manufacturers made "steady and genuine progress. Industrially and economically," he said, "it was our golden age. The balance of the trade was never more regular and equal."

There were eight schedules, each with its own *ad valorem* rate of duty, ranging from 5 per cent. on raw materials of manufacture to 75 per cent. on spirits, the average being 25 per cent.

The protectionists made futile attempts at various times between 1846 and 1857, when the tariff was next revised, to modify the act, and, indeed, to change its fundamental character, substituting the *specific* principle for the *ad valorem* in a number of schedules.

Under the tariff of 1846 such a surplus accumulated in the Treasury by 1857 that the circulating medium of the country was reduced in amount below the needs of business. There arose a general demand for a reduction of this surplus. The manufacturing interests appealed to Congress for a reduction or abolition of duties on raw materials; the agricultural interests then became alarmed, and demanded that the duty be retained on these and that it be reduced on manufactured articles. The chief contention was over wool and woolen goods. After a long discussion, extending from the middle of January, 1857, to the close of the session (March 3), a new tariff bill was passed by which the average duty was lowered to about 20 per cent. *ad valorem*. It was denounced by its opponents, who hailed chiefly from the West and such wool-growing States elsewhere as Vermont, as the result of a selfish combination of Southern hemp and sugar producers, Pennsylvania iron-masters, and New England woolen manufacturers. The manufac-

POLK VS. WOOL, OR THE HARRY-CANE

From the collection of the New York Historical Society

turers denied that it was a blow at the wool growers, claiming that, on the contrary, by building up the cloth-making industry in this country, it would create a great home market for wool of every grade.

RAW *vs.* MANUFACTURED PRODUCTS

HOUSE OF REPRESENTATIVES, JANUARY 14-FEBRUARY 20, 1857

On January 14 Nathaniel B. Durfee [R. I.] spoke as follows in favor of the manufacturing interests:

By the report of the Secretary of the Treasury [James Guthrie], it appears that the national revenues exceed the exigencies of an economical national expenditure by from sixteen to eighteen millions of dollars.

Two modes of reduction are proposed by the Secretary of the Treasury, and are understood to be favored by the Administration: first, the admission of the raw materials of manufactures duty free; second, the admission of some articles of general consumption duty free, and a reduction of the duties upon others of that description, of some seven or eight millions of dollars. It is on the former of these two modes of reduction that I wish to make a few remarks.

The great manufacturing nations of Europe admit the raw materials of their manufactures free of duty. Now, this alone gives them a manifest and uncompensated superiority over us in all foreign markets; for, other things being equal, it is plain that the manufacturer who can procure his raw material at the cheapest rate can furnish the manufactured goods at the cheapest rate; and, therefore, under such circumstances, the manufacturer who can procure his raw material free of duty can afford to undersell the manufacturer who has to procure his raw material burdened with a duty, and exclude him from any market where both present themselves upon an equal footing. The difference in the cost of production per yard may be infinitesimally small, but in the result it is all the difference between the keeping and the losing of a market. Now, insofar as this difference depends upon the enhancement of the cost of raw materials by duties, is it clearly nothing more than common justice to remove it by the repeal of the duties unless there be some cogent reason for retaining them—as a part of the necessary revenues, or for the protection of some interest which has an equal or greater claim than that of manufactures? In his greater abundance of capital and labor the foreign manufacturer has surely advantages enough without any assistance from our own Government. But notwithstanding these advantages, the proximity of the West Indies, and of South and Central America, would enable us to compete for these markets, at least in those coarser descriptions of manufactures, in the cheapness of producing which we already rival them, were it not for this duty upon raw materials.

The removal of this duty, then, will place us on the footing of equality with foreign manufactures in the procurement of the raw materials of manufactures. But the foreign manufacturer still has the advantage over us in the cheaper rates of money and of labor—so great that he can even drive us out of our own markets in many styles of manufactures unless we secure to ourselves some counterbalancing advantage in the shape of duties upon manufactured goods. Such a counterpoise the Secretary of the Treasury promises in the imposition of an adequate revenue tariff. Now, if the system will accomplish this, it is all that the American manufacturer can ask; it is all that the reasonable portion of them have ever asked. What they have sought, under the offensive appellation of protection, comes to them divested of its repulsive features in the prepossessing guise of revenue. That it comes in a form eminently calculated to win the favor of all classes and parties, and therefore to acquire the invaluable attribute of permanence, I am also convinced.

But objections have been raised to this system which are worthy of consideration. Under its operation foreign wool would cease to be a dutiable article. Now it is feared if the duty be taken off the raw material that, although the importations of woolen manufactures would diminish, yet the importation of the wool itself would increase in a far greater proportion and lead to a great and ruinous declension in the prices of domestic wool. If such would be the operation, it would be to favor the manufacturer at the expense of the producer, or, what is still worse, the foreign producer at the expense of the home producer.

But would such be the effect of the repeal? It is well known that certain qualities of wool cannot be grown in the United States. Our climate, our soil, or the culture of our flocks, is such as not to admit of its production. The experiment has been repeatedly tried, and never, I believe, with more than a very imperfect success. And there are certain styles of woolen

XII—6

manufactures in which some admixture of these foreign wools is indispensable to give them the proper fiber or the proper finish. The duty, then, as it exists at present, does not even promote the interests of the wool grower, but by checking or destroying the manufacture of all cloths which require an admixture of foreign wool is an absolute injury to him.

What we want is a reliable, steady, increasing home market, and that a repeal of the duties on wool will instantly create. The mills will be built, the spindles and the looms abide our bidding, the labor is already on our shores, or waiting an invitation to immigrate; with us only it remains to speak the word, and, with a wonder-working potency more marvelous than the magician's spell, to gladden a thousand villages with the hum of happy industry, and whiten far and wide the grassy slopes and hillsides of our extended land with millions of bleating flocks.

On February 5 Benjamin Stanton [O.] presented the case of the wool growers.

He expressed surprise that the manufacturing interest was now considered the only branch of industry requiring protection. As to the ten per cent. duty proposed on wool he did not believe it would afford the wool-growers any protection whatever. And was their protection not necessary to the independence of the country? If the wool-growing interests were broken down, and manufactures sustained on imported wool, how, in the event of war, could we supply ourselves with the necessary woolen fabrics? He said further: it is laid down as a sound principle by intelligent agriculturists that the annual animal productions of any country should equal in value its annual vegetable productions in order that the fertility of the soil may be maintained. Hence, the production of wool is an indispensable article for scientific and profitable tillage.

In regard to the abolition of the duty on wool, he wondered in what respect the wool-grower was to be benefited. It has been argued, he said, that the repeal of this duty will send the manufacturer abroad into the markets of the world; it will increase the demand for wool, and that the foreign manufacturer will be compelled to pay an increased price for it, and that consequently he must get an increased price for his cloth, which will enable the domestic manufacturer to compete with him. But here is the fallacy: the manufacturers assume that the whole population of the country that consume woolen goods is to pay an increased price for them. How far that will commend it to the favorable consideration of the committee is a question I leave them to determine. But the idea is utterly impracticable.

Mr. Stanton denied the truth of the assertion that all kinds of wool cannot be produced in this country. He gave an instance showing that a Maine manufacturer had made from Silesian wool a piece of cloth which took first prize at the World's Fair in London (1851).

He said in conclusion that the manufacturers must stand side by side with the wool-growers if they looked toward the preservation of both.

On February 5 Justin S. Morrill [Vt.] upheld the principle of protection.

It is generally conceded that we are to support the Government by revenue duties with moderate discriminations for protection. The absurdity that a duty levied upon imports is a tax *pro tanto*[1] upon exports no longer requires grave refutation. The project of a horizontal tariff—shutting our eyes to all discrimination whatever—has never yet been but *once* attempted, and never sustained with the sole object of an equalization of taxation. Nor will direct taxes ever be levied while the present provision in the Constitution stands for their apportionment. Even Secretary Walker, with all his transcendental vagaries, discarded the horizontal theory.

In my judgment *ad valorem* duties are the worst possible for either revenue or protection. They are expensive in the administration—variable at every custom house—subject to systematic frauds—offering *most* protection when prices are highest and require the *least*—and then affording the *least* protection when prices are lowest and require the *most*. *Specific* duties, on the contrary, dispense with the whole crowd of custom-house appraisers and experts, and are therefore cheaply administered—not liable to cheats, and are uniform and certain, as well for revenue as protection.

I stand on the principle of protection—moderate but certain —such as a wisely adjusted revenue tariff will abundantly afford. I am for ruling America for the benefit, *first*, of Americans, and for the "rest of mankind" afterwards. American labor has the right to find employment and reward at home. American capital has the right to some security invested in the

Correspondent tax.

development of the vast resources of our country. American skill should have sufficient encouragement to pursue "the track of glory" under our own flag.

I am aware there are some who would place wool at once on the free list. The agriculturist scarcely needs protection on anything save wool. In other things he only receives the indirect benefit of having some portion of agricultural competition withdrawn by being employed in other industrial pursuits. His cordial coöperation is expected to protect everybody else, but when the sole opportunity arrives of giving him a small boon he is told that, although he has been badly treated for ten years past or more, he must now offer himself up as a sacrifice.

> "But still the great have kindness in reserve;
> He helped to bury whom he helped to starve."

Those who urge that wool should be admitted free of duty start off with the sober assurance that the effect will be to raise the price of wool, and they assert in the next breath that the home manufacturer cannot prosper because he cannot obtain wool as cheap as the foreign manufacturer.

Now the only rise that would be likely to occur would be in consequence of American wool-growers abandoning the business and slaughtering their flocks. Deserted by their Government, why should they struggle longer? The manufacturers would find themselves disappointed in their sanguine expectations. Their domestic sources for supplying the raw material would be cut off and they would speedily be at the mercy of foreign production and foreign legislation. Should woolen manufactures fail under such circumstances as these, it would be a hopeless task to attempt their revival.

We are cited to France and to England as examples which we should follow; and it is said that wool has risen in price in those countries in consequence of the abolition of all duties thereon. Now, it is notorious that the consumption of wool over all Europe has overtaken supplies. The production has not kept pace with the demand. The prices, therefore, have risen, but not by any means so much as represented, and perhaps not more than other products of the world within the same time. The influx of gold also into the commercial world from Australia and California has raised the value of all kinds of property within the last six years from twenty-five to forty per cent. Now, the fact is, as I understand it, that wool is not admitted entirely free of duty into France, but woolen goods are absolutely prohibited. This gives the home market to the French manufacturer exclusively. For this she has fiercely struggled for two centuries. That sort of legislation would be perhaps satisfactory to both the American wool-grower and manufacturer, but it is not proposed.

Take the next case, that of England. By a system of protection the most marked and persistent ever yet witnessed, commencing in the reign of Edward III, she has reached the goal she aimed at—capability of underselling in all markets—and can safely challenge the world to meet her on the footing of free trade.

The manufacturers of England have no further step to take in the march of protection. Sir Robert Peel led them to the summit. As omnipotent as Parliament may be, it has no more power to exert in their behalf.

Such being the position of England, now, in "the bone of manhood," I submit that it is preposterous to force America, but "yet in the gristle" to adopt the same legislation which may be proper for Great Britain and all her colonies. You might as well enter a grass-fed three-year-old colt on the race course against a thoroughbred and well-trained English race horse. Naked competition must end in the extinguishment of special pursuits, or the reduction of American labor to the English level, and I am inflexibly opposed to either result. Nobody who does not desire to see the labor of this country degraded can advocate such a proposition.

Again, it is urged that we need not fear competition with England or Europe in raising wool, because our land is so much the cheapest. Those who make this statement lose sight of the vast plains and steppes of Russia, South America, and Australia, where single individuals own flocks of from ten thousand to sixty thousand, and where the cost of keeping them the year round is confined to a few shepherds and a few dogs.

It is stated that the wool-grower has been protected for the past ten years, but I deny the fact. Whenever the rate of duty upon woolens is less than that on wool, the latter receives no protection, because the former will be imported and crush both the wool-grower and the manufacturer. Our present tariff, as was obvious at its birth, and as it is now conceded by the present Secretary of the Treasury, has operated to discriminate against woolens, and, if against woolens, of course against wool.

I know of no other way of protecting wool but by putting the manufacturer's wheels in motion. To do this the duties on woolens must be higher than upon wool. When this is done to a reasonable extent, and when all, or nearly all, dye stuffs are admitted free of duty, then I think the manufacturer should say, "Hold, enough!"—and, if he attempts anything more, he may "go a wool-gathering and come home shorn."

The gentleman from Rhode Island [Mr. Durfee] the other day stated that "what we do want is a reliable, steady, increasing home market." Exactly. I agree with him. But he is for opening our ports, so far as wool is concerned, to the competition of the world. Is that the way to give the wool-grower a home market? If you entirely prohibited the introduction of woolen manufactures, that would give us the home market, and the wool-growers would need to ask no other protection. That is what France does to-day, and when she recently proposed to remove the prohibition even that was coupled with a provision for a *bounty* upon all cloths exported. If we tax cloths and afterwards find France pays a bounty equal to our tax, what protection would be realized?

The policy I have indicated would in the end be most to the advantage of the manufacturer—securing to him a home supply of the raw material and shielding him from the annual fluctuations of foreign markets and foreign hostile legislation, and it is fluctuations he has most to dread—not high prices of wool.

Without the production and control of the primary necessities of life we must remain the vassals of those who are the arbiters of our supplies. All admit that in war we should make our own cannon and our own gunpowder. Unless war be the natural state of man, and in proportion, as the years of peace are greater than those of war, it is quite as important that we shall be independent in peace as in war. Food and clothing are not less indispensable in peace than in war.

Such articles, then, of primary necessity, as there is any hope of successfully producing, should be waked into life— nursed into perennial vigor—by moderate and steady discriminations in their favor so long as their condition makes it proper, or so long as there is a probable chance of ultimate success.

On February 10 William W. Boyce [S. C.] opposed the principle of protection.

The report from the majority of the Committee of Ways and Means rests upon the idea that the protective policy is a wise policy and that the tariff should be modified in subservience to that policy. I wish to examine that question, and if I destroy the foundation upon which the report rests then the superstructure erected upon it must fall to the ground. To put the argument in the most striking and comprehensible light, I will state it in a simple and practical form. Certain persons wishing to go into manufacturing ask Government to aid them in a business naturally unprofitable by preventing the consumers of the country from buying foreign goods cheap in order that those consumers may be compelled to buy their goods dear. These are the three propositions necessarily involved in the demand for protection. Let us examine them.

As regards the first proposition, Government is asked to aid men in embarking in an unprofitable business. If it were profitable no application would be made to Government for aid. Assuming, then, that the proposed business is unprofitable, what course ought Government to take? Is it not plain that, if it did anything, instead of aiding persons to go into an unprofitable business, it should rather discourage them from it? For it must be observed that Government does not by its action increase the capital of a country; it can only give a new direction to it. The capital of a country, then, remaining the same, I insist it is unwise for Government, as a mere question of political economy, to aid in turning any portion of the capital of a country into an unprofitable channel, because, in the degree that the rate of profit upon the capital thus unprofitably directed is below the average rate of profits of the capital of the country generally, to that extent there is an absolute loss to the productive energies of the country. Therefore, it is unwise in any country to turn capital into any channel yielding a less rate of profit than the average of profits of the country. But such a policy is peculiarly unwise with us, having, as we do, a new, vast, and undeveloped country, needing only the application of capital and energy to produce the grandest and most profitable results.

As regards the second proposition, that the consumers should not be allowed to buy foreign goods cheap. I shall not dwell upon the injustice involved in this proposition, though it strikes me as a direct attack upon the right of property and the right of labor to prohibit a man from buying or selling to the best advantage. To the extent that he loses by your prohibition, to that extent you have confiscated the fruits of his industry. It is true, we are often told by the monopolists that it is ruinous to buy cheap foreign goods. But I can hardly conceive of a more monstrous fallacy than this idea. To show its infinite absurdity, let us suppose that foreign countries, instead of selling us their goods cheap, should give them to us. What would be the consequence? Why, our utter ruin, for if it is injurious to buy cheap, of course it would be utter ruin to get for nothing. Such is the logical conclusion to which this argument necessarily tends—a consequence so absurd I shall not dwell longer upon it.

Now for the third. In order that these manufacturers may succeed, they require you to make the consumers of the country purchase from them at a price enhanced to the extent of the duty on the foreign article. What justice is there in that? Why is it that one portion of the people should be compelled to buy from another portion, and a smaller portion, at a higher price than they could buy elsewhere? Why should the great body of the American people be required to pay in the enhanced price an indirect tax to the manufacturers? Is there any justice in it? If you ask what are the profits of the manufacturers, the reply is, "they do not make more than six or seven per cent." After the honorable gentleman from Rhode Island [Mr. Durfee] made his speech two weeks ago upon the subject of free wool I asked him what were the profits of the woolen manufacturers? He said that the woolen manufacturers were losing money, but that the cotton manufacturers said they were making six per cent. What is the result, then? Why, the great mass of the people have been made poorer to assist these men in making average profits. As the indirect tribute levied from the consumers by the manufacturers only raises their profits to the average profits of the country, it follows, then, that this indirect tribute is a total loss to the productive energies of the country, and the effect is the same thing to the country as if, under a free trade policy, this amount had been thrown into the sea.

I have thus gone through with the three propositions involved in the demand for protection; as they are all fallacies, it follows that the system resting upon them is also a fallacy.

I look to free trade and direct taxation as our ultimate and inevitable policy. By taking one approximating step afterwards we will be in a condition to attain the great point of free trade without any sudden convulsion.

If I could have modified the tariff exactly to my ideas I should have put the duties on articles of necessity below twenty per cent., at the lowest possible revenue standard, and luxuries I should have put at thirty per cent. In this way I would have sought to carry out, as far as possible, under an indirect system of taxation, the idea of relieving the industry of the country from taxation, and of throwing it upon property.

There is one further modification I should be willing to make in the tariff if it were reduced in good faith strictly to the revenue standard—that is, to put wool and other raw material in the free list. The effect of taxing the raw materials is that the consumer is compelled to refund the tax with interest to the manufacturer who has advanced it.

I am through; it is for the committee to say what shall be done.

Those representing the manufacturers would, I think, act wisely to consent to a reduction of duties, for the longer reduction is deferred the larger will be the surplus, and the more sweeping the reform. Besides revenue duties with the raw material free put manufactures on as good a basis as they could desire, and this point could, I think, be carried. Further, the manufacturers would find an increased demand arising from the general prosperity of the country following upon low duties. Besides, too, our manufacturers should look to the great and valuable markets of the world where gold is to be had for the gathering.

To those representing the agricultural interests I would ask what possible motive can you have to maintain the protective policy, as your interest clearly demands freedom of exchanges, and the markets of the world?

To those representing commerce I would ask: what is commerce but exchanges? To reduce duties and free exchanges is therefore to bid commerce "live and move and have its being." You gentlemen who represent the imperial city of New York should be clamorous on this subject. New York City is commerce personified. Free exchanges, and you magnify and aggrandize New York beyond the power of language to describe.

To the Democratic party I would appeal to emblazon the great ideas of free trade and low taxes on their historical banner. Cease to vex the ear of the country with infinite repetitions of the occult meanings of past measures. Seize a living, vital, actual, practical truth, and enforce it as your creed. "Free trade, anti-monopoly, equality" are the watch words for you. They appeal to the self-interest of every individual, and they fill the imagination with magnificent ideas of the future grandeur of the Republic.

Take up the great ideas of free trade, for under that sign you shall surely conquer.

HORIZONTAL REDUCTION VS. DISCRIMINATING PROTECTIVE
DUTIES

SENATE, FEBRUARY 26, 1857

When the bill came to the Senate Robert M. T.
Hunter [Va.], on February 26, moved as a substitute a
general horizontal reduction of duties on the *ad valorem*
principle.

If it be true, and I hold it to be so, that there is pressing
necessity for reducing the revenue, and that it can be done
with little injury even to those interests that are called the
protected interests, the question arises, in what way is it to be
done? It is obvious that, in the short period of the session
which is left to us, there is no mode in which it can be effected
except to take some established idea in the public mind and
modify that. It seems by general consent to have been thought,
and in that I concur, that the only plan of molding a measure
which may pass would be to take the tariff of 1846 and modify
its schedules. It is our duty so to proceed in modifying it
as to protect from sudden injury the interests which have grown
up under it.

The proper system to which we should endeavor to come
is a system of duties laid for revenue alone, and laid according
to the true principles of taxation. If we desired to raise all
the money that the imports would furnish according to this
system, we should find that duty which would make each article
yield the greatest revenue. Having ascertained those duties—
if we did not desire to obtain all that it furnished—we should
modify the duties ratably, so as to give us what we wanted,
but at the same time we do this we must do it according to
the true principles of taxation, which require that we should
lay the tax, not on production, but on consumption. That is
a principle adopted in all countries in which there is a wise
system of legislation; and it is adopted because, if you lay the
tax upon production, the people have to pay a great deal more
than ever goes into the treasury; and because, when you lay it
in that mode, you run the danger of disturbing the equilibrium
of the great industrial pursuits of the country, and turning
some which are naturally profitable out of their usual and accustomed channels; whereas, when you lay the duty on the
article when ready for consumption, the Government gets all
the duty minus the expenses of collection.

It follows, as a result of that principle, that, in regard to all those articles for which there would be no demand except such as was made by the manufacturers themselves, there should be no duty, and those should be free. Upon all articles on which you lay a duty for revenue it should be laid only for revenue purposes. Articles for which there is no demand except that which the manufacturers themselves create should be free, because we should thus cheapen the price to the consumer, and because, too, it would enable us to avoid the risk of disturbing, through our revenue system, the natural equilibrium of the various branches of productive industry.

But in proceeding to that great end I desire to go gradually. I desire to act upon a principle which is just alike to the consumer and the manufacturer; which, in short, enables the consumer to buy more cheaply both at home and abroad, because it not only diminishes the duty upon imports, but also lessens the cost of production to the domestic manufacturer. To diminish the cost of production by reducing taxation is, after all, the most legitimate protection which a Government can give to its home industry. While, then, I reduce the duties on those articles which the mass consume, I will reduce *pari passu* the duties on those chemicals, dyestuffs, etc., which the manufacturer uses, so that by proceeding on this process of reduction, when we come to the point where we have none but revenue duties on those articles consumed by the masses, we shall have the raw material, for which there is no demand save that produced by the manufacturer himself, free. Widely different is this in principle from a free list which includes articles of general consumption and fit subjects for taxation, for to make them free is to throw the whole weight of taxation upon those articles which come into competition with domestic manufactures, and to prevent those duties from ever falling to the revenue standard.

The modification which I offer will be an improvement on the act of 1846. I propose to reduce the one hundred per cent. schedule to a thirty per cent.; to reduce the forty per cent., the thirty per cent., the twenty-five per cent., and the twenty per cent. schedules one-fourth, or nearly one-fourth—that is to say, the forty per cent. to thirty, the thirty to twenty-three, the twenty-five to nineteen, and the twenty to fifteen. The lower schedules which are comparatively unimportant I propose to reduce one-fifth.

But it was not my purpose, nor do I think it would be right, to give to the manufacturer all that he desires to have free, while you tax the consumer upon a long list of articles with duties above the revenue standard. I think the two ought to go together, and I believe the substitute which I offer will accomplish that in a great degree. But how is it to operate on the great protected interests of the country? All those which have been heretofore considered as among the protected interests are in the twenty-three per cent. schedule. There you find iron, sugar, hemp, the manufactures of wool, and the finer manufactures of cotton.

Now, I ask which of these interests is it that need be afraid of foreign competition with such a protection as this? Surely not the wool interest. The woolen manufacturer gets his dyestuffs either free or at a reduced rate of duty. That is worth something to him, so that he stands in a better position than he did under the tariff of 1846. Who else, then, is there to whom I shall appeal? Is it the grower of the raw material of wool who is reduced from thirty to eight per cent.? It is manifest that if the wool-grower demands protection he admits that he cannot sell abroad. If he cannot sell abroad he cannot sell at home unless there be a home market—that is, unless the manufacturers of wool can succeed. He depends on them for that market, where he has advantages in supplying it. Now, it is known that with the thirty per cent. on the raw material the finer broadcloth factories have gone down, and that this rate of duty on the raw material has crippled and restrained the progress of the woolen manufacturer. There is reason to believe that, by diminishing this duty and allowing the manufactures to go on, you will produce a still greater demand for domestic wool. The reason is that, in order to use for certain purposes the qualities of wool which we mostly produce, we have to import finer wool to mix with them. We find it profitable, too, to import the wools of South America, which enable our own to receive the dyes better than they would without the admixture. But it is obvious that the wools which we raise for the most part stand in no danger of foreign competition. Thus the raiser of raw wool, so far from being injured, will be benefited by the change I propose.

Sir, I believe that the effect of such a change as that which I propose, a general reduction of something like one-fourth in the taxes laid on the people, will be to remove the heavy weight which now lies on the spring of productive industry, and to send forward all our great industrial pursuits as with a bound. The navigator will launch more ships on the ocean, the cotton planter will put out a larger breadth of his crop, the farmer will increase his fields, the grazier his herds, the manufacturer his spindles—yes, sir, and even the sheep master will stock his pastures and his walks with larger flocks. These great interests will grow, not at the expense of each other, but with mutual support and sympathy. The increase of one will but extend the market for another. Auxiliaries, and not adversaries, they will live and thrive together.

The bill as sent from the House of Representatives proposes that whatever advantages are to be derived from its operation shall be given to the manufacturer alone, making his raw material free, and keeping the existing rate of duties on everything else; the consequence of which must be that, when the necessity arises again for reducing the duties and changing the system, it will be to the interest of all manufacturers to combine, and resist any change; while, as long as we preserve something like the principle of which I have been speaking, it will be to the interest of the manufacturer, as well as of the consumer, to make reductions and changes when the revenue system begins to weigh too heavily upon the country. If this should prove to be heavy upon the one, it will scarcely be light upon the other. The manufacturer will gain as much by reducing the duty upon the raw material as he may suppose he loses by a reduction of that upon the manufactured article. Thus we may hope for something like harmony of effort.

Jacob Collamer [Vt.] spoke in favor of a protective duty on wool.

I advance, as an initial principle, that you cannot successfully, by any forms of financial protection in the way of tariffs, force into ultimate success and permanent prosperity any manufacture which depends for the supply of its materials upon foreign countries. That is hot-bed, forced protection. If it has to depend on the foreign supply for the raw material, the manufacture never can succeed if it be a necessary of life.

The bill of the House of Representatives provides that all wool costing fifty cents a pound or over shall be on the free list. It seems to me that will amount practically to letting in all wool free. The Secretary of the Treasury says so in his report. He says the very fine and the very coarse ought to be let in free; but that the probability is, such a law would be very difficult of execution, and might amount to nothing at all. I strongly suspect that will be made practically to bring the maximum and minimum together, and the result will be to admit all wool free of duty. If we ever mean to go on with any probability of success in manufacturing our woolens, and especially those of good quality, the protection to the material furnished in the country, and the protection to the manufacturer on the woolens, should keep pace *pari passu*. The Senator from Virginia says the reductions ought to keep pace; but how prettily has he verified that in his proposition! He has actually produced here to you a bill which he proposes to substitute for the House bill, reducing the duty on all wool to eight per cent., and reducing the duty on woolen goods from thirty to twenty-three per cent. That he calls *pari passu!*

Sir, if we ever expect to succeed and render ourselves an independent people as to our manufactures, so as not to be dependent on a foreign supply which may be cut off in war, or at any time their caprice may dictate, we should keep our duty *pari passu* on the raw material and on the manufactured article.

For these reasons, in my opinion, the House bill admitting free of duty fine wools above fifty cents a pound ought to be struck out, and that provision for letting in coarse wools free of duty ought to be perfected by striking out that part which excludes them if they have thirty-three per cent. of dirt, because that will shut them out. If you reduce the duty on woolens we cannot expect that you will keep it at its present rate on wools; but do not reduce the woolens from thirty to twenty-three, and wool from thirty to eight per cent.

I look on this whole process of changing the tariff at the present moment as temporary—I will not say temporizing. The exigencies of the moment, which press on the people in regard to the surplus in the treasury, are such that they wish to reduce the revenue.

Now, the problem of reducing duties so as to reduce the revenue is altogether too uncertain to speak of. There are so many considerations, so many elements entering into it that you cannot calculate with certainty. By reducing the duty you increase importations under certain circumstances, and again you may reduce the duties and yet reduce your importations and still increase your revenue, because of the rise of the price of the article.

Again, you may reduce revenue by increasing the duties. This, however, is altogether an experiment. It is entirely uncertain whether you will do it or not. It may be that you will increase your revenue or decrease it. You may even let the duty stand as it is, and import precisely as much as you did last year, and yet have a revenue greatly increased or greatly diminished, but especially increased, because the tendency of prices is to rise. The surplus which you now have in the treasury is not the natural and ordinary result of commerce, or of the increase of our people; it is the result of the increase of gold. I do not say there is no other element; but that is the largest element in the composition that has increased the price on everything you import. Your duties are laid *ad valorem;* and, as prices of articles rise, your revenues increase without your increasing your importations. The House bill increases the free list, and therefore it diminishes the revenue. The effects of any other changes are exceedingly problematical. The probability is that the scale of the Senator from Virginia, or the scale fixed by our Finance Committee, would increase the revenue.

George E. Pugh [O.] also spoke in favor of protecting the wool growers:

Mr. President, I do not like the principles on which this revision of the tariff has been undertaken. I am not in favor of an extensive free list. I desire to approximate equality in taxation. I believe that the Government has no rightful authority to take one dollar from the pocket of any citizen, except for its legitimate and necessary expenses, and that those expenses ought to be reduced within very narrow bounds. I wish to see this a Government of small income—one which shall be compelled to husband its resources throughout each fiscal year, lest the public expenditure should exceed the public revenue. Then, sir, we will have economy in the Government, and with it a prosperous people and honest public servants. In levying the amount thus required, I wish to see no preference of classes, interests, or individuals, one above another. For this reason, when it is proposed to reduce the amount of the Federal revenue, I object to laying a feather upon the manufacturer, and a weight upon the agriculturist.

Henry Wilson [Mass.] spoke for the manufacturing interests.

At this time, when the great interests of the nation depend upon the proper adjustment of the duties upon imports, the woolen manufacturers present their condition to the attention of Congress—to the consideration of American statesmen. They tell you, Mr. President, and they tell you truly, that the tariff of 1846 has borne heavily upon their interests. They tell you, and they tell you truly, that, under the operations of the tariff of 1846, the manufacture of the *finer* and *better* classes of woolens has almost entirely ceased—that one by one the mills for the manufacture of these finer and better classes of woolens have been compelled to succumb—that hundreds of thousands of dollars invested in these mills have been lost—that, even in the manufacture of the coarser qualities of woolens, hundreds of thousands of dollars have been sunk. They point you, sir, to many of their mills in which at least fifty per cent. of the original investments has been sacrificed, under that policy which has increased your importations of woolen goods from nine millions in 1846 to more than thirty-four millions in 1856—a policy which discriminates against the manufactures of our own country by taxing the raw material higher than the manufactured article—a policy which practically offers a bounty to the manufacturers of all nations which have the raw materials free to command our markets, and increase their wealth and power at the expense of our wool growers and manufacturers. They ask you now, in the adjustment of the tariff, to adopt the policy of admitting duty free the raw materials, the wools, the dye stuffs, and all those articles which enter into manufactures. They ask you to abandon that suicidal policy which places a higher duty upon wool than you place upon the manufactured article, and to adopt that policy which is giving to the manufacturers of England, France, Belgium, and Germany the command of the markets of the world. They ask you to abandon that policy which is closing their mills, driving American laborers from their looms and spindles, and crowding the markets of America with the products of European capital, skill, and labor.

I listened, Mr. President, as we all did, with close attention to the very elaborate speech of the Senator from Vermont [Mr. Collamer]. Without indulging in the language of reproach or denunciation, he warned the manufacturers against that policy which should diminish the production of wool in the United States. I know that I utter the sentiments of the manufacturers of my own State when I say to the Senator, to the Senate, to the wool growers of the whole country, that an increase in the production of American wool is among their first desires. The prosperity of the wool-growing interest cannot but be conducive to the prosperity of the wool-manufacturing interest. Mutuality of interests exists between the growers of wool and the manufacturers of wool.

What are the effects of the present policy upon the wool-growing interest? Is that interest keeping pace with the growth of our population—with the demands of our people for the manufacture of woolens? It may be safely assumed that the production of wool in the United States during the past five years has not perceptibly increased.

The manufacturers, Mr. President, make no war upon the wool growers. They assume that the reduction of the duty on wool, or the repeal of the duty altogether, will infuse vigor into that drooping interest, stimulate home production, diminish the importation of foreign woolen manufactures, and afford a steady and increasing demand for American wool. The experience of England, France, and Belgium demonstrates the wisdom of that policy which makes the raw materials duty free. Let us profit by their example.

In warning the manufacturers to avoid a policy which would check or repress the development of any of the agricultural interests of the country, the Senator from Vermont made the declaration that a country could not successfully manufacture articles, unless it produced the raw materials which enter into their manufacture. This declaration is too broad, sweeping, and general. It is hardly supported by the present or past experiences of nations. England, the great cotton manufacturing nation of the globe, depends not upon her own production for her supply of raw cotton—she depends upon the United States, her great commercial rival. The great manufacturing nations of Western Europe—nations which stand at the head of the manufacturing countries—draw from the United States, Mexico, South America, Asia, Africa, Australia, and the isles of the Indian seas immense supplies of the raw materials which enter into their varied manufactures. The high development of manufactures and the mechanic arts demands accumulated capital, educated labor, varied skill. Many of the raw materials which enter largely into these productions of the manufactures and mechanic arts are the rude products of less cultivated nations or the peculiar products of particular soils and climates. By this bill of the House raw silk is to come in free of duty, and we of New England expect, in a few years, to manufacture silk goods to a large extent. I concur with the Senator from Vermont in the opinion that our manufactures rest upon a safer and surer basis when our own country furnishes the raw materials; but I do not limit our capital, labor, and skill to the manufactures of those articles which our own country produces. The capital, labor, and skill of Massachusetts—of New England—will lay under contribution the raw materials

XII—7

of other States and other climes—the products which more pro-
lific soils and more genial skies, and less skilled labor contribute
to the commerce and the arts of the world.

William H. Seward [N. Y.] supported the House bill.

It seems to me, Mr. President, that the difficulties we have
to contend with, in attempting to reach a proper solution of
this question, arise from taking a view of the subject either too
broad or too narrow. Some of the gentlemen who have engaged in the debate would draw us into a whirl of political
speculation, when it is very certain that the vote of not a single
Senator will be governed by any partisan considerations whatever. It is simply a practical question, upon which no party,
as such, has expressed any opinion or adopted any policy.
Other Senators would draw us from this practical question
into one of the metaphysics of finance, and engage us in abstruse
researches into so much of the science of political economy as is
involved in the subject of revenue. Other Senators would seem
disposed to draw us into a consideration of the importance of
protecting or defending certain special interests, without sufficient consideration of the importance of maintaining other interests established or growing up in the country.

I have not looked at it in any such light. If it shall come
to be regarded as a partisan question, if it shall come to be regarded as a general question of protection or free trade, or if
it shall come to be regarded as a question of discrimination between different branches of industry, I am certain it will find
no wise solution at this stage of the session. But, sir, the light
in which I have chosen to regard the question is simply this:
it is not wise, it is not just to draw from the pockets of the
people into the treasury of the country an amount of money
greater than the current expenses of the treasury require.

Now, if we can find any plan by which six or ten, or even
fifteen millions of dollars can be withdrawn from the treasury,
or prevented from going into it, without disturbing any one of
the agricultural, or commercial, or manufacturing interests
of the country, that is the plan, under present circumstances, to adopt. In looking through the different plans with
reference to that object, I find myself prepared at once to dispense with, and lay out of view as measures which cannot receive my support, all those plans which seek a horizontal reduction of the tariff, because it would be absurd to suppose a
horizontal reduction which should disregard the special condi-

tion of the different systems of the production of the country could be made without sacrificing some of those systems, and giving at the same time unequal and undue advantages to others which do not need any protection.

The same consideration brings me also to the conclusion that the bill of the honorable Senator from Virginia, which, however, he has now offered in the shape of an amendment, is objectionable, though less so than that which is offered by the committee over which he has the honor to preside.

I find that, so far as it goes, the bill of the House of Representatives avoids all the objections which I have thought essential; and, although in some of its details it seems to me to be very injudicious, yet, at the same time, regarding it as a compromise, I am satisfied that it is a bill which is worthy of our approval and our acceptance. I do not say that it might not be advantageously modified. That bill proceeds upon the ground of certainly diminishing the revenues by transferring to the free list articles which are now paying duty. It has been remarked, as wisely as laconically, by the honorable Senator from Vermont [Mr. Collamer] that the removal of all duties on any articles imported will operate simply as a bill to effect a reduction of the revenues. I recognize also in the bill which comes from the House of Representatives the principle that, by transferring to the free list those foreign articles which are raw materials employed in the manufacture of our own country, we discriminate in favor of manufactures. In transferring to that list dyestuffs and other articles which cannot be produced in this our country at all, we encourage manufactures without injuring the agricultural or mineral interests of the United States. If by thus increasing the free list we shall effect a sufficient diminution of the revenue, then I shall be willing to stop there, and I should insist on stopping there.

Robert Toombs [Ga.] opposed the protection on wool, stating that the true policy was to encourage manufactures.

I happen to represent a constituency who get nothing at all but taxation. We ask no advantage—we claim none. You give us no protection on our productions. Cotton is in the free list; rice is in the free list; lumber is in the free list, by the reciprocity treaty. These are the chief products of my own people. We have neither sought nor asked any bounty; therefore we are impartial judges between the grower and the manufacturer of wool. It is not a Southern question. It is a question among you gentlemen who are seeking the advantages of the Government. You raise a quarrel, and I am afraid the result will be to leave us to pay taxes to a government that does not want them. You levy $20,000,000 a year, which everybody says you do not want. You say now it is going to produce a commercial revulsion, and derange your currency. If that shall be the effect, it will be a just punishment to those who levy burdens on the people without public necessity. I thank God that there is an avenging Nemesis that follows in the train of false theories in politics and wicked legislation, and teaches communities the folly of wickedness.

I would enlarge the free list on the principles I have stated, but first I want a reduction on general taxation. Take off the public burdens by reducing duties upon all articles of general consumption all over the country and among all classes. This will be beginning at the right place. Why shall you tax Maine for the benefit of sheep growers in Vermont? In this dispute between the manufacturer and the grower, I think the argument is with the manufacturer. He has my sympathies; but I hope I have equal sympathy for all my countrymen. If I could settle this dispute on any just principle, I should be glad to do so; but I believe it is irreconcilable—one or the other must go. The idea of protecting both—the wool manufacturer and the wool grower—presents one of those problems that cannot be worked out. The more you try it, the worse it will be. If you give to woolen manufacturers and to raw wool a protection of one hundred per cent., it is quite certain, even then, that you would not drive out foreign competition. It would certainly injure both interests. Its operation could only be temporary. It is futile to think of building up both interests together by equal duties, no matter what they may be. The best protection to the wool grower is to multiply and strengthen the woolen manufacturers. I believe it to be the only mode of permanently benefiting them. On no sound principle of political economy can equal duty on both which you will lay harmonize them. If woolen manufactures and wool-growing can succeed together without duty, they will succeed if you go on taxing them *pari passu;* but, if either requires a duty, neither can succeed on any such basis as I have stated. We have not the same difficulty as to cotton manufacturers, because we raise our own cotton; and we do not raise sufficient wool for the home consumption. The great complaint of the woolen manufacturers is that they have to pay a large duty on the cheap wools of South America. They are now working at a disadvantage, because the English manufacturer takes the wool from Buenos Ayres, where wool costs but little, and brings it cheaply to England duty free, while they pay thirty per cent. *ad valorem*. The result is that the duty on wool and on woolen manufactures at present being the same, our manufacturers of wool are driven out of foreign markets, and struggle hard for their own. I do not think that system is wise. In laying my duties I would protect a branch of industry which, in my judgment, will be able to support itself within a short time, and be a permanent advantage to the country.

Andrew P. Butler [S. C.], an advocate of free trade, supported horizontal reduction as a step in that direction.

I know that my State expects me to take a part in this debate, because I believe there is no State in the Union that has made as many issues on free trade as South Carolina. As to the theory which she entertains and has promulgated, I may say, without any vanity as far as I can speak of her doctrines, that she has not spoken in vain, although she was threatened with the sword for speaking. I might be considered as going very far if I were to say that I should be perfectly willing to have no custom houses at all. That is my opinion; but I know I cannot have that. I go so far as to say that, in a commercial point of view, the custom houses must necessarily, in the form of tariffs, make discriminations; and in a war point of view I know we must retain the power of discriminating, in order to protect iron or any other material which must be protected as an element of war. I have no idea now of being able to reduce the tariff to anything like the level to which the South Carolina doctrine would reduce it.

Sir, for myself, I want no tariff. I say to this Confederacy that I am perfectly willing to be placed in the original position of constituencies to pay for carrying on this Government. I am not, however, to be drawn into a discussion on that subject, for I know that anything which is untenable is a matter not to be discussed, or at least its discussion is fruitless.

We have $70,000,000 of revenue—$35,000,000 more than enough. The burden of this taxation is upon the poor and middle classes of the people, for the rich are well able to contribute their share. The persons who pay these taxes are the consumers—the humble milkmaid who pays for her calico, the humble mechanic who pays for the coat in which he works, the humble farmer who pays for the plow he uses twenty per cent. more than he ought to pay. If you could bring to the mind of the people that these classes are paying more than they are bound to pay, they would resist; but as long as you delude them with this disguised form of taxation you make this a Government more irresponsible, in my opinion, than any, as far as I have read history—I say the most irresponsible Government on earth, so far as regards the collection and disbursement of revenue. You collect it sometimes on wool, sometimes on this article, sometimes on that; but you always take it from the industrial portion of the community. They pay it, and they do not know that they pay it. It is so diffused that they never know it. If you take off the taxation in the form proposed here, you will have prosperity, particularly in my portion of the country. Cotton would rise to twenty cents to-morrow, I believe, if we had no tariff. I believe, if you let all the world compete with the manufacturers here, we should raise the raw material; that would be the result.

I desire it to be understood that your taxation comes out of delusive and fraudulent legislation in some respects, and unwise legislation in all respects. What right have you to build up the iron interest, the woolen interest, or any other interest, through the money contributed to this treasury for the benefit of the common objects of government?

I do not undertake to discriminate between my friends from Ohio, Virginia, and Georgia. If it were a matter of mere taste, I would rather go for the man who cultivates his land and feeds his sheep, and prepares the great element. But what right, in reality, have we to assume jurisdiction over matters of this kind, except to raise revenue? And in raising revenue it ought to be just. Who is to decide? Discretion. What is discretion? Interest. What is interest? Power. What is power? It is the combination of different influences; and that makes up the whole concern, so far as regards the regulation of the industrial concerns of this country. I shall vote for the amendment of the committee, and will take the best scheme I can get; but for myself I want no tariff. I would obliterate the whole concern.

The Senate adopted the substitute measure of Senator Hunter by a vote of 33 to 12. The Senate bill was accepted by the House on March 3, and approved by President Franklin Pierce upon the same day.

CHAPTER VIII

INTERNAL REVENUE

Thaddeus Stevens [Pa.] in 1862 Introduces in the House a Bill to Provide Internal Revenue—Debate: in Favor, Justin S. Morrill [Vt.], Mr. Stevens; Opposed, George H. Pendleton [O.]—Debate in the Senate: in Favor, James F. Simmons [R. I.]; Opposed, James A. McDougall [Cal.]—Bill Is Passed by Congress and Approved by the President—In 1882 William D. Kelley [Pa.] Introduces in the House a Bill to Reduce the Internal Revenue—Debate: in Favor, Alexander H. Stephens [Ga.], George M. Robeson [N. J.]; Opposed, Philip B. Thompson [Ky.], Roger Q. Mills [Tex.]—Bill Is Passed in the Following Session, and Approved by President Arthur.

ON March 3, 1862, Thaddeus Stevens [Pa.], of the Committee of Ways and Means, introduced in the House a bill to provide internal revenue. In its final form this bill established the Bureau of Internal Revenue, under the Treasury Department, with what is essentially the present system for collecting excise from manufacturers of distilled spirits and malt liquors, and from rectifiers of wine and spirits. In addition, annual licenses ranging from $5 to $100 were required from almost every kind of business or profession, the peddler on foot and the juggler being assessed, as well as the banker, lawyer, and doctor. Manufacturers of every kind of commodity, from pins to railroad iron, were taxed at various rates, specific and *ad valorem*. All sales at auction, whether of real estate, merchandise, or stocks and bonds, were taxed one-tenth of one per cent. Luxuries, such as private carriages, yachts, billiard tables, and plate, were taxed at *ad valorem* rates. Live stock slaughtered for sale had to be paid for at so much per head, according to the genus. Railroad, steamboat, and ferry companies were assessed three per cent. upon their gross receipts; holders of railroad bonds had the same percentage deducted from their dividends, as had also investors in banks, trust companies, savings institutions, and insurance companies. Three per cent. was also deducted from the salaries of those in the employ of the Government. The same rate was assessed upon the gross advertising receipts of publishers. The amount exempted by the preceding income tax bill was lowered from $800 to $600, and the rate was increased from three to five per cent. upon incomes exceeding $10,000 per annum. Stamp duties were laid upon legal papers and business instruments, as well as upon medicines, cosmetics, perfumery, and playing cards. Legacies of over $1,000, except from husband to wife, or wife to husband, were taxed at rates varying with the degree of consanguinity.

INTERNAL REVENUE

HOUSE OF REPRESENTATIVES, MARCH 3-JULY 1, 1862

Justin S. Morrill [Vt.], of the Committee on Ways and Means, supported the bill. After presenting the state of Government finances he said that the bill amply provided for all the great and unusual demands upon the Treasury.

When one of the European governments offered a reward to any person who should discover a new object of taxation, it was bestowed, I believe, upon the discovery of the stamp tax upon paper. That is not by any means our condition. There is but little more than one source, that of imposts, which we have relied upon to any extent for revenue, and that source has not been pushed to its utmost capacity. Driven, however now, like Milton's Adam, from our untaxed garden, to rely upon the sweat of the brow for support, like Adam, we have "all the world before us where to choose." In doing this we have to be just. It would not do to press any single interest with the entire burden that now weighs down upon the treasury. The weight must be distributed equally—not upon each man an equal amount, but a tax proportionate to his ability to pay— equally, yet not one that will be in the exact ratio of population, but in a just proportion to the means and facility of payment. What could be easily sustained in one quarter of the country might sink another in hopeless dishonor and repudiation. A heavy duty upon some articles would banish them from use, while upon others it would merely stimulate greater activity and industry to obtain them. A tax dependent upon the habits or vices of men is the most reliable of all taxes, as it takes centuries to change or eradicate one or the other. No matter what obstacles may be placed in the way of the introduction of opium, the Chinese will brave death itself rather than suffer the deprivation of their favorite stimulant. England taxes spirits enormously, but has her drunkards still. They raise, too, $28,000,000 (or about one dollar for each inhabitant) of revenue from duties on tobacco.

The accustomed objects of State taxation should, in some degree at least, go untouched. The orbit of the United States and the States must be different and not conflicting. Otherwise, we might perplex and jostle, if we did not actually crush, some of the most loyal States of the Union. It has not been possible, so multifarious are the systems of State taxation, and so large our wants, wholly to succeed in carrying out this idea; but it has been attempted in two modes; the first, by the avoidance of any tax or duty on live stock, and by declining to increase the direct tax on real estate—a very moderate one—levied at the last session of Congress; and the second, by a selection of new objects of taxation, and such others as for many reasons can sustain even the double taxation to which they may be for the time subjected.

Some gentlemen, and even some States, have manifested a solicitude that any taxes incident to the present rebellion should be levied in such a way as to allow the several States to assume, assess, and collect them, or, if not to include the assessment, at least to assume and collect after an assessment by the United States. If this were practicable, it might be very desirable. If State officers could be employed, and the increase of Federal patronage avoided by not creating a new corps of office holders, a great point would be gained. We provide in the present bill that the duties, if not paid at the proper time, shall be hereafter collected in the now rebellious States. Authorize the States to assume and collect, and then suppose South Carolina to set about it. How much revenue so farmed should we be likely to obtain? It would be for the interest of all State officials to collude and pay as little as possible. It is not too much to suppose some would improve the opportunity.

This idea is wholly impracticable as may be seen by anyone who looks at the scope of the bill, with its fingers spread out in all directions, ready to clutch something to buoy up the sinking credit of a nation which has hitherto generally sheltered its capital and its labor from all tax gatherers, except through the indirect process of the custom house. It is not enough to know that a debtor has means; he must exhibit the will to pay, otherwise there must be some law to coerce the will. In this emergency we cannot afford to return to the pusillanimity of the old Confederation, and request the States to make their contributions, and shiver in the wind if any should fail to do so, or declare war upon them for delinquency. The Government of the United States—the most parental and benign of all earthly governments—in its hour of need has the right to *demand* whatever may be the measure of its necessities to sustain the public credit—our honor and existence as one people.

It is indispensable that the Government shall have within its own control—responsive to it at regular and stated periods—the means of meeting all its vast engagements. This can be secured only by its own agents under its own laws. Even where the States are allowed, as they are in the direct tax, fifteen per cent. for assuming and collecting a tax, when all assume it, there is no advantage gained. The effect is to require the tax to be put fifteen per cent. higher than would otherwise be called for; and the general Government can collect the amount at a much less expense.

That the bill is perfect the committee are far from supposing. To us at best it is but an experiment, and the wisdom of Congress, now and hereafter, will judge how much of it should be permanently retained and what part must be dropped out. It is no personal or party measure, but one imperiously demanded—sharp as may be the medicine—for the general welfare.

Seeking to avoid all extremes, the committee have thought best to propose duties upon a large number of objects, rather than confine them to a narrow field, and thereby be forced to make them excessive in amount, and for that reason entirely unreliable. If the rates can be hereafter increased in any instance to the benefit of the revenue, and without inflicting any injury upon any quarter of the country, it will soon be ascertained. Meantime is it not wise to set out on a moderate scale —one that will neither shock the sense nor the pockets of the people—rather than attempt to make any one product the victim from which to torture magnificent bounties?

It is to be expected there will be a diversity of opinion concerning many features of the bill. If it will produce too much or too little revenue, if it includes objects that should be left free, or omits those which should justly be held to contribute, these are legitimate objects of amendment, as much so as matters of form or detail; but an ample and effective bill—being all for which I personally feel the slightest solicitude—is demanded at our hands by all the motives which can move a lover of his country; and if it were possible for this Congress to desert its responsibilities, and adjourn without passing some equivalent measure, it would deserve to be pickled in history as representative imbeciles. Observers living under other forms of government proclaim that our weak point is incapacity for taxation, and our securities, therefore, have no solidity abroad. Representative democracy is now on trial. Let us see to it that the Republic suffers no shame at our hands.

In starting out with a bill like the present, so important to the vitality of the treasury, which is to touch so many and such various interests, the machinery by which it is to be put into operation, with the least friction and at the least expense, becomes a question of some magnitude. We have, therefore, looked to such examples as we found upon our statutes, and have endeavored to arrange a system by which all descriptions of duties could be assessed and collected through the same officers.

For this purpose we propose a commissioner of internal revenue, under the direction of the Secretary of the Treasury, who is to have the general charge and superintendence of all matters in relation to internal revenue.

(Here the speaker described what is essentially the present system [1913] of the Internal Revenue Bureau.)

The duties proposed by the present bill rest heavily on spirits and malt liquors—being about one hundred per cent. on raw whisky, fifty per cent. on rum, and twenty-five per cent. on ale or beer—but far below the point at which even some prominent distillers thought they might be safely carried, and yet largely above the point indicated by the majority of those engaged in the business. Much the largest quantity of spirits produced in this country is from corn, and many persons engaged in the business apprehend that we shall cut them up by the roots with a duty so high as even fifteen cents per gallon, and that great injury will result to farming interests thereby. The committee were satisfied these fears are not well founded.

So long as consumption keeps equal pace with production—as in the case of all manufactures—the consumer must pay the increased cost price. And consumption will not be seriously checked by this bill.

The amount which will accrue on licenses under the present bill, embracing merchants, traders, bankers, brokers, auctioneers, distillers, brewers, peddlers, manufacturers, theaters, hotels and taverns, and other classes, will be very considerable. Licenses, though heretofore not generally adopted in this country, may be regarded among the least objectionable modes of taxation. They are a shield against unauthorized and irregular competition, and, there being no interference with the private details of business, the duty will be paid with very little dissatisfaction.

The duty proposed on unmanufactured tobacco is three cents per pound, and on manufactured tobacco and snuff an additional duty of five cents per pound. On cigars the rates are in proportion to value.

Everything used for illuminating purposes deserves to be considered with some reference to their power of competition. To be entirely impartial toward all parties, we have proposed a duty on candles, lard oil, gas, and petroleum.

The duty of three per cent. *ad valorem* proposed on all manufactures, except those specifically provided for, some at heavier rates, will not come out of the manufacturer—though a depression or glut of the market will make him suffer loss as it always does—but will increase the cost to that extent to the consumer, as much so as if added to the cost of labor or the raw material. It was not thought best to propose duties on raw materials generally, but to wait until all the cost, in the finished state at the time of sale, was added to the production, and thus assess the duty on the largest values. From this source much the largest item of revenue will be derived—in all, specific included, not less than $50,000,000.

If manufactures in the history of our Government have been fostered, they are now the strongest pillars of our support. A burden that would paralyze the agriculturists of the country will be taken onto the backs of the steam giants with alacrity and confidence. But it will be indispensable for us to revise the tariff on foreign imports, so far as it may be seriously disturbed by any internal duties—on some things the tax proposed is more than the present tariff—and to make proper reparation, otherwise we shall have destroyed the goose that lays the golden eggs. From such a revision, including some articles that hitherto it has not been considered sound policy to take from the free list and lower schedules of the tariff, it is expected also to increase the revenue several millions of dollars. If we bleed manufactures we must see to it that the proper tonic is administered at the same time. There are many articles, however, where the tariff is now high enough for revenue or protection, which will require no advance.

A tax upon railroads is easily levied and easily collected; but to adjust an equitable tax upon all railroads has been one of the difficult problems the committee have attempted to solve. If we took the basis of cost it was apparent that the nominal cost—including long interest accounts while in course of construction—would, in many instances, be beyond the present value. The market value could be no criterion, as many are not sufficiently known to have any fixed value, and of the whole five hundred and forty-one railroads in the country few are without a moiety or a prominent share of their cost represented in bonds or floating debt. If we were to take the gross receipts as a basis of taxation, many of the roads would be taxed for freights which they now transport over long distances—having competing lines, here and in Canada, by land and water—for little more than the bare cost. In these times of commercial depression it is an object to leave the transit of produce and merchandise as much unfettered as possible.

The subject has been disposed of by proposing a duty of three per cent. on the season or commutation tickets, and on the coupons or interest paid on bonds, and by a duty of two mills on passengers (other than season-ticket passengers) for each mile traveled. This, in some sort, apportions the tax between the owners of the road, whether foreign or domestic, and whether represented in the form of stock or debt.

Obviously the system had to be modified and extended to steamboats and other vessels, in order to deal justly by the roads and obtain justice for the Government.

Stamp duties upon telegraphic dispatches and express packages will not be likely to encounter opposition, especially the latter, as it is a class of business rewarded by unusual profits; nor will the duty on patent medicines, from which so many not inconsiderable fortunes have been accumulated, be regarded with disfavor.

The speaker concluded with an estimate that the internal revenue resulting from the measure would amount to $101,925,000.

The income duty is one, perhaps, of the least defensible that, on the whole, the Committee of Ways and Means concluded to retain or report. The objection to it is that nearly all persons will have been already once taxed upon the sources from which their income has been derived. The income tax is an inquisitorial one at best; but, upon looking at the considerable class of State officers, and the many thousands who are employed on a fixed salary, most of whom would not contribute a penny unless called upon through this tax, it has been thought best not wholly to abandon it. Ought not men, too, with large incomes to pay more in proportion to what they have than those with limited means, who live by the work of their own hands or that of their families?

The duty on advertisements was thought advisable on the ground that, more than any other tax, it would be likely to fall, where it should fall, upon the person for whose benefit the advertisement is published. Experience has abundantly proven that the bold, ungrudging, and even lavish advertiser is always largely repaid for all costs of advertising, and these are not the men to skulk from a picayune tax.

There is no duty proposed on the circulation of any literary, scientific, or news publication whatever. Printing paper, like any other manufactures, it is proposed to assess, but only to the extent of three mills per pound, which is equal to three per cent. *ad valorem*. It is to be assessed as a paper manufacture, but at less than half the percentage proposed on writing paper. Can it be asked that it should be exempt?

Mr. Chairman, whatever we do ought to be done speedily, as every day's delay is a resulting loss to the Government.

On March 13 George H. Pendleton [O.] opposed that provision of the bill which placed the collection of the revenue in the hands of the Federal Government.

If a scheme can be devised by which the State, rather than the Federal Government, shall take upon itself the duty of collecting this tax, I hope that it will be done. I think that it will accomplish a great good, and that we will avoid by it a great error. However much gentlemen may desire to try the patriotism of the people by their willingness to pay taxes; however much they may desire, and their constituents may desire, to express their patriotism in that way, let me tell you that when this vast system goes into operation, and these tax gatherers are abroad in the land, there will go up a voice in the country that will make this legislature tremble. Remember that never has the tax gatherer, in the history of this country, gone about under the Federal authority. Remember that never have the people been called upon to pay into the treasury these taxes. I know that, during the war of 1812, there were some instances in which land taxes were raised. But a tax bill like this which goes into every house, into every business, every neighborhood, which taxes everything a man eats and all that he wears, which enters into the consideration of every man engaged in every business of the country, which puts a tax upon every conceivable subject of taxation; such a tax bill has never before appeared in this country.

On March 15 Thaddeus Stevens [Pa.] replied to Mr. Pendleton.

The gentleman from Ohio [Mr. Pendleton] informs us in somewhat of a minatory manner of the tremendous clamor that his bill will raise. He told us that a voice is to come up here which will shake this hall, and make even the firmest of us tremble in our boots. [Laughter.]

It is not, however, the tax gatherer the people hate so much as the taxes. And, if you have no provision in the bill by which the payment of these taxes can be coerced, they will never be paid. The Representatives here will act to represent their constituents, who will turn the friends of this Administration out of power and who will, of course, desire that no taxes may be collected. Some system will then be adopted more consonant to the feelings of the people, and more in accordance with the wishes of demagogues, than that which we are devising for the purpose of enforcing this tax. We intend to lay this tax, and to take the chances of that tremendous voice which is to hurl us from power. What we desire is a tax that will last during this war, and which cannot be disturbed by mere resolutions of one branch of this legislature.

It is objected that the tax cannot be collected in the seceded States. Take Virginia, for instance.

When the Constitution is restored there, I have no doubt that under this bill we can district the State, and find loyal men enough to assess and collect this tax. If we do not collect it to-day, we will next year; and, if not next year, we will the year after; and we will pile up on Virginia her full burden of the taxes which she has brought upon us. It will be a lien upon her real estate, and we can collect it.

How can we do that, if we allow those who have caused this trouble to make the assessment? Even if there were no rebellion, how could you equalize your taxes? If every State is allowed to assess its own taxes, Pennsylvania might say, let us assess them so as to shirk our fair share, and throw it upon New York.

And, if so, where is the equalizing power? But if you keep this machinery within the power of the United States Government, and they find that anything of this sort is going on, the Government can at once discard their unfaithful agents, and see that the matter is properly adjusted.

On May 30, 1862, James A. McDougall [Cal.] delivered a speech in the Senate criticizing the unscientific nature of the bill. He declared that proper thought had not been given to its framing.

Mr. President, this bill is without system, without policy, without form, without organization; a bill that, if passed into a law, it will take a hundred years for our courts to interpret, and then they will only make it law by construction.

Early in the present session, a committee of three gentlemen from the Boston Board of Trade, gentlemen of large experience in matters of finance, came to this city to advise with the Senate Committee on Finance upon this subject. These gentlemen propose to tax trade—the very business in which they are most engaged. They say that the business of trade, the business of making the exchanges of the country, can most conveniently, economically, and justly furnish the revenue required by the Government.

It is not wealth and capital that pay taxes; it is production that pays taxes. Otherwise, if it were not production, and it depended on capital or accumulations, a country would become weaker year by year, and the result would be national impoverishment and bankruptcy. England did not pay out of her capital or her wealth the great burdens of her French and American wars. She paid them out of her energies, her enterprise, her industry, what she every year produced, or by her enterprise brought from foreign lands through the agency of her commerce spread upon every sea.

I will now proceed to state my particular objections to the measure brought forward from the committee; and the first objection I make to it is that it involves an army of officers. And what skill and knowledge in the various specialties of trade will be required to determine the quantity and quality of these various articles?

Again, I object to this measure from the complexity of the system. It has a different law for every subject of taxation.

I object to this whole system of licenses. When the Constitution was formed, the question of internal taxes was considered, among other things and, although it was conceded that there was concurrent jurisdiction in the States and the Federal Government to levy internal taxes in such form as either might choose, yet possible collision between the several authorities was regarded as a grave and not to be overlooked difficulty; and therefore Mr. Hamilton himself suggested that both the Federal and State governments, in looking to subjects of taxation, should avoid the same subjects of taxation. And there is hardly a subject of license in this bill that is not made the subject of State license.

All license systems are more or less unjust. There is the auctioneer who sells twenty-five dollars' worth a day, and the auctioneer who sells $25,000 a day, both taxed alike. There is the young fellow going to the bar who has not earned his first fee, and there is my friend from Illinois [Orville H. Browning], who accumulates his thousands per annum. This whole system of licenses is wrong. It is a system that restrains young energy, that breaks down the power of the young man full of heart, without money in his pocket. It is a system altogether unworthy of the Federal Government.

Again: I object to the tax on manufactures. I object to the tax particularly as inconveniently, unequally, and unjustly applied, and as being, as was proved by the Senator from Rhode Island [James F. Simmons], a particular burden on the laboring poor. And, again, this tax is a demand for money before money is realized. It is asking for that which the parties taxed may not have, whereas in a tax on sales the price is considered in the purchase and the money is in the hands of the vendor.

Again: the bill imposes a tax upon the salaries of all persons in the service of the Government. That is considered a happy subject of legislation. Why should men in public employment be specially taxed? It has been my impression, it is the result of all my experience, that men in office who are fit for office are, as a general rule, inadequately paid. Who is there here in the Senate who does not make a sacrifice of his personal revenue in undertaking to discharge the duties of his office? I hold a tax upon the salaries of officers in the employment of the Government to be the rankest demagogism.

XII—8

Again: I object to the tax on advertisements. Why make them a subject of taxation? A person wants to inquire for information; he is a seeker after knowledge of some particular thing; he wants to know something, and you make it a subject of taxation; and in that way tax the press, the vehicle of communication, and by taxing the press tax the person who inquires.

And now, Mr. President, I desire to enter my special protest against all those subjects of taxation which create a charge upon individual, intellectual, and commercial contact, upon moral, intellectual, and material intercommunication. Such taxation is against every rule of public policy.

It has been considered wise policy to promote the construction of railroads, canals, and telegraphs, to construct piers and lighthouses and harbors in the aid of foreign intercourse and trade.

If it is true policy to advance these interests and enterprises, there can be no good cause to disturb or impair them by impositions and charges.

You propose to tax them three per cent. on gross receipts; and what does it amount to? It amounts to at least eight per cent. on the profits of good roads, and probably takes the entire profits of inferior roads, for some of them hardly pay at all.

This brings me to the subject of coal. You say you want to reach everything. I insist that this is the great error of the bill and not any argument in its defence; we should not attempt to reach everything. Coal is the motive power that drives all our machinery, and that is enabling one man to do the work of a hundred—one of the things that when a nation finds anywhere about hidden in her earth she feels rich because of it, and promotes its development. Every development of that kind is something to be promoted, because it is a facility to the aggregation of our national wealth.

Again: I object to this universal system of stamps. Here are several pages of stamp duties. Everything is to be stamped, from the pill box to the locomotive. The child is not to be allowed to take its medicine until it is stamped. Stamps must be everywhere, presenting themselves to every eye at every moment. These things may seem expedient or necessary. I cannot think so. The idea is absurd, impracticable.

Again, Mr. President, I object to this tax on insurances. Insurance is a tax paid by the insured for protection against loss, and this is a tax upon a tax. If those who engage in insurance pay a tax upon the income they derive from their investments, this surely should be satisfactory.

Mr. President, it is vain to attempt to enumerate the multitude of objections which may, as I think, be justly raised to this bill. I will content myself with reaffirming that it is an unintelligible, as well as impracticable, measure, one which, I trust, will not be forced upon the country, particularly at this time of general privation and suffering.

The speaker here presented a substitute measure, based on the views of the board of trade previously mentioned. First, this imposed a tax on sales.

These men of commerce say—and they should be authority—that a tax on sales is the simplest, safest, and most just tax. The sale involves a money transaction. A man who sells receives the price, or what he regards as its equivalent. Having received the price, he is prepared to pay. One of the great objections to the bill reported from the committee is that it demands from people what they have not got. When you charge a tax on sales, you always charge it on what a man has received, on what he has in his pocket, which he is bound to account for to the Government.

I propose a tax on fixed incomes. I differ with the Senator from Rhode Island [Mr. Simmons] on that subject. How can you tax the income of a lawyer who keeps no books? It is not the habit of lawyers to keep an exact account either of their expenditures or incomes. They spend all the money they get generally. It is their own, unless it happens to be their clients', and then they pay it over. How are you going to get at the income of a merchant—a man whose life is engaged in venture, whose every enterprise is a risk of fortune, and who, if at the end of a lifetime of friendly and adverse fortune, is able to go quietly to his home among his people, and sit down and rest for the evening of his days, is a fortunate man? How are you going to get at his income?

SENATOR SIMMONS.—If the Senator will look at the provisions of the income tax, passed last August, he will find that that provides that a man shall render an account of his oncome for the year preceding the 1st of January of each year. His year's business ends at the 1st of January, and his income tax will be payable in six months afterward. I do not believe there is a man of business in the country who does not know his income.

SENATOR MCDOUGALL.—How is it with the men who venture in commerce, where the article they purchase at fifty dollars a ton to-day, and in which they invest $50,000, may be thirty dollars to-morrow or eighty dollars? How about those men who may be ruined or made prosperous by the accident of a day, news from Europe or from the East, war, or some treaty of peace, if you please? How about those?

SENATOR SIMMONS.—We do not tax a man's property. We tax his income. If last year he made a great income on his ships we ought to tax it. If these ships are not worth half as much this year, not paying half as much freight, then we only tax him half as much on his income.

SENATOR MCDOUGALL.—If I have any idea of commerce and its business, a man, say the master of $100,000, goes into trade; his trade runs prosperously along through a series of years, where he expects that he has means enough on hand to carry on an advancing and progressive business, but where in one day a single calamity like that which came in 1836, or came at the commencement of the present year, may destroy the most prosperous fortune: who has an income then?

I propose to tax income, but not the income of the merchant whose capital is invested in commerce, for the merchant is as much of a producer as the man who tills the soil. He who conducts it from hand to hand, who labors in that vocation, is increasing its value and producing wealth to the country. I do not tax the man who builds up machinery, workshops, and factories, whose capital is employed to support labor, for capital and labor are the two great elements of strength that enable us to pay taxes; that is active employed capital and labor. I do not tax employed capital or labor, but fixed capital, such as a man derives from rents, which comes to him as a matter of course. I tax the man who collects his interest on State and corporate securities, but not mortgages. If you tax mortgage interest, the borrower has to pay it; but bonded interests of railroad companies, of all organized companies, of cities, towns, and States of the United States, and of foreign countries, all fixed revenue where the party deriving the revenue has no relation either to active capital or to labor—they are all legitimate subjects of taxation, and have been so held by the best economists.

Then, again, I propose to tax inheritances. I am trying to avoid asking a man to give what he has not got. Inheritances are things that no one has been possessed of until they pass through administration. We have no particular or fixed right in any other person's estate, no matter how near of kin he may be; certainly none in the estate of a stranger. England has adopted a policy by which she imposes as high a tax as ten pounds per cent. where a legacy is given to a person who is foreign to the blood of the testator. We can derive as large a revenue as England from this source, and from what no other person has got any special or particular right to. It is true, we generally feel that a child has a right to inherit from a parent; but suppose there should be taken out of that a tax of one per cent. for the administration of the laws for the benefit of the child, that would be no burden. I propose an ascending scale as high as eight per cent. to persons who are alien to the blood of the testator. That is less than the English rule. Those who pay it, never having had it, never feel the loss of it. Those are taxes that can be most conveniently collected. Estates pass here more readily than they do in England, and it would be a large source of revenue.

Under these various sources of revenue, as I have stated, and putting the income of the tariff at only $50,000,000—and I try to make small figures—I make a revenue of $203,000,000, and it does not ask a person for anything he has not got, and does not employ a large number of officers.

Expenditure is immediately related to production. Production is the subject of taxation. We must every year make the subject-matter out of which taxes are taken, or else there is a loss to the national capital. Expenditure and taxation being equivalent to production, there is no loss. If production is greater than taxation and expenditure, there is a national gain. England has gained through all her wars by the strength and will and energy of her people. Our energy is being expressed now with greater force than in any previous time. We will produce every year more than the equivalent of our expenditure and our revenue.

I think we are a new people with new conditions, and when the men of commerce, the first men of our commercial cities, say commerce can best stand this tax, they should be recognized as the highest authority; and I shall maintain them as authority so far as my conduct is concerned in voting upon this measure.

The bill was passed by Congress, and approved by President Abraham Lincoln on July 1.

On March 29, 1882, William D. Kelley [Pa.], chairman of the Committee on Ways and Means, introduced in the House a bill to reduce the internal revenue. It provided for a repeal of the stamp tax on checks, etc., of the tax on banks, private and national; and of the tax on matches, perfumery, medicinal preparations, etc., and revised the entire system of taxes on tobacco, spirits, etc.

The bill came up for discussion on June 21. The Democrats particularly opposed the abolition of taxes on banks as favoring the rich, in view of the retention of the tariff on articles consumed by the people in general.

REDUCTION OF INTERNAL REVENUE

HOUSE OF REPRESENTATIVES, JUNE 21–27, 1882

PHILIP B. THOMPSON [Ky.].—Why should these taxes be taken off? Is the capital of this country to pay no taxes? We have already taken off the income tax. Are all the tax laws of this country to be framed so as to grind the face of the poor and lay heavier weights upon the backs of the laborers of this country, leaving the capitalist, the national banks, the great railroad corporations, and other monopolies, to pay no part of our taxation and contribute nothing toward the support of the Government, who feel no interest in it save the privileges and franchises which they derive from it and by which they add to their increasing wealth, already grown fabulous?

Is a Republican Congress in one way and another, upon the demand of capitalists, to take all the taxes off banking capital, national as well as State, to remit to them nearly $13,000,000 of revenue now going into the public treasury, while at the same time by its legislation it undertakes to relay upon knit woolen stockings and other goods of that kind a tax of 85 per cent., which was taken off a few days ago by decision of the Supreme Court? It is claimed that by some mistake or oversight in the codification of the statutes it was reduced to 35 per cent. It is now proposed to "rectify" this mistake in order to reimpose this tax upon the laboring classes. Are you to leave upon everything that the laboring people use the immense taxes now paid? Are steel rails, over which are transported the products of Western farmers to the seaboard for shipment to foreign countries and to the markets of the world, to pay a tax of $28 a ton—105 per cent.—while at the same time you remove taxes which are paid by the banker and other capitalists? When did these classes become the peculiar pets of this Government, that they are to have exclusive privileges and all their taxes relieved, and no other class of society is to have any relief? This bill is shaped and framed in their interest only. Other things are put into it merely as a blind—as a makeshift to carry it through. The abolition of the match tax is inserted merely to delude the minds of the people so that it may be pretended you have given them some relief? It is the Judas-like kiss with which they are to be betrayed and deceived—beguiled into the belief that the Republican party is adopting measures for their benefit, while in fact you relieve only the capitalist and increase the burdens laid upon labor.

Mr. Chairman, why should the tax upon bank checks be removed? What tax paid by the people of this country is more easily paid, or what tax is paid by people who are more able to pay it? Since the days of Adam Smith every enlightened government has adopted the principle laid down first by him and followed by every writer on political economy, that taxation should be imposed upon the luxuries of life, that taxes should be made as nearly voluntary in their payment as possible, and where not voluntary should be laid upon that class of society which has the greatest ability to pay them, and should be collected in such a way and at such times as to be least felt. Who has a greater ability to pay than the men who pay the two and a quarter million of dollars collected through the stamp tax upon checks? How many people pay this tax? You will find that the individual depositors in the national and State banks and the savings banks number about 8,000,000 of people.

Eight millions of men subscribe annually a little over two and a quarter million of dollars to support the Government. Each one of those men, according to the statistics, has $350 in the bank to his credit. It is a well-known fact the banks pay more than one-half of this tax. That is where the shoe pinches, and that is why the relief is demanded. It is not in the interest of the depositor, but in the interest of the banker, who sees his profits cut down every year to the amount of a million and a quarter of dollars, which is taken out of his pocket and given away or distributed among his depositors.

Alexander H. Stephens [Ga.] spoke on June 23. He desired to wipe out all internal taxes and rely for national revenue alone on the tariff.

I think we ought to abolish the internal-revenue system of taxation entirely. I would extirpate it root and branch. Allow me to say to both sides of the House that except in time of war these internal-revenue taxes, excise and stamp duties are in my judgment in principle anti-republican, anti-democratic, and anti-American. They are in opposition to the general principles or policy of this Government as taught by the fathers of the Republic.

The best way to raise revenue is by duties on imports. They bear less heavily on the taxpayers, and as legislators that is what we should look to. In levying duties on imports you can at the same time make foreign producers pay for the use of your markets, and in that way incidentally and properly give aid and protection to American industry. It is not true, as a general proposition, that the consumer pays all the duty imposed upon commodities brought from other countries. This is a question that I cannot now argue. In most instances where the duties are judiciously laid they are borne partly by the importer and partly by the consumer.

To allow Congress thus to raise revenue by duties upon imports was one of the main objects in establishing the Federal Constitution of 1787. This system of internal-revenue taxation by excise and stamp duties was not favored by the fathers of the Republic in times of peace. I speak plainly, and say that it was looked upon then as not only of British origin, but there was always the odium of British Toryism attached to it in the American mind. There was never any legislation more abhorrent to the people of this country, even in their colonial condition, than what was known as the infamous stamp act.

In time of war, when foreign trade is interrupted, this country has been compelled to resort to this method of raising revenue. It was thus resorted to in the Revolutionary War by the States. In the war of 1812, after the adoption of the present Constitution, it was again resorted to of necessity. But it was not adhered to one moment longer than the necessity existed. The system was adopted in the administration of the elder Adams, when war was expected with France; but nothing tended more to excite popular opposition to his administration than this system of taxation, except the alien and sedition acts. One of the first acts of Mr. Jefferson's administration was to wipe them from the statute book. The present system was adopted during the late lamentable war between the States. We do not now require its continuance.

On June 24 George M. Robeson [N. J.] supported abolition of the bank taxes.

Mr. Chairman, we hear a great deal from the other side to the effect that all taxes upon the business of the country are paid by the consumer. As a general proposition it is true; but one other thing is also true: all taxes on the business of a bank are paid by the borrower. The consumer of an article meets the manufacturer and vendor upon equal terms; he comes offering his money for the article he needs. The borrower comes asking favors of the man or institution who is to lend him money, and he is obliged to assume the expense imposed by the Government on the money he borrows. All the expenses that you put upon the machinery of banking, therefore, come out of the debtor and borrower class; they are direct taxes upon the business of the country, and upon the resources and credit of the men who carry on the business and employ the labor of the country.

Roger Q. Mills [Tex.] declared that the purpose of the bill was to prevent the payment of the public debt and so fasten the national banking system on the country, and to serve as a plausible excuse for continuing high tariffs.

Mr. Chairman, is it not a little singular that this thing was born in Philadelphia, Pennsylvania? Is it not a little strange that the first gun in favor of the repeal of internal taxes came from the gentleman from Pennsylvania on that side [Mr. Kelley], and from the gentleman from Pennsylvania [Samuel J. Randall] on this side of the House; the speech of one gentleman being delivered in the tariff convention of New York City, and the speech of the other delivered to the national bankers and the tariff men of New York City?

MR. RANDALL.—My speech was delivered before a Democratic meeting——

MR. MILLS.—I know what sort of Democrats they were.

MR. RANDALL.—And a meeting that gave response by applause.

MR. MILLS.—Yes; and it was a meeting of national bankers and high-tariff men; heretics in the Democratic party, and who have always been regarded as heretics from its very foundation.

Why is it that this thing comes from Pennsylvania? The great cry for reform in taxation comes from Pennsylvania, and the protectionists at that. You do not hear anybody in Texas or in Missouri or in Iowa or through the Western country demanding the repeal of the taxation on banks. You do not hear any great complaint from the people about the money that comes into the treasury being superabundant and about there being no necessity for it.

What man of common sense ever would think of giving away his revenues when he had his debts, bearing interest, due, and demanding payment? But the Congress of the United States is being boldly and insolently asked to-day to throw away the treasures of the people of the United States for the sole purpose of gratifying the godless greed of these monopolists; nothing else in the world. Who is to be benefited by giving away these $17,000,000 that are now reecived from the coffers of the banks? How many of your people in the West and South will be benefited by that?

The bill passed the House on June 27 by a vote of 128 to 80. It was debated at great length in the Senate, but did not come to a vote during this session.

During the next session of Congress (December, 1882-March, 1883) the bill was again extensively discussed in the Senate. It was finally passed with amendments on February 20, 1883. The House refusing to accept the amendments, a conference was held. The report of this was adopted by both chambers on March 2. President Arthur approved the bill on March 3, 1883.

CHAPTER IX

THE TARIFF OF 1870

Gen. Robert C. Schenck [O.] Introduces in the House a Bill ''To Amend Existing Laws Relating to the Duty on Imports''—Debate: Protectionists, William D. Kelley [Pa.], Horace Maynard [Tenn.], Gen. Schenck; Anti-Protectionists, James Brooks [N. Y.], William B. Allison [Ia.], Samuel S. Marshall [Ia.], James J. Winans [O.], Gen. James A. Garfield [O.]—Bill Is Passed—Subsequent Acts of Congress Providing for Further Reduction—Debate in the House [1872] Between Samuel Shellabarger [O.], Protectionist, and Job E. Stevenson [O.], Anti-Protectionist.

FROM 1857 down to the close of the Civil War the tariff question was agitated only when urgent calls for money for the prosecution of the war came up. In 1861 a bill introduced by Justin S. Morrill [Vt.] was passed, raising the tariff of 1857 one-third. This tariff remained in force only a few months. During the following years of the war the need of additional revenue caused measure after measure, revising the tariff upward, to be adopted, and it was inevitable that some protective duties should creep in.

On February 1, 1870, Robert C. Schenck [O.] introduced in the House of Representatives a bill "to amend existing laws relating to the duty on imports." It was discussed at great length throughout the session, and its provisions were finally incorporated in a bill to reduce internal revenue. The new measure became a law on July 14, 1870. Most of the protective features of the existing tariff were retained, though about 130 articles were added to the free list, and the duties on tea, coffee, sugar, spices, and pig-iron were reduced. The real burden of the war tariff was hardly lightened, as the high duties on the necessaries of life still remained.

In the debate in the House on the tariff bill leading

speakers in favor of the principle of protection were: William D. Kelley [Pa.], Horace Maynard [Tenn.], and General Schenck. Among the important anti-protectionists were: James Brooks [N. Y.], William B. Allison [Ia.], Samuel S. Marshall [Ia.], James J. Winans, [O.], and James A. Garfield [O.].

THE SCHENCK BILL

HOUSE OF REPRESENTATIVES, MARCH 3-APRIL 1, 1870

MR. BROOKS.—I do not doubt that every gentleman who now listens to the sound of my voice is abstractly for free trade, if free trade could be realized. It is the nature of man to desire the greatest freedom of intercourse, not only with his own countrymen, but with all mankind. God, who has given man dominion over fish and fowl and all living creatures in the earth, instituted no geographical or political boundaries, and He doubtless intended all to commune together as brethren in the freest intercourse and trade. He has given us different climes for different productions, and different races of men, all wonderfully fitted for their varied work of production, and all created profitably to interchange that production; whether from the sea or the soil, whether from the plow, the loom, the forge, or the anvil; whether the work of the muscle or the brain. He has planted us all upon the earth and commanded us to love one another, and not to destroy each other, neither by the sword nor the cannon, nor by what is as fatal to human happiness, by conflicting, damaging, or destructive tariffs that violate all his commands. While, and when, we have struck off the manacles of chattel slavery from 4,000,000 of men, and poured out our blood like water therefor, we have been all that while as ingloriously riveting the chains of monopoly slavery upon 36,000,000 other men in the tyrannical restraints we have imposed upon their personal liberty in trade, commerce, and intercourse; and thus what we gained in the world's estimation by the one great act we lose in the greater crime. Man's audacity, however, on the tower of Babel, inflicted upon him a confusion of languages and of tongues, and hence divided men into States or kingdoms, and with them, as punishments, have come tariffs, or supposed necessities for tariffs to support conflicting governments. In the conflict of these tariffs it has been a struggle among nations to lay countervailing duties, the one to damage the other, or to outcheat each other in inter-course and trade. This has been the policy of nations for years and years. But now, England and France, especially England, have rapidly retraced their fatal steps, while for nine long years we have been piling up tariff upon tariff. And this coun-try has become now the most tariffed, the most taxed, and in that respect the most accursed nation upon earth. While God has done everything in this vast Republic of ours to bless us, man seems to be doing his utmost to counteract the Almighty will.

What, Mr. Chairman, more beautiful spectacle exists now than that of free trade in our own country, from the rock-bound shores of Passamaquoddy in the East to the Golden Gate or Puget sound of the West? But how much more beautiful would be that spectacle, if on that long line of imaginary boundary from Miramichi on the East to the straits of Fuca on the West, among that broad-spread English-speaking people, there were but one law for customs, one rule of duties, one uni-versal free trade. On our Atlantic coast, just beyond the wa-ters of Maine, are two valuable islands—Nova Scotia and Prince Edward's. Both of them produce articles which are desirable and necessary for the food and comfort of our country, more especially for the poorer classes of our people—fish of almost all kinds in teeming abundance, potatoes, cheaper than the du-ties we impose upon them imported, oats, the best in the world, and coal, practically nearer to New England than from the mines of Pennsylvania or Maryland. We might have free trade with both these islands, but it is forbidden by our laws, and we compel the inhabitants there to turn their potatoes into pork, when on the sea coast we are suffering for the supply, and this pork, thus made, goes to Europe, there to come into competition with the pork of our Western States. These islands need and demand our breadstuffs, our cottons, and other manufactures, our boots and shoes, and leather, but we take from them little or nothing wherewith to pay for them, and so turn the whole trade over to England.

Now, if the numerous articles of production of those islands were introduced into this country free, they would enable the mechanics and laborers of New England to live from ten to fifteen per cent. cheaper than they now do. The herring of these waters are largely in demand for the colored population of the South, but our enormous duties forbid their extensive use. Mackerel are much in demand for the West, but few can afford to pay the duties and buy. Thus man fights with Providence or the laws of Providence by damaging statutes of his own, and thus the farmer of the South and West is shut off from the valuable fisheries of the East.

In our high protective, or prohibitory, tariff on wool we look only at the surface of things, forgetful of the great fact that the manufacturers of cloth need wool from all parts of the earth—from Germany, from Australia, from South Africa, as well as Buenos Ayres and Montevideo, and that when they are limited to the one producing market of wool there can be little or no variety in these manufactures, and, consequently, less production and less demand even for our own American wool. The European has open to him wool of every fiber or texture; the American, only his own. Hence, we have over-stocked the market with our own lines of production but left it free for such as demand a finer, or a more varied, or, in some cases, a cheaper article than our own. We have nearly lost our commerce with South Africa, Australia, and La Plata; and France and England have taken it. To try to raise a sheep, or an extra hide, in Vermont or Michigan, we have driven the white sails of our merchantmen from those seas.

The cold, green hills of Vermont could not compete—God forbids it—with the plains of La Plata or the savannas of Africa; and what we have seen in England and in France and in Belgium we see here now, high wool at home under a low tariff and low wool under a high tariff. While the price of Ohio wool before the high tariff of 1867 was from 54 to 51 cents a pound, it is now down to from 43 to 45 cents. And why is this? It is because the wool raisers of the world have been unnaturally driven from our markets to England, France, Belgium, Germany, and have there glutted those markets, with the millions of pounds we once brought here in our ships, and there, using and mixing the best adapted of the raw materials to the textures they would work, the softer and finer Buenos Ayres and German with the coarser or rougher wools of the world, they have commanded the markets elsewhere, and, in some degree, our own. What our farmers were supposed to gain by a heavy prohibitory tariff upon their wools they have lost in the reduced price of wool in Europe—a price so re-duced there as to underbid even the prohibitive protection we gave in 1867 to our woolen manufactures.

On all articles imported into the United States in 1869 the percentage of revenue on the values imported was 41.02 per cent. But what do you think the percentage is on the British importations? While Britain, with a less population than ours, imports about four times as much as we do, and exports annually about four times as much as we do, the proportion of revenue raised by the British tariff on all imported articles is only 7⅝ per cent. against the 41.02 per cent. of ours. Such are the contrasts of a free trade with our slave trade! Such is the strange, anomalous exhibit of a monarchy and a republic! Such the contrasting picture of the life of a subject and a citizen!

Under this presentation of facts which I have been making, Mr. Chairman, can any one doubt that it is our duty, our immediate duty, to revise forthwith the whole of our custom-house system? Our commerce in our own ships' bottoms has perished; our farmers are dissatisfied; our woolen manufacturers bitterly complain; and we are all of us taxed to death. Well, what would you do? perhaps I am asked. I would take off the duty on coal. I would make it free here as it is elsewhere. I would take off the duty on manufactured lumber and on salt. I would lower the duties on lead and copper, and would reduce the duty on pig iron to $3 per ton.

I would have timber, unmanufactured timber, free—as free as it is in almost all the countries of the world. Timber seems to be an indispensable necessity, and I would not believe men could well live without it if I had not seen them try. God has blessed a large part of our country with the finest timber in the world, and it abounds now in Washington Territory as it once abounded in Maine. But He has given us mighty prairies and uncovered mountains as well as mighty forests. From Chicago, in Illinois, to the Sierra Nevada, on the Pacific slope, there is not timber enough to house the human beings now there, to say nothing of the great hive on the way. Prairie after prairie, in Illinois, in Iowa, in Nebraska, and elsewhere, nude, naked, proclaims the indispensable necessity of timber, while, from peak to peak of the Rocky Mountains, there is the same proclamation, "no wood." And now what are we doing in our strange, unnatural, God-defying tariff? We are actually giving a heavy premium, at this very moment, to the people of Michigan and Maine for the spoliation of their forests, instead of giving them a bounty, as we should, for their protection. Far wiser would it be for us to give 25 per cent. protection to every man who would plant a tree and never use his axe upon the forest than to give a bounty as we do for the destruction of those forests.

I say nothing here in all this of the wrong and injustice in depriving the poor man of the East and center of the cheapest

timber and boards wherewith to build him a house, while the
rich can build in brick, or freestone, or marble, or iron. I say
nothing of the folly of giving the manufacturer of the East a
bounty on his cottons and his woolens when you thus tax his
timber and planks and boards of which his manufactory is
made. All is folly, all is wrong, from beginning to end, and
the wonder is that such folly has advocates in a free-school land.

I come now to the article of pig iron. It should be recollected that two or three years ago we reduced the internal revenue taxes on all manufactured articles. It will be recollected,
too, that when at the opening of the war Congress imposed a
high internal revenue duty upon all manufactured articles it,
at the same time, as a matter of equity, made a corresponding
tax increase on imported articles of the same kind. But, though
we have greatly reduced internal revenue from the manufacturers and manufactured articles of the country, we have not
yet made one cent of reduction in the external tariffs. We have
not at all relieved the consumer of the four or five thousand
taxes on what he imports. We took off the internal revenue
tax upon iron, but we have left the external tax upon iron just
where it was.

Mr. Kelley had denied that the bill increased the duty
on manufactured iron. Mr. Brooks analyzed the bill
to show that it did. He then continued:

Mr. Chairman, I shall not detain the House longer, further
than to call its attention to one document which has been sent
to us by the Secretary of the Treasury, and that is the report
of the gentleman who has the custody of the statistics of the
commerce and the navigation of the country, Mr. Nimmo. He
records that there are now 117 foreign steamers bringing imports and emigrants into the country, and carrying off our exports, and all under a foreign flag.

When I recapitulate these melancholy facts, Mr. Chairman,
with difficulty do I repress the pulsations of my heart, and the
passion such a record of national folly and crime inspires. Our
great Republic opens upon two oceans, upon the Gulf of Mexico south, and the great lakes north; our continent overflows
with all the material necessary for shipbuilding. We have
harbors unrivaled; we have seamen, who, from the days of
Paul Jones to the days of Farragut, have known no fear nor
shrunk from any adventure, who have stormed the fires of
Tripoli and of New Orleans, and yet now our commerce scarcely

ventures beyond our capes and headlands, or, if so, it is swept
from the open seas by the superior and better maritime administration of England, France, Germany, and even Sweden
and Norway. We, who in the Old World have seen, in Asia
and in Africa as well as in Europe, the star-spangled banner
everywhere—and who have seen it with pride and pleasure—
we, who have traced it from the Arctic to the Antarctic, from
the Pacific and the Atlantic to the Indian Sea, and from the
Indian Sea to the Behring Straits—we, who have seen that flag
carried in grandeur and glory all over the earth, now see it
scarcely anywhere on any of the broad seas of that earth. It
has been banished, swept away, killed, damned, by our accursed tariff. It is gone—almost all gone; the wrecks of it only
saved by our exclusive coastwise navigation, or upon the distant shores of the Pacific, too far from England, too far for
the mariners of the Baltic to crush it, as it is otherwise crushed
and crumbled everywhere upon the open seas.

The most melancholy picture now on the earth, the most deplorable for the American who loves his country, is to see in
the harbor of New York, flying from the fleets of shipping
there assembled, the British cross of St. George, the tri-colors
of France, of Belgium, and of Italy; the red, black, and gold
of Germany, and the yellow of Spain—foreign flags everywhere, and the star-spangled banner nowhere but upon some
coastwise craft. How is this? Why is this? Are the days of
Preble and Decatur rubbed out of the American calendar?
Are the *Constitution* and the *Guerrière* forgotten? Are the
memories of Tripoli and of the Algerines no more? Have the
industry and enterprise of our country gone—all gone? Do
we, the sons of glorious ancestral fame, mean to give up the
dominion of the seas? Never, never, sir. Even now, while the
accursed tariff is pouring into our ships its fatal grape and
canister, and the star-spangled banner is going down, every
true-hearted American reëchoes the dying words of Lawrence:

"Don't give up the ship."

The effects of the enormous duties which are levied upon
our shipping we find set forth in Nimmo's "Statistics," which is
a most valuable work. The duties upon a ship are so numerous
that it is difficult to remember them all. Even upon the flag
that floats over an American ship—the flag of freedom—one,
one only, I believe, grasping manufacturer in Massachusetts
has laid his clutches and demanded a bounty from that flag;

XII—9

so that every part of a ship, from its keel and the copper on its sides to the bunting that floats from the masthead, is enslaved to monopoly.

One hundred and forty per cent., and that a bounty to one bunting manufactory on the flag of our country! And, sir, it is but justice that such a tariffed flag should float over such a tariffed country; for the 140 per cent. prohibition bounty on it but represents the almost innumerable bounties of the four or five thousand tariffed articles upon which forty millions of people are now paying taxes.

There will be no finality until justice is done to the great body of the people. There will be no finality until monopoly is brought down and equality is brought up. There will be no finality as long as legislation is so wielded as to make the rich richer and the poor poorer. There will be no finality so long as immense fortunes, with the sluiceway of a Niagara, are pouring into the coffers of a few men to the impoverishment of the great masses of the people.

On March 25 Mr. Kelley[1] replied to Mr. Brooks.

Mr. Chairman, I apprehend that no enlightened student of political economy regards a protective duty as a tax. Even the gentleman from Iowa [William B. Allison] admitted that in most cases it is not; yet influenced, as I think, by a clever story which the chairman of our committee, who is somewhat of a wag, tells, he does not think the principle applies to pig iron. It runs thus: some years ago, during the days of the Whig party, when the chairman of the committee [Mr. Schenck] was here as a Representative of that party and a friend of protection, he met as a member of this House a worthy old German from Reading, Pennsylvania, a staunch Democrat, but strongly in favor of protection on iron. The gentleman from Ohio, who is fond of a joke, said to him one day, "Mr. R., I think I shall go with the free-traders on the iron sections of the tariff bill, especially on pig iron." "Why will you do that?" was the response. "Well, my people want cheap plows, nails, horse-shoes, etc." "But," replied the old German, "we make iron in Pennsylvania; and if you want to keep up the supply and keep the price down you ought to encourage the manufacture." "But you know," said our chairman, "that a protective duty is a tax, and adds just that much to the cost of the article?"

[1] Mr. Kelley was familiarly known as "Pig Iron" Kelley from his faithful advocacy of high duties upon that article.

"Yes, I suppose it does generally increase the cost of the thing just so much as the duty is; all the leaders of our party say so, and we say so in our convention platforms and our public meeting resolutions; but, Mr. Schenck, somehow or other I think it don't work just that way mit pig iron." [Laughter.]

The gentleman, while admitting that protective duties do not always or even generally increase the price of the manufactured article, thinks "that somehow or other it don't work that way mit pig iron." Now, I think that iron in all its forms is subject to every general law, and that the duty of $9 per ton on pig iron has reduced the price measured in wheat, wool, and other agricultural commodities and increased the supply to such an extent as to prove that the duty has been a boon and not a tax. On nothing else produced in this country has the influence of protection been so broadly and beneficently felt by the people of the country at large.

A few years more and we will produce from our own coal and iron our entire supply of iron and steel and compete with England in supplying the demands of the world. The gentleman from Iowa was constrained to admit yesterday that the price of English iron has gone up steadily during the last year, because the demand is in excess of her capacity to produce; yet the price of American pig iron has fallen at least $6 per ton on all grades within the last 10 months. What is the cause of this reduction? Not British competition—and that is the only possible competition—for the price of British iron has risen. No, sir; the price of American iron has gone down under domestic competition and the general depreciation of prices. Keep your duty high enough to induce other men to build furnaces and rolling mills and before five years you will find American iron cheapened to the level of the markets of the world, and that without a commensurate reduction of wages.

The friends of free trade say we do not import enough English iron; we do not import enough English cotton goods; we do not import enough English woolen goods, considering how cheap we can buy them all. If we are to reduce our duties and import more I beg the Representatives of the farming States of the West to demand something like reciprocity on behalf of their constituents, for whose grain there is no market. Every yard of cotton and woolen goods and every ton of iron represent the grain and meat consumed by the families of the men who produced it; and, while our grain goes to waste for the want of purchasers, the friends of protection protest against importing that grown in other countries, even when converted into cloth or iron. The cloth and iron would be as good if made where well-paid laborers eat freely of American wheat, butter, and meat; and to those who cannot sell their crop at any price a neighboring furnace, factory, or rolling mill would be a blessing, even though they could not buy cloth or iron at English prices.

Of the $108,000,000 England raises by her tariff she gets $32,712,300 by duties on one of our agricultural staples. Her duties on tobacco are taxes, for England has no tobacco fields to develop. They are, therefore, not protective duties. England's duty on spirits is an absolute discrimination against our grain. Were that duty removed the farmer and distiller would be working together, and instead of exporting wheat and corn at prices that will not cover the cost of production and transportation their produce would be manufactured into alcohol, pork, and lard oil; and while our own laboring people would have cheaper provisions the farmer would greatly reduce the cost of transportation and have an ample market for his grain manufactured into alcohol, pork, and oil. Yet gentlemen representing agricultural districts plead with us to admit British goods at lower rates, while she gathers $54,599,865 in a single year by imposing such duties on tobacco as greatly diminish its consumption and such on spirits as preclude the importation of our grain in the only forms in which it can be profitably exported.

MR. BROOKS.—Let me state that our great agricultural products—cotton, which is an immense product, and wheat, corn, etc.—are admitted duty free.

MR. KELLEY.—To that I reply that they take our cotton because they cannot live without it, and our wheat and corn when they cannot buy cereals cheaper elsewhere. France has a duty on wheat and flour even when imported in French vessels. We are too far from the seaboard, and the cost of transportation from our grain fields is too great for us to send them grain in bulk at present prices. The cheapest way of transporting corn is in the form of alcohol. In this form we could send it profitably were their duties not prohibitory. England will take raw materials from countries from which she can buy cheapest. But her much-lauded free trade does not offer any advantage to the American. Gentlemen talk about monopolists, and aver that protection fosters monopolies. Sir, the world has never seen so heartless, so unrelenting, and so gigantic a monopoly as the British Government and the manufacturing power that sustains it. It is a monopoly which has desolated

Ireland and swept her factories from the face of the earth. The manufacturing and landed monopoly of England but a few years ago huddled into their graves the decaying bodies of more than 1,000,000 of the people of Ireland, who died of starvation in a single year.

By peaceful arts, without the clash of arms, we can emancipate the hundreds of millions of people England now oppresses. The source of her power is her commercial and manufacturing supremacy, and this we can and should undermine, as we are its chief support. With our cotton fields, our widespread and inexhaustible deposits of all the metals, and our immense sheep walks, we should supply all our wants. When we do this our commerce will revive, for populous nations that supply their own markets always produce a surplus which they can export at low prices. But now England properly regards us as a dependency more profitable than "all the English-speaking dependencies of the empire."

The gentleman from Iowa [Mr. Allison] says that we are offering inducements to thousands to go at wheat growing; that the homestead law is tempting immigrants to engage in wheat growing and add to the unsalable and unavailable stock. That is true, and how would he improve matters? He agrees with me that the homestead law is beneficent and should not be repealed. What, then, is the gentleman's proposition? It is identical with those we have heard from so many gentlemen— reduced duties on coal, salt, hides, lumber, iron, and woolen goods. This is the burden and refrain of all the sweet singers trained in the musical academy of David A. Wells, Commissioner of Revenue.

Is free trade a specific for all or any of our ills? No, sir, it is sheer quackery, charlatanism. The only cure for the evil of which Western grain growers complain is to increase the number of consumers and decrease the number of growers of wheat; raise, if possible, the wages of workmen so as to make mechanical employments attractive; say to the farmers' sons, "There is work and good wages for you in the machine shop, the forge, the furnace, or the mill"; say to the men whose capital is unproductive on farms, "Build mills, sink shafts to the coal bed which underlies your farm; avail yourselves of the limestone quarry and the ore bed, whether of iron, lead, copper, zinc, or nickel; employ your industry and capital so that it shall be profitable to you, your country, and mankind"; and in a little while you will cheapen iron and steel and make an adequate market for all the grain of the country. The gentleman's remedy is the theory of the homeopathic physician, that like cures like, which, though it may be correct in physics, is not an approved maxim in social science.

Mr. Allison.—I would like the gentleman to state how long it will be before that happy period will arrive?

Mr. Kelley.—As the price of iron goes down here it is going up in England; and under the present duty we will soon be able to supply our own demand, and meet England in common markets at equal prices.

Sir, I want to show gentlemen from the West what effect the tariff has on immigration. I have before me the tariffs from the organization of the Government down to the present time, given in *ad valorem* percentages, and a statement of the number of immigrants that arrived in each year, from 1856 to 1869 inclusive. By comparing them I find that whenever our duties have been low immigration fell off, and whenever our duties have been high the volume of immigration increased. This seems to be a fixed law.

It is thus demonstrated historically that, precisely as we make our duties protective of high wages for labor, so do we bring skilled workmen from Germany, Belgium, France, and England to work in our mines, forges, furnaces, rolling mills, cotton and woolen factories, and create a home market for the grain of Iowa, Illinois, and the other States whose farmers complain that they have no market for their grain.

General Schenck.—We have free trade in men.

Mr. Kelley.—Yes, men are on the free list. They cost us not even freight. Yet how they swell the revenues and help us pay the debt of the country! They are raised from helpless infancy, through tender childhood, and trained to skilled labor in youth in other lands, and in manhood, allured by higher wages, they come to us and are welcomed to citizenship. In this way we have maintained a balance of trade that has enabled us to resist without bankruptcy the ordinary commercial balance that has been so heavily against us. We promote free trade in men, and it is the only free trade I am prepared to promote.

On March 30 Mr. Maynard spoke as follows:

It has been confidently asserted that "a tariff is a tax," and "that a tariff on imports is, under all circumstances, a tax which is paid wholly or in part by the consumer." A tax, in political science, is a sum of money levied by authority, directly or indirectly, from the citizen for the support of the Government.

A tariff is a sum of money exacted from the importation of foreign merchandise. It is a duty, not a tax, a burden *in rem* and not *in personam*,[1] enforced when necessary by a proceeding against the property itself. "Taxes, duties, imposts, and excises," is the language of the Constitution, never tautological. But it is assumed that the importer, in turn, exacts it from the citizen to whom he sells; or, to state the proposition differently, that the tariff invariably and necessarily forms a part of the price and is paid by the consumer. And it is insisted that the price of all like articles of domestic production is equally enhanced as a necessary effect of the tariff; that the duty of $1.25 per ton on bituminous coal, for instance, increases the price just so much to the consumers not only of the 100,000 tons imported from England and the 230,000 from Nova Scotia, but of the 4,000,000 tons from the mines of the United States; and it is further argued that, while the Government receives but $412,500 duty on the coal imported, the American miners receive on their production $5,000,000, and that it all comes from the hard-used, overtaxed consumers. This has been asserted so often, with respect especially to coal, salt, iron, and wool, that a belief has resulted from the continued reiteration. It would follow, then, as a corollary, that no duty should be imposed upon these articles, or indeed upon any others that compete with the growth or production of our own country.

If this doctrine is true of these articles, it is true of all others; for example of butter, cheese, potatoes, and wheat. The duty on butter and cheese is 4 cents per pound, on potatoes 25 cents per bushel, and on wheat 20 cents per bushel. Now, will any man be bold enough or reckless enough to assert that the duty of 4 cents per pound upon butter enhances to the consumers by so much the price not only of the 6,650,000 pounds imported from Canada, but also of the entire produce of our own dairies; or that the duty of 20 cents per bushel on wheat adds that sum or any sum to the price either of American wheat, or of the 1,500,000 bushels imported from Canada. The prices are regulated by the home supply, and the importer must conform to them and pay duties and other expenses out of the proceeds of his sales. How much these amount to the purchaser neither inquires nor cares. Such is the result invariably and under all circumstances when the domestic production approximates the demand so nearly as to regulate the price

[1] "On the thing and not the person."

in our market, as is the case with the articles enumerated above.

He who takes coals to Newcastle for sale must sell at Newcastle prices and pay all expenses. A load of Canadian wheat in the market of Chicago, Milwaukee, or Buffalo sells no higher than a similar load from Iowa, Minnesota, or Illinois. Yet the owner must pay the duty of 20 cents per bushel, besides all his other expenses, and pocket only the net proceeds.

JAMES A. GARFIELD [O.].—With the gentleman's permission, I would ask him a question. I ask the gentleman whether what is brought in from abroad, together with what is produced at home, does not undoubtedly form the total supply upon which must necessarily be based the prices? I ask if prices are not based on the whole supply made up from both these sources, and if it is quite correct, therefore, to say that the Milwaukee supply regulates the prices of Milwaukee products; if it is not rather correct to say that the price results from the total of the Milwaukee product, plus the foreign product, added to it?

MR. MAYNARD.—I think when I have stated my propositions the gentleman will see that we are not very wide apart. The profession to which he and I belong recognizes the principle *"de minimis non curat lex."* [1] I was attempting to show that, when the domestic production is so great in comparison with the demand as to fix the market price a small importation does not affect it either with respect to the imported or to the domestic article. It follows, then, that the duty on all such articles is paid by the importer for the privilege of our market, and does not under any circumstances fall upon the consumer. It is not, therefore, a tax—not being levied from the citizen, but from the stranger who brings his commodities for trade. This our English brethren and our Canadian neighbors understand perfectly well; nobody better. Hence the loud complaints and bitter invectives against what they denounce as our unenlightened and illiberal policy.

But it is especially as the Representative of a Southern constituency that I advocate the policy of protecting and fostering our manufactures. The opposite doctrine had prevailed for a whole generation prior to the war; and during the war we experienced the bitter consequences. Isolated from the rest of the world, seaward by the blockade and landward by the military lines, we endured privations altogether incredible and difficult to appreciate. With three thousand miles of sea coast, and naval stores and material in abundance, we had neither

---

[1] "The law looks not at little things."

ships nor seamen. With an unlimited supply of cotton, and wool, and hides, and oak bark, and falling waters, we had neither shirts, nor coats, nor blankets, nor shoes. But for the household industry prevalent in the South beyond other parts of the land, not a few would have been reduced to stark nakedness.

It would be a disastrous policy for the South to repeal the present protective tariff and return to the old condition of things before the war. Let New England and Pennsylvania with their superior mechanical skill and capital; let New York, with her great *entrepôt* of foreign commerce; let the free and mighty West, proud of her growth, satisfied in her abundance and *insouciant* of the future—let them unite, if they will, to discard protection to their labor and to their springing enterprises; the South cannot afford to do it; she is behind them all in the race of prosperity.

But let her industry be protected and fostered for a few years to come as they have been for a few years past and she will be abreast of the foremost.

If, therefore, she is wise she will discard the pernicious counsels of a school of economists whose teachings in the past brought her to a state little better than vassalage, dependent and in debt in time of peace, without resources in time of war. She will embrace the same policy which has made other parts of our common country wealthy, prosperous, and great. I appeal, then, to my Southern associates. I invoke a common interest. Differing as we have differed in the troubled past or as we may differ even now on questions of political expediency and justice, we surely can agree on a line of policy which will develop our commerce, our mines, our manufactures, no less than our agriculture.

On March 31 General Schenck defended his bill.

The speeches which have been made have generally been presented by gentlemen as embodying their views in regard to free trade on the one side, and a system of protection to the industry of the country upon the other. And, if there were really any great and marked difference among the people of the country in respect to two policies of this kind, then, perhaps, the most significant debate indeed would be that which we have already had. But, Mr. Chairman, I cannot see that the arguments made have to any great extent approached, much less settled and disposed of, the various questions that are involved;

for the simple reason that I do not understand that there is any such thing as free trade to talk about.

What is free trade? A myth! A fancy! If the phrase have any meaning at all it must convey one of two ideas—perhaps only one. That one idea would be strictly this: that we should permit all articles imported into our country from abroad to come in without any charges at all in the shape of impost duties. That would be really free trade. There may be, however, by courtesy, allowed to the expression another signification or definition. Persons might be held to favor a doctrine of free trade who should advocate the plan of admitting articles of every kind and description upon the same footing and with equal charges, uniform percentage of duty being imposed upon all alike.

But free trade, as described in either of these two ways, has no existence, never has had, and never will have in any civilized country. We recognize by our legislation, and have in this country from the beginning recognized, the expediency of allowing some things to come in without any charges at all, while we put charges upon other articles, and discriminate in reference to those upon which we do impose duties, admitting some of them at higher and some at lower rates than others; and wherever there is this condition of things to talk about free trade is to my mind the sheerest nonsense. It is giving the name of a theory and an abstraction to that which is above all others a purely practical thing.

Perhaps the gentleman upon this floor who comes nearest the idea of favoring pure free trade is my colleague from one of the Cincinnati districts [Job E. Stevenson]. In the course of his remarks he took occasion to say that he longed for the time to come when no duty should be imposed upon any article imported; but that the Government should be carried on and have all its needs supplied by direct taxation imposed upon all property and articles of every kind in proportion to their value. Now, if I understand that, it is going a little beyond the platform of the Democratic party, and is going entirely beyond all practice and all experience of this or any other civilized country in the present day.

Try this, and what shall we come to? This theory, if reduced to practice, according to the longing desire of my colleague, would bring us to a condition of things when every acre of land would be directly taxed for the support of the general Government, and every cow, and every horse, and every part of the whole property of the country would have to pay the same as articles of luxury, the same as accumulated capital. Give up a tariff, give up discrimination, adopt this scheme of equal, horizontal, direct taxation, dreamed of and hoped for by my worthy colleague, and milk, which costs about the same to produce it as whisky, would be taxed the same as whisky, and potatoes would be charged the same as tobacco. Now, sir, I object to all that. I am for discriminations in our internal taxation, with reference to which it is not proper that I should speak now; and I am equally for discriminations in the charges made in the shape of duties upon articles brought in from abroad.

Another colleague of mine, my friend from the Xenia district [James J. Winans], meets at the very threshold this question, whether it be right or expedient to discriminate in the rates of duties imposed, by claiming that, as in his opinion he has proved from the Constitution that a tariff levied for any other purpose than revenue is totally against the provisions of that instrument, therefore to extend protection by any discriminating duty to the industries of the country or interests of the country in any shape is clearly unconstitutional. In this I think he, too, goes a bowshot beyond anything that even the Democrats of the country, as a party, have ever maintained. He certainly disagrees with the fathers who made the Constitution.

Here General Schenck read the preamble to the first tariff act passed by Congress.

Mr. Marshall [Ia.].—The decision of the framers of the Constitution upon a question of this kind, supposing it to have been brought to their attention and decided deliberately, would be entitled to great weight. But I submit that a mere expression in a preamble, which for aught that we know was not carefully considered, which may not have been brought to the attention of one-fifth of the members who voted for the bill, which there is no evidence to show was considered at all, is entitled to no weight. How often in this House do bills for which we all vote have preambles that not one in twenty knows anything about? There is no evidence that the men composing the Congress to which the gentleman has referred decided deliberately that the power to enact a tariff for protection was granted in the Constitution. The tariff act which they passed was not in fact a protective tariff in the sense in which the term is now used. The duties which it imposed amounted on the average to but $8\frac{1}{2}$ per cent.

Mr. Schenck.—My friend from Illinois begs the whole question. He stultifies the fathers, and endeavors to get rid of a solemn, clear expression of their opinion, embodied in such shape as to be spread upon the statute book of the country, and there taking the form of the most authentic record, by supposing that they did not know exactly what language they were using or what was its significance. I have no reply to make to such an assumption—none whatever.

But my colleague from the Xenia district [Mr. Winans], approaching the question of discrimination for protection as involved in this bill, and as it is found in the present and all former tariff laws of the United States, announces another proposition which struck me as exceedingly extraordinary.

He said it might happen that even in a tariff imposed only for the purpose of revenue some benefit or good might come to some interest of the country; but, if it did, it was a matter that could not be helped and was to be deprecated.

Mr. Winans.—One of the reasons for that was this, that, while it increased the price of the goods to the consumer, it gave no benefit to the Government, and therefore ought to be deprecated.

Mr. Schenck.—I have nothing to do with my colleague's reasons.

His doctrine is this: a tariff can only constitutionally be laid for revenue; it may be that in laying it even for revenue alone some citizen or some home interest will be helped; but that is a pity and to be deplored. Great Heaven! is that to be our idea of government? I always thought every government, most of all every free government, every nation under any organism of government, ought to be regarded as the great *alma mater* of her children, and if, by her legislation, designed even for the purpose of carrying on public affairs and supplying her ordinary needs, she could shower plenty broadcast over the land, it was a thing every patriot ought to congratulate himself on rather than think it, as my colleague does, a pity! something to be "deprecated"! What a narrow, selfish, heartless, hard policy of government that must be which shrinks from building up anything, from helping anybody, from advancing any interest even by accident! No, my colleague not only denies us incidental, but he will not let us have even accidental protection. "Incidental protection" used to be the favorite phrase, but he goes one step further, intensifies the idea, and then deplores it if we should by any chance, and without cost or increased burden, get advantage to any interest in the country.

We must not have any protection by discrimination, says my colleague; and why? He claimed that protection to be of any avail must so far be prohibition, and that all prohibition being wrong there should therefore be no protection. According to such reasoning you cannot shut out cholera or the small-pox. You cannot prohibit the importation of venomous snakes. You must put so many dollars or so many cents of duty on the head of each serpent, or else let the snakes come in free. I have no such narrow idea of the Constitution of the United States as that. Under its wise provisions and distinctly given authority we cannot only levy taxes and pay debts, but regulate commerce and provide for the general welfare. I believe it is a mere question of discretion, a discretion to be properly exercised, to prohibit anything from coming which may be hurtful to the country, or to prescribe the conditions on which anything shall come in. We may say that whatever it is desirable to have, and upon which we do not want to raise revenue, shall come in free; we may impose duties upon any class of articles we see fit; and we may discriminate between the different classes of those articles, so as to let some come in at a higher and some at a lower rate of duty. That is my idea; and I venture to say that such is not only the practice of this Union and of all civilized nations, but that it has been the true and unvarying interpretation of our Constitution, settled and declared first by those who made that instrument, and adhered to by all parties, Administrations, and Congresses ever since.

On April 1 General Garfield spoke.

The great Coleridge [1] once said that abstract definitions had done more injury to the human race than war, famine, and pestilence combined; and I am not sure that a philosophical history of the struggles and difficulties through which the civilized world has passed would not prove the truth of his observation. I trust no such disasters are likely to result from this discussion, and yet I think we are approaching the verge of a great danger from a similar cause. The most acrimonious utterances we have heard in these speeches were made concerning the abstract ideas of free trade and protection; and I fully agree with my colleague [Mr. Schenck] in his declaration that a large part of the debate has not applied to the bill, but to abstractions.

There is no doubt a real and substantial difference of opin-

[1] Samuel Taylor Coleridge.

ion among those who have debated this subject; a difference which discloses itself in almost every practical proposition contained in the bill; but I am convinced that the terms used and the theories advocated do not to any considerable extent represent practical issues. There are, indeed, two points of the greatest importance involved in this bill and in all bills relating to taxes. One is the necessity of providing revenue for the Government, and the other is the necessities and wants of American industry. These are not abstractions, but present imperative realities. As an abstract theory of political economy free trade has many advocates and much can be said in its favor; nor will it be denied that the scholarship of modern times is largely on that side; that a large majority of the great thinkers of the present day are leading in the direction of what is called free trade.

MR. KELLEY.—The gentleman says no man will deny that the tendency of opinion among scholars is toward free trade. I beg leave to deny it, and do most positively. The tendency of opinion among the scholars of the continent is very decidedly toward protection. This is strikingly illustrated by the recent publication in six of the languages of the continent of the voluminous writings of Henry C. Carey, and their adoption as text books in the schools of Prussia. I think the gentleman's proposition is true of the English-speaking people of the world, but that the preponderant tendency is the other way.

MR. GARFIELD.—With the qualification which the gentleman makes, we do not greatly differ. Take the English-speaking people out of the world, and civilization has lost at least half its strength. I detract nothing from the great ability and the acknowledged fame of Mr. Carey when I say that on this subject he represents a minority among the financial writers of our day. I am trying to state as fairly as I can the present condition of the question; and in doing so I affirm that the tendency of modern thought is toward free trade. While this is true, it is equally undeniable that the principle of protection has always been recognized and adopted in some form or another by all nations, and is to-day to a greater or less extent the policy of every civilized government.

The economic doctrines known as the Mercantile System, which prevailed throughout Europe during the seventeenth and eighteenth centuries, gave shape and character to the colonial policy of all European governments for two hundred years. It is a mistake to suppose that in planting colonies in the New World the nations of Europe were moved mainly by a philanthropic impulse to extend the area of liberty and civilization. Colonies were planted for the purpose of raising up customers for home trade. It was a matter of business and speculation, carried on by joint stock companies for the benefit of corporations.

While our Revolution was in progress Adam Smith, when discussing and condemning the colonial system, declared that "England had founded an empire in the New World for the sole purpose of raising up customers for her trade."

When the colonies had increased in numbers and wealth, the purpose of the mother country was disclosed in the legislation and regulations by which the colonies were governed.

Whatever did not enhance the trade and commerce of England was deemed unfit to be a part of the colonial policy.

Worse even than its effects on the industry of the colonies was the influence of this policy on political and commercial morality. The innumerable arbitrary laws enacted to enforce it created a thousand new crimes. Transactions which the colonists thought necessary to their welfare, and in no way repugnant to the moral sense of good men, were forbidden under heavy penalties.

They became a nation of law-breakers. Nine-tenths of the colonial merchants were smugglers. Nearly half of the signers of the Declaration of Independence were bred to commerce, to the command of ships and to contraband trade. John Hancock was the prince of contraband traders; and, with John Adams as his counsel, was on trial before the admiralty court, in Boston, at the exact hour of the shedding of the first blood at Lexington, to answer for a $500,000 penalty alleged to have been incurred as a smuggler.

Half the tonnage of the world was engaged in smuggling or piracy. The war of independence was a war against commercial despotism; against an industrial policy which oppressed and tortured the industry of our fathers, and would have reduced them to perpetual vassalage for the gain of England.

In view of these facts, it is not strange that our fathers should have taken early measures not only to free themselves from this vassalage, but also to establish in our own land such industries as they deemed indispensable to an independent nation. The policy I have described prevailed throughout Christendom, and compelled the new Republic, in self-defence, to adopt measures for the protection of its own interests.

No one now fails to see that the European policy of the seventeenth and eighteenth centuries was as destructive of national industry as it was barbarous and oppressive. Political philosophers did not hesitate to declare that a general and devastating war among other nations was desirable as a means of enhancing the commerce of their own. The great Dryden, poet laureate of England, was not ashamed to begin one of his noblest poems, the Annus Mirabilis, by invoking the thunders of war on Holland for the sole purpose of reducing her commercial prosperity.

A better civilization has changed all this; has expanded the area of commercial freedom, and remanded the industry of nations more and more to the operation of the general laws of trade. But it must be borne in mind that the political millennium has not yet come, when all nations belong to one family, with no collision of interests and no need of distinct and separate policies. Until that happy period arrives, each government must first of all provide for its own people. Protection, in its practical meaning, is that provident care for the industry and development of our own country which will give our own people an equal chance in the pursuit of wealth, and save us from the calamity of being dependent upon other nations with whom we may any day be at war.

In so far as the doctrine of free trade is a protest against the old system of oppression and prohibition it is a healthy and worthy sentiment. But underlying all theories there is a strong and deep conviction in the minds of a great majority of our people in favor of protecting American industry. And now I ask gentlemen who advocate free trade if they desire to remove all tariff duties from imported goods? I trust they do not mean that. Do they not know that we are pledged, by all that is honest and patriotic, to raise $130,000,000, in gold every year to pay the interest on our public debt; and will they not admit the necessity of raising $20,000,000 more a year, in gold, as a sinking fund, to apply to the principal of the public debt? Will it be wise statesmanship to raise less than $150,000,000 in gold a year? If this be admitted we have the limit within which we may reduce the duties on imported goods.

Let us next inquire in what way this reduction may be so made as to give most relief to industry. And here let me say that, in my opinion, the key to all our financial problems, or at least the chief factor in every such problem, is the doctrine of prices. Prices exhibit all fluctuations of business, and are as sure indicators of panics and revulsions as the barometer is of storms. If I were to direct any student of finance where to begin his studies I should refer him to the great work of Thomas

Tooke on the "History of Prices," as a foundation on which to build the superstructure of his knowledge.

But to make the study of prices of any value we must examine the elements which influence prices. Some of them lie beyond our control, while others are clearly within the reach of legislation. Among the most prominent influences that affect prices are seasons, crops, the foreign markets, facilities of transportation, and the amount and character of taxation and of the currency. All these combine to regulate and determine the prices that prevail in one country as compared with prices in others. "The early and the latter rain," abundance and famine, war and peace in other nations and sometimes in our own are elements beyond our control. But we are responsible for the statutes which regulate trade, transportation, currency, and taxation. It is in our hands to place the burdens of taxation where they will impede as little as possible the march of industry, and least disturb the operation of the great laws of value, of supply and demand.

I stand now where I have always stood since I have been a member of this House. I take the liberty of quoting, from the *Congressional Globe* of 1866, the following remarks which I then made on the subject of the tariff:

"We have seen that one extreme school of economists would place the price of all manufactured articles in the hands of foreign producers by rendering it impossible for our manufacturers to compete with them; while the other extreme school, by making it impossible for the foreigner to sell his competing wares in our market, would give the people no immediate check upon the prices which our manufacturers might fix for their products. I disagree with both these extremes. I hold that a properly adjusted competition between home and foreign products is the best gage by which to regulate international trade. Duties should be so high that our manufacturers can fairly compete with the foreign product, but not so high as to enable them to drive out the foreign article, enjoy a monopoly of the trade, and regulate the price as they please. This is my doctrine of protection. If Congress pursues this line of policy steadily, we shall year by year approach more nearly to the basis of free trade, because we shall be more nearly able to compete with other nations on equal terms. I am for a protection which leads to ultimate free trade. I am for that free trade which can only be achieved through a reasonable protection."

While in 1871 the tariff question was again agitated no legislation was enacted. During the following year revenue was decreased, first, by removing the taxes on tea and coffee on May 1, and, second, by admitting large classes of manufactures to a reduction of ten per cent. on June 6.

XII—10

During this session of Congress the tariff was discussed to a great extent. Among the most notable speakers in the debate in the House were Job E. Stevenson [O.] and Samuel Shellabarger [O.]. Stevenson was, with the possible exception of Samuel S. Cox [N. Y.], the most powerful exponent of "tariff reform," which was clearly indicated as a leading issue in the presidential campaign that was just beginning, and Shellabarger, who, though recognized as the strongest and most thorough-going advocate of Republican principles, had heretofore kept out of the tariff discussion, was led to come forward in support of his party, and to demolish the arguments, not only of Stevenson, but of the great economist, David A. Wells, who had recently made an exhaustive report on the tariff.

It was understood that Mr. Wells had also inspired the plank in the platform of the new Liberal Republican party, which, inviting Democratic and Republican free trade adherents to the support of Horace Greeley, a protectionist, declared in favor of taking the tariff out of partisan politics.

PROTECTION AND POLITICS

HOUSE OF REPRESENTATIVES, MAY 1–16, 1872

On May 1 Mr. Stevenson spoke on the inconsistency of protectionists.

The great obstacle to reform is the "hostility" of prohibitory protectionists to moderate measures. These propagandists appear to consider every effort at relief as an attack of an enemy which they are justified in repelling by all means in their power; hence they discard candor and fair dealing, and act upon the maxim that "all is fair in war." With such antagonists there is no possibility of agreement. They use every weapon of logic and fallacy, fact and fiction. They are ready to assert whatever is denied, to deny whatever is asserted, and no proof satisfies them. They maintain contradictory statements and theories in the same speech, if not in a breath, as combatants fight before and behind, at the right hand and the left, caring only to defend themselves or offend their assailants.

Inconsistent as are the arguments of those who advocate the exclusive policy, their practices are more contradictory.

Here the speaker dwelt at length on the contradictory policies of the States favoring the national exclusive theory. Pennsylvania, for instance, in her internal taxation system, laid special taxes on manufactures.

Mr. Stevenson continued:

If we accept the claim of ''protection'' as the giver of wealth, and begin to cast accounts with favored interests and States to see what they have gained by the policy, its advocates turn about and indignantly deny that it increases the price of protected articles, and denounce those who assert or assume the fact.

If the opposite theory be true, then how can the reduction or the repeal of duties on imports injure domestic manufactures? And why do manufacturers come to Congress on every rumor of a change of duties? What fills our committee rooms and lobbies and this hall with interested men? What prevents our proceeding at once to adjust the tariff to a revenue standard? If duties do not aid the American producer, surely we should consult the wishes of consumers and the interests of the treasury.

On May 16 Mr. Shellabarger replied to Mr. Stevenson.

I venture to copy the words of my most excellent colleague, Mr. Stevenson, who leads the ''revenue reformers'' of our party from Ohio in Congress, and say as he said in the great debate of March, 1870, to General Schenck:

''We are much nearer together than you think we are.''

Now let us see if our differences go deeper than to the mere surface, the ''incidentals,'' the matters of differences as to how best we shall get at what we all want—the things ''tentative'' —and as to which experiment, trial, experience, will, by their teachings, bring us quickly together.

First. Who in the Republican party does not revolt at the idea of making a law that shall confessedly tax out of one man's earnings parts of them and give it to another without giving to the taxed man a pecuniary equivalent of some sort? There is no such man.

Second. Neither is there an intelligent man in the country who favors protecting interests here which are not "legitimate." That is, nobody is for fostering industries by legislation whose products, owing to the permanent conditions under which they must ever be produced here, cannot be produced without much greater expenditure of human labor than is required in other countries. For illustration, nobody is for what was rendered famous by the epigram of an English statesman, "Making protected wine out of grapes raised in hothouses in Scotland."

Third. So, on the other hand, no Republican fails to insist that any law which really does have the effect of here creating or augmenting a great and legitimate industry does by necessity bring to every member of the nation other benefits than the revenues it may yield to our treasury, benefits precisely as real and compensatory, as clearly within the cognizance of just legislation, and just as much to be counted in estimating the wisdom of a revenue law or tariff law as is the item of what revenue it gives the treasury.

Among these benefits claimed for a law which really has this effect of creating or augmenting in our country a great industry or industries may be named these: that by adding a home to a foreign competition you secure an ultimate reduction of prices; that the presence in our country of these industries creates a home market for some of the productions of the consuming class, which, owing to their weight, or perishable qualities, or the state or distance of transportation, or the state of foreign custom laws, or the like, he could get no market for abroad. Or the benefit the consumer gets may be in the fact that his lands are enhanced, or his business or profession or trade, by having this country built or filled up with these industries.

Every civilized government in the world, every practical and eminent ruler in our own history, every modern code of commercial law enforced by enlightened states, unite with our own entire and wondrous history in pronouncing it the first duty of government to "protect" as well the industries as the lives and properties of their people.

CHAPTER X

A Tariff for Revenue Only

[PROPOSED WOOD BILL OF 1878]

Fernando Wood [N. Y.] Introduces a Bill in the House for a Revision (Downward) of the Tariff—Debate: in Favor, Mr. Wood, John R. Tucker [Va.]; Opposed, William McKinley [O.], William D. Kelley [Pa.], Gen. James A. Garfield [O.]—Bill Fails to Come to a Vote—General Winfield S. Hancock on the Tariff.

ON March 26, 1878, Fernando Wood [N. Y.] reported in the House, from the Committee on Ways and Means, a bill reducing customs duties and reforming the entire system of the tariff. It came up for discussion on April 9.

Reform and Reduction of the Tariff

House of Representatives, April 9-June 4, 1878

MR. WOOD.—It will be remembered that taxation simply consists in imposing exactions for the support of the Government. It was not designed that any other considerations should enter into the discharge of this trust. The burden, whether great or small, was to be borne by the whole people upon principles of equity and equality.

The United States has never had a permanently established system by which to procure revenue and to regulate its commerce with other nations. Nor is this singular in view of the fact that we have been undergoing remarkable changes since our national birth. Within the century of our existence the policy that was desirable at one time would have been very unfortunate at another, and at no time have we been so circumstanced until now that we could adopt political economies purely American. That period has arrived. For the first fourth of our century of life we were emerging from a colonial chaotic

149

condition, struggling to cement fraternity among ourselves and to furnish mutual protection against others. The next quarter of the century was devoted to the ascertainment of our resources, and an assertion of our independence upon the seas. The third quarter was distinguished by the expansion of our territory, the acquisition of mineral resources of incalculable value, and a gradual growth of the nation toward becoming a great maritime power. While the last fourth of the century has marked the most extraordinary epoch in our history—distinguished for its extinction of slavery—the greatest civil war of any time, and its consequent demoralizing and stimulating effects upon values, and the vicious legislation which of necessity followed. The nation, in consequence, lies weakened and prostrated, and sick almost unto death.

We are now brought face to face with the solemn consideration of the present, and the great duties of the future. Doubtless those who shall write the history of this century hereafter will not fail to discover that in this latter period to which I have referred, comprehending the present time, could be traced the germ of the subsequent national grandeur, wealth, and power, which I now see clearly are, with wisdom in our legislation, susceptible of accomplishment. There is now no pending question which is within itself of sufficient importance to the people to make it worthy of a moment's consideration as compared with that of establishing a policy of international commercial intercourse, connected with a policy of taxation, which shall be wise in its inception, permanent in its character, less onerous in its exactions, and have for its prime objects a fuller development of our material resources, and a more profitable disposition of the fruits of labor, the results of enterprise, and the security and profits of capital.

These objects are to be secured by the application of principles in legislation which shall take from labor and capital the minimum of taxation with a maximum of advantage in return, by economy in administration, and the fullest possible development of the resources of the country, from which both production and commerce shall derive an equal, honest, and legitimate advantage in the prosecution of their industries.

The fundamental basis upon which our legislation to promote these objects should rest is that production and commerce are twin sisters, and should go hand in hand—that one is indispensable to the other. There can be no antagonism between them. While it may be true that the present cost of internal transit in this country has imposed and does impose an undue burden upon production, arising altogether from a monopoly of the power of transmission, yet this will not be the case either upon the land or the ocean if in our new departure we shall adopt enlightened principles.

The levying the duties upon foreign goods and direct taxes upon domestic goods and interests may be considered not only as questions of revenue, but also as susceptible of being made the methods by which all interests can be subserved and the national resources more fully utilized. If the authority to impose taxes can be used to advantage one class, is it not well for us to consider whether it cannot be used as well for all? not only to promote the home industries, but to advance the prosperity of all sections and every enterprise, whether commercial, agricultural, mechanical, or manufacturing.

While unquestionably the power to tax if confined to its legitimate object is restricted to that duty alone, yet if it can be made an instrument so as to combine other objects not inconsistent with just and equal taxation, by which the whole nation, as well the people as individuals, shall be alike advantaged, then is it not our duty to adopt it? To this end we should connect with our system a more enlarged and comprehensive scheme than that which now exists.

With a larger seaboard than any other nation, and with material resources in excess of our capacity of consumption, we must encourage and promote the adoption of such relations with other nations as will open up the markets of the world, and make the whole universe contribute to our prosperity.

But the further development of our material resources will avail us little if commerce does not stand by to utilize the results. The large surplus yield of our agriculture would be of trifling value if it could not be carried to other consumers than those who produce it. The same principle applies to manufactures and minerals. We should therefore adopt a policy which shall create facilities purely American for the transmission of the excess over our own consumption to foreign buyers and consumers. Nor will this be the only advantage of such a policy. It will lead to a larger interchange of commodities between other nations and ourselves, in which we will be the gainers. We shall take from them the articles which our soil or climate will not enable us to produce, and return them back in manufactured form, thus deriving profit from our superior capacity, energy, or ingenuity.

Before proceeding to consider how best to avail ourselves of these advantages by legislation, it may be well to look at the laws as they now exist and to see in what regard the present tariff operates as an obstruction to the enlargement of our foreign trade. I approach the subject with a full appreciation of the difficulties attending any change, however desirable it might be.

The laws as they now exist are mainly the creation of the last fifteen years. Within the period from 1861 to 1876 were passed one hundred and eight laws relating to the tariff and the collection of duties. Nearly every one of these acts was the creation of some special domestic interest or to subserve some partisan purpose.

The evils of the present tariff laws are so outrageous that it is difficult to speak of them with patience. They are the results of a series of assaults through legislation upon the pockets and labor of the people. They are immoral in theory, utterly indefensible in practice, and without any merits upon which their most ingenious and well-paid beneficiaries can maintain their defence. And yet we do not propose to deal with them as their demerits deserve. I recognize an implied moral right to a little longer continuation of the favor which they afford to the manufacturing interests. The bill reported affects them, so far as the rates of duties are concerned, but little. Its reductions are trifling as compared to what they should be, and in my opinion they could well afford to bear. If I had the power to commence *de novo* I should reduce the duties 50 per cent. instead of less than 15 per cent. upon an average, as now proposed.

The committee has not undertaken to reform all the abuses of the present tariff. Though fully conscious of the necessity of effecting many radical changes sooner or later, we were content with a simplification of methods of assessing the duties, changing the phraseology, so as to avoid ambiguity and doubt as to the proper duty to be levied, a large curtailment in the number of articles to be assessed for duty, and ingrafting upon the law important provisions looking to a more liberal commercial intercourse with foreign nations.

The changes proposed are designed to be the foundation for a permanent measure, comprehending new principles and a lopping off of the complications and contradictions now existing in the present laws.

The bill reported has but one list so called, and that is the dutiable one. It has no compound rates, the duties being either *ad valorem* or specific, and the latter as far as practicable. It has no free list as such; all articles not enumerated and specifi-

cally named are to be admitted free. In lieu of the duties now
levied upon the cost and charges added to the original cost or
value of the articles imported at place of production or export,
which has been the source of so much litigation between the
Government and the importers, the bill fixes an allowance of 5
per cent., equally applicable to all merchandise coming in under the *ad valorem* principle. It levies a discriminating duty
of 10 per cent. additional upon all merchandise imported from
and the growth and production of any country which discriminates against the United States in the admission of our products
to their ports.

This provision is not intended as retaliatory, but is designed
as an inducement to those foreign countries whose treaty stipu-
lations prefer other nations to our own to make commercial
regulations with us which shall place us upon an equally favorable footing. The bill in this, and in its general scope and
tenor, looks to an enlargement of our foreign commerce, not
only in its navigation, but also in facilities for the profitable
sale of American-grown products of every character. Another
and important provision is that which proposes to establish
manufacturing bonded warehouses, and the benefit of drawback upon all exported goods containing any foreign material
subject to duty. It is designed to encourage the exportation
of American manufactured products of every character, by
affording them the raw material free of duty, so that they can
compete with any other like manufactures in the markets of the
world. We believe that it is only necessary to afford our people
an equal chance with all others in order to prove to foreign nations that we are equal if not superior to them in our manufactures.

The bill will materially reduce the cost of collecting the customs revenue. I may safely claim that the simplification, together with the curtailment of the number of dutiable articles
and the abolition of the free list, will reduce the cost at least
15 per cent. Another considerable saving will be gained in the
authority given to the Secretary of the Treasury to consolidate
the collection districts, now the source of a large and unnecessary outlay; many of them are kept up at several thousand dollars' expense without producing any return whatever in the way
of duties collected.

Some apprehensions have been entertained that the reduced
rates proposed will cause a loss of revenue. There is no necessity for fear on this account. The removal of the ambiguities
of the present tariff and the easy and speedy liquidation of

entries which will follow will operate as much to increase the importations as the proposed reduced rates will cause loss of revenue.

The many obstructions now existing in entering goods at the custom houses and of speedily ascertaining the amount of duty to be paid will under the new system be very much if not altogether removed.

A merchant will know in advance the exact amount of duty to be paid, which will facilitate commerce and the Government will collect the duty without delay or litigation. Those who are not familiar with the present machinery used in the collection of duties will be slow to believe the great losses to the treasury which are constantly occurring in consequence. It has been estimated that the Government loses from 10 to 15 per cent. of the amount it should collect.

The losses occurring by evasions of the law, collusion with officials, and smuggling will, if the reforms proposed be carried out, be much lessened, and the opportunity for frauds and the demoralizing effect upon Government officers prevented.

The reductions proposed in the present tariff will afford much relief, and, as I have shown, without injury to the treasury. A corresponding reduction can be made in direct taxes, and yet sufficient revenue can be relied upon to meet the interest upon the public debt and defray all the necessary expenses of administration, if conducted upon a like scale of economy, as the taxpayers are now compelled to apply to their own individual affairs.

The principal opposition to a change in the tariff emanates from the friends of extreme protection to the manufacturing interests.

Whatever may have been the excuse originally for the governmental bounty to the then infant manufactures, it does not now exist and should not be continued, because the necessity for it no longer remains. They have reached so high a degree of excellence and grown so strong that they not only need not fear foreign competition here, but are able to maintain themselves in other countries against any opposition or rivalry there. This is the fact, especially with regard to the leading and the most protected interests. The iron and steel, the woolen, the cotton, and the silk productions of the United States are now forcing themselves into foreign markets by no other aid than their own superiority and conceded merit.

It is only necessary for us to have the opportunity to establish reciprocal trade with all the nations of the world in order to show our superiority. Certainly American industries, so far as manufactures are concerned, have reached so high a degree of perfection that we can have nothing to fear. An exclusive policy, like that which the protective system implies, is not applicable to modern times. No nation now lives within itself. Science has served to unite the human race into one common family. While political institutions and language separate them into individual communities, yet in interests, in social ties, in rapid and constant intercommunication, in interchange of products, they have become solidified and concentrated. The former barriers which prevented general fraternal concord have been shattered, if not altogether broken down. The telegraph and the rapidity by which intercommunication is constantly conducted have caused a similitude of thought and action. The result of this will speedily effect reciprocal interchange of products and commodities, and that people which can supply another to the best advantage will command appreciation.

As a consequence the United States will receive universal recognition in all things in which we strive to excel. Hence the removal of any obstructions upon our part to the full consummation of this coming assimilation and consolidation is demanded by every consideration of self-interest.

As we have set the example of free political institutions and the recognition of the rights of the people, holding up to other nations the example of free political thought and action, it is our duty to lead off in the free interchange of productions and the removal of those barriers which serve only to dwarf human energy and to keep fettered in a subordinate condition the manual power of labor.

While firmly convinced of the justice and necessity of an abolition of the protective policy, I do not propose at this time to make the application. The bill reported by the committee makes but slight reductions from the existing tariff. These reductions are made in a way and in a direction that will not affect existing manufacturers. They are rather intended as an indication that the special favor which has been so long extended must sooner or later be materially modified and finally be withdrawn altogether. I recognize in consequence of the present tariff a moral right in the interests affected for a little longer enjoyment of the sustenance so liberally dispensed to them. I think that the advantages which the bill extends to them very much outweigh any injury inflicted by a reduction of the rates. New principles are sought to be ingrafted upon

the policy of the Government extending facilities for the ex.
portation of American manufactures which are not now enjoyed.

In contemplating the needs of the country, is it not time for
statesmen and thoughtful men to raise themselves above the
mere conflicts of party? Is there no higher object worthy of
their effort than to become mere partisan retainers and gladi-
ators? Is it not the duty of the intellect of the nation, with
opportunity in public life, to initiate and shape legislation looking to a fuller development of our material resources and a more
profitable use of the advantages which God and nature have
given us? However desirable a reform in the civil service may
be and however important the preservation intact of the political organizations to which we belong may be, yet these and all
other pending questions are secondary to that of the political
economies, involving in their consideration the highest interests
of the present as well as of succeeding generations, by an intelligent utilization of existing yet hidden superior possessions.

On April 15 William McKinley [O.] opposed the bill.

I am opposed to the pending bill from a high sense of duty,
a duty imposed upon me by the very strong conviction which
I entertain, after an examination of its several features, that
should the proposed measure become a law it will be nothing
short of a public calamity. It scales down the much needed
revenues of the Government. Although this proposition was
denied by the distinguished gentleman who opened this debate
[Mr. Wood], I desire in this connection to call attention to a
carefully prepared statement by Mr. Young, superintendent of
the Bureau of Statistics, in which it is shown that the revenues
to be derived under this bill, if it shall become a law, estimated upon the basis of the importations of 1877, will fall short
of the revenues of that year something more than $9,000,000.

This bill not only impairs the revenues of the Government,
but it is a blow well directed at the mining, the manufacturing,
and the industrial classes of this country. It will not be denied
that any material readjustment of the tariff system at this time
is a delicate and hazardous undertaking, and should be approached if at all with great care and circumspection, with a
thorough knowledge of the business and commerce of the country, their needs and relations, which it proposes to affect. Its
consideration should be unincumbered by individual or sectional interests, and should be free from any attempt or desire
to promote the interests of one class at the expense of the many.

William McKinley

The highest good to the greatest number should guide any legislation which may be had. I believe if this rule shall be adopted the proposed measure will find little favor in this House.

I do not doubt that free trade or its "next of kin," tariff reform, might be of temporary advantage to a very limited class of our population and would be hailed with delight by the home importer and foreign manufacturer; but no one, I predict, who has thoughtfully considered the subject and its effect upon our present state and condition can fail to discern that free trade or tariff reform introduced into this country now will produce still further business depression and increased commercial paralyzation.

Our once prosperous manufactories are barely able now with the present duties upon imports to keep their wheels in motion; and what, I ask, must become of them if the foreign-manufactured product which competes with the manufactured product of the United States shall be suffered to come into this country free of duty or at reduced rates of duty?

But, Mr. Chairman, the defeat of this measure is not only demanded by the popular judgment of all classes, but it is alike the dictate of every just principle of morals and of fair dealing. The present tariff has existed almost without alteration for the past sixteen years. Men have embarked in business under the existing law regulating the tariff; great enterprises have been projected; vast amounts of capital are invested all over the country upon the faith of the existing law and relying upon its permanence, and to-day millions of dollars are invested in buildings, machine shops, and factories all over this land, built up under the fostering care of protection. It is proposed by this bill, without any note of preparation to the manufacturing classes, without any word of warning, without any service being made upon them, by a swift and certain blow to destroy these vast investments of capital and labor.

Even Mr. Wood admits that there is a high moral right resting upon the Congress of this country to continue still further the protection which in the past has been given to the industries of the country. I can assure the gentleman that his bill does not recognize this right, but as to many industries wholly ignores it.

Free trade and tariff reform are captivating phrases, and to one unacquainted with their true meaning and import are deceptive, while the arguments urged in their behalf are alike deceptive and delusive.

The chief consideration that is urged by the advocates of

free trade or tariff reform, so called, is that the duties fall
upon the consumer; in a word, that the great mass of consumers in this country will get their products, their goods, their
merchandise at a very much less price than they now do if
free trade or tariff reform shall prevail instead of the present
policy.

Mr. Chairman, history and experience both teach us that
the agricultural products of this country have in the main increased in price since the tariff of 1824, but that substantially
all manufactured articles, articles that have been protected by
that or successive tariffs, have been secured to the great body
of the consumers at a very much less cost than they formerly
were. And, Mr. Chairman, the price of articles has not only
been diminished and the consumer benefited by the reduced
price, but the quality of the article has in every instance been
improved.

Our proud position to-day is due in great part—indeed I
had almost said in most part—to the wise protection and the
fostering care thrown around American manufactures and labor
and enterprise by the early statesmen of this country and continued down to the present time. No other policy would ever
have given us the advanced stage in manufactures that we enjoy to-day.

The policy of the manufacturers of Europe is to keep "the
growth and the increase in the United States in check"; and
it can be done, say they, in one way only, and that is by a
reduction of the tariff. The American Congress is to-day engaged in that, to the European trade, commendable work; and
for what purpose? To keep the growth of manufactures in the
United States in check and increase the board of trade returns
in Europe. If we did not know better, Mr. Chairman, we would
be justified in believing that we were in the British house of
commons, legislating for British subjects, rather than charged
with the high and sacred duty of making laws for the citizens
of the United States, to protect them in their labor, their industries, and their investments.

But it is said, Mr. Chairman, that our present system is an
obstruction to foreign trade, while the fact stands out before
us, so bidding us read, that our foreign trade has uniformly increased under the tariff policy, and always when the tariff policy has been withdrawn our foreign trade has invariably diminished.

I invite your attention to the following extract, which I
take from Mr. Bigelow's excellent work upon the tariff policy:

The foreign trade of Russia and of the United States increased during the past ten years, under the policy of protection, in a greater ratio than that of Great Britain under the policy of free trade; and, also, in a greater ratio than that of France, which the English claim as a free-trade ally.

Mr. Chairman, a wise tariff protects American industries and manufactures, while it does not destroy foreign competition. Prohibition is no part of the American system. It builds no wall about commerce and trade, shutting out the great world from us; it does not exclude foreign importation; it prevents monopolies from absorbing the wealth of this nation, while it encourages growth and enterprise among our own people. I have said that it encourages enterprise; it opens our mines; it erects our machine shops, our furnaces, and factories; it enlarges our cities and builds up villages.

It adds to the material wealth of the nation. It enhances the value of real estate. More than that, it gives to the farmer a ready market for the products of his farm. It brings a market almost to his very door. It imparts value to many articles which he raises which otherwise would be of little or no value; articles which it would not pay to ship to a distant market have ready sale at home. It does more than this: it furnishes employment to the laborer and subsistence to the poor, and all the while is adding to the nation's wealth.

The bill means reduced wages to operatives. It means the closest, sharpest competition among manufacturers at home with manufacturers abroad. It means the closest economy of the price in the article produced. And the very first step taken in the direction of economy on the part of the manufacturer is to reduce the wages he pays to his laborer; not because he loves to do it, but because the exigencies of his business demand it. That has always been so, and the present and future will be no exception to the past.

Mr. Chairman, self-preservation is the first law of nature, as it is and should be of nations. The general welfare is of paramount importance, and any measure which does not keep this steadily in view, which does not foster and encourage American labor and American industry, is in opposition to the great law of life, and subversive of the principles upon which governments are established. We want to be independent in that broad and comprehensive sense, strong within ourselves, self-supporting and self-sustaining in all things.

I listened attentively to the carefully considered speech of the gentleman from New York [Mr. Wood], waiting to hear of some American interest which was demanding this new legislation, and at last I was rewarded for my patience. He sent a letter to the clerk's desk to be read from Messrs. Worthington & Co., of Jackson, Michigan, manufacturers of agricultural implements, who declared themselves in favor of the bill, and that they were able to import steel to this country, manufacture it into agricultural implements, and send it back again at a profit. This was a strange statement and entirely inexplicable until the distinguished gentleman from Michigan [Omar D. Conger], always on the alert, stated to the House that this firm, which was well known to him, did their work with the convict labor of Michigan at thirty-two cents a day. No other statement was needed. This was the only interest in the whole country over which the gentleman published as satisfied with the proposed change. Comment is unnecessary, for when we commence to employ convict labor I will concede free trade is practicable.

This committee have imposed a duty of 20 cents a bushel upon wheat and they have suffered wheat ground into flour to come into this country free: an unjust discrimination against every flour manufacturer in the land. Again, they have under their bill suffered cloths, manufactured cloths, to come into this country at 50 per cent. *ad valorem;* and in that same bill they allow the cloths made into clothing for wearing apparel to come in for 45 per cent. duty; a discrimination against every manufacturer of clothing, every tailor, every sewing woman the country over.

They have reduced the duty upon scrap iron, wrought and cast; and what will be the result? Why it will throw thousands of men out of employment and will wholly destroy the profession of the puddlers of the land.

The bill in some cases protects the raw material, while the manufactured article is practically free of duty or largely reduced.

They have destroyed the entire classification of wools. They suffer non-competing and competing wools to come in at the same rate of duty. They have broken down the more reasonable classifications which have been approved by the wool grower and accepted by the trade, and now they are all to come in at the same rate, whether we grow the wool in this country or not.

Mr. Chairman, the proposed bill is a piece of patchwork and abounds in inconsistencies. It is an attempt to conciliate two schools of political science and pleases neither. It has marched

out into the broad field of compromise and come back with a
few supporters, it is true, who were opposed to the original bill
as reported. It is neither free trade, nor tariff reform, nor
protective tariff. It has none of the virtues of either, but the
glaring faults of all systems. It is an attempt to change a law
which does not improve the old one. It is an experiment opposed by all experience. It introduces uncertainty into the
business of this country when certainty is essential to its life.

Mr. Chairman, there never was a time in the history of this
country more inauspicious than the present for the dreamer and
the theorist to put into practical operation his impracticable
theories of political science. The country does not want them;
the business men of the country do not want them. They want
quiet to recuperate their wasted forces; and I am sure I utter
no sentiment new or original when I say that if this House will
promptly pass the appropriation bills and other pressing legislation, following this with an immediate adjournment, the people will applaud such a course as the work of statesmen and
the wisdom of men of affairs.

On May 8 John R. Tucker [Va.], a member of the
Committee on Ways and Means, supported the bill.

He argued that the Constitution intended that the
power to lay duties on imports should be distinctly and
only a revenue power, and that the present use of it to
regulate commerce and to put into the pockets of a privileged class bounties extracted from other industries is
a perversion of this intention as well as violative of all
principles of right and justice.

If I am right in maintaining that the Constitution vested
this power to ''lay and collect'' (coupling those two words together so that there should be no duty laid which was not to
be collected), I next inquire what is a revenue tariff as contra-
distinguished from a protective tariff, which uses the revenue
power for another and a different purpose? On this point I
read from an article which I have printed elsewhere.

In all the modes of taxation which may be adopted upon all articles
of consumption, the quantum of revenue raised is the result of two factors:
the rate of tax and the amount of consumption. The amount of consumption may be regarded for practical purposes as the proper factor, for
under a tariff the consumption will regulate the import, and in excises the
consumption will limit the production. So that in every tariff the revenue
derived from each article will be the result of the duty multiplied by the

XII—11

amount of import and in every excise the tax multiplied by the quantum of product.

In the case of the tariff system, it follows that as the rate of duty increases the amount of consumption on importation will decrease. When the duty is nothing, the revenue will be nothing, however great the importation. When the importation is nothing the revenue will be nothing, however great the duty. And as the importation falls off with the increase of the rate of duty, until the duty becomes prohibitory, by so increasing the price of the import as to prevent any consumption, it follows that between the point of no duty and the prohibitory rate there will be an ascending scale of revenue to a maximum point of revenue and a descending scale of revenue from that maximum point to the point of prohibition. So that on either side of that duty, which raises the maximum revenue on any article, there will be a lower and a higher duty which will raise the same amount of revenue.

Therefore, as no higher duty ought to be laid than is needed to raise the requisite revenue on any particular article, it follows that the true revenue duty is the lowest duty which will bring the required revenue. To lay the higher duty to obtain the required revenue, instead of the lower, which will achieve the same result, is an oppressive violation of right, in making the burden heavier than the needs of the Government require for its support. Such higher duty is not a revenue measure, but is a needless limitation upon consumption, oppressive to the citizen and an improper restriction upon freedom of commerce. In other words, the lowest rates of duty which will secure the required revenue may be termed a revenue tariff; the highest rates securing the same will be a protective tariff. The former enlarges consumption, the latter diminishes it, and both bring the same amount of revenue. The one decreases the comforts of the people by decreasing ability to consume; the other increases their comforts by enlarging their capacity of consumption.

In view of what I have said these rules may be laid down as within the spirit of the Constitution: first, no duty should be laid higher than the maximum revenue point; second, that under that maximum revenue point luxuries may be made to pay a higher rate of duty than necessaries; third, that it is more just to have an *ad valorem* duty, and, where that is impracticable because of danger to revenue from frauds in invoices, that the specific duty should be so laid upon the article by classification as to make it as nearly as possible equivalent to an *ad valorem* duty; and, fourth, that, unless necessary for revenue, raw materials may be admitted free of duty in the interests of the manufacturer as well as of the consumer of the products from such materials.

It is in this view that I hold the protective system contrary to the true spirit of the Constitution, because—

First. If the power to lay and collect duties be granted to raise revenue from imports, it cannot be in accord with the spirit of the power so to use it as to prevent imports and defeat revenue.

Second.   Nor can it consist with a grant of power to raise revenues for the Government to use this power as a means of extorting bounty from one class to be lavished on another.

Third.   Nor can this system, so unjust and unequal, be sanctioned by a constitution whose preamble declares it was formed "to establish justice," and "to secure the blessings of liberty" to the people of all the United States.

Fourth.   And besides, as the Constitution forbids that any tax or duty shall be laid upon articles exported from any State, and as a restriction upon imports by duties operates by indirection to restrict exports, as if the duties were laid upon them, it is contrary to the true purpose of the Constitution by such indirection to accomplish an end which cannot be done, but is forbidden, by any direct means.   It is an evasion of a prohibition and kills the spirit by a seemingly strict conformity to the letter of the Constitution.

Tested by the principles already advanced, I ask is the existing tariff a revenue tariff?

To speak algebraically, you may formulate the amount of revenue by an equation, as I have already shown; revenue equal to the duty multiplied by the import.   Now, as the duty increases the import will decrease, and *vice versa*.   Therefore, it is not improper to say, as has been so often said by political economists—I think as far back as Adam Smith—that two and two do not always make four in political economy.   You do not double your revenue when you double your duty; you very often double your revenue by halving your duty.   The great error that has been made, in my judgment, by the honorable gentleman from Massachusetts [Nathaniel P. Banks], who spoke yesterday, and by the estimate of the Secretary of the Treasury and Dr. Young at the Bureau of Statistics, is in supposing that the revenue under the present law will be decreased because of a reduction of duties under the proposed bill.   In many cases the revenue will be increased on account of that rduction.

The question we come now to consider is whether, tested by the rules which I have laid down, the present tariff—not the bill proposed here—is a revenue measure.   Why, sir, I will show that so far from being a revenue measure the framers of that tariff and those who now support it seem to prefer it because it does not (in many cases) raise any revenue.   The present tariff is such that in the statistical tables all along the column of duties you will find the figures very high, but in the column in reference to the quantum of revenue you will find the amount sometimes down to zero, or a few hundred or a few thousand dollars; showing that the duties are laid to prevent revenue and not to raise it. And what is this for? Not to support the Government, but to benefit a privileged class.

In proof of this, I call attention to pig iron. I mean no unkindness to this "infant industry," this little "pig" from Pennsylvania, whose infancy is perpetual. Ever since the year 1816, when the first duty was laid on pig iron, a duty of $9 a ton, it has been an "infant industry"; unless indeed it came to its maturity during the period of our revenue tariff, and is now again and still an "infant," because it has fallen into the decrepitude of its second childhood.

You will find that as the duty fell the revenue increased; and as the duty rose the revenue fell; thus the revenue from all iron was $21,922,127 in the year 1872, and it has fallen in the year 1876-77 down to $3,765,846; and the revenue from pig iron alone has fallen from say $1,500,000 in 1872 to about $557,000 in 1877. I am met, when I ask for reduction of the tax on tobacco, by the objection that by reducing the burdens on that industry we will diminish the revenue; but when I ask for a reduction of the duty on pig iron so that the consumer may get it cheaper and may thus increase revenue, they say, "Oh, no; we do not want to increase the revenue on pig iron; we want to protect our pig iron, by destroying the revenue from it." In other words, it is proper to keep the Government out of revenue on pig iron at the expense of the consumer for the benefit of the manufacturer, but very wrong to lift the burden from the tobacco interest lest we decrease the revenue!

To show that the purpose of the duty is to prevent importation and thus prevent revenue, I will read from the June, 1877, annual report of the American Iron and Steel Association, page 24, which they have done me the honor to send me. Listen to the tone of self-gratulation:

During the year 1876 we did not import a single steel rail; in 1873 we imported 159,571 net tons. Our imports of iron rails in 1876 amounted to only 287 tons; in 1871 they amounted to 515,000 tons. While these results are gratifying—

That is, that the duty has excluded the importation and thus decreased the revenue—

it is nevertheless a source of mortification that we should last year have bought abroad ten million dollars' worth of pig-iron, bar-iron, steel, &c., which our own iron and steel makers could have manufactured with the help of idle workingmen. So long as it is possible to import into this country ten million dollars' worth of foreign iron and steel in a year of such great industrial depression as last year, so long will a protective tariff be a necessity to American iron and steel interests and to every American citizen whose prosperity does not depend upon the sale of foreign goods.

That is to say, the power to raise revenue by a tariff is, according to the ideas of these gentlemen who represent the iron and steel interest, to be purposely perverted from its constitutional object of raising revenue into a scheme to support the iron and steel interest by diverting revenue from the treasury and furnishing rich bounties by a tax upon the consuming classes of the country.

It is a misnomer to call this system of duties protection. Protection against what? Protection to whom? It is simply a means by which the Government makes an enforced contribution, or, as they used to call it in the days of the Stuarts, "a compulsory benevolence," in behalf of certain people who, having a fancy to go into certain enterprises which are not profitable, are by this legislation enabled to hand round the hat to eke out the profit they cannot make by their occupations.

What is the true national policy? In this era of expanding energies, of all-embracing sympathies, of far-reaching aspirations for a better and higher destiny for our race, are we to be told that our true policy is to clip the wings of our commerce, to block the wheels of our trade and industry; to cramp our enterprise, to shrivel our sympathies, to exult in the stoppage of our imports, to live within ourselves, and, hugging our petty interests within the narrow circle of our contracted selfishness, close the gates of our new world to intercourse with mankind?

Mr. Chairman, I cannot believe this is according to the Divine plan. Christianity bids us seek in communion with our brethren of every race and clime the blessings they can afford us, and to bestow in return upon them those with which our new continent is destined to fill the world.

Our lot is cast upon a virgin continent whose rich soil can feed and clothe the human family. It is ours to develop and fill the markets of all nations with the exuberant harvests of our fruitful earth. The wage of labor is high. I am thankful to God for it; that "in our Father's house there is bread enough and to spare and none need perish with hunger." There is no place for the footprint of a tramp upon the Western prairie nor upon the fields of the sunny South, whose teeming products will abundantly feed a hungry world, clothe a naked world, and shelter a homeless world!

Now, sir, why should it be our policy to crowd labor into cities upon profitless employments and then eke out the lack of profit and wage by governmental aid, in the shape of a compulsory benevolence or a forced contribution, to furnish a profit their enterprise cannot afford.

That people, Mr. Chairman, whose inventive genius and natural resources can best supply the needs of the world's crowded population with food and raiment and human comfort, and whose commerce reaches out to do so, will hold the van in the march of civilization; and that people which is content to supply only its own needs and limits its commerce to itself, and confines its sympathies within the sphere of its own petty interests, will shrivel into poverty and shrink into insignificance. Hence it is that in all ages, and now more than in any former age, the exports and imports of every nation are the typical tests of its prosperity and the splendid symbols of its progress. They form the great balances of international trade. They must coexist. Check the one and the other withers. Destroy the one and the other perishes.

Now, suppose this House should prohibit all importations, what would be the effect on our agricultural products? They would perish on our hands. As you limit the imports of the country, which furnish the means of paying for our exports, to that extent you limit the value of our exported products and limit the prosperity of the agricultural interests in this country.

Look at the results of this policy for the privileged classes. Agriculture languishes for markets; manufactures are ruined because overproduction, induced by excessive bounties, first brings on a fall in prices and then bankruptcy; labor is thrown out of employment; ships rot at our wharves for lack of trade, and the country is in great distress from the panaceas prescribed for it by the empirical economists. What the patient needs is to "throw physic to the dogs," and let the *vis medicatrix naturæ* do its proper work. Strike the fetters from the limbs of the American Hercules, and he will with giant strides take the lead in human progress.

Here let me notice in brief the doctrine of Mr. Henry C. Carey, that the producer and the consumer are best related when closest to each other. To carry this idea to its logical conclusion, the result would be that the producer and the consumer are closest together when a man is at once both producer and consumer; so that the whole effect of Mr. Carey's policy would be to limit all human sympathy and interchange of human ideas and their products to our own dear selves.

Now, whenever by commercial treaties, as with the Hawaiian

Islands, we have established free trade with foreign countries, the immediate results have been mutually advantageous, and exports and imports in the case of the Hawaiian Islands doubled in one year. Enlarge the system, embracing all countries, and our export and import trade would soon rival that of Great Britain. Our revenues from our billions of imports at a duty of 20 per cent. would nearly double our present revenue; our debt would be diminished, our export trade would enlarge, prices would advance, and all our industries would thrive and grow in the vigor and strength of healthful maturity.

In truth, free trade, which is based on the golden rule, "Do unto others as you would that others should do to you," by commingling and intertwining the interests of all peoples through free commerce would be a guaranty and bond of peace. The antagonisms of commercial policies have bred wars which have drenched the earth with blood. Free trade, promotive of social intercourse and the interests of mutual exchanges, will spread the banner of peace over the world and promote the glory of God, in "peace on earth and good will toward men." Free trade, the product of the divine doctrines of Christianity, would be the peace-maker of the world!

How far does the proposed bill bring down the duties to the revenue standard? It is true the reduction is not what a revenue tariff requires. The duties are still too high; but the precedent of the tariff compromise of 1833 justifies a moderate and gradual reduction, and not a radical one. Still the reduction is considerable and the movement is in the right direction of a revenue tariff, and is not so radical as to convulse the manufacturing interest of the country. The duties on iron are too high and should be further reduced even now, and yet that interest is dissatisfied at any reduction.

It is much to be regretted that this system of specific duties must still be largely retained. They operate oppressively on the poor, by making the duty as large on the cheap as on the dear article. But this has been remedied as far as possible by the classification of the same kind of articles according to their value.

Some objection has been made that there is no free list. This objection is not well founded. It is according to sound principles that nothing be taxed which is not clearly intended by the express terms of the law. It is contrary to principle to require a party to exempt his property from taxation by showing terms indicating such a purpose. Let all be free which is not clearly taxed; not, let all be taxed which is not clearly free.

The *onus* should be on the executive officer to show that the legislature has imposed it in clear terms and should not be on the citizen to show he is excepted from the universal imposition of burden.

Mr. Chairman, we need in the present state of the country a well-defined policy. Permit me, in conclusion, to indicate some of the elements of one which it seems to me would be wise and successful:

First. We need a judicious economy in disbursements, which, while securing efficiency by commanding the services of intelligent and capable agents, will avoid the extravagance which tends to corruption through the influence of patronage.

Second. The times demand a strict adherence to the Constitution as a sacred duty, as needful to an efficient administration of the powers granted, and to prevent the evils of centralism. The danger of our future is that in the absorption of power by the Federal Government we not only incur the perils of a consolidated government, but make an effective discharge of our duties under the Constitution well-nigh impracticable. In my judgment, in the enlarged area of the country and with its increasing interests, we will have our hands full to do well what is expressly devolved upon us without attempting to exercise doubtful powers.

Third. We need to have free trade and to relieve production from the burdens of internal taxation; to lift the load which presses upon the producer and consumer of tobacco and other domestic productions, and to open our ports to an unshackled commerce with all nations, except so far as revenue for an economical administration of the Government requires the laying of duties on imports.

Let us render to Cæsar the things that be Cæsar's, but let tribute to privilege and bounty to favored classes cease forever!

Fourth. We need a sound and stable currency which will give to labor a real, and not a fictitious, value; which will shun artificial inflation, that buoys enterprise with false hopes; and avoid compulsory contraction, which crushes the debtor class by requiring more in payment than was agreed, and shrinks values to the ruin and detriment of all classes of society.

Fifth. We need integrity to public faith—paying all which contract of honorable obligation requires and guarding jealously against all claims which justice, right, and public law do not sanction.

And then we need the cultivation among ourselves of mutual

respect for the opinions and sensibilities of each other. We need forbearance and charity, a spirit of justice and moderation, and a profound regard for the equal rights of all under the Constitution and laws of the land.

Brothers in a common humanity, we are coheirs of liberty under constitutional law and copartners under Providence of a virgin continent, midway between European progress and Asiatic stagnation, washed by two great oceans and permeated by innumerable channels for interstate trade; with a soil teeming with products, which will bless the world with abundant food and raiment; with a coast and harbors for boundless commerce and unlimited merchant marine. Oh, my brothers of America! God helping us, have we not something nobler to do than to rake up the ashes of our former strife and stir again its fires? Something higher and better than to revive the enmities, the jealousies of the past, and to fill these halls with criminations and outbursts of passion? Yes, let the dead past bury its dead; let us cease bickerings and disputings as to the right and the wrong of the great struggle; let us strive to forgive and forget the angry feuds which filled the land with blood and mourning and desolation; and, turning from these passions which disturb the balances of the judgment, paralyze duty for the busy present, impair faith and hope in our great future, with mutual respect for each other's virtues and mutual forbearance for each other's faults, let us clasp hands and join arms in the pledge of earnest coöperation, under the dictates of a divine duty, in pressing forward the destiny of this mighty people in a career of honor, prosperity, and civilization, which will make our constitutional Union of States the glory of the world and a blessing to our children's children to the remotest generations. [Great applause.]

On May 9, 1878, William D. Kelley [Pa.], a minority member of the Committee of Ways and Means, opposed the bill.

Doctrinaires and editors of commercial organs have persistently criticised some of the details of our present tariff law and objected to the principles upon which our revenue system is based; but no part of the people have petitioned Congress to engage at this time in a revision of the tariff.

The loom and the spindle stand still. The mine is unwrought and the fires are out in the forge, the furnace, and the rolling mill. The captains of industry by thousands are passing into bankruptcy and the laboring people of the country by millions into want, if not into absolute pauperism. They are not permitted to endure the primal curse and earn their bread in the sweat of their brows. They implore us to relieve them, but not one of them has suggested that it can be done by a revision of the tariff in the interest of foreign producers and their agents who are supplanting American merchants in New York and elsewhere. They are told by school men and the organs of these foreign commercial agents that they are suffering from "over-production"; that they are hungry because they have produced too much food; that they are naked or in rags because they have spun and woven too many fabrics; that they are shoeless and footsore because they have produced too many boots and shoes; and that they are houseless "tramps" because they have erected too many homes and constructed too much furniture.

They do not believe these preposterous assertions and ask us to legislate in quite another direction than the revision of the tariff in the interest of the employers of foreign labor.

I must ask the committee to pardon a brief digression. I cannot abstain from saying in this connection that I am more than half persuaded that the magnificent denunciations of the protective system uttered yesterday by the gentleman from Virginia [Mr. Tucker] were, notwithstanding his apparent earnestness, only in a Pickwickian sense. In support of this surmise I refer to the facts that, while the highest manufactures of the North are stricken at by this bill, the blossoms or leaves of sumac, an indigenous bush which infests the hillsides of Virginia and which are gathered by old women and children as an amusement, are to be protected by a duty of 10 per cent. and tobacco shooks are made free by special provision.

I do not think it will be suspected that any gentleman outside of Virginia caused those provisions to be inserted in the bill; and from their presence there I infer that the gentleman would accept a little protection if Virginia had any manufacturing industries to be protected. [Laughter.]

I do not complain, Mr. Chairman, that these articles are made free. They ought all to be free except perhaps the shooks. Were competition in that important article possible it might stimulate some stalwart Virginian to cut a few trees and shape them into shooks. But I take no special exception even to that item. What I do complain of is that there is not a full and specific free list. I assert without the fear of plausible contradiction that the absence of such a list is a fatal defect.

No tariff has ever been made by a manufacturing nation that did not embody a specific free list. The commercial and manufacturing nations of the world have agreed that raw materials which cannot be produced within the country of their conversion, especially those which come from tropical or other countries which will take their manufactures in exchange for raw material, should be admitted free of duty. We alone impose duties upon any of them and if we are to manufacture either for home consumption or in the hope of reaching a foreign market we must adopt this part of the policy of other nations which puts us under bonds to maintain a free list embracing all such raw materials.

Now, a tariff is not a matter of inspiration. It is a thing of slow growth and of adaptation to the extent, resources, and development of a country. Switzerland, with her few miles of territory, her snow-capped mountains, and her lakes, enriched with no native resources in the way of metals, may need free trade. But it is not adapted to a young and sparsely populated country which extends, as ours does, from ocean to ocean, embraces all climates, is more richly endowed than any other country with soil and climate for varied agricultural productions, and is still more richly endowed with minerals, useful and precious, and whose people, having been trained in the industrial centers of all countries, are in the enjoyment of schools of art and science such as the magnificent one founded by the munificence of the venerable man who does me the honor to listen to me (Mr. Peter Cooper), which, with its stores of literature, its models, its drawings, its scientific apparatus, and other educational appliances, is open to the poorest child of either sex in the country.

Such a country needs a protective tariff that will enable its people to employ whatever faculties Heaven has endowed them with; the feeble, with a taste for art to embellish our productions and adorn our homes and public halls; the vigorous and enterprising, to explore our mountains and develop their wealth; those with mathematical or mechanical gifts, to advance the arts and industries and carry them forward with the advancing line of civilization into our unpeopled wastes. The inhabitants of such a country develop their faculties and aptitudes by laboring to supply and gratify each other's needs and desires; but to enable them to do this the Government must secure to them at least equal chances with the foreigner in their own markets; and this can only be done by a tariff ample for the purpose of protection. This is all that a judicious tariff is.

It is all that the manufacturers of this country ask, and had the Committee of Ways and Means met them they would have indicated reductions of duties that could be made with safety and extensions of the free list which might be made and which when made would justify a further reduction of duties upon the articles derived from such materials. They do not seek to injure their countrymen by the establishment of protected monopolies.

There is unhappily much evidence in the bill that its aim is to prostrate manufacturers as a class. But the blows are often aimed so unskillfully and awkwardly that over the shoulders of the manufacturer they strike the head of the farmer.

The bill is a nondescript. When going over it to make an analysis of its provisions, I could not help thinking of the mule so pathetically described by the witty Senator from Oregon, Mr. Nesmith, and made up my mind that like it this bill was a thing that could have no pride of ancestry, for it was unlike anything that had ever gone before, and could have no hope of posterity as it was not possible that any deliberative body would accept it as a model.

It retains duties which yield little or no revenue, and repeals those which yield large sums. It retains duties on some things and repeals them on other articles identical in character and use. It imposes duties on materials and removes them from the articles into which these materials have been wrought.

Gentlemen say we can go through this bill in Committee of the Whole and correct these errors. They are mistaken. It is utterly wanting in governing principle, and its provisions are so helter-skelter and incongruous that it would be easier to blot the whole thing out and begin anew. From now until next December would not be long enough for the Committee of the Whole on the state of the Union, proceeding as rapidly as I have ever seen it proceed with a tariff bill, to correct the blunders, stupidities, incongruities, and absurdities embodied in the committee's bill.

But time will not permit me to examine details. Let me, however, hastily consider some of the doctrines of the chairman of the committee. He assumed throughout his speech, and so did the gentleman from Virginia, that duties add themselves to the price not only of imported articles but of like articles produced in this country. Let me ask them do competition in the market and increase of supply increase prices? Are the prices of cotton, woolen, worsted, and silk goods, of locomotives, iron or steel rails, machine tools, agricultural implements, mechanical toys, or any of the thousand other articles we now produce, as high as they were under the free-trade tariff of 1857 or at any time prior to the increase of the rates of duty in 1861? No, sir; all kinds of American goods can be bought cheaper under the higher duties of to-day than they could be under the lowest rates ever fixed by our tariff laws, and it is the very madness of theory to assert, as the gentlemen have done, that duties which stimulate production and add to the world's supply enhance prices.

I was amused by the chairman's expression of sympathy with the overtaxed farmer. It was so amusing to note the gravity and pathos with which he started his poor farmer out to buy taxed hardware, shoes, etc., for himself and clothes and medicines for his wife. When I first read that gem of his speech in my youth or earliest manhood, just after Sydney Smith had produced it, it made an impression upon my mind that still lingers. [Laughter.]

Sir, for the last twenty years I have been so in the habit of laughing, at least in my sleeve, when hearing gentlemen reproduce that admirable novelty that I could not help doing so when the chairman of my committee startled me by reciting it. I have it before me as uttered by the gentleman, then from Ohio, but who has carpet-bagged to New York [Samuel S. Cox], and who is sometimes known by the *sobriquet* of "Sunset," as he delivered it in 1864. [Laughter.]

Subsequently I heard it from my friend the late James Brooks. Then from our friend, Samuel S. Marshall, of Illinois, and there has never been a tariff bill under discussion that I have not heard it three or four times; and I repeat that I could not help laughing when the chairman of the committee got it off with such solemnity.

MR. COX.—As original?

MR. KELLEY.—He did not indicate that he had ever read Sydney Smith's works or heard of Sam. Marshall or Sam. Cox or any other Sam who has sent the poor farmer out to make purchases? [Laughter.]

Now, concerning the witty remark of the gentleman from Virginia, that, if Mr. Carey's theory that brings to proximity the producer and the consumer was sound doctrine, then the man was best off who made everything for himself and consumed all he made, I must say that it was hardly worthy of him, as it showed that he had not made himself familiar with the principles of the great matter of social science. Mr. Carey starts out with the proposition that association is the first and paramount want of a human being. He also teaches that from diversity of employment come unity of interests and freedom of association, and shows that this diversity is produced by protection.

A duty, no matter how high it may be, if required to enable an ingenious and industrious people to supply their own wants out of the raw material with which Providence had endowed them, is the proper duty; and being high enough to do that it will so increase production as to reduce prices; and this is in accordance with Mr. Carey's doctrines. Therefore a duty is never too high when in a country of such native resources as ours the supply of the home market may be vitally interfered with by foreign competitors nothwithstanding that duty. That question furnishes the measure of a just duty, in the mind of an intelligent protectionist.

And now let me state that the gentleman from Virginia [Mr. Tucker] has unconsciously paid me what I shall cherish as the most magnificent tribute received during my now somewhat extended congressional life. Referring to the tariff of 1870, he said that it had placed on the free list a large number of articles; and he added that in consequence our manufactures had grown and our exports had increased from $60,-000,000 to $160,000,000 a year.

I had the honor of initiating that enlargement of the free list. It cost me the labors of a whole vacation and correspondence with consumers of raw material in every branch of industry. By this work and my labors in that Congress I earned the honorable *sobriquet* of "Old Pig Iron." Those who hoped by inaugurating what they called revenue reform to destroy the industries of this country saw that to make raw materials free was to enter wisely on the march toward free trade. While by the prevalence of the teaching of British economists they could keep our raw material under heavy duties they could compete with us in our own market and prevent the growth of our foreign trade. Then it was that their well-paid lobby, with its open rooms in every elegant portion of Washington City, set upon my devoted head the scribblers of the nation and bestowed upon me the *sobriquet* that I now cherish of "Old Pig Iron," which is said to be significant of the fact that through good report and ill report I had stood by my intelligent convictions and the interest of the laboring people of the whole country.

The gentleman from Virginia and the chairman of the committee support the proposed bill as a free-trade measure. Is it that or something else? Its provisions are so haphazard and incongruous that no man can tell whether it most promotes free trade or protection. Mr. Moore, the Parsee merchant, protests against it, because of its violations of free-trade principles, and Mr. D. C. Robbins protests with even greater emphasis that it is violative of every principle of free trade; while I and gentlemen around me say that its provisions would prove to be alike destructive to the free-trader and the protectionist.

But, if it could be shown that it favors free trade, it would simply prove that it is an attempt to resist the tendency and drift of the age. England herself begins to realize the sad mistake she made when she failed to confine freedom of trade with her ports to raw materials and food. Many of the ablest thinkers of that country are now asking that the errors of Cobden and Bright may be corrected. On the 3d of last month, Mr. Ernest Seyd, than whom there is no more proficient statistician in England, addressed the British Society of Arts in London. He said:

Although I am a thorough free-trader, I am of the opinion that, unless there is soon a better balance between our imports and exports, there is really no other method of effecting this than by a partial return to protection.

The cotton lords of England, as her manufacturers were called, are demanding the protection of their investments against the terrible competition from India.

In characterizing the last quarter of the first century of our existence the chairman of the committee alluded to the Civil War as its distinguishing feature. History is made up of the story of great wars, and, though ours may have had distinguishing features, it did not characterize the last quarter of our first century. The crowning glory of that period was a triumph of the arts of peace and the testimony the United States gave to the world of the power of the protective system in developing the resources of a continent and the attributes of a people. The crowning glory of that century of American history centered in the buildings in the shadow of whose magnificent proportions stands my humble home, and to the construction and maintenance of which a niggardly Congress refused to permit the Government to contribute a dollar. It was an illustration of the capacity of a free and self-governing people. We behold it in the display there made of machinery the most wonderful that man had ever beheld; in the products of genius, taste, skill, and industry put forth in the field, the workshop, the mine, the mill, the laboratory, and the studio. It was there in the habits, manners, and apparel of our people who gathered there by millions, and who, thanks to the general principles of the protective system, and especially to the tariff of 1867 on wool and woolens and to the stimulus the additional duties it imposed on ready-made clothing gave to that industry, were clad, the rich and the poor, the capitalist and the laborer, the farmer and the denizens of cities, in garments of the same texture, cut, and make, and presented to foreigners an undistinguishable mass, so that, as they loitered through the immense buildings or among the crowds which swarmed in the beautiful grounds, they inquired of their American friends, ''Where are the people, the artisans, the *paysans*, the laborers?'' No matter from what country they came, none of them had ever seen the laborer and farmer so clad and so orderly that they could be crowded together a quarter of a million within a single inclosure without the presenec of troops, or *gens d'armes*, or even the appearance of a palpable police. This exhibit of the developed resources of our country, of the skill and attainments of our people, of the influence of self-government upon the social habits of a people, was the crowning glory of the first century of our history. It came as the result of our challenge to the world to peaceful competition, and it is for this that we are receiving the benedictions of the scholars, statesmen, and thinkers of the world in grateful recognition of the instruction the American people have imparted to all nations by their example.

On June 4, James A. Garfield [O.], a member of the Committee on Ways and Means, spoke upon the bill.

A few days ago the distinguished gentleman from Virginia, who now occupies the chair [Mr. Tucker], made a speech of rare ability and power, in which he placed at the front in his line of discussion a question that was never raised in American legislation until our present form of government was forty years old; the question of the constitutionality of a tariff for the encouragement and protection of manufactures.

He insists that the two powers conferred upon Congress, to levy duties and to regulate commerce, are entirely distinct from each other; that the one cannot by any fair construction be applied to the other; that the methods of the one are not the methods of the other, and that the capital mistake which he conceives has been made in the legislation of the country for many years is that the power to tax has been applied to the regulation of commerce, and through that to the protection of manufactures. He holds that if we were to adopt a proper construction of the Constitution we should find that the regulation of commerce does not permit the protection of manufacturers, nor can the power to tax be applied, directly, or indirectly, to that object.

I will not enter into any elaborate discussion of that question, but I cannot refrain from expressing my admiration of the courage of the gentleman from Virginia, who in that part of his speech brought himself into point-blank range of the terrible artillery of James Madison, one of the fathers of the Constitution, and Virginia's great expounder of its provisions. More than a hundred pages of the collected works of James Madison are devoted to an elaborate and exhaustive discussion of the very objections which the gentleman [Mr. Tucker] has urged.

I will close this phase of the discussion by calling the attention of the committee to the language of the Constitution itself:

The Congress shall have power to lay and collect taxes, duties, imposts and excises, to pay the debts and provide for the common defence and general welfare of the United States.

Language could hardly be plainer to declare the great general objects to which the taxing power is to be applied.

It should be borne in mind that revenue is the life-blood of a government, circulating through every part of its organization and giving force and vitality to every function. The power to tax is therefore the great motive power, and its regulation impels, retards, restrains, or limits all the functions of the Government.

What are these functions? The Constitution authorizes Congress to regulate and control this great motive power, the power to levy and collect duties; and the objects for which duties are to be levied and collected are summarized in three great groups: First, "to pay debts." By this, the arm of the Government sweeps over all its past history and protects its honor by discharging all obligations that have come down from former years. Second is "to provide for the common defence." By this the mailed arm of the Government sweeps the great circle of the Union to defend it against foes from without and insurrection within. And, third, is to "promote the general welfare." These are the three great objects to which the Constitution applies the power of taxation. They are all great, beneficent, national objects and cannot be argued out of existence.

Protection has received the support of the most renowned names in our early history; and, though the principle has sometimes been carried to an unreasonable extreme, thus bringing reproach upon the system, it has nevertheless borne many of the fruits which were anticipated by those who planted the germ.

Gentlemen who oppose this view of public policy tell us that they favor a tariff for revenue alone. I therefore invite their attention to the revenue phase of the question. The Secretary of the Treasury tells us that it will be necessary to cut down the expenditures eleven millions below the estimates in order to prevent a deficit of that amount. The revenues of the last fiscal year failed by three and a quarter millions to meet the expenditures required by law. In the face of these facts can we safely diminish our revenues? But we are told that some of the reductions made in this bill will increase rather than diminish the revenue. Perhaps on a few articles this will be true; but as a whole it is undeniable that this bill will effect a considerable reduction in the revenues from customs.

Gentlemen on the other side have been in the habit of denouncing our present tariff laws as destructive to rather than productive of revenue. Let me invite their attention to a few plain facts:

During the fifteen years that preceded our late war—a period of so-called revenue tariffs—we raised from customs an average annual revenue of forty-seven and a half million dollars, never in any year receiving more than sixty-four millions. That system brought us a heavy deficit in 1860, so that Congress was compelled to borrow money to meet the ordinary expenses of the Government.

Do they tell us that our present law fails to produce an adequate revenue? They denounce it as not a revenue tariff. Let them wrestle with the following fact: during the eleven years that have passed since the close of the war we have averaged one hundred and seventy and one-half million dollars of revenue per annum from customs alone. Can they say that this is not a revenue tariff which produces more than three times as much revenue per annum as that law did which they delight to call "the revenue tariff"? Can they say that the present law does not produce revenue? It produces from textile fabrics alone more revenue than we ever raised from all sources under any tariff before the war. From this it follows that the assault upon the present law fails if made on the score of revenue alone.

I freely admit that revenue is the primary object of taxation. That object is attained by existing law. But it is an incidental and vitally important object of the law to keep in healthy growth those industries which are necessary to the well-being of the whole country. If gentlemen can show me that this is, as they allege, class legislation which benefits the few at the expense of the many, I will abandon it and join them in opposing it. This is the legislature of the nation; and it should make laws which will bless the whole nation. I do not affirm that all the provisions of the existing tariff law are wise and just. In many respects they are badly adjusted and need amendment. But I insist that in their main features they are national, not partial; that they promote the general welfare, and not the welfare of the few at the expense of the many.

What sort of people should we be if we do not keep our industries alive? Suppose we were to follow the advice of the distinguished gentleman from Virginia [Mr. Tucker] when he said:

Why should we make pig-iron when with Berkshire pigs raised upon our farms we can buy more iron pigs from England than we can get by trying to make them ourselves?

For a single season, perhaps, his plan might be profitable to the consumers of iron; but if this policy were adopted as a permanent one it would reduce us to a merely agricultural people, whose chief business would be to produce the simplest raw materials by the least skill and culture, and let the men of brains of other countries do our thinking for us and provide for us all products requiring the cunning hand of the artisan, while we would be compelled to do the drudgery for ourselves and for them.

The gentleman from Virginia [Mr. Tucker] is too good a logician not to see that the theory he advocates can be realized only in a state of universal peace and brotherhood among the nations; for, in developing his plan, he says:

Christianity bids us seek, in communion with our brethren of every race and clime, the blessings they can afford us, and to bestow in return upon them those with which our new continent is destined to fill the world.

This, I admit, is a grand conception, a beautiful vision of the time when all the nations shall dwell in peace; when all will be, as it were, one nation, each furnishing to the others what they cannot profitably produce, and all working harmoniously together in the millennium of peace. If all the kingdoms of the world should become the kingdom of the Prince of Peace, then I admit that universal free trade ought to prevail. But that blessed era is yet too remote to be made the basis of the practical legislation of to-day. We are not yet members of "the parliament of man, the federation of the world." For the present, the world is divided into separate nationalities; and that other divine command still applies to our situation, "He that provideth not for his own household has denied the faith, and is worse than an infidel"; and, until that better era arrives, patriotism must supply the place of universal brotherhood.

For the present Gortchakoff can do more good to the world by taking care of Russia. The great Bismarck can accomplish more for his era by being, as he is, German to the core, and promoting the welfare of the German Empire. Let Beaconsfield take care of England, and McMahon of France, and let Americans devote themselves to the welfare of America. When each does his best for his own nation to promote prosperity, justice, and peace, all will have done more for the world than if all had attempted to be cosmopolitans rather than patriots. [Applause.]

Too much of our tariff discussion has been warped by narrow and sectional considerations. But when we base our action upon the conceded national importance of the great industries I have referred to, when we recognize the fact that artisans and their products are essential to the well-being of our country, it follows that there is no dweller in the humblest cottage on our remotest frontier who has not a deep personal interest in the legislation that shall promote these great national industries. Those arts that enable our nation to rise in the scale of civilization bring their blessings to all, and patriotic citizens will cheerfully bear a fair share of the burden necessary to make their country great and self-sustaining. I will defend a tariff that is national in its aims, that protects and sustains those interests without which the nation cannot become great and self-sustaining. The system adopted by our fathers encourages the great national industries so as to make it possible at all times for our people to equip themselves for war, and at the same time increase their intelligence and skill so as to make them better fitted for all the duties of citizenship both in war and in peace. We provide for the common defence by a system which promotes the general welfare.

I have tried thus summarily to state the grounds on which a tariff which produces the necessary revenue and at the same time promotes American manufactures can be sustained by large-minded men for national reasons. How high the rates of such a tariff ought to be is a question on which there may fairly be differences of opinion.

Fortunately or unfortunately, on this question I have long

occupied a position between two extremes of opinion. I have long believed, and I still believe, that the worst evil which has afflicted the interests of American artisans and manufacturers

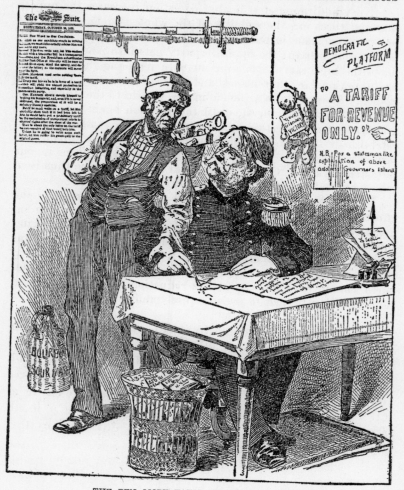

THE PEN MORE FATAL THAN THE SWORD

Democratic Workman—"STOP, GENERAL; WRITE NO MORE ABOUT FREE TRADE; YOU ARE MAKING AN AWFUL MESS OF IT"

From the collection of the New York Public Library

has been the tendency to extremes in our tariff legislation. Our history for the last fifty years has been a repetition of the same mistake. One party comes into power, and, believing that a protective tariff is a good thing, establishes a fair rate of duty.

Not content with that, they say: "This works well, let us have more of it." And they raise the rates still higher, and perhaps go beyond the limits of national interest.

Every additional step in that direction increases the opposition and threatens the stability of the whole system. When the policy of increase is pushed beyond a certain point, the popular reaction sets in; the opposite party gets into power and cuts down the high rates. Not content with reducing the rates that are unreasonable, they attack and destroy the whole protective system. Then follows a deficit in the treasury, the destruction of manufacturing interest, until the reaction again sets in, the free-traders are overthrown, and a protective system is again established. In not less than four distinct periods during the last fifty years has this sort of revolution taken place in our industrial system. Our great national industries have thus been tossed up and down between two extremes of opinion.

During my term of service in this House I have resisted the effort to increase the rates of duty whenever I thought an increase would be dangerous to the stability of our manufacturing interests; and, by doing so, I have sometimes been thought unfriendly to the policy of protecting American industry. When the necessity of the revenues and the safety of our manufactures warranted, I have favored a reduction of rates; and these reductions have aided to preserve the stability of the system.

The bill failed to come to a vote during this session of Congress.

In the presidential campaign of 1880 Gen. Winfield S. Hancock, the Democratic candidate, tried unsuccessfully to eliminate the tariff as a major issue, writing a letter in which he declared that "the tariff is a local issue." A great deal was made of this statement by the Republicans during the campaign.

CHAPTER XI

A TARIFF COMMISSION

[ACT OF 1882]

ON January 9, 1882, John A. Kasson [Ia.] introduced in the House a bill to appoint a commission to investigate the tariff and internal revenue. It was referred to the Committee on Ways and Means. On February 8 he reported a bill to this effect from the majority of the Committee. It came up for discussion in the Committee of the Whole on March 7.

TARIFF COMMISSION

HOUSE OF REPRESENTATIVES, MARCH 7-MAY 5, 1882

Edward K. Valentine [Neb.] raised the point of order that the bill, not being a revenue one, could, by the rules, have no precedence over others on the calendar. In this he was supported by other Representatives, among them George D. Tillman [S. C.], who said:

Mr. Speaker, instead of this being a bill to raise revenue I think it is a bill to spend revenue, yet not being a ''general appropriation'' bill it is not a privileged bill. Instead of proposing to raise funds for the Government it proposes, as I understand, to pay nine gentlemen ten dollars a day and expenses.

Another view is that instead of being a bill to raise revenue it is simply a bill to raise a commission to make suggestions to this body. It seems to me analogous to a resolution calling on one of the departments for its opinion upon certain subjects, and is therefore entitled to no precedence over other bills.

The Chairman (George D. Robinson [Mass.]) sustained the point of order. In his statement of the reason for his decision he incidentally gave a summary of the provisions of the bill.

The Chair finds on inspection of the bill, in the first instance, that it provides for a commission called the ''tariff commission''; that in the second section it gives the number of such commissioners, provides for their salaries, and the payment of such officers and assistants as may be provided. In the third section the duty of such commission is prescribed. It is to take into consideration and thoroughly investigate all the various questions relating to the agricultural, commercial, mercantile, manufacturing, mining, and industrial interests of the United States so far as the same may be necessary to the establishment of a judicious tariff, or a revision of the existing tariff; and for the purpose of fully examining the matter which may come before it such commission in the prosecution of its inquiries is empowered to visit such different portions and sections of the country as it may deem advisable. The fourth section provides that the commission shall make to Congress final report of the result of its investigation at certain times prescribed in the bill.

The bill in due order came again before the Committee of the Whole on March 28.
Mr. Kasson spoke in its support.

This proposition, Mr. Chairman, needs but very little debate. I know of very few people in the United States who admit they have no complaint to make against some part of the details of the present tariff. Whether you are free-traders or prohibitory tariff men, protective tariff men, or advocates of a tariff for revenue only, I take it for granted that you all agree that in some manner the present tariff should be reviewed and more or less modified.

For the last twenty years, subject to some slight partial modifications, this country has been conducting its business under the present tariff laws. The interests of the country have become greatly modified and in some respects radically changed in the course of these twenty years.

The free-trader denounces the whole tariff system in principle and detail, and demands revision for his destructive purposes. I may assume, then, sir, I think without dispute, that there is common consent on both sides of the House that there should be a revision of the tariff. It being admitted that a revision is necessary, the next question is as to the manner of the revision. Three methods are proposed. One of them is the ordinary method of the action of your Committee on Ways and Means reporting a bill to the House and obtaining action on that bill. The second is a proposition to combine members of the two Houses of Congress with civilian experts, and thus make a commission for the revision of your tariff; and the third mode is the selection of commissioners, civilian experts, if you please, who shall devote their whole attention to the subject, investigate the facts, the relation of one industry to another, the relation of raw material to the manifold forms of its finished product, its relation to the manufacture of the same things abroad; and, having completed that investigation, shall put it in compact and logical form, and so give us the facts upon which we shall revise and adjust the tariff. That is the third proposition, and it is the one presented by this bill. The Committee on Ways and Means, by a majority, considered the latter mode the best mode; and I think the House, upon candid consideration, will agree with them that the first mode, which involves a report simply from your Ways and Means Committee, is not the one that will bring us to union and harmony in the action of the House. Later experience is against it.

During the last three Congresses, as well as in many instances before in previous Congresses, all your efforts by the Ways and Means Committee to procure a revision and procure action upon your tariff have utterly failed and the House has accomplished nothing in the way of results. Now, sir, what is the reason of that? I think we can all perceive it. We in the Ways and Means Committee go to our work upon that subject with fixed opinions and prejudices sharpened by political contact and fastened to a great extent upon us by the articles of the platforms of the respective parties. We are always antagonizing politics with the business of the country, so that everything that we report to you is more or less colored by the allegation that it results from our party affiliations and our partisan feeling. The House divides itself in that way. And in addition to that there come up special interests that the committee has failed to get hold of. This is a great country in territorial extent and in the character of its industries. Will any member of the Ways and Means Committee rise in his place here and say he knows all of these vast industries and their relations to each other and to their foreign rivals? Is any man vain enough to say that he is master of all the labors and all the industries of this continent or even of this Union?

I affirm that politicians as we are, with here and there rare exceptions, we are not enough practically acquainted with the industrial interests of the country to be able to tell the House and to satisfy the country that we have adjusted their relations and their taxation in the right way.

When you come to detailed questions there is but one safe source of action, that is the practical knowledge of practical men. Gentlemen may ask, do we not get this in the Committee on Ways and Means by summoning witnesses? I answer yes, partially, but only partially. The richest manufacturers come to us, those who perhaps least need protection. The poorer manufacturers do not come to us. Every man who comes to us voluntarily, all the way from the seat of his own industry, which is usually limited within a certain radius from Washington—every such man comes here for the purpose of taking care of his own interest, not the interests of the whole country.

Now, what is desired above all things is that there shall be men selected who will advise in the general interests of our whole country, not those of an individual manufacturer or the manufacturers of a single article in the market. The advantage of the system proposed is that it directs the commissioners to visit the places where these industries are carried on. It gives them power to call men before them as well as to hear those who come voluntarily. They have their whole time to pursue this inquiry and to reach a result in harmony with the prosperous development of all our diversified labor.

I venture to say that not a tariff bill could be presented here by any number of men upon this floor now getting together and preparing such a bill that would not call forth complaints of the country that some interest had been omitted, injuriously affected, others destroyed, and still others unduly benefited. That would be inevitable, because the information we get in ordinary forms is partial and the result of personal interests in contradistinction to national interests.

What would you gain if, as proposed by some gentlemen, we should combine with this expert commission, so called, a representation of the Senate and the House, having three members of the House, two Senators, and four civilians? The same objections exist, because the majority of the elements of the commission would be subject to the same prejudices and the same political influences as our own committees are here, and their action would not advance us a step in the revision beyond that of the civilian commission.

An additional reason for our objection to both the first and the second methods which I have named is this: our congressional election comes off this year. How many members of this House are willing to devote their entire time from now till December next in the pursuit of these inquiries? How cool and persistent would they be in that pursuit during an exciting electoral contest involving their own political fortunes? Sir, every day of the vacation is required for the commission to reach results. Your Committee on Ways and Means devotes three hours a week to the consideration of this question.

But a commission selected from civilians would give forty-eight hours a week to its consideration, where we now give but three hours, and they would thus arrive at the result we desire vastly sooner than it could be arrived at by the Committee on Ways and Means or by a mixed commission, part of whom must absent themselves during the political contest. You cannot successfully get your work done by the first Monday in December next, except through an independent and free commission.

Gentlemen have often said to us, "Oh, you do not mean anything by this tariff commission except delay; you do not want to touch the tariff or modify it at all; you have held this policy before us for one, two, or three years for no other purpose than to shield the manufacturers against a revision of the tariff." Mr. Chairman, I take this occasion to say that this allegation does not come with the proper grace from our friends on the other side, who had it in their power in the last Congress to have allowed that bill to be taken from the Speaker's table and acted upon, as was desired by every member on this side of the House. Had that been done, then by January of this year a report would have been before you, a bill would have been prepared, and your revision of the tariff would have been now in full progress.

It must be evident that if we can do anything at all in this Congress it must be through this bill, and by the aid of a commission including neither Senators nor Representatives, but only men who can give their whole time to the subject and who can visit the seats of our great industries.

This method is not new—the method of inquiring by commission. Frequently it has been had by the House of Commons in England, by royal commission, on various subjects. Everywhere except here on this floor and at the other end of the Capitol governments recognize the advantage of consulting their own people, consulting practical business interests, before they adopt legislation that may sweep industries out of existence and convert the prosperity of the country into equally great adversity by the destruction of its vital interests.

Now, Mr. Chairman, I admit that there is one class of men who may justly protest against any delay in the revision of the tariff in order to obtain trustworthy information by a commission or otherwise. Those gentlemen who care for nothing but "revenue only" are justified in asking immediate action. If you do not care what effect your action has upon the business interests of this country, then you want no commission. You may take your tables of returns in the treasury, find how much each article has yielded under the tariff, make your estimates as to how much revenue you want, and grade your rates of duty accordingly. If, on the other hand, you believe that there is such a thing as a national system, that there is such a thing as protection, whether absolute or incidental, and that national industries are worth preserving, then you must be careful what you do; it is then your duty to consult the interests that are to be affected by your action.

Here Mr. Kasson replied at length to the general arguments for free trade. He said in conclusion:

Let others sing the theoretical beauties and blessings of free trade. Enough for me that I find the sure path which has led to the prosperity, the greatness, and the glory of my country. Lend your ears if you will to the melody of free trade, which is like the scholar's story of the music of the spheres, never yet heard by mortal sense. The American patriot will rather incline his ear to that music which is made by the blade that cuts the waving grain, by the hum of the spindle, the sharp ring of the anvil, the whistle of the plane, the crash of the great roller upon masses of iron and steel, the blow of hammers, the rush of machinery, and the whir of the railroad trains which exchange food and manufactures in an unceasing stream among our people. As fire and water, light and heat, electricity and magnetism are elemental forces producing the infinite variety and utility of nature, so do these represent the formative physical forces of our organized prosperity as a nation. This is the song of education. It means wages for the laborer, bread and clothing and education for his children, and hope for the future. It means that employment of capital which distributes its earnings among the largest number. It means diversity of national industries, which defends us against privations in war and secures our independence in peace. It means national enrichment by buying at home instead of spending abroad. It means accumulation of national wealth, which in turn flows back in a thousand channels to fertilize new enterprises, and develop new sources of wealth. It means the beneficence of boundless charity and the endowment of schools and colleges and churches. It means the progress, the prosperity, the comfort, and the happiness of a people already great, and with a yet greater destiny in the future. [Applause.]

John G. Carlisle [Ky.], of the minority on the Ways and Means Committee, replied to Mr. Kasson.

My objections to this bill do not require a discussion of its provisions in detail, for, while there are many reasons why it should not become a law, the great and controlling reason with me is that in my judgment it is the duty of Congress, in the discharge of its constitutional obligations, and in obedience to the demands of the country, to proceed immediately to revise and modify the existing tariff in the ordinary way. While the intelligent representatives of every industry in the country are almost unanimous in their complaints against the unjust and incongruous provisions of the present system, and many of them are demanding immediate relief from its hardships, it is no time to resort to measures which, however they may be intended, can produce nothing but delay and prolonged agitation to the great injury of every interest involved.

This is not a bill to facilitate the revision of the tariff. It is a bill to pay out of the public treasury about $200 per day for a period of six or seven months, to compensate and defray the traveling and other expenses of a commission to perform duties which we are sent here to perform, and which the people are paying us to perform. It is a bill to create unnecessary offices and to incur unnecessary expenses; and, worse than that, it is a bill to postpone a revision and to take the question, for a time at least, away from the forum to which the Constitution has committed it, and send it to an irresponsible roving commission whose report cannot possibly be considered and disposed of during the existence of this Congress.

MR. KASSON.—I want to ask my friend and colleague upon the committee, if this revision has been a duty demanded of Congress, and can be well done by the Committee on Ways and Means, why has it not been done by them in the last three Congresses, when men of the gentleman's views were in power?

MR. CARLISLE.—I will state in reply to the gentleman a fact very well known to him and to the whole country, that there never has been a time since this House came under the control of the Democratic party when there has not been a very large majority on this side of the House in favor of revising the tariff system; and the efforts in that direction have been defeated in every instance by an almost unanimous vote on the other side of the House, acting in conjunction with a small minority on this side. The records of Congress bear me out in this assertion.

Mr. Chairman, if this measure shall be passed it requires no gift of prophecy to foresee that there will be no revision of the tariff or any relief from its admitted hardships in particular instances for the next two or three years. All legislation must be suspended, and all consideration of the subject must be postponed until these executive appointees have informed the legislative department what its duties are, and then we are to be graciously permitted to resume our constitutional authority to determine how our own constituents shall be taxed.

What is this wandering commission to do? Is it to assume the right to fix and determine the policy of the Government with respect to the amount of revenue it will raise by the imposition of duties on imports, a question which necessarily involves the whole financial policy of the country? It is perfectly evident that it cannot possibly propose a scheme or plan for the revision of the tariff without first determining how much money ought to be raised; and it is equally evident that it cannot even approach the consideration of that question until it has determined when and how the public debt shall be paid, what the ordinary expenditures shall be, what shall be appropriated for pensions, for public buildings, for the improvement of rivers and harbors, and, in fact, occupied the whole ground embraced within the scope of congresisonal power over these great subjects. In view of the magnitude of the interests involved in the determination of the questions which are inseparably connected with the revision of our customs-revenue system, and especially in view of the favorable circumstances under which we can now enter upon the consideration of the subject, it is not extravagant or intemperate to say that the surrender of our control over it, even temporarily, would be an inexcusable dereliction of duty.

But it may be said, and has been said in substance by the gentleman from Iowa, that the proposed commission can collect evidence in relation to the condition and necessities of the various industries of the country and, without undertaking to decide what amount of revenue shall be raised, or what particular rates of duties shall be imposed, can determine what principles shall or ought to govern us in our legislation upon the subject; that is, whether we shall impose taxes for the purpose of raising revenue for the Government or simply for the purpose of increasing the profits of capital engaged in certain industries, or for both of these purposes. Here again the commission would be treading upon ground which belongs exclusively to Congress. The power to tax the people is the highest prerogative of sovereignty, and the right to determine upon what principles and for what purposes taxes shall be laid and collected—if these be open questions under the Constitution—is one which we can neither surrender nor delegate without virtually yielding the principal power itself. I do not assume that the action of the commission would absolutely bind Congress or actually deprive it of any power it now possesses over these subjects, but I do assume, what every gentleman here very well knows, that its report is expected to have, in fact, a controlling influence over our deliberations when we come finally to make a revision of the tariff. If this is not the intention and expectation, then the whole scheme is utterly devoid of any intelligent purpose except mere delay.

There is but one really substantial ground upon which this measure, or any measure of a similar character, can be justified, and that is the assumed incapacity of the majority in Congress to deal with the subject. I believe that this Congress is entirely competent to perform its duties, and I shall not abandon that opinion until a majority of its members have deliberately pronounced their judgment to the contrary. And we who have been chosen by the people, and who are directly responsible to them, are better qualified than any nine men appointed by the President, and responsible to nobody, to determine what shall be the financial policy of the Government, and upon what principles taxes shall be imposed upon our constituents. This is our right and our duty. It must come to this at last, no matter

what any commission may say or do, and, in my opinion, we
ought to commence this work at once and not leave the present
law, with all its inequalities and incongruities, to harass and
oppress the industries of the country two or three years longer.

Under this tariff the rates of duty run from less than 10
per cent. all the way up to 780 per cent.; from revenue to protection, and from protection to absolute prohibition. Considerably more than two-thirds of our annual importations are
subject to these various rates of duty, the average on all dutiable goods being, for the last fiscal year, nearly 43¼ per cent.

Let us inquire as briefly as possible whether such a system
as we now have is beneficial to the great body of the people who
are compelled to purchase and use manufactured articles, or
only a comparatively small number who have invested their capital in particular enterprises. That the prices of such articles
are generally lower now than twenty or thirty years ago is undoubtedly true, but I deny that the protective policy has brought
them down. That it has not done so, but that on the contrary
it has retarded the process of reduction in this country, is conclusively shown by the fact that the diminution of prices here
has not been so great under this system as it has been in other
countries, and especially in Great Britain, the country which is
constantly held up to us as an example of the evil effects of
what is erroneously called free trade. The very object of protection is to increase prices. If it did not have that effect it
would be of no possible advantage to the manufacturer, and he
would not want it.

We are accustomed to hear some very strange and inconsistent arguments upon this subject from the advocates of the
protective policy, arguments which no degree of skill in dia-
lectics can possibly reconcile with each other. We are assured
that the inevitable effect of a protective tariff upon an article
which is or can be produced at home is to cheapen its price, and
at the same time we are assured with equal earnestness that the
raw material should be free of duty in order to reduce its cost
to the manufacturer and to enable him to use it profitably in
his business. In brief, we are told that a duty on the raw material increases its cost to the manufacturer, but that a duty on
the manufactured article reduces its cost to the consumer.
[Laughter.] When the consumer demands a reduction of duty
he is informed that it would not reduce the price to take it off,
but when a duty is proposed to be put upon the raw material
it is immediately protested against as imposing an unjust charge
upon the manufacturer who is compelled to use it.

WILLIAM D. KELLEY [Pa.].—Will the gentleman permit me to suggest that it is raw material which cannot be or is not produced in this country to which that argument is applied?

MR. CARLISLE.—I so stated a moment ago.

MR. KELLEY.—The duty on wool as raw material operates to benefit our farmers, and counts in the *ad valorem* duty on woolen goods.

MR. CARLISLE.—The gentleman admits, then, that the duty on wool increases the price of the article. [Laughter.]

MR. KELLEY.—I think not, sir. I think it has led to so great a production that the price, notwithstanding the duty, is down.

MR. CARLISLE.—Now, Mr. Chairman, I am glad the gentleman from Pennsylvania has introduced the subject of wool and woolen goods. Whenever a proposition is made to reduce the enormous duty on woolen goods, the gentleman from Pennsylvania very well knows—no one knows better—that we are invariably met with the statement that a large part of that duty was imposed to compensate the manufacturer for the high rates on wool, which is his raw material; that is, to compensate him for a duty the effect of which, according to one part of the argument, is to reduce the price of the article he has to buy. [Laughter.]

ROSWELL G. HORR [Mich.].—Is the gentleman in favor of repealing the tariff on wool?

MR. CARLISLE.—Not entirely; but there should be a reduction. I assert that no manufacturer, no friend of the protective system, can be found, notwithstanding his constant reiteration of the argument that the duty reduces the price, who is willing to take the tariff off the finished product and leave it on the raw material. In other words, there is no gentleman to be found among them who has sufficient confidence in his theory to subject it to a practical test. [Laughter.] Notwithstanding their assertion that the imposition of a duty reduces the cost, they all want free trade in raw material, whether it be produced at home or abroad, and free trade in labor, no matter where it comes from. [Applause.]

Now, what is the true policy of legislation upon the tariff and all kindred subjects? I think that a policy which gives to all a fair chance in the great contest for wealth, and for social and political distinction, is the only one that will fully develop the material resources of the country and awaken all the energies of its people; and, more than that, it is the only policy consistent with the principles of free government.

XII—13

Mr. Chairman, it is our duty to legislate for all, and not for a part; to encourage all if we can, and to injure none if we can avoid it.   Such a course will develop every industry of the country, do justice to all its people, and demonstrate to the world the wisdom and beneficence of the free institutions under which we live.   We have now an opportunity to enter upon such a course, and we ought not to let it pass away from us. [Great applause.]

On March 30, Abram S. Hewitt [N. Y.] opposed the bill.

I take my first proposition, directly antagonizing the gentleman from Iowa.   I assert that *legislation cannot create value nor can it determine the rate of wages*.   The issue is fairly made up.   There is no source of wealth in any country except that which is derived from the soil by the application of labor, machinery, and capital.

It is not possible by any human contrivance, by any amount of abstract thought, by any schemes of legislation, to add to the natural resources of any country.   Whatever there may be is in the soil, and in the rain and sunshine that fructify it.   Capital can only support the labor which is necessary to bring about the annual harvest, and machinery can only be used to economize the amount of labor bestowed.   With labor and skill sufficient for the cultivation of the soil, the economy of production will be proportioned to the amount of capital and machinery employed in its cultivation.   There is no royal road to wealth— there is no patent process by which the resources of nature can be augmented.   "Can a man by taking thought add a cubit to his stature?"   In the absence of any legislation the work of production will proceed in a natural channel, and all that legislation can by any possibility do will be to divert labor and capital from the direction which they would have taken under natural laws.   I feel it necessary to make this statement, because many persons who have not given much reflection to this subject seem to think that there is some potency in legislation which can add value to the forces of nature.   This fallacy underlies a great many of the propositions which are made in regard to money as well as industry.   It is the key to the fiat-money delusion, and it is the explanation of the mistake which is made by those who advocate protection for the sake of protection.   When it is once realized that value cannot be created by legislative action, and is the offspring only of hard and

honest labor aided by actual capital—that is, by the possession of accumulated wealth either in the form of money, struc-
tures, materials, or machinery—most of the difficulties in the
way of intelligent legislation and of placing our industry upon
a secure basis will disappear.

But, if legislation cannot create value, it can prevent the
growth of wealth by misdirecting industry into unprofitable
channels, and by depriving us of the profit which is realized
when we exchange the products of our labor, properly applied,
for commodities which can be produced in other countries with
less expenditure of labor than is necessary to produce these
commodities at home. In other words the profits of legitimate
commerce may be altogether or partially destroyed by artificial
obstructions to the free natural interchange of commodities.
These obstructions constitute a deduction from the amount
which our producers would otherwise receive for their labor
and skill, and are therefore to be avoided, and not created by
the action of government.

From this simple statement it will be apparent that I do
not believe in the efficacy of taxation in any form as an aid to
the development of industry. If we could dispense with taxation altogether it must be evident that the producers of this
country would have more to spend and the consumers would
get more for the money which they have to expend. The only
possible effect of taxes imposed upon foreign commodities must
be to alter the direction or distribution of human effort. To
understand the bearing of this proposition we must go back
to the origin of the Government. In order to secure sufficient
revenue, duties were placed upon imports, and those imports
were selected upon which the duty could be most readily collected. The duty imposed added to the price of the article,
and hence, as this article was raised artificially in price, labor
directed to its production would be better rewarded than labor
devoted to the production of the untaxed article—assuming
always that the labor and capital in each case were not mis-
applied. In such cases the revenue duty necessarily becomes
protective, the labor devoted to the production of the protected
article being thus better paid. Thus there is a diversion from
the unprotected channels of business into the protected channels, until an equilibrium is produced between the wages paid
in both divisions of production.

The exchanges made between these divisions very soon adjust themselves upon a common standard of wages, so that
labor and capital are equally rewarded, whether employed in

the protected or the unprotected branches of business. This proposition is true of a country which has no surplus products to export, and in such a country the tax levied upon foreign imports distributes itself equally among the whole mass of the consumers. But whenever there is a great surplus of natural products to be exported the price of these products is not made at home, but in the foreign markets where they are sold, and the wages which can be paid to the laborer engaged in the production of these articles are therefore and thenceforth fixed and determined by what they produce in money, not at home, but in the foreign markets where they are sold. When the time comes that these products constitute the great bulk of the industry of the country, then it is clear that the wages which can be paid for labor are fixed abroad, and not at home; in other words, by free trade and not by protection.

Wages in this country are therefore not regulated by the tariff, because whatever wages can be earned by men engaged in the production of agricultural products, the price of which is fixed abroad, must be the rate of wages which will be paid substantially in every other branch of business. If other branches pay better, labor will quit agriculture and take to manufacture; and, *vice versa*, if agriculture pays better, manufactures will decline and agriculture will progress. Wages, like water, seek a level. Thus we dispose of the first great fallacy of the protective system, which declares that a high tariff produces high wages. The wages of labor at any given time depend upon demand and supply. They will be high when our products are all wanted; they will be low when there is a surplus which the world will not take. Our great products are agriculture. In years of famine the world will take all we have to spare; in years of plenty there will be a surplus for which there is no foreign outlet. And, in the absence of markets for our manufactured products, we are reduced to the unnatural position of basing our prosperity upon the misfortunes of mankind; when in fact the happiness and comfort of the human race ought to be proportioned to the abundance and not the scarcity of the necessities of life.

Now, by our protective system interests of a vast and complicated nature have been created, intertwining and interlacing with each other, so that any injury to one immediately reacts upon all the others. Reforms must therefore be so made as not to cripple or interfere with any considerable existing interest. The object must be not to cripple but rather to remove obstructions which interfere with the natural and healthy growth of business. We must proceed slowly so as not to interfere with the occupations of people, and not to dislocate industry to such an extent that men are compelled to seek new occupations by a sudden stoppage of those in which they are engaged. This has happened in Germany, where the new revenue system of a highly protective nature has positively destroyed many branches of business and reduced whole towns to a condition of destitution.

But, on the other hand, if reforms are not introduced we come upon another condition of affairs which is even worse than the one which we have described and desire to avoid. That condition of affairs springs from what is mistaken overproduction—that is, from the production of articles which the world wants but from whose markets we are excluded by an unnatural revenue system, shutting us up as if we were bounded by an impassable stone wall. This is the condition in which we shall find ourselves whenever by good harvests abroad we shall no longer have a foreign market for the surplus products of our farms and our plantations. In the ordinary course of nature this condition cannot be far distant, and it is for that reason that I fear the delay which will be inevitable if action upon the tariff is to be postponed until we get the report of any commission, no matter how constituted.

Although the French commissions of inquiry on the tariff simply delayed legislation for five years, and then bore no valuable fruits, against commissions I have no prejudice. In the English system of jurisprudence they do most excellent work, and they can be introduced with great advantage into many branches of our own administration, where we are suffering from the lack of a comprehensive knowledge of the facts necessary to secure reform. But now the time for a commission has passed by. The country cannot afford to wait for the results of its investigations.

This brings me to my second proposition, which is, *that access to the open markets of the world for our manufactured products is essential to the continuance of our prosperity.*

If we could consume our surplus food in the production of manufactured articles which could find an outlet in the open markets of the world, which we could sell in competition with other nations, who are not impeded by charges upon raw materials, we could at least, if no longer able to draw into our coffers the accumulations of gold and silver with which our industry has been fructified—we could at least find occupation for our working population, and gradually establish our industries upon so broad a basis that failure or superabundance of a single harvest would not affect their general stability. It is true that we cannot hope to provide remedial measures which will produce immediate results, but any improvement in the conditions for production by which our markets may be widened will moderate the impending calamity and shorten its duration.

In reforming the tariff I would select first the raw materials of industry and waste products as proper subjects to be transferred to the free list. This change will lead at once to the extension of many branches of business and the establishment of many new avenues for labor. No injury will be done to any existing interest, because on these raw products the freight is always sufficient to compensate for the difference of the rate of wages prevailing in this country and in the countries from which these products are imported. Many of these raw materials are needed for mixing with our own materials, and indeed many branches of industry cannot be successfully conducted without such admixture. Every pound of foreign material thus imported will enable an additional quantity of our own materials to be used, and in this way the market for these materials and the area for the employment of labor will be greatly and steadily enlarged. The abolition of the duty on raw materials will then enable us to make a corresponding reduction in the duties imposed on the manufactured products of which they are a component part. This reduction of duty on the manufactured product will lead to lower prices, which in their turn will produce a larger consumption, whereby the area of employment will again be enlarged. Notably in this class of reduction will be placed the manufactures of cotton, wool, iron, steel, and many chemical products. This will relieve us from the necessity for raising duties in any case, as was proposed in what is known as the McKinley bill. In the rearrangement of the tariff upon this basis, I shall be able to produce the testimony of the most intelligent manufacturers engaged in these great branches of industry that the result will be beneficial and not injurious.

The principles I have laid down can be applied without the aid of any commission. The information is already in the possession of the Committee on Ways and Means, or within the knowledge of members of this House. If the committee is disinclined to undertake the task of applying these principles, then let the Representatives in Congress assembled undertake it and constitute special committees for the work. There is no leading branch of business which is not represented in this

House. Members here know what measures of reduction can be permitted and what raw materials can be admitted free. To this work of reform both parties are committed. President Arthur in his letter of acceptance used the following language:

Such changes should be made in the present tariff system of taxation as will relieve every burdened industry and enable our artisans and manufacturers to compete successfully with those of other lands.

On the other hand, the Democrats, when they planted themselves upon a tariff for revenue only, declared through their leading men, and by every authority whose utterances are worth considering, that their only intention was to remove the obstructions to the growth of industry by making raw materials free and by establishing a rate of duty which would be just as between the producer and the consumer, protecting each at the time when each needed protection.

Now, in revising the tariff, taxation should be made to fall as far as possible upon the rich, and removed from the articles consumed by the working classes. Hence I would not tax tea, coffee, or tobacco. I would reduce the duties on common sugar, and, by the removal of duties on raw materials, cheapen clothing and all articles which are consumed by the working classes. Thus may we in a measure prepare for the great alterations which are impending and will change the face of the world from causes more powerful than any mere human devices, bringing about the time when all trade shall be free and all men shall be brothers—

When the war-drums throb no longer, and the battle-flags are furled,
In the parliament of man, the federation of the world.[1]

This transition may either be gradual and natural or, if we attempt to dam up the stream of progress, it may come by a convulsion which will shatter the very framework of society. If the change is provided for by intelligent legislation we shall begin by exporting our coarse cottons, as we did before the war; we shall extend the foreign markets for our admirable products of steel and iron in the form of labor-saving machines, and gradually supplant England in the markets of the world, with the productions which we can turn out at a less cost in labor than will be possible for her to do, after paying freights on our raw cotton and our food. The primacy of industry will be transferred gradually but steadily from the Old World to the New, and free trade will give us the markets of the world which

[1] From Tennyson's *Locksley Hall.*

are now controlled by the mother country, and this without impairing our ability to pay the higher rate of wages due to cheaper food, lower taxes, and greater personal intelligence in work.

But let us reverse the picture, and see what is likely to happen in case we delay the reforms in the tariff which are demanded by both political parties and by every consideration of public interest. If good harvests should be secured abroad we shall have a great surplus of food upon our hands and the price will fall; wages will go down with the fall in price; the reduction of wages will be restricted by strikes and lockouts; the conflicts between capital and labor will be reopened, and indeed have already begun; the prosperity of the country will be arrested; railroad transportation will fall off; new railroads will cease to be constructed; our shops will lack work; there will be a dearth of employment all over the country; the volume of immigration will fall off, and the career of expansion and general development will be brought to a disastrous conclusion.

Such a calamity ought never to come to pass, and it never will come unless this generation of men and the representatives of this generation upon this floor fail to comprehend the spirit and the warnings of the time; when capital and labor, mobilized by the discovery of new laws of force and by the progress of invention, demand and will secure the same free interchange for their products which they have already achieved for themselves; when all thoughtful men now see and know that the "glad tidings of great joy," proclaimed two thousand years ago, "of peace on earth and good-will toward men," are, after the lapse of ages, to be made a reality, through the untrammeled intercourse of men and nations with each other, bringing to naught and utterly confounding the doctrine, born of passion, prejudice, and ignorance, which regards men as natural enemies, instead of proclaiming them to be the children of the same Heavenly Father, "whose service is perfect freedom." [Great applause.]

On April 6 William McKinley [O.] spoke in favor of the commission.

While the present tariff laws need some revision, any wholesale change would be unhealthful and unwise. A large part of our industries has been built up under their fostering care; trade has conformed to them, and has been prosperous and progressive, and no genuine American interest wants them overthrown or materially disturbed. If we could secure some slight changes, conceded by all as necessary, which would endanger no existing interest in the United States, and then establish a clear and unmistakable rule of construction, to guide our customs officers in their interpretation of the law, any general revision of the tariff might well be left for many years to come.

Manufacturers, farmers, laboring men, indeed all the industrial classes in the United States, are severally and jointly interested in the maintenance of the present or a better tariff law which shall recognize in all its force the protection of American producers and American productions. Our first duty is to our own citizens.

Free trade may be suitable to Great Britain and its peculiar social and political structure, but it has no place in this Republic, where classes are unknown and where caste has long since been banished; where equality is the rule; where labor is dignified and honorable; where education and improvement are the individual striving of every citizen, no matter what may be the accident of his birth or the poverty of his early surroundings. Here the mechanic of to-day is the manufacturer of a few years hence. Under such conditions, free trade can have no abiding-place here. We know what we have done and what we can do under the policy of protection. We have had some experience with a revenue tariff, which neither inspires hope or courage or confidence. Our own history condemns the policy we oppose and is the best vindication of the policy which we advocate. It needs no other. It furnished us in part the money to prosecute the war for the Union to a successful termination; it has assisted largely in furnishing the revenue to meet our great public expenditures and diminish with unparalleled rapidity our great national debt; it has contributed in securing to us an unexampled credit; has developed the resources of the country and quickened the energies of our people; has made us what every nation should be, independent and self-reliant; it has made us industrious in peace, and secured us independence in war; and we find ourselves in the beginning of the second century of the Republic without a superior in industrial arts, without an equal in commercial prosperity, with a sound financial system, with an overflowing treasury, blessed at home and at peace with all mankind. Shall we reverse the policy which has rewarded us with such magnificent results? Shall we abandon the policy, which, pursued for twenty years, has produced such unparalleled growth and prosperity?

No, no. Let us, Mr. Chairman, pass this bill. The creation of a commission will give no alarm to business, will menace no industry in the United States. Whatever of good it brings to us on the first Monday in December next we can accept; all else we can and will reject. [Great applause.]

On April 20 James A. McKenzie [Ky.] opposed the commission.

This bill is an organic injustice. It delegates powers of a quasi-legislative character to nine civilians or experts. And, by the way, gentlemen of the House, the word expert in the last ten years has been made as odious in the American world as the Shakespearean word "occupy." It has a vague, general, indiscriminate signification that is extremely repulsive to all thinking minds.

This bill has one of two objects in view: either to secure delay in the matter of revising the tariff or to secure a revision in the interest of a high protective system.

I say to you gentlemen over on that side of the House that, if this bill becomes a law by your votes, in all conscience you ought to contribute out of your salaries enough to pay the expenses of these nine civilian experts. You were sent here to revise this tariff. You were elected to devise ways and means for carrying on this Government. If you admit your incapacity and delegate your powers and prerogatives to nine paid civilians, by every principle of common honesty known among men you ought to pay the expense yourselves. That would make an enormous difference, I take it, in the votes on that side if it were tacked on as an amendment. [Laughter.]

Amid all the screaming and howling virtue on the Republican side of this House reduction of salaries is not one of their distinguishing and peculiar characteristics. Seventy-five cents a day would be very fair pay for a man who votes for this bill. [Laughter.]

Mr. Chairman, the time has come when the people of America demand relief from this odious, this infamous protective system. We have a country too broad and too grand for such a miserable and restricted policy. It may do in France, it may do in any country of Europe whose territory is equal to only one of our great States; but for a country like ours, a country bounded on the north and the south almost by the poles of the earth, a country reaching through dozens of degrees of longitude, a country rocked and cradled in the roar of two oceans, the idea of applying a principle so protective, contracted, and proscriptive is ridiculous and unjust, and will eventually be repudiated by the American people. We cannot, as the representatives of fifty million people living under a system of government that guarantees to every man equal rights under the law, afford to foster and protect and further foist upon the people a system that is in contravention of every principle of their laws and of their civilization. [Great applause.]

On May 3 Samuel S. Cox [N. Y.] opposed appointment of the commission.

These are some of the points as I see them against the commission bill:

1. There is an immediate necessity for curtailing the Government revenues. Reason: If we do not, we must use the surplus in one of two ways:

First, in schemes of extravagance, an alternative which is not to be thought of; not alone because of the injustice of bleeding an overtaxed people for reckless wasting, but also because such wasting is corruption to every energy of the Government.

Second, to redeem the bonds. But the Government bonds are the standard security of the country. Our whole financial system (of banks of deposit, banks of issue, trust companies, savings banks, insurance companies, and general trust funds) is built on the bonds. It will be dangerous to draw away that foundation suddenly. *Ergo,* we must not pay off our national debt too fast until our financial system is changed. I know what to say when such a change is before us.

2. There is an immediate expediency in reducing taxation. Taxes stand for more than the amount of the burden represented in dollars. They enter into the cost of production; and, supposing they enter into the cost of the raw material, they make part of an initial value, which is added to at each change and sale—both by profits, interest, and expenses—until when the finished article reaches the consumer the "tax" may have been rolled up to ten times its original bulk. The industries of the country are even now having strikes and a struggle to live, and especially to take their way in the world's markets; they need immediate relief from needless taxation.

3. While it is easy to bring about a conviction that the

tariff is a very complex structure and needs experts to understand it, it is absolute folly to say that glaring abuses are not apparent to the eye of even a superficial analyst. It needs no expert testimony to prove that the duty on steel rails is a fraud. The present rate was put on when the cost of manufacturing rails was five times as great as it is to-day. The duty on copper and copper ore is an obvious swindle. We have the most productive copper mines in the world, and American copper is actually sold cheaper to Englishmen than to Americans. The duty on raw wool is a sop to the farmers which is as much a sham as the duties on wheat; American wools have ruled lower in price since the duty was on than before. The duties on wool and copper are fatal to the extension of our trade with the River Platte countries and Australia.

In a word, there are numerous cases where the slightest examination would discover the advisability of reduction or abolition of duties. Take these cases now, reduce or abolish the duties at once; and let your commission go to work too, if you wish!

4. The findings of the commission would be of no more value than the findings which may be now brought out by the opposing discussions of free-traders and protectionists in Congress. Free-trade Congressmen are of course bound to insist that one side of every tariff case is already made up—namely, the side of the people. The reasons for the abolishment of the duty are established by the universal principle. The only testimony, then, is the testimony of the defence, and it is safe to trust those interested to be at Washington in full force to present their views. [Laughter.]

My friend from Kentucky, in an interview, placed the whole matter in its proper light, with a gleam of felicitous *facetiæ*. J. Proctor Knott was asked as to his opinion of the proposed tariff commission:

"I consider the whole protective system as a cunningly devised scheme to rob Peter in order to enrich Paul, and I think the main object of this proposed commission is to convince poor Peter that he is robbed for his own good, and that he ought to feel very happy when he sees Paul growing rich at his expense. Not to put too fine a point on it, in my judgment the sole purpose of the proposed commission is to collate a batch of specious protection sophisms in the form of a 'report,' to be printed at the public expense and circulated by the million through the mail under the frank of members of Congress just in time for the next presidential campaign; and I think that will be precisely the result should the bill become a law. A very smart trick, well worthy of the sagacity of a set of sharp-sighted patriots who can see a three-cent piece farther with the naked eye than an honest farmer can the full moon through a telescope."

The men who will be on this proposed commission are already in the public mind. They create and subsidize politics. They expect their compensation.

The tariff we seek to revise is a monument of war necessity, and of subsequent treachery. It was promised to be reformed after the war when the internal taxes were reduced on home manufactures. The protectionists know that it stands on shaky ground. They would postpone its modification, because one link in the common bond which binds its selfish enactments and mutual aggrandizement once severed the whole chain falls to pieces. Hence they are anxious for changes, but do not want to begin. The commission is a convenient expedient with which to promise and not perform.

The assertion that protection makes wages high is probably the most potent defence which protectionists at this time possess. But it is an assertion purely; and it is a most preposterous assertion. So utterly bare of argument is this favorite postulate that the moment you attempt to combat it with argument the protectionist sops his ears, shuts his eyes, and opens his mouth to shout "Theory!" Logic is "theory"; reason is "theory"; to think at all is to theorize, when the question "Does protection raise wages?" is propounded. The protectionist solemnly appeals to "facts," and the "facts" put forward are unauthentic, unverified, undigested statements, which, even were they as true as truth, could not possibly prove anything at all.

The usual thing is an elaborately constructed table—figures arranged in symmetric columns; for do they not carry an air of authority? Are they not wonderfully effective even with those who do not read them? The usual thing, I observe, is an elaborate table, professedly comparing wages in England and the United States. It exhibits a low scale of wages for England and a high scale for the United States. And thus run the wonderful syllogisms:

1. Major premise: England has free trade. Minor premise: England has low wages. Conclusion: Free trade produces low wages.

2. Major premise: The United States has protection. Minor premise: The United States has high wages. Conclusion: Protection produces high wages. [Laughter.]

Really, Mr. Speaker, this sort of logic is very easy. There is no end to the propositions we might prove. Thus:

3. Major: England has a queen. Minor: England has low wages. Conclusion: Queens make wages low. [Laughter.]

4. Major: The United States is infested with snakes. Minor: The United States has high wages. Conclusion: Snakes make wages high. [Laughter.]

"But this is nonsense!" says the protectionist. "Exactly so," responds the free-trader; "as pure nonsense as the stock protection argument about wages." The thing you pretend to do is to prove that the alleged low wages of England result from free trade, and you simply assert it. You are asked to prove that the high wages which exist in the United States are the result of protection, and again you simply assert that such is the case. Why do you not carry out your pretence of reasoning? Of all the advanced countries of Europe, England pays the highest wages. Wages are higher in England than in France; higher in France than in Germany. Why do you not treat your followers to this sort of argument:

In England, free trade and high wages. In France, protection and low wages. Therefore: Free trade makes wages high, and protection makes wages low.

Now, I wish to offer here a curious bit of figuring. Suppose that the reasoning from protection premises is correct, and that the 5 per cent. of our workingmen do actually get the higher wages. The number of our working population to-day is not far from 15,000,000. Five per cent. of these gives us 750,000. Now the lowest estimate I have ever been able to make of the total tax paid by consumers on protected goods is $750,000,000 per annum. But $750,000,000 among 750,000 men would be just $1,000 apiece. Whence it would appear that we might just as well have free trade and pay the "protected" workingmen $1,000 a year for remaining idle!

It is the unprotected industries whose steadiness of profits and products enables them to pay the best and steadiest wages. When we tax expenses and not income, it is the workingman who suffers, not capitalists.

In short, the protected industries, like all other industries, take the rate of wages as they find it, and the rate obviously cannot be fixed by a demand which covers only 5 per cent. of the field. Wages are made high in this country by the 95 per cent. demand—by the unprotected grain of the West, the unprotected cotton of the South; by the wonderful bounty of nature to this fruitful land, and by the intelligent brains and cunning hands of all our people.

Now, do you not see that this tariff, which hangs as an incubus on labor in country and city, is one of the monopolies by shameless legislation, by purchased and interested nabobs?

What have you done to lighten the labors of the poor? You would keep up a great surplus by continued taxation. You make provisions dear by making transportation dear, by Bessemer steals. You would perpetuate the mean little taxes on matches and checks and keep the taxes uneconomically high on spirits and beer, by the aid of a pestilent internal system of spies and informers. You are safe while your commission sits, for your exactions continue. You fail to give relief as to the hours of labor or by removing the competition of striped scoundrels in the penitentiary. You force them into "unions," and then, with pretexts of mob and violence, with bayonet and bullet, drive them into desperation. You have legalized oil companies in a gigantic form of greed to grease the wheels of liveried coaches. You would take river fronts in great cities to increase your corporate gains. You create great overland routes and allow them to be gutted, watered, and handled so as to defy and defraud the Government which gave them land and bonds. You make them the supple instruments of heavy interest and a privileged, expensive, political banking system; you have done it by your votes; and, when the devil you have harbored turns and rends in its desperation, you stand here and ask for a commission to report to you, at the end of two years or more, some plan of relief, which will be when reported seven other devils of despair. The men who raise your products, make your cloths, roll your iron, and build your houses are entitled to a fair share of the inheritance of the earth and the blessings of government. They will have their inheritance or know "the reason why." [Cheers.]

This tariff commission will result in nothing. There will be no agreement if the two sides are represented; and, if one side only, it will be partial about any important matter. And Congress at last will simply have to inquire anew for itself.

Now, as to instructions. They will be ruled as not in order to the pending bill, except in so far as they instruct the commission. I suppose as this is not a "revenue measure," so called, the point of order on all amendments directing the Committee on Ways and Means to report a tariff measure, or in any way changing or revising it, will be ruled out. Not being able to vote for any amendment dealing in the rise and fall of wages, and taking my ideas from Silas Wright and Robert J. Walker, the great economists of 1846, I cannot vote for the unequal system of specific duties unless they be discreetly arranged so as to protect the poor man.

Protection is insectivorous. It feeds on the larger body. It is parasitic. It was said by Professor Riley, a naturalist of the Smithsonian, in a humorous illustration, that there are birds of ill omen who tear holes in cows and sheep and deposit their eggs therein. These hatch out lizards. They fatten on the animals just as protectionists fatten on agriculture. But the animal does not die at once. The lizards in time are driven off the body and buried in the ground and come forth again in the form of birds like their parents. It is the analogue of protection. It may not kill, owing to the native strength of the cow or sheep, but it is very troublesome. [Laughter.]

This clamor of protection is a croak; it is not a rational speech. It began after developing its infantile ways as a tadpole in search for worms and insects. It grew so in damp weather, in the land, that people thought it rained frogs. After a surfeit, the infant began to appear in public as a leader of fashion; he works out of his old skin deftly and swallows it, then he begins to croak again at the satisfaction of consuming part of himself. [Laughter.]

Mr. Kelley.—Will the gentleman from New York allow me a question?

Mr. Cox.—No, sir; my time is limited. I draw the line of prohibition on you.

Mr. Kelley.—I only wanted to say that the last Democratic Committee on Ways and Means could not dispose of the single subject of sugar alone during the whole Congress.

Mr. Cox.—The gentleman from Pennsylvania [Mr. Kelley] is speaking; but I do not *value* his remarks specifically. [Laughter.] In fact he is prohibited. [Laughter.]

John R. Tucker.—He is smuggling.

Mr. Cox.—He is an instance of all high tariffs. It leads to smuggling, even in debate. [Laughter.] The gentleman's policy taxes little children, babies even.

Mr. Kelley.—Not yours. [Laughter.]

Mr. Cox.—I have no doubt somebody has lost something by the fact of my not being perpetuated; but before I call attention to these taxes on the babies I desire to say that if I had a child and he did not oppose these high-tariff bounties I would disown him. [Laughter.]

The little girl cannot play with her doll, nor the boy whiz his top, nor the mother wash her offspring with soap, except at an expense of from one-third to one-half of their cost for the domestic privilege. [Laughter.] If the mother gives her child castor-oil she pours down 148 per cent. *ad valorem* [laughter]; if the child does not enjoy the dose, there is a 25 per cent.

bowl as the recipient of the contents of its tender stomach. And though she "wash it with niter and take to it much soap, yet the iniquity is marked before me, saith the Lord," for the soap is taxed 40 per centum! God help the child!

RICHARD W. TOWNSEND [Ill.].—How about candy?

MR. COX.—I am coming to that in a moment, my honey. [Great laughter.]

If she wraps the little dear in a plain bleached cotton nightshirt, it has a nightmare of 5½ cents per square yard specific [laughter]; when the child awakes in the morning fretful, she combs its little head at 35 cents *ad valorem* [laughter]; if she would amuse it, she rolls it over a Brussels carpet at 90 cents per square yard, or gives it confectionery made of refined sugar at 4 cents a pound tax, and 25 per cent. *ad valorem;* if it tears its little panties, the gentleman from Pennsylvania [Mr. Kelley] sews them up with spool-thread taxed at three-quarters of its value. [Laughter.] Why, if she used a shingle to bring the little "toddling wee thing" to its senses, as the honorable gentlemen can recall, the cost would be enhanced at the rate of 17 per cent. taxation. [Laughter.]

If the youngster has a patriotic inclination on our Fourth of July, his firecrackers are taxed as a patriotic luxury at $1 extra a box, and the bunting which furnishes the flag, though but 23 cents a pound, costs 121 per cent. extra, while the band plays on instruments taxed at 30 cents. She takes him to the menagerie to study natural history. There is the zebra, symbolic of a mixed *ad valorem* and specific [laughter], and the stately giraffe, high protection [laughter], the royal tiger, and unicorn of Holy Writ at 20 per cent. And the procession of elephants. Every one 20 per cent. True, Jumbo, for purposes not to be mentioned, is excluded by the affidavit of a consistent protectionist! but the log-chain that holds his huge legs binds the monster in protective chains! [Laughter.]

Mr. Chairman, I have come to this debate with no very sanguine hope. The commission bill will pass. We are speaking at a funeral, but it is a funeral which suggests the resurrection and the hope of liberty. America, sir, may yet pioneer the way among the nations in the cultivation and elevation of science, art, manufactures, taste, and amenities which are the result of that intellectual and moral condition that flows from unrestricted interchange, when the differences of soil, climate, production, and society will be so far obliterated that the human race will be advanced in its spiritual and loftier aspirations.

This progress commands the inner and solemn agencies that mark our own race, land, and era. The pauseless energy of steam and the fleet forces of lightning are harnessed for the triumph of liberty—liberty to the plow, the loom, and sail— liberty to dispose of one's labor, the precious pearls of which upon the brow of this century are set as crown jewels of democratic-republican exaltation of individual and national life.

Is it not time for the toilers of our time, so fruitful in progressive thought, to recognize the idea that the greatest economy and morality is to be found in freedom? If, sir, to conserve law with liberty burdens must be laid upon labor, then let it be remembered when we create taxes and tariffs that

> All that freedom's highest aim can reach,
> Is but to lay proportionate loads on each.

[Applause.]

On May 4 William R. Morrison [Ill.] opposed the bill.

The highly protected manufacturing industries do not sustain 10 per cent. of our people. Rates of wages are fixed by what is earned by nine men employed in agricultural, railroad, and other industrial pursuits, not by the one in manufactures. Changes from one employment to another for any cause often bring with them some hardships, but laboring men have the intelligence common to their fellow citizens. If wages are higher in one industry than another, protected or unprotected under like conditions, labor goes from one industry to another and thus wages are equalized in all. When labor is oppressed in the Old World its only escape is to the New, over what is too often an impassable sea. It is compelled to accept the wages offered by its taskmaster, and wages therefore are low. In this newer and better country democratic statesmanship blazed the trees to the other ocean toward which laborers find homes and profitable employment, and therefore wages are not so low. When we have no more cheap lands labor will be lower.

In protected and unprotected industries employers pay what will obtain the needed service and no more. But the gentleman from New York [Mr. Hewitt] seems to be one protected manufacturer who continued his business in the interest of labor at the expense of his own interest, and this is not the only inconsistency of which he is accused. Both politician and manufacturer, he is actually accused of abandoning the protective policy which those who accuse him say is supported by the majority of all the people.

Sir, let us all take courage, when the protective era produces a man, both legislator and manufacturer, who can be accused of devoting himself to the public interest at the expense of his own.

The opponents of revenue reform convert untruths a century old into arguments by restating them. Their first argument was based on a home market for farm products as one of protection's promised results. In 1860 we sent to foreign markets 4,153,153 bushels of wheat, and 153,252,795 bushels in 1880. The value of grain, flour, and meal exported was $23,-493,510 in 1860 and $284,126,760 in 1880, with other agricultural products in like increased proportion. The price for our surplus in foreign markets regulates the price of the entire product sold at home or abroad. Two of every three bales of cotton go to a foreign market and one-third of our wheat. Large as our harvests have grown, we must find a foreign market for a larger proportion than before the enactment of the present tariff, and each succeeding year finds us farther from the promised home market. Less than one-fifth of our population produces the manufactures which all consume. Protected or unprotected, the country can sustain less than one-fifth of its population in manufacturing for its own consumption.

At our second centennial, when our people number two hundred millions, manufactures can sustain but forty millions. The value of our agricultural export, now $730,000,000, will be then twice two thousand millions to be sold in competition with the product of the cheapest labor in the Old World, whose cheaper goods our agricultural labor is not permitted to buy in exchange for its own products.

And then, as now, the advocates of this doctrine will produce from the protective storehouse of broken promises and false pretences arguments based on the necessity of protecting our infant industries, to provide a home market for farm products.

The protectionists, who credit this tariff with all they consider good and see nothing but evil in every proposed reduction, present us with a long list of useful inventions, the alleged result of genius inspired by a tariff which puts a tax on salt for cattle and hogs and makes it free for fish, gives bounty to the manufacturer of the iron and steel in the plow, to be paid by him who holds it. Statistics are not so complete as to justify an estimate of the number of useful discoveries to be credited to the manufacturer who receives bounties and the number to be credited to those whom they pay 68 cents for a day's labor. When that list is furnished I venture the prediction that the useful inventions to be credited to highly protected manufacturers will be made up chiefly of useful inventions and methods for producing Congressional legislation, so largely as to justly entitle our tariff system to the dignity of a science, the science of winning ways.

This paternal policy now affects great solicitude for new industries. It asks us to believe it would develop new industries, or old industries in new homes, and is especially concerned about the undeveloped resources of the new South. If the South needs protection from Old England, who will protect her from the New? Who from Pennsylvania's one-hundred-year-old and long-established industries and her capital accumulated from the bounties of a century? When capital invested in manufactures ceases to be pensioned on our own people it will successfully contend for the world's commerce, depending, it may be, upon the difference in cost of one-eighth of a cent per yard or one-twentieth of a cent per pound. Then capital will avoid waste and must go to the cotton and the ore. The manufacturing industries of the country, chiefly in the older States, are nearly or quite equal to the production of what all our people can use. If it be true that manufactures to prosper or survive must be protected in our own markets, as protectionists assert, and they cannot therefore compete in the world's markets, what is to become of our old "infant industries" in Massachusetts and Pennsylvania when new "infants" are born in Georgia, Alabama, Illinois, and Iowa? Who, then, will pay for Massachusetts school-houses and the musical instruments upon which the honorable chairman [Judge Kelley] has his laboring people playing whenever he does not have them starving? The anxiety of Pennsylvania and Massachusetts to cut off their own markets in the interest of the new South is another evidence that protection quickens inventive genius and develops resources for securing Congressional legislation.

In conclusion, sir, this question in its higher aspects is not a party but a political question, affecting the distribution of property and the proceeds of labor and going back to the foundation rocks of our political system. But it is also a business question. In this view what we need is a business settlement of a business question—reasonable and practical treatment to avoid excessive changes, and we must begin at once, for our surplus revenue is becoming the great corruption fund of the age.

Wages in shops and mills are the same as in other works of like kind, or less. Wages are not the criterion of cost; it is efficiency of labor that counts. Our wages are higher; they should be; and our cost is lower because the labor is more effective. When the courage of our textile manufacturers and our iron and steel makers is equal to their skill they will demand freedom from commercial shackles and bring the world's commerce to their feet.

On May 5 William D. Kelley [Pa.] supported the bill. In conclusion he said:

Mr. Chairman, it has been said that "events are written lessons glaring in huge hieroglyphic picture-writing that all may see and know them." Let me, therefore, turn from the unseemly wrangle into which I have been forced, and from the consideration of imperfect tables, which, like cobwebs, "will hold no conclusion," and contemplate our subject in the light of events—events not of mean but of magnificent proportions. The loss by England of the commanding position in commerce and manufactures she so long maintained and the recognition of the United States as the foremost member of the family of nations are events that all will read and know. By what terrible contest of arms has this reversal of the relations of these nations been wrought! What carnage and desolation marked its progress! Sir, this is the work of peace. It has been wrought by legislation and not by war; and it illustrates the importance of gravely considering every revenue measure which can influence the productive forces of a country.

About thirty years have elapsed since Great Britain entered fully upon its present commercial system, and, throwing down the barriers of defence which secured her home market to her laborers, challenged the nations of the world to competition in manufactured goods in all its markets. The period was well chosen for the success of the experiment. The change was coincident with the discovery of the gold fields of California and Australia, which, by opening to settlement Australasia and the Pacific coast of North America, created large demands for wares and fabrics of every variety in new and highly remunerative markets. The sudden and unprecedented augmentation of the world's stock of gold caused great movements of people, great increase of production, and a great enhancement of prices. Oblivious to the relation of the increase of the supply of gold to prices and the power of people to pay for and consume commodities, and of the effect of the settlement of the rich and remote states to which I have alluded, British statesmen ascribed the wonderfully increased demand for British goods and ships exclusively to their newly applied economic theories. They deceived themselves into the belief that England was invincible and would forever remain as she then was—the workshop of the world and the mistress of the sea.

We had then recently repealed the protective tariff of 1842, and were under the free-trade Walker tariff of 1846; and, if free trade were a specific for the relief of depressed people, our share of prosperity should have been relatively commensurate with that of England. Indeed, many circumstances favored our growth and prosperity in a higher measure than that of England. The gold fields of California were ours, and she could obtain the gold we mined but by purchasing it from us. Our mercantile marine was superior to hers, and London merchants paid a shilling more per chest for tea on an American clipper ship from Hong Kong to London than they would to a British ship. The potato rot devastated the fields of Britain and much of the Continent, and opened a large market for our cereals. During the decade from 1850 to 1860 we mined $1,100,000,000 of gold; but notwithstanding this, and that ocean freight charges were in our favor and not against us, as now, 1857 found the people and the Government bankrupt. Our banks were unable to redeem their notes; our Government unable to borrow money; our laborers idle, and our merchants and manufacturers in a condition almost as deplorable as they had been in 1840, when universal insolvency forced the adoption by Congress of a bankrupt law as the only means of redeeming from mortgage the future of a generation of business men.

If England's augmented prosperity was the result of her adoption of free trade, the history of that decade shows that it did not operate as favorably in this country as it did in that, and that it is therefore not a specific of universal application. Mr. Chairman, in contemplating the history of that decade I am forced to the conclusion that the Almighty, in pursuance of His beneficent purposes, had determined to compel the American people to develop and apply to the relief of suffering mankind the resources of the virgin continent to which He had

led them; and to demonstrate to them by a series of grand
events that to accomplish this work they must defend and protect against all competitors by whatever means might be required a people's right to supply their own wants when this
could be done by the use of their own raw materials.

The protective tariff of 1842 had lifted us from the prostration to which we had been brought by the compromise tariff
of 1832. It was succeeded by Mr. Walker's revenue tariff of
1846; and now in 1857, having mined and squandered on perishable foreign commodities more than a thousand millions of
gold, we were again in the condition that 1840, 1841, and 1842
had found us, and in which we remained till the protective
tariff of 1861 went into effect.

Since then the provisions of that tariff have defended our
industries, our right to develop our resources, and, so far as
our insufficient stock of machinery would permit, to supply
our own markets. These are events the world must take heed
of. In contemplating them it will behold the gradual loss by
England of many of her markets; it will see that, to borrow
the words of M. Léon Say, her "capital account" is being
closed, and that her industry has entered on its decadence;
that her people of moderate means in all ranks of life are flock-
ing from the best portions of her farming land to better their
fortunes in the wilds of America; and that her manufacturers
are not only deserting her, but are bringing their capital, their
arts and mysteries, their machinery, and their skilled and
trusted workmen to enlarge our "capital account" and add to
the wealth and prospective power of our country.

Samuel J. Randall [Dem.], of Pennsylvania, supported the bill.

I do not favor a tariff enacted upon the ground of protection simply for the sake of protection, because I doubt the
existence of any constitutional warrant for any such construction or the grant of any such power. It would manifestly be
in the nature of class legislation, and to such legislation, favoring one class at the expense of any other, I have always been
opposed.

In my judgment this question of free trade will not arise
practically in this country during our lives, if ever, so long as
we continue to raise revenue by duties on imports, and therefore the discussion of that principle is an absolute waste of
time. The assertion that the Constitution permits the levying

of duties in favor of protection "for the sake of protection" is equally uncalled for and unnecessary. Both are alike delusory and not involved in any practical administrative policy. If brought to the test I believe neither would stand for a day. Protection for the sake of protection is prohibition pure and simple of importation, and if there be no importation there will be no duties collected, and consequently no revenue, leaving the necessary expenses of the Government to be collected by direct taxes—for internal taxes would interfere with the protective principle, and when the people were generally asked to bear the burden of heavy taxation to sustain class legislation and the interests of a portion of our people at the expense of the great bulk of our population there would be an emphatic and conclusive negative. So, too, with free trade, there is hardly a man in public life who advocates it pure and simple. Nobody wants direct taxation, although it would bring taxation so near and so constantly before the people that Congress would hesitate long before it voted the sums of money it now does, if not for improper, at least for questionable purposes.

The real question which is presented and in controversy is the revision of taxes, so we may hold the control of the markets of the world for the benefit of our excess of productions over the home consumption.

I favor what Mr. Jefferson declared to be "discriminating duties," what General Jackson described as "a judicious tariff," and what Silas Wright designated as "incidental protection." To accomplish these ends wisely and well requires the greatest circumspection and the exercise of the most careful judgment.

I favor a commission "to take into consideration and to thoroughly investigate all the various questions relating to the agricultural, commercial, mercantile, manufacturing, mining, and industrial interests of the United States, so far as the same may be necessary to the establishment of a judicious tariff."

It will, in my judgment, bring about a revision, absolutely essential, at an earlier day than in any other way now feasible. If I did not sincerely entertain this conviction, no member on this floor would be more opposed to the pending proposition than myself. I believe that the arrangement of our system of tariff duties should not rest upon any partisan policy regulated by existing parties, but that, on the contrary, it should in a measure be divorced from politics, and not be a bone of periodical contention in and out of Congress. It should occupy the higher level and command the best efforts of statesmanship of every party. Mentchikof,[1] one of the ablest as well as one of the most successful ministers of modern times, said: "Statesmanship is a practical knowledge of a state's resources."

We now really have only a choice between no action and this proposed commission. It was originally introduced into Congress by a Democrat. A bill for such a commission was passed during the last Congress by a Democratic Senate. It has again passed the Senate this year with the aid of Democratic votes. It was very generally approved upon the "stump," in my section, at least, during the recent presidential contest.

The Senate has shown at this session an indisposition to respond to any effort which might have been made in this House, for it has anticipated the House in the creation of a tariff commission by an overwhelming vote. It has been frequently charged in this debate that the object of this bill was delay. There is no justification, in my opinion, for such an assertion. Its inevitable tendency and effect must be in the nature of things to hasten a thorough and speedy final adjustment of all questions in dispute as to tariff amendment and reform.

The charge that we are improperly parting with our constitutional functions in the passage of this bill is invalid and should have no influence upon our deliberations and action.

The duties delegated to the commission do not extend beyond the power of recommendation. Yet I hope and believe their review when presented will be of so broad, comprehensive, and catholic a character as to command as a basis of action in reform of taxation the approval of thinking men of all parties.

The fourth section of the bill provides that the commission shall make its final report of the results of its investigation and the testimony taken in the course of the same not later than the first Monday of December, 1882, and it shall cause the testimony taken to be printed from time to time and distributed to members of Congress by the public printer, and shall also cause to be printed for the use of Congress 2,000 copies of its final report, together with the testimony.

Can language be more explicit to prevent delay? It means tariff revision, intelligent and just, at the earliest practical moment. I trust that after the passage of this act—of which at present there seems but little doubt—authority will be given to the Committee on Ways and Means by this House to enable

[1] Alexander Danielovitch Mentchikof (1670-1729), minister under Peter the Great, Catherine I, and Peter II.

it to assemble about the 10th day of November next, and proceed immediately to formulate a bill based upon the testimony taken, and which they will have with all other members received from time to time. Then at the opening of the session in December that committee will be ready to report forthwith its measure of relief to the House for action before the Committee on Appropriations will require the time for general appropriation bills.

Now, I might add that while I have no direct assurance of the fact, yet I am led to believe that the President will, in the composition of this commission, whether exclusively of civilians or only partially, select men who have given a lifetime to the study of the history and philosophy of tariff taxation.

It will not do for any public man to narrow his mind on such a momentous question as that which affects not only the integrity of the Government, but brightens or darkens the home of every citizen just as we shall legislate. Speculative philosophers have contrived the most fascinating forms of government, but wherever they have been subjected to the touchstone of practical operation they have gone most shamefully to pieces. It will not do for men to say, I have laid down this theoretical landmark and you must not go beyond it.

> There's a divinity that shapes our ends,
> Rough-hew them how we will.

If Canute had not moved his chair upon the seashore the incoming tide would have overwhelmed him and his weak advisers under the mighty waves of the sea.

We are no longer a few scattered, isolated colonies of three millions of people, hugging the coast from Massachusetts to Georgia. In 1880 we were a united nation of fifty millions of inhabitants, with industries of the greatest diversity, and grown to such size and power as to contest the markets of the world, and with a military prestige that has surprised and kept in awe the most warlike nations.

In the year 1903 we are told that, according to the ordinary rate of increase, we will have one hundred millions of people. Is there any human mind that can foresee all the possibilities of a free republic of such vast proportions, leading the coming century in wise legislation? Is there one so foolhardy who will stand up and say he knows all about it, and that the wondrous ways of God shall bend to his peremptory dictation? If there be, he can vote against this bill. [Great applause.]

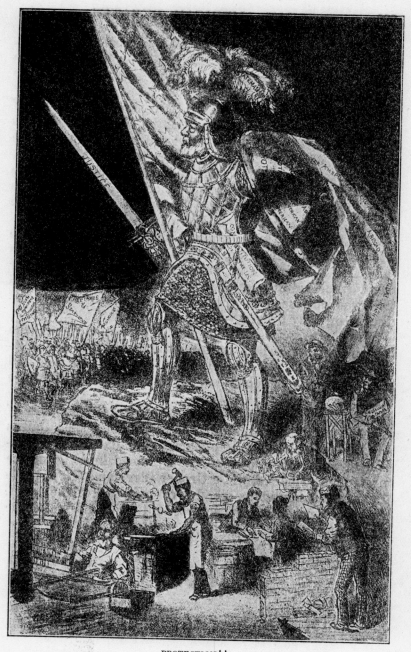

PROTECTION!!

Cartoon by Frank Beard

From the collection of the New York Public Library

219

The bill was passed on May 6 by a vote of 151 to 83. It was passed on May 9 by the Senate, by a vote of 35 to 19. President Chester A. Arthur signed the bill on May 15, 1882.

The commission reported in December, 1882. Out of this report the House Committee on Ways and Means framed and reported a tariff bill which made an average reduction of about 20 per cent. In the midst of discussion thereon the House bill reducing internal revenue came back from the Senate amended in such a way as virtually to revise the entire system of the tariff. The House adopted this bill in lieu of the tariff bill.

On March 11, 1884, a tariff bill was reported in the House by Mr. Morrison, from the Committee on Ways and Means, of which he was chairman, making a 20 per cent. "horizontal reduction" of customs duties. This bill was discussed at great length, and was finally defeated on May 9 by a vote of 159 to 155.

As the principle of "horizontal reduction" had been previously applied in revising the tariff [see the compromise tariff of 1833—chapter vi), and this new bill failed to pass, the debates upon the latter are therefore omitted.

The tariff entered into the presidential campaign of 1884 as an important, although not crucial, issue. James G. Blaine [Me.], the Republican candidate, was represented by his followers as the "plumed knight" of the protective principle, while Grover Cleveland [N. Y.], the Democratic candidate, stood for "reform" of the tariff, no less than of the civil service and other affairs of the Government.

CHAPTER XII

Reduction of the Surplus

[MILLS TARIFF BILL OF 1888]

.ssional session of 1887-88 the
.f subject of legislation. Not
.agreed as to the necessity
.was the general opinion
.e collection of revenues
.ing of this session John
.e House, had urged a
.aid in part:

.RPLUS

.taken even a partial
.w come when a re-

vision of our revenue laws and a reduction of taxation are a[bso]
lutely necessary in order to prevent a large and danger[ous]
accumulation of money in the treasury. Our effort should
to afford the necessary relief to all without injury to the i[nter]
ests of any; and it seems to me that course of legislation s[hould]
be pursued which will guarantee the laboring people o[f the]
country against the paralyzing effects of a general an[d pro]
longed financial depression, and at the same time n[ot inter]
fere with their steady employment, or deprive the[m of any]
part of the just rewards of their toil. If this can [be done,]
and I believe it can, if our deliberations are conduct[ed with]
wisdom and patriotism which the gravity of the [case de]
mands—this Congress will have cause to congr[atulate]
upon an achievement which promises peace and [benefit to]
the country for many years to come. [Loud a[pplause.]

On December 6, 1887, the third an[nual message of]
President Grover Cleveland was read. [It is rare for]
all such messages to deal with only on[e topic; this one,]
entirely on revenue reduction.

REDUCTION OF THE [TARIFF]

THIRD ANNUAL MESSAGE OF PR[ESIDENT CLEVELAND]

You are confronted at the thr[eshold of your]
duties with a condition of the nati[onal finances which im]
atively demands immediate and car[eful consideration.]

The amount of money annually [exacted, through the opera]
tion of present laws, from the in[dustries and necessities of the]
people largely exceeds the sum[necessary to meet the expenses]
of the Government.

There seems to be no [. . . that the with]
drawal from use of the pe[ople's money . . . the busi]
ness community may not[. . . and]
the same distress whic[h . . .]
same cause. And w[hile . . .]
ury should be few a[nd . . . the point]
would be reached, I b[elieve, . . . when . . .]
private business interest[s . . . legitimate pur]
poses, it idly holds mone[y withdrawn from the chan]
nels of trade, there seem[s . . . no reason why . . . some]
legitimate means shoul[d not be devised . . .]

store in an emergency, without waste or extravagance, such money to its place among the people.

If such an emergency arises there now exists no clear and

IT IS TIME TO GET THIS UNTANGLED

Grover Cleveland—"What a mess you have got this into by leaving it wound so long. There are so many snarls and knots that it will take much longer than you think to get this yarn to rights."

Cartoon by Thomas Nast

undoubted executive power of relief. There are no bonds outstanding the payment of which we have the right to insist upon.

In the present state of legislation the only pretence of any existing executive power to restore, at this time, any part of our surplus revenues to the people by its expenditure consists in the supposition that the Secretary of the Treasury may enter the market and purchase the bonds of the Government not yet due, at a rate of premium to be agreed upon. The only provision of law from which such a power could be derived is found in an appropriation bill passed a number of years ago; and it is subject to the suspicion that it was intended as temporary and limited in its application, instead of conferring a continuing discretion and authority. If it is deemed wise to lodge in the Secretary of the Treasury the authority in the present juncture to purchase bonds, it should be plainly vested, to relieve him from undue responsibility.

Our scheme of taxation, by means of which needless surplus is taken from the people and put into the public treasury, consists of a tariff or duty levied upon importations from abroad and internal revenue taxes levied upon the consumption of tobacco and spirituous and malt liquors. It must be conceded that none of the things subjected to internal-revenue taxation are, strictly speaking, necessaries; there appears to be no just complaint of this taxation by the consumers of these articles, and there seems to be nothing so well able to bear the burden without hardship to any portion of the people.

But our present tariff laws, the vicious, inequitable, and illogical source of unnecessary taxation, ought to be at once revised and amended. These laws, as their primary and plain effect, raise the price to consumers of all articles imported and subject to duty by precisely the sum paid for such duties. Thus the amount of the duty measures the tax paid by those who purchase for use these imported articles. Many of these things, however, are raised or manufactured in our own country, and the duties now levied upon foreign goods and products are called protection to these home manufactures, because they render it possible for those of our people who are manufacturers to make these taxed articles and sell them for a price equal to that demanded for the imported goods that have paid customs duty. So it happens that, while comparatively few use the imported articles, millions of our people, who never used and never saw any of the foreign products, purchase and use things of the same kind made in this country, and pay therefor nearly or quite the same enhanced price which the duty adds to the imported articles. Those who buy imports pay the duty charged thereon into the public treasury, but the great majority of our citizens who buy domestic articles of the same class pay a sum at least approximately equal to this duty to the home manufacturer. This reference to the operation of our tariff laws is not made by way of instruction, but in order that we may be constantly reminded of the manner in which they impose a burden upon those who consume domestic products as well as those who consume imported articles, and thus create a tax upon all our people.

It is not proposed to relieve the country entirely of this taxation. It must be extensively continued as the source of the Government's income; and in a readjustment of our tariff the interests of American labor engaged in manufacture should be carefully considered, as well as the preservation of our manufacturers. It may be called protection, or by any other name, but relief from the hardships and dangers of our present tariff laws should be devised with especial precaution against imperiling the existence of our manufacturing interests. But this existence should not mean a condition which, without regard to the public welfare or a national exigency, must always insure the realization of immense profits instead of moderately profitable returns. As the volume and diversity of our national activities increase, new recruits are added to those who desire a continuation of the advantages which they conceive the present system of tariff taxation directly affords them. So stubbornly have all efforts to reform the present condition been resisted by those of our fellow-citizens thus engaged that they can hardly complain of the suspicion, entertained to a certain extent, that there exists an organized combination all along the line to maintain their advantage.

It is also said that the increase in the price of domestic manufactures resulting from the present tariff is necessary in order that higher wages may be paid to our workingmen employed in manufactories than are paid for what is called the pauper labor of Europe. All will acknowledge the force of an argument which involves the welfare and liberal compensation of our laboring people. The standard of our laborers' life should not be measured by that of any other country less favored, and they are entitled to their full share of all our advantages.

The question imperatively presented for solution should be approached in a spirit higher than partisanship and considered in the light of that regard for patriotic duty which should characterize the action of those intrusted with the weal of a confiding people. But the obligation to declared party policy and principle is not wanting to urge prompt and effective action. Both of the great political parties now represented in the Government have, by repeated and authoritative declarations, condemned the condition of our laws which permits the collection from the people of unnecessary revenue, and have, in the most solemn manner, promised its correction; and neither as citizens nor partisans are our countrymen in a mood to condone the deliberate violation of these pledges.

Our progress toward a wise conclusion will not be improved by dwelling upon the theories of protection and free trade. This savors too much of bandying epithets. It is a *condition* which confronts us—not a theory. Relief from this condition may involve a slight reduction of the advantages which we award our home producers, but the entire withdrawal of such advantages should not be contemplated.

The simple and plain duty which we owe the people is to reduce taxation to the necessary expenses of an economical operation of the Government, and to restore to the business of the country the money which we hold in the treasury through the perversion of governmental powers. These things can and should be done with safety to all our industries, without danger to the opportunity for remunerative labor which our working-men need, and with benefit to them and all our people, by cheapening their means of subsistence and increasing the measure of their comforts.

I am so much impressed with the paramount importance of the subject to which this communication has thus far been devoted that I shall forego the addition of any other topic.

In accordance with the recommendation of the President in his message on January 16, 1888, Roger Q. Mills [Tex.] introduced in the House a bill to authorize the Secretary of the Treasury to purchase bonds which were not yet due, in order to reduce the surplus. It was referred to the Committee on Ways and Means, of which Mr. Mills was chairman. He reported the bill from the committee on February 14. It came forward for discussion in the Committee of the Whole on February 29, 1888.

GOVERNMENT PURCHASE OF BONDS

HOUSE OF REPRESENTATIVES, FEBRUARY 20, 1888

William McKinley [O.] declared that the bill was unnecessary.

Does any man within the sound of my voice doubt that the President had a perfect right, from the 4th day of March, 1887, aye, from the date of his inauguration down to this very hour, to have applied every dollar of the fifty-five or sixty millions in the treasury to the purchase of outstanding bonds? He had that power fixed by a law passed in a constitutional way, which passed by the unanimous vote of both Houses, which stood unassailed and unassailable, and, declining to avail himself of it, he lectures Congress because it did not provide for paying out the surplus.

I charge here to-day that the President of the United States and his Administration are solely responsible for whatever congested condition we had in the treasury and whatever alarm prevails about the finances of the country. [Applause.]

He may lecture that side of the House as much as he will. Doubtless they deserve it. [Laughter.] But he cannot avoid or evade the responsibility that rests on him. What does a man do who has got a surplus balance in the banks and has outstanding debts bearing interest? He calls in the evidences of those debts and pays them off with his surplus deposit. That is what a business man would have done. That is what a business administration would have done, and we would have had fifty millions less of interest-bearing bonds in circulation to-day if the President had followed the way blazed for him by the Republican party.

Well, now, I wonder, Mr. Chairman, if there was any ulterior motive in piling up this surplus. I wonder if it was not for the purpose of creating a condition of things in the country which would get up a scare and stampede the country against the protective system.

Well, if the President thought that he was going to get up a storm of indignation and recruit the free-trade army, break down the American system of protection, and put the free-traders on top, he has probably discovered his blunder by this time; and the best evidence of that is that he now wants the law which he has discredited; and so he comes here through his Secretary and asks us to pass this bill which is a duplicate of existing law.

Why pass it? He has got the authority now, and whatever vote we may give we give with the distinct understanding and the positive declaration that an authority just as full and just as ample exists to-day which the President and Secretary have refused to use, and no higher power will be imparted by this law when put on the statute books. But I am willing to do anything in an honorable way in aiding the Administration to get out of its dilemma and put in circulation the sixty millions of money which it has been hoarding and pay off that amount of Government debts. [Applause.]

THOMAS B. REED [Me.].—Mr. Chairman, I believe that the present financial condition of the country is a part of the conspiracy against protection. I believe that this surplus in the treasury has been accumulated with reference to its effect upon the people of the United States, so that they might without investigating, without quite understanding, clamor for something to be done, they cared not what, which would lead to the impracticable legislation to which chairman after chairman of the Committee on Ways and Means has endeavored in vain to lead the House.

⸙ Why, sir, when we came here what spectacle met us? The President with a message, a message which neglected every interest of this vast empire, which placed to one side every question except that of a tariff bill. That was pressing upon us— that and the surplus—and we must act, act instantly, and what have we done? Three months have rolled by and the Committee on Ways and Means have never spent one day upon the tariff. [Applause.]

A special message declaring that there was only one thing on earth which demanded the attention of the Congress of the United States, and that subject utterly unmentioned for three long months in the committee to which that unique message was consigned; and they call that business! [Laughter on the Republican side.]

Mr. Chairman, this method of piling up money in the treasury to affect the general business of the country, for the purpose of attacking the system of protection, deserves and will receive the reprobation of thinking men. [Applause on the Republican side.]

WILLIAM C. P. BRECKINRIDGE [Ky.].—Mr. Chairman, the condition which confronted the President and the Secretary of the Treasury on the 1st of October last was a condition for which the present Administration was in no way responsible.

The Forty-ninth Congress must take its due share of responsibility. That Congress alone had the power of providing some mode by which the revenue could be reduced, so that the bonds payable at the option of the Government might absorb the accumulating surplus. That Congress knew that before December last the Administration would have to meet that condition when the 3 per cents. would all be called, the expenditures provided for, and a surplus accumulating daily; and, thus knowing, it adjourned without action.

Surely no one will for a moment propose to keep up revenues larger than the public necessities require, unless the mode in which those revenues are raised indirectly fills his pockets

There is something in power that creates a craving for more.
If monopoly is an infant *now* and needs "protection," what will he be when he becomes of age?

Cartoon by Thomas Nast

with somebody else's money. Therefore the ready excuse of the Forty-ninth Congress for failing to pass any measure which would reduce the public revenues was that so to do would touch the private revenues of the constituents at whose will the gentlemen who refused to reduce the revenue held their commissions in this Hall. [Applause on the Democratic side.]

Now, the President, under the solemn pressure of his sense of duty, has given utterance to his honest judgment and delivered a message, which has been taken out of the mere dull sequence of official documents and caused a discussion from one end of America to the other that neither the wit of the gentleman from Maine [Mr. Reed] nor the eloquence of the gentleman from Ohio [Mr. McKinley] will cause to cease until the iniquitous protection of the present tariff has been reformed. And if the gentleman from Maine will just wait we shall have as much of a tariff bill as he is able to consider, and far more, I think, than he will be able to defeat [applause] ; a tariff bill, I hope, that will gather to its support every Democrat on the floor of this House [renewed applause] ; a tariff bill which will gather to its support all Republicans who are not given over to "strong delusion that they should believe a lie" [applause] ; that will gather to its support all the fair-minded manufacturers who only want what is just; a bill, whether wise or unwise, which will be the product of great labor and a very strong desire on the part of the committee to do what is fair and just. It will relieve the President, whether it be Mr. Cleveland or somebody else, in the next four years from the dilemma of last fall; and instead of finding surplus revenue accumulating in the treasury we will find this surplus left in the pockets of the men who make it. [Applause.]

To-day we only ask of the Congress of the United States to take more explicitly, if it has once done it, to take now, if it has never done it, the responsibility of authorizing the Secretary of the Treasury of the United States to buy the bonds of the United States, even at the premium that they now bear, and in the name of a part of the Democratic party I avow that the fact that it has to buy these bonds at a premium does not rest upon our shoulders; that we did not tie the hands of the American people by putting these bonds out of their power to pay, nor did we perpetuate the taxation which caused this unnecessary accumulation of money in the treasury. [Applause.]

The bill was passed without division. It was amended and passed without division by the Senate on April 5. A conference committee was appointed, which did not report during the session.

The long-delayed tariff bill was reported in the House by Roger Q. Mills [Tex.] from the majority (Democrats) of the Committee on Ways and Means on April

2, 1888. The bill came forward for discussion on April 17.

REDUCTION OF THE TARIFF

HOUSE OF REPRESENTATIVES, APRIL 17, 1888

Mr. Mills supported his measure.

Mr. Chairman, during our late Civil War the expenditures required by an enormous military establishment made it necessary that the burdens of taxation should be laid heavily in all directions authorized by the Constitution. The internal-revenue and direct taxes were called into requisition to supplement the revenues arising from customs, to aid the Treasury to respond to the heavy demands which were being daily made upon it. It was stated by the distinguished gentleman [Justin S. Morrill, of Vermont] who then presented to the House the bill so largely increasing the duties, and which to-day bears his honored name, that it was demanded by the exigencies of war and must cease on the return of peace. In his own words he said: "This is intended as a war measure, a temporary measure, and we must as such give it our support."

More than twenty years have elapsed since the war ended. A generation has passed away and a new generation has appeared on the stage since peace has returned to bless our common country; but these war taxes still remain; and they are heavier to-day than they were on an average during the five years of the existence of hostilities. Yet Congress lent a willing ear to the demands of wealthy corporations and individuals and took all the burden from them.

Here Mr. Mills spoke of the abolition, since the war, of various internal taxes, such as the income and corporation taxes, taxes on certain manufactures, etc.

Now, sir, what has been the result of this high-tariff policy? Enormous taxation upon the necessaries of life has been a constant drain upon the people—taxation not only to support all the expenditures of government, but taxation so contrived as to fill the pockets of a privileged class, and taking from the people $5 for private purposes for every dollar that it carries to the public treasury.

The benefits of the tariff all go one way. They go from the consumer to the manufacturer, but not from the manufacturer to the consumer. Suppose that the tax on the 60,000,000 of consumers amounts to $10 per head, then it is a tax of six hundred millions; if it is only $5 per head, it is three hundred millions taken out of the pockets of the consumer and put into the pockets of the manufacturers. The tax on the four hundred millions of goods imported goes into the public treasury; the tax levied on domestic manufactures, by raising their price, goes into the pockets of the manufacturers.

But, Mr. Chairman, it is said that this bill will injure our labor. It is said that if we reduce the tariff wages must be reduced. I deny this. Why is it that our rate of wages is higher than anywhere else in the world, that England is higher than France, and that the rate of wages is higher in France than in Germany? Germany and France both have a protective tariff to guard against the free-trade labor of England. What then is it that makes higher wages? It is coal and steam and machinery. It is these three powerful agents that multiply the product of labor and make it more valuable, and high rate of wages means low cost of product. A high rate of wages means that cheap labor has got to go; and the history of our country in the last fifty years demonstrates that as clearly and as conclusively as any mathematical problem can be demonstrated.

Mr. Chairman, Mr. Edward Atkinson, one of the clearest thinkers and writers on political economy of the present day, in his little book on "The Distribution of Products," lays down the principle that high rate of wages means low cost of product, and low rate of wages means high cost of product. He says that "the cheapest man is the one who works the greatest amount of machinery with the least stops."

Here the speaker quoted from Mr. Atkinson various statistics, showing the improvement in labor conditions in several New England manufacturing establishments since the introduction of machinery. He then spoke at length on the rate of wages paid to workers in various industries in England and the United States, and alleged that American laborers are not receiving, in proportion to the amount of work they accomplish, as much pay as the English laborers. He said in conclusion:

Now, gentlemen, the time has come, after the people of this country have been bearing for years these enormous burdens that have been levied on the necessaries of life; now, when "trusts," and "combinations," and "pools" are arising all around us to limit production, to increase prices, to make the laborer's lot harder and darker—now the time has come for us to do something, not for classes, but for the great masses of our people.

I hope and trust that the bill which we have presented to you and which has met with favor throughout the whole country will receive a majority of your votes, a majority of the votes of the Senate, and become a law. I earnestly hope when the treasury is full to overflowing of the people's hard earnings you will lighten their burden, and reduce the taxes on the necessaries of life.

Although the bill we propose is not all that we could have asked, although it is a very moderate bill, yet it will send comfort and happiness into the homes and bosoms of the poor laboring people of this country, and I ask you now in behalf of them to consider their claims and help to reduce the burdens that have so long been laid upon their shoulders.

[Enthusiastic applause on the Democratic side, and cries of "Vote!" "Vote!"]

William D. Kelley [Pa.], of the minority of the committee, replied to Mr. Mills.

The enactment of this bill would instantly paralyze the enterprise and energy of the people. Under the baleful influence of such a law the report of the census of 1890 will announce the overthrow of our manufacturing supremacy and the reduction of our commanding commercial position to that of colonial dependence. It is studiously designed to produce these dire results, and nicely adapted to its purpose. [Applause.]

None of the provisions of the bill are in harmony with the spirit of the age: for they antagonize the aspirations of the American people and are not adapted to facilitate their efforts to supply their wants, gratify their desires, and provide for the future of their families. Its first effect, should it be enacted into law, would be to arrest the magnificent development of mineral wealth, of manufacturing power, and of the diversification of agriculture now taking place throughout the South, and to paralyze the organized industries of the North.

By putting wool on the free list it would abolish sheep husbandry, destroy the immense capital embarked therein, and impoverish the more than a million men who own the flocks or are employed in their care, and by working this ruin it would diminish the supply of cheap and healthful animal food now furnished by wool-growers to the mining and manufacturing laborers of the country. It would also render the production of American tin-plates and cotton-ties impossible by placing those articles on the free list with wool.

By the transfer of these and other products of coal and iron ore to the free list, and by reducing the duties on steel rails, structural iron, and many other forms of iron and steel sufficiently to withdraw protection from them and permit foreign producers to flood our markets, it would, though it maintained existing duties on coal and iron ore, close a majority of the bituminous coal fields and ore banks which are now giving profitable employment to hundreds of thousands of laborers.

Let me now turn to President Cleveland's free-trade message. His assumption that the duty is always added to the cost, not only of imported commodities, but to the price of like commodities produced in this country, shows how profoundly ignorant he is of economic science. To illustrate the puerile absurdity of this assumption I invite the President's attention to the fact that, though the duties imposed by our Government on sugar when reduced to *ad valorem* standards were never so high as they now are, the price of sugar was never so low in this country as it now is. This condition of things is not exceptional, but is consistent with the history of the production of saccharine plants and the conversion of their juices into marketable sugar.

Here Mr. Kelley spoke at length against the reduction of the duty on sugar. He then concluded by saying:

The purity of the Government, the safety of business, and the morals of the people demand the abatement of the surplus by the repeal of the special war taxes from which it flows. If we shall fail to abolish these taxes, and, in addition to the hoarding of millions of dollars in the treasury of the United States, we also maintain a system of securities by which from seventy-five to one hundred million dollars more of our money shall be applied exclusively to the use of the whisky trust in its war upon our industries and national independence, history, when referring to the surplus and its demoralizing influence, will impute the crime that perpetuated it and the consequences with which it is fraught to the Fiftieth Congress. [Great applause.]

On April 24 Benton McMillin [Tenn.], of the majority of the committee, replied to Judge Kelley. He said in conclusion:

I have no apprehension as to who will be victor in the battle about to be waged between legitimate taxation and that oppressive taxation which is invoked to aid trusts and make pooling profitable. The people have waited long and patiently. But at last they are aroused. Their voice comes thundering through these halls demanding reduction of taxes. "Justice has had to travel with a leaden heel, but is ready to strike with an iron hand." The procession for the relief of the tax-payer is moving. There are but two places about this procession— one after it, the other under it. Seek to-day, sirs, whether you prefer to follow and aid it, or go down under it and be crushed by it. [Prolonged applause.]

Julius C. Burrows [Mich.], of the minority of the committee, then spoke. Addressing his remarks to the President's message, he said:

That the plan of the President and his party, if carried into execution, as proposed in this bill, would prove disastrous to American industries and American labor cannot be questioned. It is impossible to secure the necessary reduction of revenue by the abolition or lowering of duties without exposing our domestic industries to the most ruinous foreign competition. But the President seeks to allay public apprehension in this regard by declaring that in the execution of this plan care will be taken not to cripple or destroy our manufactures or work "loss of employment to the workingman or the lessening of his wages." As if his plan could be carried out without working such a result!

On April 25 William D. Bynum [Ind.], of the majority of the committee, spoke exhaustively, answering, one by one, the objections to the bill. In conclusion he said:

Mr. Chairman, the last and certainly the weakest argument that has been urged against the passage of the bill under discussion and in favor of higher duties upon imports is that we should increase duties so as to prohibit importations and thereby raise the price of all products, in order that we may not, in case of a sudden attack or invasion, be dependent upon

other countries for supplies. To declare that it is necessary
for us to compel one class of citizens to pay tribute to another,
in order that we may constantly be prepared for a sudden
invasion upon every side, is to declare that the great lights
which have illumined the world and inspired the hopes of
mankind for two thousand years may go out in a twinkling.
As for myself, I indulge in no such fears. Rather than dwell
in the ages of the past, clad in armor, with spear in hand, I
prefer to live in the present, and in the glorious anticipation
of a higher and grander future, when all nations shall be
banded together in one solemn compact to peaceably arbitrate
all differences. [Great applause.]

On April 30 Isidor Rayner [Md.] spoke, ending with
an appeal to his fellow Democrats to unite in support of
the bill as presented by the committee.

I am for revenue reform because I am a Democrat; not of
that sort of democracy that gathers its inspiration from the
blast furnaces of Pennsylvania or the woolen mills of New
England, but a democracy that can point to Mount Vernon's
shades and Monticello's heights and say that from the day of its
birth it has been the mortal enemy of monopoly; and when it
strikes it down, as strike it down it will, upon its ruins it will
live. Its manhood asserted, its promises fulfilled, and its honor
vindicated, it will receive under the leadership of him who
leads it now, and who, in my opinion, is as fearless a foe as
corruption ever encountered, the renewed fealty of the people;
but if it yields to the tempter's touch, if it breaks its ranks
and locks hands with the monopolists who have been gathering
their iniquitous toll for a quarter of a century at the ports of
entry of this Republic, and who are here now infesting the
avenues of legislation, then in my opinion its handwriting is
on the wall and its destiny is closed, for treachery can never
triumph and a lie can never live. [Great applause.]

William L. Wilson [W. Va.], of the majority of the
committee, spoke on May 3.

That which confronts us to-day is a condition of prolonged,
excessive taxation, of a surplus flowing into the treasury which
can be gotten out again only by using it to buy the bonds of the
Government at the market premium; of a surplus that by the
end of the present fiscal year, without such purchase, will drain

away from the channels of trade and commerce one-tenth part of all the money usually in circulation among the people.

That, sir, is the condition, and, as in the past, so now there is no statesmanship on the other side of this House that can meet it. Acknowledging an allegiance higher than that which they owe the people in framing a tariff system, they stand helpless before the great task of tariff reduction. Even in their debates here they are "many men of many minds."

We have had twenty-five years of protection in this country and the fruits of it. Proposing to be a policy for the making and maintenance of wages, it tells us nothing of the growing antagonism between labor and capital that has marked the recent history of our country; of the unsatisfactory relations between employer and employed; of the long industrial depressions; of the twenty and odd thousand strikes, and the twenty and odd hundred lockouts in our industrial establishments during the past six years alone, with the resulting loss of $60,-000,000 in wages to labor; of the building up of great wealth by favoritism, which tries to hold on to its privileges by corrupting the ballot box and intimidating voters; of the centralization of manufactures into a few great corporations, and the recent combination of these into trusts. Of all these, Mr. Chairman, we hear nothing in our discussions.

It urges the restoration of our merchant marine, which it has helped to sweep from the seas, by subsidies, that word of evil omen in a republic, contact with which has never failed to bring shame upon Congress and a stain upon our national honor.

Such, Mr. Chairman, are some of the fruits of twenty-five years of protection; such are some of the ideas with which it is educating our people; such is the career of profligate expenditure along which it is urging us in order to escape any reduction of taxes which may work a lessening of its bounties.

Here the speaker denounced the protective system as the builder of trusts. He said in conclusion:

All we can hope for the future greatness of this country hangs upon the present issue; and in the sentiment and somewhat in the words of Mr. Speaker, whoever may falter and whoever may fail, the people of the country mean that its glorious destinies shall be preserved; that they shall be transmitted unimpaired to posterity; that the country shall not belong to monopolists on the one hand or to communists on the other, but shall be, as it was designed to be, a government of the people, by the people, and for the people. [Great applause, and cries of "Vote! Vote!"]

Nelson Dingley [Me.] opposed the bill. He addressed his remarks principally to Mr. Mills' speech.

Where are the facts to support the ingenious theory of the gentleman from Texas that the American laborer receives less pay than the foreign laborer in proportion to the amount of work he accomplishes? How does he arrive at this conclusion? Why, the simple fact that so many hundreds of thousands of foreigners come to our shores to improve their condition, and that none go to Europe from this country for this purpose, is a complete demonstration that they secure better wages for the same amount of work.

Driven to the wall, the last refuge of the free-trader is in the assumption that our protective policy has nothing to do with maintaining our higher wages, but that these wages are the result solely of our cheap land and our abundant natural resources.

"Demand and supply make wages," says the gentleman from Texas. True. But the protective policy comes in to encourage and establish new industries and new opportunities for labor, and thus increases the demand and necessarily tends to raise the rate of wages, not simply in manufacturing industries, but also in every other employment within the reach of the demand for labor which they create.

The gentleman from Texas devoted much time to an attempt to show that manufacturers, and not their employees, reap the whole benefit of protective duties.

The simple answer to this allegation is that the active competition going on in all kinds of business in this country prevents manufacturers from reaping larger rewards for their investments than is obtained in other kinds of business. Statistics of dividends, furnished by Mr. Edward Atkinson, an authority which the gentleman from Texas accepts as reliable, show that the average annual profits of the manufacturing establishments of New England in the last fifteen years were only 6 per cent.

Indeed, Mr. Atkinson states that the proportion of product received by capital has been steadily declining, and that received by labor steadily increasing.

Now, the gentleman from Tennessee [Mr. McMillin] congratulated the country that "we have reached a point for the consideration of a bill looking to the reduction of the taxes on the necessaries of life." Surely there is not much reason for congratulation on this score in view of a bill which proposes to impose a "tax" of 65 per cent. on rice and 68 per cent. on sugar—two articles which by common consent are as necessary as flour in every poor man's family, and articles, too, produced to so small an extent in this country that the duty is nearly all added to the price. [Applause.]

But let us look further into this bill. It proposes to make wool, lime, manufactured lumber, wood and chemical pulp, and farm products cheaper by allowing them to be imported free of duty from other countries where the labor required to produce these materials is cheaper than here.

Mr. Chairman, what I desire to ask the distinguished chairman of the Ways and Means Committee is, if it is a good thing to avail ourselves of the manufactured lumber, the wood pulp, the lime, the wool, and the farm products supplied by the cheaper labor of other countries, and give up producing these articles here, or else bring our labor down to the foreign standard, why then is it not a good, aye, a better, thing to also allow all the more advanced manufactures which can be made abroad more cheaply by labor paid less wages than here to come in free of duty? [Applause.]

The chief reason given by the gentleman from Texas for placing on the free list these so-called "raw materials" was to thereby cheapen our manufactured products, so as to be able to better compete with European manufacturing nations in foreign markets.

The gentleman from Indiana [Mr. Bynum] seemed to think that if we only had free wool our woolen mills would at once be able to find valuable foreign markets for their goods.

Now, if with the raw material of cotton cheaper than our British competitors we have been able to export only a few goods, in which there is but a fraction of labor, how does the gentleman suppose we should be able to compete in foreign markets with woolen goods in which the labor is a much larger element?

No, Mr. Chairman, free wool would not add to our foreign markets for woolen goods so long as our labor costs so much more than does the labor of our foreign competitors. That is the sole reason why we cannot compete in foreign markets with manufactured articles into which much labor enters, except in cases of specialties which circumstances have made peculiar to this country.

Here the speaker discussed at length the question of the foreign market. He said in conclusion:

Mr. Chairman, it ought to be sufficient to deter us from hazardous experiments which look attractive in the figures of rhetoric, that under the protective policy which has prevailed for more than a quarter of a century the United States has grown so wonderfully in population, agriculture, manufactures, and all the elements which have to do with material prosperity, that even the most distinguished and most highly honored statesman of Great Britain—the peerless Gladstone—has spoken of her in debate in Parliament as the most marvelous and prosperous nation in Christendom. [Prolonged applause.]

General Joseph Wheeler [Ala.] supported the bill in a long speech which consumed parts of two days (May 4 and 5). He gave a summary of our tariff legislation from the first Congress down. Coming to the present, he dwelt particularly upon high tariffs as a basis for the formation of "trusts." He said in conclusion:

In revising the tariff, let us have laws so that we can ship our products in our own vessels, officered and manned by Americans, and we will defy every nation on the earth.

There are many things which should be done to bring about this desired end. We should reduce the tax on machinery, so that mills could be established at less expense; we should reduce the tax upon all necessaries of life; we should encourage reciprocal relations with all the nations whose trade we desire to obtain, so as to induce them to enact friendly tariff laws instead of the retaliatory measures now on the statute books of those countries, some of which were provoked by unnecessary and unwise discriminations in our laws; we should build up our merchant marine, and have American sailors upon every sea and in every foreign port. The sailors of our country are its commercial missionaries; they meet the persons who are to handle, purchase, and use our goods in their own country and at their own homes. We must have American sailors in every port to uphold and defend our merchandise.

On May 5 Richard P. Bland [Mo.] supported the bill. He replied to Mr. Burrows' speech of April 24, and then addressed his remarks particularly to the argument of protectionists that, in order to avert a financial panic, the present system must be maintained.

He continued:

The gentleman from Michigan [Mr. Burrows] took occasion the other day to criticise somewhat sarcastically the majority of the Committee on Ways and Means for the manner in which they had produced this bill. He even went so far as to say that it was a bantling without parentage. This comes with bad grace from the minority of the committee, who up to this hour have shown to the country that they are financial and tariff eunuchs, not having the virility or the manhood to present to this House a bantling of any character. [Laughter and applause on the Democratic side.]

Is it true, Mr. Chairman, that in this stage of our history we have reached a point where we have encumbered ourselves with a boomerang of tariff, a system of taxation that cannot be touched or interfered with without bringing disaster to the business interests of the country; while, on the other hand, it takes from the pockets of the people and piles up in the treasury a surplus amounting, I assert to-day, to $300,000,000 that ought not to be there? If this is true, and if this system is to be continued, sooner or later it will absorb the whole circulation of the country, reducing enormously property values, and bringing bankruptcy and general financial disaster upon the people. Is it true, I ask, that if we touch the tariff we are to be bankrupted, and if we do not touch it we are still to be bankrupted— that we are to be damned if we do and be damned if we do not? [Laughter.]

On May 10 Joseph G. Cannon [Ill.] opposed the bill. He talked particularly on the "trust" question.

Much has been said, Mr. Chairman, during this debate about trusts or combinations to limit the production and control the prices of products. It is claimed that our customs legislation is responsible for the same. These combinations are common in the country and throughout the world, and from time to time have existed for ages past. I submit, however, that the protective policy is one of the principal means of combating such organizations. Before our industries were diversified, and while we were dependent upon Europe for our manufactured products, the foreign manufacturer who wanted a good price and the importer who wanted a good profit and commis-

XII—16

sion in handling the foreign product fixed the prices as they chose, but wherever protection was sufficient to afford the home manufacturer security against the cheap labor and capital of the foreign manufacturer home manufactories have been established and home competition has cheapened the product.

The manufacturer produces side by side with the agriculturist and other producers. Exchanges of products have been made upon smaller commissions and small charges for transportation. All over the country manufacturers come in direct contact with the retailers and consumers. This does not suit the importers, especially at New York, who with our Southern brethren are the most persistent enemies of the protective system. Let it be noted that a trust or combination between the importer and the foreign manufacturer cannot be reached by legislative penalty.

Mr. Chairman, these combinations are against public policy, and the American people can and will subdue and destroy them. We can reach "trusts" formed in the United States by legislative penalty, but "trusts" of foreign growth are beyond our reach, except as we reach them by development of home industries.

Seth L. Milliken [Me.] opposed the bill. He spoke particularly of the free raw materials proposed by it.

The proposition of free raw material which the President makes, which is in every Democratic speech made in this House, and which is a continual song in the mouth of the free-trader, is about as absurd as any part of the free-trade argument. What is raw material? Nothing that has been made valuable by human labor; nothing that has been wrought or developed by the skill or muscle of man. But free-traders make their classification to suit themselves. Some place raw material at one stage of manufacture and some at another, and when an article has been wrought to the condition next to the last degree of perfection, so that they would not protect any workman except him whose labor has been applied to the last process of production, most of our free-traders cease to call it raw material.

John M. Allen [Miss.] followed. He spoke particularly upon the question of cotton.

Many of the arguments against this bill remind me of the discussion between Mr. Baps and Mr. Toots and Sir Barnet Skettles, given by Dickens in "Dombey and Son." Mr. Baps solemnly and seriously propounded the question to Mr. Toots: "What are you going to do with your raw materials when they come into your ports in return for your drain of gold?" Mr. Toots, to whom the question seemed perplexing, replied that he'd cook 'em. [Laughter and applause.]

But Mr. Baps did not seem to think this would do, and when he met Sir Barnet Skettles he propounded the same interrogatory to him. Sir Barnet had much to say upon the question and said it, but it did not appear to solve the question, for Mr. Baps retorted, "Yes, but suppose Russia stepped in with her tallows," which struck Sir Barnet almost dumb, for he could only shake his head after that and say, "Why, you must fall back on your cottons." [Laughter.]

Now, gentlemen, we have been told here upon this floor that "the tariff has made New England what it is, and is going to give you people in the South, whenever you accept all the beneficial provisions, all that great prosperity that pertains to New England." To hear these gentlemen talk you would suppose that they put the tariff upon the same ground as the plan of salvation; it is a thing you have to accept in order to get the benefit of it. [Laughter and applause on the Democratic side.]

THOMAS M. BAYNE [Pa.].—Is the price of cotton fixed at London or at Boston?

MR. ALLEN.—It is fixed at Liverpool.

MR. BAYNE.—Does not the British manufacturer treat you in the same way as the Boston manufacturer?

MR. ALLEN.—Yes; but he does not levy any tariff on us. It is the Boston man who gets the tariff, not the British man. [Applause.] If the Boston man gave us any more for our cotton than the Britisher, it would be a reasonable exchange, but he does not. [Applause.]

Now, sir, let me state that the Southern people are a people who would like to avail themselves of all the privileges that are within their reach. Gentlemen are attempting to make them out as a stubborn people, and a people who will not reach out their hands and take what is offered. When I hear the gentleman from New Hampshire and the gentleman from Ohio coming up here and making love to each other, billing and cooing, it reminds me, and if I had my voice I would give it to you in song, of the cooing of Bettina and Pippo in "The Mascot," when New England says: "I my factories love," and Ohio responds, "And I my sheep," and New England says, "When they make their biggest gobble, gobble, gobble" [great laughter], and Ohio says, "When they softly bleat, bah, bah." [Renewed laughter and applause.]

Mr. Chairman, if in the course of these few feeble and hurried remarks [laughter] I have said anything that is calculated in the least to reflect on or wound the tender sensibilities of the New England hen or the Ohio sheep, I ask pardon now, sir, and trust it will be granted. [Prolonged applause.]

William H. H. Cowles [N. C.], a Democrat, favored raising all revenues from the tariff, abolishing internal revenue. He spoke particularly against the taxes on whisky and brandy. He said in conclusion:

The people feel, sir, that all such taxes should be left to the regulation of their States respectively. They love their State governments, and more blood and treasure, including the days of the Revolution, have been spent to maintain the right of local self-government than for any other cause on this continent.

Mr. Chairman, it is not the whisky-making or the whisky-drinking element of society that I represent in this argument, but I feel that I voice the sentiment of the law-abiding, God-fearing Christian people of my country when I say, Down with the demoralizing system of internal revenue! The moral element of the land have got the true idea of this institution at last, which for so long a time—God save the mark—has run as an adjunct to morality and temperance, and their opposition will grow more and more intense as they learn more about it.

On May 16 Benjamin F. Shively [Ind.] supported the bill. He concluded his speech as follows:

Mr. Chairman, the issue is broad, plain, and distinct. The Government must have money to pay its expenses, its debts, the pensions to its soldiers. A large proportion of this money must be raised by customs taxation. Sufficient taxes must be thus collected, added to our internal revenue, to defray all the expenses of the Government economically administered. Within these limits I favor a discriminating tariff. At every point I would give American labor the benefit of the doubt, but let a measure of the regulating power of competition loose among the American combines, and compel them to allow freer raw material to our manufacturers and cheaper necessaries of life to our consumers. Reduce the surplus in the public treasury, and leave the present excess of taxes in the pockets of the people.

Opposed to all this stand the privileged combinations of the country to whom has been farmed out the power of taxation. They are arrayed in solid phalanx in favor, not of protection to infants, but monopoly for gains; not in favor of keeping up the price of what labor has to sell, but of what labor has to buy; not in favor of moderate taxation and economic government, but in favor of excessive taxation and profligate expenditures; not in favor of that fundamental principle of equal justice to all which forms the very substructure of this Republic, but in favor of the principle of special privileges to the few, which corrupts government and destroys the welfare of the many. On such an issue, and with such a cause, we confidently appeal from the clamor of greed, of privilege, and of power on this floor to the millions on the farms and in the workshops of the country, on whose shoulders at last fall the burdens of government, and in whose hearts at last rests the safety of our institutions. [Prolonged applause.]

On May 17 Samuel S. Cox [N. Y.] replied in a humorous vein to various remarks of the protectionists preceding him. He said in conclusion:

With all this country's wonderful experience and accomplishment, beyond the wildest dreams of that classic genius which pictured a new Atlantis and an ideal commonwealth beyond the Hesperian star—shall we be shackled by a wrongful constraint? Shall Economy, which ever walks white-handed along with her sister—Liberty—fail of that guiding effulgence which makes glad the heart of our people? Why should not our struggling millions aspire to a better future? Why should they lay up the treasures of their enterprises, if, indeed, the spirit of freedom be wanting? Freedom not only to work as we please, but to dispose of the product of our work as we please; freedom to spend our means where we can get the most for them; freedom to invest our means without the ignominy of enslaving statutes, and freedom to symbolize with our enstarred ensign that beauty and unity with which nature has glorified our beloved land, and to inspire other nations with the same constitutional order wherewithal that we have been made free.

> What avail the plow and sail,
> Or land or life, if freedom fail!

[Long continued applause.]

Samuel J. Randall [Pa.] spoke on May 18. He presented a substitute for the Mills bill.

The bill which I have introduced embraces a revision of the entire tariff system on principles believed to be in harmony with the last authoritative declaration of the Democratic party. The principles of this bill are as follows:

It carries to the free list many articles which enter into consumption as raw material, or otherwise, and in the production of which there is no injurious competition between this and other countries.

In fixing the tariff rates the aim has been to adjust the duties as nearly as possible to cover the difference in the cost of production in this and other countries, arising from the different conditions I have stated. This rule has been extended to all the industries embraced in our system where climate or other causes do not put us at a disadvantage in carrying on production.

In working out the details of the bill under these principles it has been my purpose to lower the duties wherever possible and reduce the revenues.

But here we come upon principles that require careful attention. Between the extremes of free trade on the one hand and a prohibitory tariff on the other there are three principles, one or the other of which must govern in levying a tariff. First, revenue only, or an even rate of duty on all imports, just high enough to yield the revenue needed to support the Government.

Second, maximum revenue; that is, a tariff that will yield the largest possible revenue.

Third, a tariff to cover the difference in cost of production in this and other countries.

The important points to consider in connection with these principles is that the line of "revenue only" falls below either of the others, and that the line of maximum revenue (which is the largest product resulting from multiplying the rate of duty on any article by the quantity imported) is always and necessarily below the line of difference in the cost of production. Consequently, to lower the rate of duty, until the line of maximum revenue is passed, must result in an increase of revenues and not a decrease. To reduce the rate from the line of maximum revenue down will result, of course, in reduced revenues. On the other hand, to raise the rate until the line of maximum revenue is reached is to increase the revenues; but, from the line of maximum revenue up, an increase in the rate of duty necessarily results in reduced revenues. To ignore these principles is to act blindly, and any computations calculated to show the results of changes in the tariff that do not take these facts into account are utterly worthless.

William McKinley [O.] followed Mr. Randall.

Mr. Chairman, there are a few striking things in this bill which the country ought to understand.

Here is a single item, steel billets. The present duty on steel billets is 45 per cent. *ad valorem.* In this bill it is increased to $11 per ton, which is equivalent to 68.33 per cent.—an advance of 45 per cent. Do you know what is made out of these steel billets? Wire fencing, which incloses the great fields of the West; and the raw material is increased 45 per cent. by this bill; and if the principle of the gentlemen who advocate the bill be true, that the duty is added to the cost, every pound of wire fencing that goes to the West will be increased from one-quarter to one-half a cent a pound; all this under a Democratic bill. What else is made out of steel billets? Nails, which everybody uses, which enter into the everyday uses of the people. The duty upon nails is reduced 25 per cent., and the raw materials is increased 45 per cent. [Laughter.] As a friend near me suggests, when one end goes up the other goes down; and the latter, I trust, will be the fate of this bill. [Laughter.]

Why, sir, the duty on wire fencing is only 45 per cent. *ad valorem,* yet the billet from which wire fencing is made must pay in this bill 63 per cent. Here [illustrating] is a piece of wire rod drawn from these steel billets, and which finally goes into fencing. That is dutiable at 45 per cent. under this bill; and the steel from which it is made is dutiable at 63 per cent. What do you think of "raw material" for manufactures? [Laughter.] No account is here taken of the labor required to draw the rods.

Then here are cotton ties, which present another queer freak in this bill. Everybody knows what cotton ties are; they are hoop iron cut into lengths just large enough to go round a bale of cotton. Now, if the Southern cotton planter wants some of this hoop iron with which to bale his cotton, he goes to the custom house at New York or Charleston and cuts off all he wants; and he does not have to pay a cent of duty; but if the farmer-constituent of my friend who sits before me [Mr. Nelson], or your farmer-constituent, want some hoop iron of precisely the same width and thickness, and goes to the custom house to get it, the Government makes him pay one cent and a half of duty upon every pound he takes, while it lets the cotton planter take his for nothing.

Gentlemen, is that fair? I appeal to Southern men who sit before me; I appeal to Northern Democrats who sit around me; is that fair upon any principle of justice or fair play? Talk about sectionalism! You raise the question in your bill; you make a sectional issue which I deeply regret, and I am sure you must upon serious reflection.

Why, what in the world, Mr. Chairman, has this bill done for the people anyhow? What has it done for the farmer? It has taken the duty practically off of everything he grows; I will not stop to give the items. It makes free practically every product of the farm, the forest, and mine.

It takes the duty off of wool. What does it give the grower in return? Everything he buys is dutiable.

Now, I shall not tax you further with the details of the bill. I might spend hours in pointing out inconsistencies. I only give these samples so that my honorable and learned friend from Kentucky [Mr. Breckinridge], who replies to me, shall take them up and explain the principle on which these rates are fixed and these duties levied.

Mr. Chairman, there is another thing which I wish to call attention to in connection with this bill, and that is the internal-revenue part of it. It seems to have escaped attention. Now, so far as the abolition of the tax on tobacco is concerned we are all in accord; but this new feature of the bill provides for the repeal of the law which authorizes the destruction of illicit stills when found in unlawful use. Under the present law if you find a man engaged in unlawful distilling, not having paid the tax or secured the license, the officer is authorized to go and destroy the whole outfit. This bill repeals that section of the law and provides that the still shall neither be mutilated nor destroyed, but preserved presumably for future violations of the law. [Laughter and applause.]

And in this bill further provision is made that, in case a man is arrested for illicit distilling, the judge is charged especially with the duty of looking well to his comfort and to his well-being while he is in the custody of the officials of the law. [Laughter on the Republican side.]

Now, Mr. Chairman, there is one leading feature of this bill which, if it stood alone, ought to defeat this entire measure; and that is the introduction of the *ad valorem* system of assessment to take the place of the specific system now generally in force.

It is a system, sir, that has been condemned by all the leading nations of the world. There is not a leading nation that adheres to any considerable extent to the *ad valorem* rates of duty upon articles imported into its borders; and England has abandoned all *ad valorem* duties except one, for the very reason that there can be no honest administration of the revenue laws so long as the value is fixed thousands of miles away from the point of production and impossible of verification at home.

The expectations of cheaper clothes is not sufficient to justify the action of the majority. This is too narrow for a national issue. Nobody, so far as I have learned, has expressed dissatisfaction with the present price of clothing. It is a political objection; it is a party slogan. Certainly nobody is unhappy over the cost of clothing except those who are amply able to pay even a higher price than is now exacted. And besides, if this bill should pass, and the effect would be (as it inevitably must be) to destroy our domestic manufactories, the era of low prices would vanish, and the foreign manufacturer would compel the American consumer to pay higher prices than he has been accustomed to pay under "the robber tariff," so called. Let us examine the matter.

[Mr. McKinley here produced a bundle containing a suit of clothes, which he opened and displayed amid great laughter and applause.]

Come now, will the gentleman from Massachusetts know his own goods? [Renewed laughter.] We recall, Mr. Chairman, that the chairman of the Committee on Ways and Means talked about the laboring man who worked for ten days at a dollar a day, and then went with his ten dollars wages to buy a suit of clothes. It is the old story. It is found in the works of Adam Smith. [Laughter and applause on the Republican side.] It is the old story, I repeat, of the man who gets a dollar a day for his wages, and having worked for the ten days goes to buy his suit of clothes. He believes he can buy it for just $10; but "the robber manufacturers" have been to Congress, and have got 100 per cent. put upon the goods in the shape of a tariff, and the suit of clothes he finds cannot be bought for $10, but he is asked $20 for it, and so he has got to go back to ten days more of sweat; ten days more of toil; ten days more of wear and tear of muscle and brain to earn the $10 to purchase the suit of clothes. Then the chairman gravely asks, Are not ten days entirely annihilated?

Now, a gentleman who read that speech or heard it was so touched by the pathetic story that he looked into it and sent me a suit of clothes identical with that described by the gentleman from Texas [Mr. Mills], and he sends me also the bill for it, and here is the entire suit, "robber tariffs and taxes and all" have been added, and the retail cost is what? Just $10. [Laughter and applause on the Republican side.] So the poor fellow does not have to go back to work ten days more to get that suit of clothes. He takes the suit with him and pays for it just $10. [Applause.]

And now, Mr. Chairman, I never knew of a gentleman engaged in this business who sold his clothes without a profit. [Laughter.] And there is the same $10 suit described by the gentleman from Texas that can be bought in the city of Boston, can be bought in Philadelphia, in New York, in Chicago, in Pittsburgh, anywhere throughout the country at $10 retail, the whole suit: coat, pants, and vest, and 40 per cent. less than it could have been bought in 1860 under your low tariff and low wages of that period. [Great applause.] It is a pity to destroy the sad picture of the gentleman from Texas which was to be used in the campaign, but the truth must be told.

Mr. Chairman, this bill points to the overthrow of the protective system; that is its tendency and mission. It puts no languishing American industry on its feet; it sets in motion no idle spindles; it starts no new fires; it creates no increased demand for labor; if an industry is down it keeps it there, its very breath is paralyzation, it injures what it touches and touches that it may injure. [Great applause.]

William C. P. Breckinridge [Ky.], of the majority of the committee, supported the bill. He replied particularly to the criticisms made against the majority of the committee.

This bill does not pretend to change a system, to set aside the present system and substitute in lieu of it another and different system. It leaves the average rates of duty higher than they were under the Morrill tariff, and it is a protective-tariff bill. The committee did not believe that it was its duty to do more than to propose a moderate reduction of taxation by increasing the free list, reducing certain rates, and removing as far as practicable unnecessary restrictions, and to make an effort to render the administration of the law more efficient to the protection of honest importers and the detection and prevention of fraud.

While it is true that reduction of rates sometimes produces increased importations, and in certain articles affected by the proposed changes this may occur, it is believed that this bill will enable the home manufacturer of woolen and other textile fabrics to so equally compete with his foreign competitor as to supply the home market with much of what is now supplied by importation, and that this will continue until the foreign goods of certain characters will be entirely driven from our market.

The changes proposed by this bill are designed to give to the farmer, by whom all provisions are raised, a market for his breadstuffs and for raw materials, which is only profitable when he has a prosperous manufacturer for a purchaser; to the laborer, the hope of a constant market; and to the manufacturer, freedom from unnecessary burdens. We have, therefore, put upon the free list, as far as we felt it was just, the materials necessary for the manufacturer. We have reduced the rates, wherever we have touched them, to a point that gives to the home consumer the hope of fair competition whenever a demand may be made by an internal trust to advance the prices beyond a fair consideration for the article to be sold, and yet we have left the rates so that the protection afforded is greater than any necessity, and makes all competition of foreign manufactures upon terms of great advantage to the American manufacturer. We do not believe there is a single instance in the bill where the duty left upon an article is not more than the difference between the cost of production in America and the cost of production abroad, plus the freight.

In the twenty-five years in which the internal-revenue system has been in force certain statutes have been found to admit of an administration which is oppressive and irritating. The committee have thought it wise to repeal so much of these statutes as were not necessary to the proper administration of the system and the collection of the revenue under it. We propose the repeal of special retail licenses, the revenues from which we do not need, which licenses we do not believe to be necessary to the administration of the law and the collection of the remaining revenues, and which are a continual source of oppression and irritation, as is shown by the fact that more than 50 per cent. of all the prosecutions in the Federal courts are for the alleged violation of those provisions of the statute which are proposed to be repealed.

Here Mr. Breckinridge spoke upon the committee's views in regard to the question of repealing the internal tax on alcohol for use in the arts. He said they had concluded that no provision could be framed that would effectually accomplish this and be at the same time just to those who paid taxes on other spirits. After discussing the relation of the tariff to the "trust" question, he said in conclusion:

The boast has been made on this floor that the chairman of the Committee on Ways and Means in the Forty-eighth and Forty-ninth Congresses—that gallant and pure gentleman, brave of heart, clean of life, loyal to friend, frank to foe, with a conscience void of offence and a love for truth that nothing could daunt [William R. Morrison]—has been stricken down because he opposed these "trusts." Greatly as I deplore his defeat and much as I miss his presence, it may be that his defeat, compassed as it was, will be of greater benefit than his presence. His very absence arrests the attention of the Republic, and all the people ask, "Are such elections necessary to the maintenance of this system?" Gentlemen protectionists, I warn you that the vacant seat of Morrison cries louder than the virtues of Duncan "against the deep damnation of his taking off." [Great applause on the Democratic side.]

Mr. Chairman, if one standing here in this hall to-day, and looking into the future, could be able to see what the years would bring us under a system where the untrammeled activities of a free Christian people find fruition, under a climate so salubrious and with a soil so fertile, all burdens to progress thrown aside, all the passions of the past removed, and everyone engaged in a generous and unselfish rivalry to make for and out of the opportunities to which he is called all that is possible, no hand could paint and no orator picture what would be the result.

Slowly will this future come. We have had our backs to it; to-day let us turn our faces to its rising sun. If we can do no more, we can lift our eyes toward this east of new hopes and resolve that from this hour our steps shall be in that direction. [Loud and long-continued applause.]

Thomas B. Reed [Me.], of the minority of the committee, spoke on May 19. He addressed his remarks particularly to Mr. Mills' speech.

People say that these tariff discussions are dull and tiresome, but there are always delightful things in them. I don't know when I have bathed my weary soul in such a reverie of bliss as I did while the Chairman, by the aid of Edward Atkinson, and the great doctrine of labor cost, was explaining that the high wages of our work people were not an obstacle, but the very reason itself why the whole circumambient atmosphere should be flooded with the pauper sunshine of Europe. [Laughter.]

The more you pay the workman the less the "labor cost." The more you give your shoemaker the less the shoes cost. The former, he explained, is the cause of the latter. Less "labor cost" is produced by higher wages. The higher the wages the lower the labor cost. No limitation, of course, was set to so divine a principle. The only limit to lowness of "labor cost" is our generosity to the laboring man. Give infinite dollars to the laboring man and things will cost nothing. [Laughter.] Surely no frantic orator on Labor Day, the session before election, ever offered to the horny-handed sons of toil such a sweet boon as the great doctrine of "labor cost."

But the pleasure given by the great doctrine of "labor cost" is soon lost in the admiration at the cool courage of what follows. Stimulated by the theory of "labor cost," the chairman ordered an investigation into the oldest manufactories in New England. What was the result? Why, constantly increasing wages and constantly decreasing cost; the two very things his side has sneered at since tariff debates were invented, higher wages for the worker and lower prices for the consumer.

What industries did he select? Cotton sheetings and cotton prints; cotton goods, the very articles, and perhaps the only articles, which have had continuous, unbroken, effective protection since 1824. He selects industries which, under all tariffs, have had sixty-four years of solid protection, shows by them higher wages for labor and lower prices for consumers, then boldly wraps the flag of labor cost about him and proclaims to a wondering world that tariff has nothing to do with wages. I wonder what Edward Atkinson thought of his new disciple at that moment.

Oh, no; tariffs have nothing to do with wages. It is coal and steam and machinery. But what set up the machinery? What caused the cotton factory to be built? Why, the tariff. So, then, the tariff built the mill, set up the machinery, the machinery increased the wages, but the tariff did not. Is not that very much like saying your father was your progenitor, but your grandfather wasn't? [Laughter.] How could you improve machinery you didn't have? How could you increase the efficiency of machinery that didn't exist?

Mr. Chairman, we have now spent twenty days on the discussion of the Mills bill. Have you noticed what has been the most utterly insignificant thing in the discussion? The most utterly insignificant thing in the discussion has been the Mills bill. How do you account for it? I will tell you. If the principles you have enunciated are true, it is an unworthy compromise with Satan. If the principles we have stated are true, it is an unworthy ambuscade, and you know it. You mean this merely for one step. You mean to cut deeper next time. You mean the destruction of the system which now exists. That is your aim and purpose.

John G. Carlisle [Ky.] followed Mr. Reed.

Although the question now presented is purely a practical one, it necessarily involves, to some extent, a discussion of the conflicting theories of taxation which have divided the people of this country ever since the organization of the Government. There is a fundamental and irreconcilable difference of opinion between those who believe that the power of taxation should be used for public purposes only, and that the burdens of taxation should be equally distributed among all the people according to their ability to bear them, and those who believe that it is the right and duty of the Government to promote certain private enterprises and increase the profits of those engaged in them by the imposition of higher rates than are necessary to raise revenue for the proper administration of public affairs; and so long as this difference exists, or at least so long as the policy of the Government is not permanently settled and acquiesced in, these conflicting opinions will continue to embarrass the representatives of the people in their efforts either to increase or reduce taxation.

The opposition to the bill has been directed mainly against that part of it which proposes to repeal or reduce the tax upon certain classes of imported goods; and gentlemen, speaking for the interests which have long ago been relieved of all the burdens imposed upon their industries, earnestly protest that the consumers of their products shall have no relief, or at least that they shall not have the full measure of relief contemplated by this bill.

It seems that our friends on the other side have at last concluded that there ought to be a reduction of the revenue, and many gentlemen who have spoken in opposition to the pending bill have foreshadowed their policy. Its main feature, in fact about its only feature as regards the tariff, is the total repeal of the duty on sugar and the payment of a bounty to the producers of that article; not to the laborer who tills the soil and converts the cane juice into sugar, but to the capitalist who owns the plantation and the refinery. After all their professions of love for the laboring man, after all their arguments to show that labor receives the benefit of the tariff, after all their harrowing descriptions of the deplorable condition to which our laboring classes would be reduced if the tariff were removed, when they come to put their propositions in the form of practical legislation the mask falls off and the natural features of the system are exposed.

Here Mr. Carlisle spoke at length against the sugar-bounty plan. He then discussed the effect of the present tariff upon the farmer. He said in conclusion:

In revising the tariff let us diminish the cost of production in our agricultural and manufacturing industries, not by diminishing the wages of labor, but by reducing taxation upon the necessaries of life and upon the materials which constitute the basis of our finished products, and by removing, as far as we can, the restrictions which embarrass our people in their efforts to exchange the fruits of their own toil which they do not need for the commodities of other countries which they do need. [Great applause, loud and prolonged.]

The bill was passed on July 21 by a vote of 162 to 149. The Senate, on the same day, referred the bill to the Committee on Finance, which reported a substitute measure on October 2.

REDUCTION OF THE TARIFF

SENATE, OCTOBER 3-4, 1888

On October 3 John Sherman [O.] explained the Senate bill. The House bill had, he said, been referred by the committee to a subcommittee consisting of four Republicans and three Democrats. The latter advocated the endorsement of the Mills bill, but the former preferred to frame a substitute, and, being in the majority, had done so. The Republicans were William B. Allison [Ia.], Nelson W. Aldrich [R. I.], John P. Jones [Nev.], and Frank Hiscock [N. Y.].

Referring to the Mills bill Senator Sherman said:

The subcommittee quickly came to the conclusion that the bill sent by the other House was not a sufficient bill to answer the purposes demanded, that it was totally inadequate, that it was not a revision of the tariff law. It was only an amendment of the tariff law. It affected only a portion of the paragraphs or schedules of the tariff law. It did not aim to be a revision of the law nor to provide machinery to carry into execution the law, but cut here and there—I was about to say at random— at the various provisions of existing law. When it came to be examined in detail, there were many incongruities in the bill, provisions that were totally inconsistent with each other, taxes levied on raw materials at a higher rate than on the finished article, and many other incongruities and uncertainties necessarily involved in the framing of the bill owing to the manner in which it was framed, however honest may have been the intention. This bill is also marked in its discriminations. Of the duties modified in the Mills bill to the injury of American production $1,200,000,000 of the competing domestic articles were grown in the North, and I believe it was but $60,000,000 that were grown in the South. So that the Mills bill is a wide and general discrimination, as we think, against Northern industries; while this bill avoids that and makes a fair and impartial reduction of revenues and a fair and impartial classification of the revenues.

Here Senator Sherman gave the details of the Senate bill. This bill prescribed the manner in which all internal and external taxes should be collected, and introduced safeguards against frauds and undervaluations. It provided a reduction of revenues to the extent of about $70,000,000. The duty on sugar was greatly reduced, and the taxes on manufactured tobacco and alcohol for use in the arts entirely removed. Duties on a few other articles, such as copper and nickel, were slightly reduced, and there was also a small addition to the free list. Wool, however, was subjected to a slight increase.

Senator Sherman said in conclusion:

I believe if this bill was taken up free from the party asperities, free from party feelings and prejudices that necessarily attend a presidential election, and if it could be considered on its merits with such amendments as might be proposed and debated and considered and adopted, after full investigation, it could be made the most perfect revenue measure ever placed upon the statute books of the United States.

On October 4 Nelson W. Aldrich [R. I.] presented the detailed report of the majority of the committee. It elaborated the arguments of Senator Sherman. A minority report followed, signed by Isham G. Harris [Tenn.], Zebulon B. Vance [N. C.], and Daniel W. Voorhees [Ind.]. It was concurred in, with modifications of some of the rates proposed, by John R. McPherson [N. J.].

This report said in part:

It is safe to say that all the interests benefited by a high protective tariff have been fully heard and have had much influence in shaping this substitute, while the great body of the people, the taxpayers and victims of this policy, have not appeared and have not been heard.

The essential difference between the House bill and the Senate substitute is apparent and radical at the outset in the matter of revenue. The one is framed in the interest of the public treasury; the other in the interest of private pockets. The one is framed in the interest of the whole people; the other in the interest of a few thousand manufacturers. The one is designed to reduce both government revenue and taxation, the taxation especially which bears heaviest on the necessaries of life; the other is intended to raise public revenue indeed, but to maintain private revenues by increasing and retaining taxation on all the necessaries of life.

Practically, the substitute offers to the people free whisky and free tobacco, leaving all the expensive machinery for the collection of the revenue and enforcement of the law in full force, while it increases taxation upon the actual and indispensable necessaries of life, and this, too, when there is a large surplus in the treasury, and under existing laws that surplus is being increased at the rate of over $10,000,000 per month; thus withdrawing and withholding from the channels of trade, com-

merce, and business of the country money absolutely necessary
to their successful operations.

James B. Beck [Ky.], of the minority of the committee, presented a separate report.

Not having seen the bill proposed by the Republican majority of the Finance Committee of the Senate until within the
last few days, I can only enter my protest against the principles presented, and give in a general way the reasons I have
for supporting the principles presented by the House bill. That
bill is an earnest effort to reduce taxation by diminishing the
cost of the raw materials used by American manufacturers, so
as to enable them to compete in the markets of the world with
their foreign competitors who produce similar goods. It proceeds upon the recognized fact that raw materials are not consumed in that form, but are necessary for the production of
commodities to which the industry of the country may be properly applied; and it is an honest effort to reduce the cost to the
American consumer of the goods which they must necessarily
have, retaining, as far as possible, such taxes as are imposed
upon articles which the people may use or not just as they
please, and the proceeds of which taxation, less the cost of collection, reach the treasury of the United States. It seeks to
promote trade with all the world, to restore and build up our
lost commercial marine, and thus exchange commodities with
other people upon somewhat fair and equal terms.

The Senate substitute, when carefully examined, will show
that in every feature it aims to increase the cost of the goods
he needs to the home consumer, and to close the markets of the
world against imports and exports as well, except such as are
purely agricultural and have to be sold abroad for any price
they will bring in free open market with foreign competition.
Under it we can have no successful commerce, no return cargoes, indeed, no ships in the foreign trade, and no sailors except such as hover around our coasts protected by the combinations and monopolies in our coastwise trade where all competition is excluded.

The pretence that the Republicans are going to aid chem-
ists, machinists, and others by giving them free alcohol is a
sudden conversion, because every report that has been made by
the Treasury Department from the time of Secretary Sherman
to the present shows that any effort to do that would simply be
the breaking down of all barriers against fraud in the collec-

tion of revenue on distilled spirits. It would, however, have the effect, which perhaps is desired by the Republican gentlemen who deny the existence of trusts, of giving the whisky trust of Peoria, Ill., the right to sell their alcohol at any price they please free from all competition at home or abroad.

Here Senator Beck presented a comparison of the principles of the Democratic and Republican parties.

DEMOCRATIC DECORATION

Only a little English grave,
But oh! so dear to them.

Cartoon by Victor Gillam in "Judge"

He spoke in praise of President Cleveland's stand upon the tariff question. In conclusion he said:

If any President ever satisfied the American people that he subordinated private ends to public interests, and had the courage to express his convictions, regardless of personal consequences, President Cleveland in this message, in his veto of the dependent pension bill, and in his enforcement of absolute integrity in the conduct of public officials, high and low, has satisfied them that he is acting with an eye single to the public good. He can say, as the Marquis of Montrose said to those who urged temporizing measures on him as the safest:

> He either fears his fate too much,
> Or his deserts are small,
> Who dares not put it to the touch,
> And win or lose it all.

The debate in the Senate repeated the arguments on the general subject of the tariff, which had been presented in the House, and entered extensively into the discussion of the schedules of the Senate bill. Owing to the fact that the presidential campaign was at its height the speakers often lost sight of the particular issue before them and entered into general indictments of the opposing party and eulogies of their own.

The session closed before the bill came to a vote. Republican success in the presidential election of 1888 killed the bill. Senator Benjamin Harrison [Ind.] was elected President.

CHAPTER XIII

The Tariff of 1890

[THE MCKINLEY BILL]

William McKinley [O.] Introduces in the House a New Revenue Bill—
Debate: in Favor, Mr. McKinley, Julius C. Burrows [Mich.], John H.
Gear [Ia.], Joseph H. Walker [Mass.], Sereno E. Payne [N. Y.], Daniel
Kerr [Ia.], Robert M. La Follette [Wis.], Nelson Dingley [Me.], David
B. Henderson [Ia.]; Opposed, Roger Q. Mills [Tex.], Benton McMillin
[Tenn.], Roswell P. Flower [N. Y.], Benjamin F. Shively [Ind.], Charles
F. Crisp [Ga.], William McAdoo [N. J.], William M. Springer [Ill.],
Amos J. Cummings [N. Y.], John M. Allen [Miss.]; Joseph McKenna
[Cal.] Opposes Free Sugar; Joseph G. Cannon [Ill.] Opposes Free
Works of Art; Mr. McKinley, Henry Cabot Lodge [Mass.], William
C. P. Breckinridge [Ky.] Defend Free Works of Art—Bill Is Enacted—
Grover Cleveland Is Re-elected President.

ON April 16, 1890, William McKinley [O.] reported
from the Committee on Ways and Means the
tariff bill which bears his name. It came forward for discussion in the Committee of the Whole on
May 7.

The McKinley Tariff Bill

House of Representatives, May 7-21, 1890

Mr. McKinley explained the measure.

In the bill which the Committee on Ways and Means have
presented we have not been compelled to abolish the internal-
revenue system that we might preserve the protective system,
which we were pledged to do in the event the abolition of the
one was essential to the preservation of the other. That was
unnecessary. [Applause.]

The bill does not amend or modify any part of the internal-
revenue taxes applicable to spirits or fermented liquors. It
abolishes all the special taxes and licenses, so called, imposed
upon the manufacture of tobacco, cigars, and snuff, and dealers

261

therein, reduces the tax upon manufactured tobacco from 8 to 4 cents per pound, and removes all restrictions now imposed upon the growers of tobacco. With these exceptions the internal-revenue laws are left undisturbed.

From this source we reduce taxation over $10,000,000, and leave with the people this direct tax which has been paid by them upon their own products through a long series of years.

The tariff part of the bill contemplates and proposes a complete revision. It not only changes the rates of duty, but modifies the general provisions of the law relating to the collection of duties.

Here Mr. McKinley went into detailed discussion of several of the modifications. Among these were the following:

1. A repeal of the provision which allows the United States to import any article for its use free of duty.

2. The value of personal effects accompanying the passenger returning from foreign travel to be limited to $500.

3. Foreign merchandise imported into the United States to be stamped with the name of the country in which such articles are manufactured.

4. All articles manufactured in whole or in part in any foreign country by convict labor to be prohibited.

Mr. McKinley continued:

By way of encouraging exportation to other countries and extending our markets, the committee have liberalized the drawbacks given upon articles or products imported from abroad and used in manufactures here for the export trade. Existing law refunds 90 per cent. of the duties collected upon foreign materials made into the finished product at home and exported abroad, while the proposed bill will refund 99 per cent. of said duties, giving to our citizens engaged in this business 9 per cent. additional encouragement, the Government only retaining 1 per cent. for the expense of handling.

We have also extended the drawback provision to apply to all articles imported which may be finished here for use in the foreign market. Heretofore this privilege was limited. This, it is believed, will effectually dispose of the arguments so often made that our tariff on raw materials, so called, confines our own producers to their own market and prevents them from entering the foreign market, and will furnish every opportunity to those of our citizens desiring it to engage in the foreign trade.

Now, the bill proposes that the American citizens may import any product he desires, manufacture it into the finished article, using in part, if necessary, in such manufacture domestic materials, and when the completed product is entered for export refunds to him within 1 per cent. of all the duty he paid upon his imported materials.

That is, we give to the capital and labor of this country substantially free trade in all foreign materials for use in the markets of the world. We do not require that the product shall be made wholly of the foreign material. Already, under special provisions of laws and regulations of the Treasury Department, the fact that parts of a finished product are made here and attached to the finished article does not deprive the exporter of his drawback.

We have extended this provision and in every way possible liberalized it, so that the domestic and foreign product can be combined and still allow to the exporter 99 per cent. upon the duty he pays upon his foreign material intended for export; which is, in effect, what free-traders and our political opponents are clamoring for, namely, free raw material for the foreign trade. And, if you are desirous of seeing what you can do in the way of entering the foreign market, here is the opportunity for you. [Applause on the Republican side.]

In the same direction we have made, by section 23, manufacturing establishments engaged in smelting or refining metals in the United States bonded warehouses, under such regulations as the Secretary of the Treasury may prescribe, and have provided that metals in any crude form, requiring smelting or refining to make them available in the arts imported into the United States to be smelted or refined and intended for export in a refined state, shall be exempt from the payment of duties. This, it is believed, will encourage smelting and refining of foreign materials in the United States and build up large industries upon the sea coast and elsewhere, which will make an increased demand for the labor of the country.

Here Mr. McKinley discussed the important changes in the rates of duty which the bill proposed. The committee, he said, had recommended increased duties upon glassware, carpets, and tinplate. He continued:

An advanced duty is placed also upon wheat and other agricultural products. Though we are the greatest wheat-producing country of the world, the increased product of other nations during the past few years has served to diminish proportionately the demand for ours; and if we will only reflect on the difference between the cost of labor in producing wheat in the United States and in competing countries we will readily perceive how near we are if we have not quite reached the danger line so far even as our own markets are concerned.

In the further interest of agriculture the committee has recommended an increase of duty in the wool schedule. It is also to be noted that having increased the duties on wools we have also increased the duties on the product—the manufactures of wool—to compensate for the increased duty on the raw product.

Now as to the free list, Mr. Chairman, we have taken from it and placed upon the dutiable list eighteen articles, ten of which are products of agriculture. If these eighteen articles are imported in the same quantities dutiable as now the revenue will be increased in the sum of $2,456,030.14.

We have taken from the dutiable list and placed upon the free list forty-four articles, which last year yielded a duty of $60,936,536, $55,975,610 from sugar alone.

Here the speaker discussed at length the question of foreign trade. He said in conclusion:

If our trade and commerce are increasing and profitable within our own borders, what advantage can come from passing it by, confessedly the best market, that we may reach the poorest by distant seas? In the foreign market the profit is divided between our own citizen and the foreigner, while with the trade and commerce among ourselves the profit is kept in our own family and increases our national wealth and promotes the welfare of the individual citizen. Yet in spite of all the croaking about foreign trade our exports were never so great as they are to-day. We send abroad what is not consumed at home, and we could do no more under any system.

And, if the United States would give the same encouragement to her merchant marine and her steamship lines as is given by other nations, her commerce on the seas under the American flag would increase and multiply. When the United States will expend from her treasury from five to six millions a year, as do France and Great Britain, to maintain their steamship lines, our ships will plow every sea in successful competition with the ships of the world. [Loud applause on the Republican side.]

Experience has demonstrated that for us and ours and for the present and the future the protective system meets our wants, our conditions, promotes the national design, and will work out our destiny better than any other.

With me this position is a deep conviction, not a theory. I believe in it and thus warmly advocate it because enveloped in it are my country's highest development and greatest prosperity; out of it come the greatest gains to the people, the greatest comforts to the masses, the widest encouragement for manly aspirations, with the largest rewards, dignifying and elevating our citizenship, upon which the safety, and purity, and permanency of our political system depend. [Long continued applause on the Republican side and cries of "Vote!" "Vote!"]

Roger Q. Mills [Tex.], of the Committee on Ways and Means, replied to Mr. McKinley. He dwelt at length on the injustice of putting sugar and hides on the free list and increasing the duties on woolens, cottons, iron and steel. He continued:

Now, I do not believe in protecting hides or anything else against competition. I am for free raw material, and I am for putting a low revenue duty on the finished product that goes to the consumer, for that is the cheapest taxation you can impose upon him. But you increase the duty on wool, and you take camel's hair off the free list and put it upon the dutiable list, and you do that because you say it displaces a certain amount of wool, and you put the duty on to check its importation. You increase the duty on wool in order to develop the shoddy industries of the country, and judging from the price you put upon wool and woolen goods in the judgment of the Republican party to wear a piece of woolen goods is a crime in this country. [Laughter.]

Now the committee are greatly alarmed about our wheat growers. That great industry is imperiled by "a most damaging competition." They have increased the duty on wheat and that great product is safe. How many bushels of wheat are imported into this country? Last year we exported 90,000,000 bushels and imported the inconsiderable amount of 1,946 bushels of wheat. [Laughter and applause.] And that duty has been put on to protect American farmers against the damaging foreign competition.

And what do you suppose that wheat was imported for? It was seed wheat, imported by the wheat grower of the West to improve his seed. And you have made it cost him that much more to improve his agricultural product so that he can raise a better character of wheat and better compete in the markets of the world, where he has to meet all comers in free competition.

We exported 69,000,000 bushels of corn last year and we imported into this country 2,388 bushels, an amount, we are told, that imperils the market of those who raise 2,000,000,000 bushels. [Laughter.]

How much rye did we import last year? Sixteen bushels! [Laughter and applause on the Democratic side.] It could all have been raised on a turnip patch. [Renewed laughter.]

Mr. Chairman, why have we not the prices of 1881? Because we have cut off importation from our European customers, and they have cut off importation from us. Our surplus is increasing with our population, and we have no markets to consume it. What ought we to do?

We should reduce the duties on imports, put all raw materials on the free list, increase our importation four or five hundred millions or more if we could, and thus increase our exports to that extent. That would raise the prices of agricultural products and the aggregate value of our annual crops $1,500,000,000 or $2,000,000,000 per year. That would distribute a large amount of wealth that would be expended in the employment of labor, and thus unbounded prosperity would be brought to the whole country.

Instead of this the committee have prepared a bill increasing taxes, raising duties, restricting importations, shutting in our farm products and decreasing prices. They are going in the opposite direction and struggling to intensify the distress of the country.

My friend from Ohio [Mr. McKinley] is alarmed at the importations from Canada. He showed the rapid increase of imports from Canada during the reciprocity treaty [1854-1856]. But it escaped his mind that exports also increased during that time, and when the treaty expired and imports fell off the exports fell off, too. If his bill shall check imports from Canada, he will also check the exports of many of our people.

Now, Mr. Chairman, my friends on the other side have discovered something new to tell to the manufacturers and to the working people. They say "We propose to give you a drawback on everything, except to the extent of 1 per cent., which will cover the cost to the Government; we will let you make your importations of materials, and when you send out your manufactured articles you can withdraw from the treasury the duty that you advanced on the materials.'' That looks all right, but let us see whether it is so or not.

A few months ago, while in the State of Massachusetts, I went into one of the largest manufacturing mills, I suppose, in that old commonwealth; it was located at Lawrence. I saw there a hall larger, I think, than this, containing a large number of mills which had been imported from England. I asked the gentleman in charge what those mills had cost. My recollection is that he said $800 apiece. I asked him what was the life of one of those mills. I think he said eight or nine years. The duty was 45 per cent. on every mill.

HOW WE TREAT OUR GUESTS

Anxious to Trade Behind the Wall of Protection, but Not Willing to Deal with the Rest of the World

Cartoon by D. McCarthy in the "New York Herald".

Now, I want somebody to tell me whether a manufacturer in Massachusetts, if he had everything else free, could import his mills from England, paying 45 per cent. duty, and then manufacture goods in competition with anybody outside of the United States? Do not gentlemen know—of course they do—that in the markets of the world a difference of half a cent on the unit of quantity is sufficient to turn the scales? A man who can offer goods at half a cent less on a pound or a yard or a dozen of anything than his competitor takes the market and holds it. If we import coal we must pay a tax upon it, while the Englishman, the Frenchman, and the German get their coal free. There cannot be any rebate on the coal; the coal is consumed in generating the steam that drives the machinery, and, like the tax on the machinery, cannot be reëxported; and the cost must be charged up to the consumer in the product.

The case is the same with the oil that lubricates the machinery. And thousands of gallons are used in manufacture.

Now, what about this sugar-bounty plan? Why have you started this demoralizing and vicious policy?

You are going to give bounties on steamships, too. My friend from Ohio spoke most eloquently in advocacy of this plan. He said we ought to check importations, obstruct foreign trade; that it is demoralizing our labor; that we ought to build up home markets and home trade; and yet he maintains that we ought to have a bounty on American ships, so as to put our flag on the sea and increase our foreign commerce. [Applause on the Democratic side.] Mr. Chairman, I do not want to bribe anybody to put an old hulk on the ocean. [Laughter.] I do not want to hire anybody to display our flag somewhere in the world. [Applause on the Democratic side.] When that proud emblem of our country goes to the uttermost parts of the earth, on all the seas and among all the nationalities and tongues of the globe, I want to see it riding as free as the air and as fearless as the eagle that nestles in its folds, the symbol of the proudest and the freest people in the world, a people whose liberty and genius and spirit have enabled them to carry their commerce wherever they please. [Applause.]

Mr. Chairman, we promise our friends that we will examine their bill; we will discuss some of its provisions, for they intend to cut off our debate and prevent us from discussing all of them. It needs discussion, and will get whatever we are permitted to give it; and then when we have done that you will pass it. We will content ourselves by giving our votes against it, and, when you leave this House and Senate with this enormous load of guilt upon your heads and appear before the great tribunal for trial, may "the Lord have mercy on your souls." [Great applause and cries of "Vote!" "Vote!" on the Democratic side.]

On May 8 Julius C. Burrows [Mich.], of the Committee on Ways and Means, spoke in favor of the bill. Reversing the famous epigram of President Cleveland in his tariff message of 1887, he said: "It is a theory and not a condition that confronts us."

In addition to the specific criticisms of the various provisions of this measure we shall be confronted with the usual objections to the whole theory upon which it is framed and there will be no end of denunciation of the protective system as a whole, and all the ills flesh is heir to will be charged to this policy.

It will be reasserted with increased emphasis that the imposition of a duty on imports is a tax paid by the consumer and that the effect of such imposition is not only to raise the price of the foreign article, but to advance the price of the domestic article in an equal degree. While this is true of a strictly revenue tariff raised on articles not produced in this country, yet it is not true when the duty is levied on articles the like of which are manufactured at home in sufficient quantities to meet the home demand.

Without entering into particulars I challenge any man to name a single article on which a duty is imposed, under which the production of such article has grown to the extent, or nearly so, of the home demand, that the price of such article, if competition is not interfered with, has not been materially reduced to the consumer. This results from the inexorable law of supply and demand.

Benton McMillin [Tenn.], of the Committee on Ways and Means, replied to Mr. Burrows.

The gentleman began his speech with the announcement that "It is a theory, and not a condition, that confronts us." He seems to be anxious to put himself in antagonism to one of the greatest men of this country, and has done it in that way. I invite him to call in his eloquence and bestow a little of his thought to home affairs. What is the condition there? There are 47,720 farms in Michigan on which are mortgages, and only

43,079 that are not mortgaged. Is that a "condition" or a "theory" that confronts the gentleman at home? [Applause.]

When these words were spoken in reversed order by President Cleveland, they applied to an overflowing treasury obtained by excessive taxation, which he was trying to induce Congress to remedy. But since that the Republican party has come into power. It has diminished the surplus and is proposing to get rid of the balance. This play on President Cleveland's words is probably a delicate and unique way the gentleman from Michigan has of telling the House his party has squandered the "condition" and left the taxpayer nothing but "theory."

It would seem when there is a surplus flowing into the treasury there could be no diversity of opinion as to what should be done; that, when the people are being taxed beyond the needs of economic government, wisdom of statesmanship and purity of patriotism would alike suggest reduction in taxation. That is our condition to-day.

Roswell P. Flower [N. Y.], of the Committee on Ways and Means, discussed minor features of the bill. The bounty principle, he said, if applicable to sugar was equally applicable to tinplate and all other articles more cheaply produced abroad than here. The increased duties on leaf tobacco would tend to drive cigarmakers to Cuba and elsewhere. The tax, he said, was an unwarranted interference of the Government with the tastes, aptitudes, and occupations of the people.

It will throw many persons out of employment and sacrifice large interests to the greed of a few growers of a kind of tobacco that consumers do not desire to purchase, and it is extremely doubtful if it will result in a benefit to even this small class of the people.

Benjamin F. Shively [Ind.] opposed the bill.

In good faith this should be entitled a pension bill. Its only purpose and effect is to pension off its beneficiaries on the rest of the community. The sugar planter is pensioned directly from the public treasury, and the wire, twine, tinplate, and other select industries are armed with the taxing power of the Government to secure domestic monopoly and pension themselves out of the pockets of the people. The pension is not for

wounds received in battle, nor for disability contracted in the
line of duty. Nor is it for honorable service rendered in defence of the flag or free institutions. It is a pension to selfishness and greed. It is a pension to the men who reap where
others sow and gather where others plant. It is a pension to
the men who debauch the ballot and gamble in public trusts. It
is a pension to the men who seem to have no possible use for
the grandest government on earth except to prostitute it to
their individual profit and private gain.

On May 9 John H. Gear [Ia.], of the Committee on
Ways and Means, spoke in favor of the bill. He discussed in particular the bounty principle, which, he said,
was not a new one, for bounties had been given by many
of our States to develop various industries. He pointed
out that many of the great sugar-producing countries
of the world, such as France and Germany, had used to
great advantage the bounty system. He continued:

Sir, I do not see why the American people should not be encouraged by the same means which has accomplished such great
results in other countries. If we can do this, it seems to me that
we shall have conferred a great blessing on the agricultural interests of the United States—an industry which we all know to-
day is in a languishing condition—by opening to them a new
avenue of production which will be more certain and more remunerative than the raising of some other products. In addition, when you stimulate the beet industry you at once cause
the erection of sugar factories in every hamlet which produces
beets.

Charles F. Crisp [La.] opposed the bill. In speaking
upon the general results of a protective policy he said:

Our Republican friends point to the fact that in the past
twenty-five years there has been a great reduction in the price
of manufactured articles, and claim all this as due to the present protective system. They forget that something is due to
science and art and invention.

Why, sir, twenty-five years ago one man perhaps was engaged all day in making a pair of shoes; the pay that he received for that pair of shoes had to include a sufficient sum for
labor to support him, and, therefore, necessarily, the price of
shoes was considerable. Now a machine has been invented

which, with the aid of two or three men, will make 100 pairs or perhaps 200 pairs of shoes in a day. Under such circumstances ought not the price of shoes to be reduced?

JOSEPH H. WALKER [Mass.].—I want to ask the gentleman whether those machines were invented by mechanics or by farmers, and whether it is not the fact that every machine which is used for making boots and shoes was invented in this country.

MR. CRISP.—It is altogether absurd to claim what my friend here claims for protection. He claims every invention that is made. Why, sir, the stimulus to invention is the protection provided in the patent law for the inventor.

Sereno E. Payne [N. Y.], of the Committee on Ways and Means, at the close of a long speech, replied to Mr. Crisp.

The gentleman from Georgia asks, Do we claim that the protective system has had anything to do with invention? Why, Mr. Chairman, "necessity is the mother of invention," and when you create the necessity here for the supply of our wants by the manufacture of our hands you stimulate the inventive genius of the country. Take away protection, take away the chance to manufacture the article invented, and what incentive is there for men to spend their brains, their time, and their talents in invention if the seventeen-year patent right is not to inure to their benefit? because they are defenceless without a protective system and cannot manufacture profitably the articles which they invent.

Daniel Kerr [Ia.] supported the bill, though he objected to the bounty plan.

If we pay a bounty on sugar to the amount of 2 cents a pound it will cost in the beginning $9,000,000 a year, and if successful it will cost the nation every year $66,000,000, and at the end of fifteen years, if the policy proposed in one section of this bill was adopted, it would cost this nation $100,000,000 a year. I protest, in the name of other American industries, against this policy of taxing one American industry for the benefit of another American industry [applause on the Democratic side] when they are both subjected to local taxation and to all the charges incident to our institutions.

On May 10 William McAdoo [N. J.] opposed the bill. He dwelt especially on the question of labor.

The present bill and the attitude of the majority form a step backward in civilization, and an attempt to outwit the laws of nature and to evade the rules of common honesty.

When under unreasonable restrictions, made to prohibit the landing of foreign products on the quays of New York, you force the human stream of the unemployed of other lands to join the multitude competing for the right to work in our own, and bring to our shores the powerful foreign syndicates now rapidly purchasing and controlling the very industries which you have unduly protected, how are you protecting American labor? If you desire absolute isolation, the logic of this bill leads to prohibition of immigration and stringent laws against the investment of foreign capital; then behind these barricades against the universe, these fortifications against human intercourse, paternal and class government will undoubtedly prevail, and, having made your country a huge jail to imprison commerce and foreign intercourse, boast of freedom if you will.

If the foreigner cannot compete under reasonable terms in the open market, he will of necessity bring his capital within the shelter of the prohibitive law—but still open to the labor of the world—control your industries, and drain our land of the profits of the toil of our people to benefit himself and his own country. If you dam the water at one point, allowing no egress, it must of necessity overflow your dam or force a vent in some other way.

Is it any wonder, therefore, that your railroad and steamship stations cannot accommodate the throng of immigrants, and that the English newspapers bristle with the advertisements of syndicates to purchase American industries or to control American land and interests?

Why did you and the manufacturers, at least some of them, retreat from a demand for the reduction of wool duties and actually propose an increase? The true history of this movement reveals the inherent viciousness of your present policy. Wool was considered as ripe for shearing on the tariff list, but wool was well organized, and its organizers stood up and said to you, "Men and brethren, in the day that puts the knife of tariff reduction on wool, in that day we demand free cloth and many other such things. Nay, more, we demand forthwith an increase." No consideration of the merits of an item standing by itself, but a confraternity of extreme selfishness and rapacity, is the existing order.

I warn the blinded selfishness that urges these abuses of legislation. If wealth can increase its gains by law, are you not preaching "bloody instructions" to want to prostitute the same enginery to undo wealth? If wealth by such laws can reap undue advantage and close out competition, what answer will you make to want, which has the most votes, when it demands paternal government at first hands and for itself? You close out competition by law and form a trust to regulate domestic consumption, and then profess surprise at the radical demands coming every day from organizations, more or less socialistic in principle, asking that government itself shall enter into active competition with these Frankensteins it has created, and which, under the present policy, have become more powerful than their creator.

Robert M. La Follette [Wis.], of the Committee on Ways and Means, supported the bill. He contrasted it with the Mills bill, and then continued:

Mr. Chairman, I maintain that the question of labor should be the prime consideration in all revisions of our tariff system.

No article can be found upon the dutiable list in the bill under consideration which is not in whole or in part the product of labor, and we have endeavored to make it dutiable in proportion to the labor in it. The material upon which the labor is wrought has no value except as it is capable of being wrought. If you would find the real raw material of which it is composed go to the standing tree in the forest, worth no more in its place than the shade it affords; to the ore lying deep in the earth, worth no more in its bed than the rocks and dirt which cover it. When did it cease to be raw material? When the hand of labor was first placed upon it. Then, when it was turned out finished for the market, a thing of value, what was there in it which made it valuable? Why, the labor in it. And when shipped to the United States to compete with a like article produced here, and we met it at the custom house with a protective tariff, what was that tariff on? Why, it was on the valuable part of that article, the labor in it. And what was protected by that duty? Why, the valuable part of the domestic article which the foreign came to crowd out, the labor in it. [Applause.]

Mr. Chairman, it is to protect the labor of this country in

the field and in the factory, to maintain existing occupations, to acquire other new and useful ones where possible, to hold certain the advantages of our country, that we have guarded the American industrial system as we would the very liberties of our people in this Republican bill. It is to preserve the markets of this country to our own producers that we have kept the duties like a breastwork, high enough at every point to protect the man who is busy adding to the sum of its wealth from assault from any foreign source. Whenever foreign products the like of which we can supply our own people with have been taking the market from us, there we have raised the barrier to the protective point, and we have no apology to make for it. We believe that in so doing we have responded to a patriotic duty. [Applause on the Republican side.]

Here Mr. La Follette discussed the world-wide depression in agriculture. The sharp decline in prices, he said, was due to overproduction in India, Russia, the United States, and other countries. In conclusion he said:

This Republican bill not only seeks to give the farmers of this country a much larger body of consumers for their products right here at home, by multiplying the factories, adding to the millions engaged in mining and manufacturing pursuits, but it also proposes, in direct opposition to the Democratic plan, to encourage the development of the largest diversity of production upon the farm; to add millions on millions of acres to the production of barley and flax and hemp and tobacco and hops and vegetables and fruits and fibers, and to seed down to pasture vast areas now cropped in corn and wheat, for the 60,000,000 additional sheep required in this country to produce all our own wool. [Applause on the Republican side.]

Mr. Chairman, as I listened to the distinguished gentleman [Mr. Mills] there passed before me a comparison of the two economic systems, the one gathering the whole world into one family, leveling up and leveling down till all the nations of every race and grade tread at the same pace, work at the same bench, eat at the same board, take from toil the same meager returns, share and share alike; the other gathering this nation unto itself as one family beneath the protecting arm of the Government, holding sacredly for us our higher advantages, yielding nothing we have except our labor be made whole and the exchange even, giving to our workers—and they are all workers—a better and a better chance, a larger and larger share of profit and longer hours of leisure, opening the way to every citizen for the highest American achievement and to the nation the grandest possible development and destiny. [Loud and long-continued applause on the Republican side.]

William M. Springer [Ill.] opposed the bill. Speaking of the proposition to allow drawbacks on raw material, he said:

The gentleman from Ohio [Mr. McKinley], in reference to drawbacks on imported merchandise, said the reduction of the amount retained by the Government from 10 per cent. to only 1 per cent. would enable the manufacturers of the country practically to have the benefit of free raw material, or within 1 per cent. of it. He contended that with this advantage raw material of every kind could be imported, converted into a finished product, and then exported. The duty paid on the raw material in such exports would then be refunded within 1 per cent.

I asked at the time if this would apply to wool. He said it would, that it would apply to everything. But will any one tell me how the imported wool in a finished piece of cloth can be traced and identified so as to permit a drawback to the amount of the duties paid on its importation? It is imported in the grease; it is then washed, then scoured. It has shrunk by these processes from 33 to 60 per cent. It is then put into the mill, carded, spun, and woven. It loses at least 25 per cent. in these processes, and when it has reached the finished product thus reduced in quantity it is found to be mixed with native wool, with shoddy and other adulterants.

How is anybody to determine what amount of drawback is to be allowed? It would be impossible, or, at least, utterly impracticable. As of wool, so of nearly all other articles which are known as raw material. How is iron-ore to be traced into a pocket-knife or a chain? Can an American tobacconist import Havana tobacco and Sumatra wrappers, manufacture them into cigars, ship them to Canada, and get a drawback of all the duties, save 1 per cent.? If so, the Canadian will be able to smoke a pure Havana cigar while our own people will have to smoke clay pipes.

If there were any virtue in the drawback provision, if it would really accomplish what the gentleman claims for it, its highest virtue should condemn it in the estimation of every American citizen. It will no doubt prove successful in some cases, but the effect would simply be to enable our manufacturers to sell their goods to foreigners at from 25 to 50 per cent. cheaper than they could afford to sell them to our own

THE TRUE INWARDNESS OF THE "HOME MARKET"

It Costs Money to be a McKinleyized American, but it is Fine for the Foreigner

Cartoon by Dalrymple in "Puck"

people, for when selling to the foreigner the manufacturer would get a portion of his price from the United States Treasury and could sell to his foreign customer for that much less.

Nelson Dingley [Me.] supported the bill. He spoke chiefly on the question of wool.

Mr. Chairman, the wool and woolen-goods schedule has received the severest criticism of the gentleman from Texas [Mr. Mills] and the gentleman from Illinois [Mr. Springer].

The main difference between the woolen schedule of the pending bill and the bill reported by Mr. Mills in the last Congress lies in the fact that his bill abolished the duty on wool and consequently the specific compensatory duty on the cloth intended to be the equivalent of the duty on the wool of which it is made, but left an *ad valorem* duty of 40 per cent. to protect the manufacturer. The manufacturer was protected, but the farmer abandoned to the unrestrained competition of South America and Australia. The gentleman from Texas was able to say that he had reduced the "tax" on woolen cloth, but all the reduction was at the expense of the wool-grower. [Cries of "That's so!"]

In order to understand clearly the difference between this bill and the Mills bill as to the woolen schedule, it must be borne in mind that in any tariff which proposes to protect the wool-grower, as well as the wool-manufacturer, against the competition of a foreign country which has free wool it is necessary to impose upon imported woolen cloth a double or compound duty. First, a sufficient specific duty equivalent to the duty which would be paid upon the wool if imported, which goes to the wool-grower; for the farmer can not get the benefit of the protective duty on his wool unless the domestic manufacturer is able to buy it and make his goods in competition with the foreigner. And, secondly, a sufficient *ad valorem* protective duty for the manufacturer to cover the difference in cost of manufacture between this country and Europe.

The two duties added together make an apparent large equivalent *ad valorem* of duty, not, however, represented in the price at which common goods are sold, simply because the wool-growers' duty and the manufacturers' duty come together.

The Mills bill did not propose to reduce the manufacturers' duty, although, in making one uniform duty of 40 per cent. for manufactures of wool, it gave more than is necessary for coarse, unfinished goods like blankets and flannels, and less than is necessary for fine finished cloths and dress goods. In this bill, while the average protective duty for the manufacturer is about the same as the Mills bill provided, yet the duty is distributed according to the proportion of labor in different kinds of goods, and is therefore better adapted to the situation of this industry.

The practical difference, therefore, between the woolen schedule of the pending bill and of the Mills bill is that this bill gives the farmer the same protection on his wool that it gives the manufacturer in making his cloth, while the Mills bill entirely wipes out the farmer's part of the duty and preserves the manufacturer's part intact.

For myself, Mr. Chairman, and speaking, as I believe, the sentiments of this side of the House, I favor this bill because I know that it will increase the home market for American manufactures and products of the farm; will increase our importations of articles which we do not produce here and thus enlarge our foreign trade; will largely add to the opportunities and wages of labor, and will promote the prosperity of the people of the United States. [Applause.]

Amos J. Cummings [N. Y.] spoke against the bill.

Mr. Chairman, from its organization down this Congress has been a raging sea of ravenous legislation. Its rules are a complex battery trained on the treasury. The friends of the people have only a moment to cry out before they are swept overboard to make their moans to the winds and the waves. It is not the voice of the people. It is an instrument of tyranny. This proposed tariff bill is only a lever in its complicated machinery.

There is hardly a beneficent interest or industry in the country that this bill does not assail. It robs labor under the guise of friendship. It laps dry rivulets of toil which it pretends to replenish. Its abominations are almost countless.

Here Mr. Cummings dwelt particularly on the question of our foreign commerce. In conclusion he said:

Commerce is the life of all nations. A nation without it is, like ore in a mine, dead. Abram S. Hewitt was pleased to call it "the angel of civilization," and so it is. It takes charge of the interests, the movements, the thoughts, and the intercourse of all mankind. New York is a child of commerce. Great as she is, she is only an epitome of its work. This bill strikes at her as though she was a viper, an unclean reptile, such as Paul shook from his finger. On behalf of her toiling millions, often dependent upon commerce for food, fuel, clothing, and the necessaries of life, I protest against the passage of this bill. [Prolonged applause on the Democratic side.]

Joseph H. Walker [Mass.] supported the bill as in the interest of the small manufacturers as opposed to the large, who would use free trade to force them out of business and thus establish monopolies.

These rich, greedy, and unscrupulous free-trade manufacturers who (and their fathers before them) made every dollar of their present fortunes under protection, and now are willing to see their young, enterprising, energetic, and courageous competitors of small capital ruined, that they may gobble up their factories to increase their fortunes, would coin money out of the sufferings of their fellow-men.

On the other hand, these smaller manufacturers, in patriotic love of country and a fellow-feeling for the men at the loom and work-bench, some of whom are their fathers, brothers, and cousins, and all of whom were so recently their companions as wage-earners, are fighting a hard battle with greedy importers and traders, whose profits at the expense of their customers are from twice or four times as much on many imported goods as on better goods of the same kind which are sold at the same prices to the consumer.

David B. Henderson [Ia.] supported the bill. He spoke particularly upon the question of trusts.

Trusts have only been born and become able to walk during the last four or five years under Mr. Cleveland's administration. How does it come that the ninety-five years when there were no trusts and when there was constant protection are lost sight of? Does any intelligent person wish to be understood as believing that the tariff creates the trusts?

If any facts could be presented to support this theory, then would come this question:

Where do you get the four leading trusts of this country— the Standard Oil trust, the cotton-seed trust, the anthracite-coal trust, and the whisky trust, the greatest and most powerful in the country? Have they any parent? Are these four great Democratic trusts bastards? [Laughter and applause.]

It will not do to bring up and maintain such a doctrine on the floor of the House of Representatives. The tariff has created no trusts. But I will tell you what is true, Mr. Chairman. Strike down protection, leave the industries of this country to grapple unprotected against the cheap labor from abroad, and the combinations and trusts that now control every industry in Europe, reaching with strong arm into the tea and the coffee and the sugar industries of every country, yes, and reaching out to control the markets of this country—strike down that protective barrier and what must be the result? The industries of this country will be forced into combinations and trusts in order to save their very life. Protection is a great panacea for the very evils of which you complain, and it will do much to solve the question of destroying the trusts and combinations. [Applause.]

Joseph McKenna [Cal.] opposed putting sugar on the free list, saying this was a blow to the principle of protection and a repudiation of Republican declarations.

Mr. Chairman, we can not make sugar the scapegoat of the surplus without involving the protective system itself; and, believe me, sir, we have struck it a harder blow than any tariff-reformer or free-trader has ever struck or can strike, unless he strike on our principles; and, sir, will it not be odd if future Democratic Congresses shall quote a Republican Congress and put wool on the free-list on protection principles? [Laughter and applause on the Democratic side.]

I think the Committee on Ways and Means has made a mistake. It appears to have acted under the influence of a scare about the surplus, and has cast to the pursuit of the tariff reformer the most precious thing we have, as the Russian woman tossed her children to the pursuing wolves.

On May 20 John M. Allen [Miss.] opposed the bill. In the conclusion of his speech he said:

I have noticed through this whole debate the representatives of the "jute-bagging trust," that has been preying on our cotton-planters for a few years back, sitting in the galleries watching the McKinley bill, in which they have so much interest and which is to be passed without our having an opportunity to vote an amendment to put jute bagging on the free-list. Our cotton-planters ought to feel very grateful to the Republican party for increasing the duty or tax on cotton-ties from 35 per cent. to 115 per cent. This certainly ought to earn for the Republican party the everlasting gratitude of the colored Republicans of the South. This is one of the greatest outrages of this outrageous measure.

I had hoped that I might have an opportunity before the final vote was taken to offer as an amendment to this bill a bill I have prepared providing for an income and succession tax. I wanted to make some of these great fortunes pay some of the taxes, bear some of the burdens of the Government. I made application to the Chairman of the Committee of the Whole several days ago to get recognition for the purpose of offering such an amendment. I did want a vote on it so as to let the people see where the members of this House stand. But it is very evident the Ways and Means Committee do not mean to let us vote on that, or but very few other amendments. Never mind, gentlemen, the income tax will come.

Now, Mr. Chairman, I must close; but before doing so I had promised to give some word of consolation to the representatives of the combinations, trusts, and struggling infant industries, who are watching this debate with so much interest from the galleries, and as I have discussed this bill in poetry and prose I will now close the discussion in song, which is really my strong suit. This is for the struggling infants.

SEVERAL MEMBERS.—Sing, sing!

MR. ALLEN, of Mississippi.—It is—— (Singing)

> Rock-a-bye, babies, you are on top,
> When the fat fries the cradle will rock;
> When the fat stops the cradle will fall,
> And down come Republicans, babies and all.
> Rock-a-bye, rock-a-bye; nothing to fear;
> Rock-a-bye, rock-a-bye, the G. O. P.'s here.

[Great laughter.]

Joseph G. Cannon [Ill.] moved to retain the existing duties upon works of art, which the bill placed on the free list.

I believe, Mr. Chairman, that the law had better stand as it is touching these productions. They are luxuries. They go to the few, and the policy of the Republican party, as outlined in its platforms and illustrated by its practice heretofore, requires that they shall be upon the dutiable list. I offer this amendment at the request, I believe, of the majority of the members of this side of the House, and I hope it will be promptly adopted.

Mr. McKinley opposed the amendment.

I should regret very much if this provision of the bill were stricken out by the Committee of the Whole. It has been asked for by substantially all the artists of the United States. A committee of the Union League Club of the city of New York two years ago sent inquiries to every artist in the United States whose address could be found, in order to obtain an expression as to the desire of members of the profession touching the question whether works of art should be dutiable or should be admitted free.

There were 1,435 replies received from artists in the United States, and out of that entire number 1,345 petitioned the Congress of the United States to remove this onerous duty upon art which is for educational purposes. And I want to simply read to the committee what the artists themselves have said upon the subject.

JOSEPH H. WALKER [Mass.].—They are the workingmen.

MR. McKINLEY.—They say:

We, as American artists, proud of our country, confident of its future, and jealous of its honor and credit, are opposed to all special privileges and discrimination in our behalf. We ask no protection, deeming it worse than useless. Art is a universal republic, of which all artists are citizens whatever be their country or clime. All that we ask is that there should be a free field and no favor, and the prize adjudged to the best.

[Applause on the Democratic side.]

HENRY CABOT LODGE [Mass.].—An impost is either a tax, pure and simple, for the purpose of raising revenue only, or is a duty imposed to protect home industries. In the nature of the case this duty must belong to the former class. It is not a protective duty, for no one, of course, pretends for a moment that you can create artistic genius by a protective tariff. The artists of America, who are the producers in this case, desire free art and they desire it in the interest of art alone.

I say let us encourage the importation of works of art in the interests of the people, for it is really and in the end in their interest, and in theirs alone. All the greatest works of art in the world to-day belong to the people, and are gathered in the galleries and museums, which are open to mankind, and which give pleasure and instruction to all alike, to gentle and simple, to rich and poor. The rich man buys them, it is true, but in the end the people own them, and the ownership of the people is perpetual.

Let us encourage the importation of all that is best in painting and sculpture, and not, by degrading them to the rank of a luxury, put a tax upon education and popular pleasure and instruction. Let us leave them free, too, for the sake of our artists and for the benefit and development of American art. [Applause.]

Our own artists are now forced to go to Europe, where schools of art are thrown open to them, owing largely to the fact that we put a burden of this character upon art here and keep pictures and sculpture out of the country, drying up the springs from which the museums and galleries are fed.

WILLIAM H. H. COWLES [N. C.].—How about the copyright bill? We want free knowledge as well as free art.

MR. LODGE.—It stands on exactly the same principle as the copyright bill. Universal copyright, which places all writers on the same footing, is free copyright. I would make art and literature free, and every artist and every literary man asks for the same thing. They ask justice and a fair field, nothing more and nothing less.

MR. CANNON.—The gentleman from Ohio says the artists in this country are not demanding protection. I do not vote for this bill as a matter of protection for the artist. I vote for it in harmony with the platform of my own party, recognizing that these works of art are luxuries and therefore, in the language of the platform, the men who buy them in this country to the extent of a round million of dollars every year can afford to pay 30 per cent. *ad valorem* upon them. [Applause.] That is the reason I propose the amendment.

Now, a further word about this matter. For schools of art, for art purposes, and for institutions of education, under the law now and in this bill, these works come in free for that purpose, and there is the education of the people to which reference has been so strongly made.

Another thing: over on the other side, in Italy, the sculptor who does the mechanical work and carves out the slab of marble works cheap. It is not done by the artist who conceives the sculpture himself; and therefore I can readily understand how parties of great wealth in this country, who are able to buy these works of art when they do come over, and how people of this country who desire to avail themselves of that kind of labor on the other side, can go to the marble quarries there and make this statuary out of cheap marble, utilizing the cheap labor for that purpose.

I think this provision should be stricken from the bill, and I ask a vote upon the amendment. [Cries of "Vote!" "Vote!"]

WILLIAM C. P. BRECKINRIDGE [Ky.].—Mr. Chairman, extremes meet. The artist is indeed the highest form of skilled labor. You cannot think of a man having higher art and more skill than he; and with the eye and intellect of genius and the hand of skill he produces a great picture; and therefore he is in favor of free trade, and the more you get of skilled labor the less protection you will need for anything. [Applause on the Democratic side.]

I am in favor of the provision of the bill because it is a step in the right direction. I am in favor of it because it is becoming in a great and imperial republic to open her doors as she does her heart to works of genius of the past or of the present.

When, Mr. Speaker, the French found we were excluding her works of art it touched her heart, because she loved her art next to glory; so she sought to hurt our feelings. When she saw we had stabbed her art she undertook to hurt us in our most sensitive part; and so she excluded the American hog. [Laughter and applause and cries of "Vote!" "Vote!"]

The amendment was defeated by a non-partisan vote of 54 ayes and 77 nays.

The bill was passed on May 21 by a strictly partisan vote of 164 to 142.

The Senate referred the bill to the Committee on Finance, which, on June 17, reported it back with amendments. It came up for discussion on July 7, and was debated almost to the exclusion of other matters until September 10, when it was passed by a vote of 40 to 29.

Almost every Senator spoke upon the bill, many of the speeches being able, and several of unusual brilliance, but, as their arguments were necessarily repetitions of those in the preceding House debate, they are not presented here.

The House refused to concur in the Senate amendments, and a conference was appointed. After considerable debate the report of the conference was agreed to on October 1, 1890, and approved by President Harrison on the same day.

In the presidential election of 1892 the tariff was the chief issue, and upon it Grover Cleveland was elected to a second term of office.

CHAPTER XIV

THE TARIFF OF 1894

[THE WILSON BILL]

William L. Wilson [W. Va.] Introduces New Tariff Bill in the House—
Debate: in Favor, Mr. Wilson, Tom L. Johnson [O.], William C. P.
Breckinridge [Ky.], Jerry Simpson [Kan.], W. Bourke Cockran [N. Y.],
William J. Bryan [Neb.], Charles F. Crisp [Ga.]; Opposed, Julius C.
Burrows [Mich.], John Dalzell [Pa.], Joseph G. Cannon [Ill.], Thad-
deus B. Mahon [Pa.], Nelson Dingley [Me.], Sereno E. Payne [N. Y.],
Joseph H. Walker [Mass.], Charles A. Boutelle [Me.], Thomas B. Reed
[Me.]—Bill Is Passed—Senate Amends Bill in Direction of Protection
and Passes It—Mr. Reed Taunts Democratic Representatives—After
Futile Joint Conferences House Accepts Senate Amendments—Debate:
Mr. Wilson, Mr. Reed, Lafe Pence [Col.]—Bill Becomes Law Without
Signature of the President.

ON December 19, 1893, William L. Wilson [W. Va.],
chairman of the Committee on Ways and
Means, introduced in the House a bill of the
majority of the committee revising the tariff. On December 21 Thomas B. Reed [Me.] presented the minority
report on the bill. On January 8, 1894, the bill came up
for discussion in the Committee of the Whole.

THE WILSON TARIFF BILL

HOUSE OF REPRESENTATIVES, JANUARY 8-FEBRUARY 1, 1894

Mr. Wilson supported the bill in a speech consuming
the greater part of two days (January 8-9).

The majority members of the Committee of Ways and
Means have had to deal with a system that has grown up
through thirty years of progressive legislation. They do not
profess that they have been able, at one stroke of reform, to
free it from injustice or to prepare a bill directly responsive

286

to the command of the people. They have dealt as intelligently and as fairly as they could with existing conditions. Even in their desire and purpose to do this they have been hampered

CAUSE FOR WORRY

The Discharged Nurse (peevishly)—Dear me! It grieves me to death to see how that child's wasting away since they changed its food.

Cartoon by J. S. Pughe in "Puck"

by the usual difficulties of reform and by some very unusual difficulties. We knew and expected that some friends would fall away from us whenever we presented any definite measure of legislation. We knew from all experience of the past that not all who march bravely in the parade are found in line when the musketry begins to rattle. [Applause.]

But in addition to this usual and expected embarrassment we are called upon to take up this work in the shadow and depression of a great commercial crisis. I shall pursue no inquiry into the causes of our present stricken industries and paralyzed trade. But, sir, from whatever causes originated, whether produced and fostered, or merely aggravated and intensified, by bad legislation, it is to us a hindrance in the performance of our duty, if for no other reason than that it has been eagerly seized upon by the enemies of tariff reform to kindle hostility against that movement. Yet, Mr. Chairman, if there ever was a time when the burden of taxation ought to be lightened it is when men are struggling for the necessaries of life. [Applause.] If there ever was a time when the fetters of trade should be loosened it is when trade is held in the paralysis of a commercial crisis. [Applause.]

Again, Mr. Chairman, we undertake to relieve the people of taxes at a time when government revenues are falling behind government expenditures, and when we must daily scrape the bottom of the barrel to gather meal enough to make our daily bread.

We begin our task by an effort to free from taxation those things on which the industrial prosperity and growth of our country so largely depend.

Of all the reductions made in this bill there are none in their benefit to the consumer, none in their benefit to the laborer that can be compared with the removal of the taxes from the materials of industry. We have felt that we could not begin a thorough reform of the existing system, built up, story by story, until it has pierced the clouds, except by a removal of all taxation on the great materials that lie at the basis of modern industry, and so the bill proposes to put on the free list wool, iron ore, coal, and lumber. [Applause on the Democratic side.]

Sir, I have no doubt, speaking in the light of experience, that, with wool on the free list and moderate duties on finished products, we shall have such a growth of manufacturing in this country as will steady and improve the market for American wool, and greatly cheapen the cost of woolen goods to the American people.

Now, Mr. Chairman, if there is any one great industry as to which we could throw down to-day our tariff walls and defy the world's competition, it is the great iron and steel industry of this country.

We have found along the Appalachian Ranges of the South,

around the Great Lakes of the North, deposits of iron ore, so rich, so easily worked, so accessible to other materials, and so convenient to our cheapest systems of transportation, that we can now mine the ore and make the pig at less cost than anywhere else in the world.

Sir, there has been no more oppressive monopoly in this country than that of the makers of steel rails. [Applause.] Under a tariff which gave them first $28, then $17, and now $13.44 a ton protection, the rolling mills have combined to keep up prices to the people of this country far beyond the cost of production, and now, when we have reached a point where we shall soon be able to make steel rails as cheaply as they can be made in any country, they are raising their angry outcry against a bill carrying a duty of 25 per cent. on steel rails.

TOM L. JOHNSON [O.].—Will you tell us why you still give them 25 per cent. protection?

MR. WILSON.—A maker of steel rails asks me why we leave this duty at 25 per cent. I suppose the best answer I could give is that we could not well make it less according to the general scale of duties in the iron and steel schedule.

So as to coal. There is now a duty of 75 cents a ton on bituminous coal—a duty which is in excess of the entire cost of production, either in the United States or elsewhere.

We are not only the great iron-producing country, we are the great coal-producing country of the world. With exhaustless supplies, so close to the surface that the cost of mining has been reduced to a minimum, to less than is possible in Nova Scotia, to less than is actually paid in England, the question of a tariff on coal is neither a question of protection nor a question of revenue, but simply a question of subsidy to the great railroad corporations of the country. [Applause on the Democratic side.]

We are exporters of coal for sale in neutral markets. We have a steadily and of late years a rapidly growing export trade, and retain this duty only to hold onto markets so remote from the coal mines that railroad transportation is their chief item in the cost of fuel.

As to lumber, another article put on the free list, I need say but a few words. Logs, as everyone knows, have been free for years. Under the existing tariff we are denuding our forests and rapidly destroying the most valuable part of our timber. It is not contended that the cost of lumbering in this country is materially higher than in the countries from which we might import such products. Along the Canadian border the

XII—19

work is largely done by the same labor on both sides of the line and I presume at practically the same rates. Here, again, we are a large exporter. Our export of dressed and finished lumber is one of the growing, as it is to-day one of the largest, items in our export trade. If we can send our lumber to Europe, to the West Indies, to South America, we can certainly compete, we can certainly hold our home market without the aid of a tariff.

Mr. Chairman, the question of wages is, in my judgment, the vital question of tariff reform. If protection makes or increases wages, if it improves the well-being of the American worker, I am a protectionist from this time forward. But, sir, neither reason nor experience gives countenance to any such idea. The wages of labor are paid from the products of labor. The general productiveness of every country determines the wages of the laboring people of that country. The skill and intelligence of its labor, the character of its institutions, and the abundance of its resources determine that general productiveness. We have higher wages in the United States than are attainable elsewhere, first, because we are a great, new country with all the elements of production and of industrial supremacy in unsurpassed abundance, for whose development we command all the resources of art and skill, of science and invention; and, secondly, because we have the most intelligent and the freest laboring men in all the world.

Mr. Chairman, while this bill will, at first, effect some reduction, some substantial reduction of revenue, the experience of the past justifies us in believing that this reduction will soon be compensated for by an increase of revenue under the lower duties.

The Committee on Ways and Means expect to follow this bill with an internal-revenue bill that will provide for the temporary deficiency in the revenue, or with an amendment to the present bill making such provision. Their plan contemplates an income tax of 2 per cent. on the net earnings of the corporations of the country, a tax of 2 per cent. on personal incomes in excess of $4,000, an internal-revenue tax of $1.50 a thousand in place of the present tax of 50 cents on cigarettes; and also an internal-revenue tax of 2 cents a pack on playing cards, and an increase of 10 cents a gallon on whisky.

Now, Mr. Chairman, in closing these remarks I want to say that if the economic objections to protection are so great, if it unbalances trade, if it causes fluctuations and gross inequalities in the industries of the country, if it robs labor of employment, if it lessens the wages of the toiler, if it throws crushing burdens upon the American farmer, if it makes the support of government an onerous burden upon every man or woman who works for a living, a still stronger condemnation of the protective system is that its inevitable effect when persisted in is to undermine free institutions in this country and all just sense of equal citizenship.

So I say to my friends on this side of the House, let us go forward until we make this a country in which every man shall see the gateway of opportunity opening before him, in which the great avenues of industry shall no longer be the private possession of the wealth of the country, but every youth in its borders shall be inspired to rise by his own merits and his own efforts—not born to labor for others, not beaten back in contempt by those who speak of him as rebel when he seeks his own rights. Let this be a country free to all, equal for all, with the golden ladder of opportunity planted in every cabin, in every home, and at every humble fireside in the land. [Long-continued applause.]

Julius C. Burrows [Mich.] of the minority of the Ways and Means Committee, replied to Mr. Wilson.

I desire to say that this measure as a whole stands without a parallel in the history of proposed tariff legislation in this country. It was framed with the evident intention of carrying out that portion of the Democratic platform and policy which declared for a "tariff for revenue only," and is the boldest step yet taken by any party in the United States in the direction of free trade—a step which, if it shall find popular following in this country, will certainly lead to individual disaster and national bankruptcy.

The first proposition arresting attention in this bill is the proposed transfer of one hundred and thirty-one articles from the dutiable to the free list.

It will not escape notice in this connection that upon examination of the list of articles thus transferred from the dutiable to the free list the interests of the farmer seem to have been selected for special assault and destruction, as nearly one-half of the items embraced in this proposed transfer are the fruits of domestic husbandry. Even the duty of 20 per cent. *ad valorem* accorded the American farmer on his wheat, corn, rye, oats, buckwheat, and their manufactures is to be removed, and all these products admitted free of duty from any country extending like privileges to us. The way is thus open to the Canadian farmer to invade our markets at will.

The one hundred and thirty-one articles proposed to be transferred to the free list are not exclusively of foreign origin. They are of domestic production, built up and sustained by the investment of American capital and the employment of American labor. They are the products of our factories, our mines, our forests, our mills, our flocks and our fields, which you propose thus to expose to the merciless and unrestrained assault of our foreign rivals. And to what end? That the manufacturers, forsooth, may have the advantage of "free raw material."

I notice every "tariff reformer" urges free raw material as an indispensable adjunct to the consummation of his theory. "There is method in his madness." No one understands better than he that free raw material will be swiftly followed by free manufactured goods. It will be protection for all or protection for none. [Applause.] When you force the producers of raw material into unrestrained competition with the world the manufacturers of this raw material into the finished fabric will speedily share the same fate.

Yet I confess that in the light of this measure it is somewhat difficult to understand the Democratic idea of raw material.

For example, you put one class of clays on the free list, while another, adapted to the use of the same industry, is made dutiable. One would suppose that clay was about as "raw" a material as could be imagined. Yet, while putting the clays of New Jersey on the free list, you impose a duty of $2 a ton on the clays of Florida, Georgia, and other Southern States. One would surmise what was raw material in New Jersey would be "raw material" in Florida. But it seems not. One would suppose that hoop iron would be the same, regardless of the uses to which it is applied. Not so. On the farmer's bucket it is taxed, around the planter's cotton it is free.

Passing from the consideration of the free list to the dutiable schedules, we find here the same spirit of hostility manifested in every provision. There is not a schedule in which there are not some industries which will be imperiled by the passage of its bill—many will be utterly destroyed. On the other hand, if there is any provision in this bill which will stimulate a single domestic industry or give increased employment to labor it has not been pointed out. The measure as a whole looks only to lessened industries and lower wages.

I would call attention to the many incongruities in this bill.

The committee may be able to explain why pig iron is taxed, and cotton ties are free. Why the Northern farmer, with harvest labor at $2 a day, is allowed 20 per cent. on his wheat,

THE AMERICAN WORKMAN

He Killed the Goose that Laid the Golden Eggs

Cartoon by Victor Gillam in "Judge"

and the rice producer of the South, with 75 cents day labor, secures 71 per cent.

Why tallow, wool grease, and degras are made free as tanners' materials, while the sumac of Virginia and North Carolina, used for the same purpose, is protected. Why the farmers' potatoes secure only 10 per cent. consideration, while peanuts of Virginia grow in security behind a Chinese wall of 35 per cent. Why in many instances the duty on the finished article is less, or no more, than on the articles entering into its manufacture.

But the most startling feature connected with and running through the entire dutiable schedules is the general substitution of *ad valorem* for specific rates. It is urged as an objection to specific rates that they operate unequally on the consumers of cheaper goods. But it must be remembered that on all the cheaper class of fabrics it is a matter of comparative indifference whether the rate is specific or *ad valorem,* as domestic competition has reduced the price of such articles in many cases to the consumer even below the duty itself.

Furthermore, specific duties serve to keep out of our markets cheap adulterated fabrics which are practically worthless to the purchaser, and insure a better grade of goods for the poor and rich alike.

Against the opinions of the mere theorists of to-day I interpose the substantial judgment of practical business men, experienced officials, and the practice of the most enlightened nations on the globe. In all continental nations excepting the Netherlands *ad valorem* tariffs have been substantially discarded.

It is not surprising, however, that the party of free trade in the United States should make this method of levying duties the leading feature of its policy. It is a fit accompaniment to this bill. It removes the last safeguard to American industries and strikes down the last hope for our protective system. If there was nothing else in this measure deserving public condemnation, this alone ought to be sufficient to insure its overwhelming defeat.

I implore you to abandon this suicidal policy. Have you not pursued it far enough to become convinced of its disastrous consequences? It is no longer an experiment—it has become a public crime. You have it within your power to instantly relieve this appalling situation. You have only to substitute for the pending measure a joint resolution declaratory of your purpose to maintain existing law in full force and effect during the continuance of this Administration, and business activity would instantly take the place of business depression. It would arrest the slaughter of our flocks, open our mines, relight the fires of our furnaces, unchain the wheels of our industries, start every spindle and loom; while whistles and factory bells would call the tramping starving millions back from enforced idleness to profitable employment and the American Republic would leap with a bound to its accustomed place in the van of industrial nations. [Prolonged applause on the floor in the galleries.]

On January 10 Tom L. Johnson [O.] criticized the course of his party on the tariff as timorous.

Mr. Chairman, I am like the man who *could* eat crow. I will vote for this bill if I can get nothing better. But I do not like it. That it does contain some good points is true. The McKinley bill contained some good points; it put raw sugar and some other things on the free list. This bill goes further, and puts wool, coal, iron ore, and undressed lumber on the free list, and in so far makes some show of redeeming our pledge to abolish protection. This is its little sprinkle of saving salt, which commends it to me. Even if it were a proposition to reënact the McKinley bill, with the single exception of free wool, I would still vote for it if I could do no better, for every addition to the free list is a step toward free trade; every break in the link of protected interests lessens the power of the league of plunder to further squeeze the people.

But, though I might vote for this bill with pleasure if it came from a Ways and Means Committee representing a Republican House, I am disgusted and dismayed that it is presented by a Democratic committee to a Democratic House, as representing their idea of what the Democratic party, with all branches of the Government in its hands, proposes to do for a suffering people.

Perhaps it may satisfy what are called tariff reformers, but if this is a tariff reform bill I am all the more rejoiced that I am not now and never have been a tariff reformer. I am only a plain free trader. [Laughter.]

A fear of irritating the trusts seems to run through the bill. I can see no trust that it has struck at, or at all injured, except this sugar trust. The nominal reductions made on many articles still leave so high a duty as to close our market to foreign importations and secure to combinations of American manufacturers as full power to squeeze the American consumer as they have under the present tariff.

Take steel rails, of which I happen to know something, as I am a manufacturer of steel rails. I appeal to the Democrats of the House to join me in putting steel rails on the free list. The present duty on steel rails is estimated to be equivalent to

50.44 per cent. *ad valorem*. The committee have reduced this to 25 per cent. This seems like a great reduction. But it is only nominal, for 25 per cent. is all the steel rail trust want. It is as good to them as 1,000 per cent., for it is practically a prohibitory duty.

JOHN DALZELL [Pa.].—Does the gentleman speak now from the attitude of a steel rail manufacturer?

MR. JOHNSON.—I do. Our mill makes about one-thirtieth of all that are produced in the United States.

MR. DALZELL.—Is the gentleman a party to the steel rail trust?

MR. JOHNSON.—I am not; but whether I am or not would make no difference. Outside of this hall, as a steel manufacturer, I might be perfectly willing to enter a trust, but I will not defend trusts here. [Applause.]

Here Mr. Johnson opposed the continuance of the McKinley tax on imported books. He then dwelt on the need of immediate revision of our tariff system.

That you can injure industry and hurt labor by abolishing tariff taxes too quickly and too completely I deny. You will injure monopoly and hurt trusts; but you will stimulate industry and give labor relief. Take the business in which I am interested. If you put steel rails on the free list, as I intend to move, you will not shut up mills; on the contrary, you will open them, for the steel-rail pool can then no longer, out of the extra profits the tariff gives it, afford to pay for keeping mills idle. There will be greater activity and a greater demand for labor in the making of rails. And so with structural steel. But the benefit will not end there. The men engaged in making steel rails and structural steel are but a handful compared with those engaged in laying rails and erecting buildings and bridges, and even they are few compared with the men such erections set at work. You will lessen the profits of some of us steel manufacturers, but you will stimulate industry, give idle labor a chance for employment, and so tend to raise wages.

I am far from asserting that the bottom cause of the present distress is the tariff. It is something greater than that— it is the monopolization of land, the natural opportunity of all employment, the natural prerequisite of all wealth, and such distress must recur again until we come to the only true mode of raising revenue, the only full free trade—the single tax. But a quick and sharp reduction of taxation and breaking down of the trusts and monopolies that have grown up from the Republican tariff will give large present relief and start again the wheels of industry.

It is bad politics to ignore the friends who voted for you in order to please enemies who opposed you. That is what the majority of the committee have done in reporting such a protectionist bill. What have they gained by their "moderation"? Simply the sneers of the minority. Every Republican member will oppose their bill; every Republican paper will denounce it; every ring and trust will fight it just as strongly, just as bitterly, just as persistently as they would oppose the bill that I would like to introduce. That bill would be short and simple. It would read:

SEC. 1. All import duties and corresponding internal-revenue duties are hereby abolished, and all officials engaged in collecting such duties are hereby discharged.

SEC. 2. The Secretary of the Treasury is hereby directed to sell all custom houses and revenue cutters, and pay the proceeds into the treasury.

SEC. 3. This act shall take effect immediately.

Such a bill would excite no more protectionist opposition than this poor, timid, little Wilson bill will. But it would not be sneered at, and it would arouse a mighty support, that this bill cannot get.

Such a bill as that I do not hope for now, but if we want to see another Democratic victory let us stand up to the platform of our party, and, retaining what free list the committee have proposed, add to it such things as steel rails and bicycles, and strike out all the protection they have filled into the bill.

JOSEPH G. CANNON [Ill.].—The gentleman has given us the bill that he would like to enact, repealing all the present revenue laws; will he be kind enough now to give us also the brief bill he would put in their place?

MR. JOHNSON.—I would put the tax upon the monopolization of natural opportunities; upon land values irrespective of improvement—the values which are created by the community and which the community has the first right to. [Applause.]

Now, Mr. Chairman, I know it is a long way from a protective tariff to the single tax, but I want to make the start. Of all the known methods of raising revenue the worst is a tariff, and of all tariffs the worst is a protective tariff.

The best of all taxes is the one I have indicated—the single tax. I will vote with you, gentlemen, on every step between the worst and the best. If, on the way, you want an income tax,

I will vote for it, though I do not like income taxes. But any
tax on what men have is better than a tax on what men need.
[Applause.]   Any tax on wealth in any form is better than a
tax on consumption in any form. I am far from charging that
our present difficulties—this great depression through which
we are passing—is due to the acts of either political party. I
do not believe that the tariff cuts anything like the figure in
this distress that people generally give it credit for.

We have to look further than that to find the cause, for
there is no civilized country on the globe, except perhaps New
Zealand, where the single tax has been begun, that is not suffering at this time from depression. We must look further
than tariffs. But the measure I would propose in answer to
the gentleman from Illinois would go to the heart of this world-
wide question, would solve the labor problem—it is the single
tax. [Prolonged applause on the Democratic side.]

Thaddeus M. Mahon [Pa.] opposed the bill. He particularly denounced the omission of the reciprocity
clause which was in the McKinley bill.

One of the greatest achievements of the Republican party
was accomplished during the closing days of the Fifty-first
Congress, by the adoption of section 3 of the McKinley tariff
law. I refer to the reciprocity clause. The measure now under
consideration will repeal the same, and with its repeal all of
the advantages secured in the trade markets of the countries
we have made treaties with will be destroyed.

On January 11 William C. P. Breckinridge [Ky.]
supported the bill. He said that it was a decided step in
advance of the Mills bill, although it did not go so far as
he would have gone, "for, until yesterday, I considered
myself the most ultra free trader in this House."
[Laughter.]

My friend and kinsman, Mr. Johnson, of Ohio, who was born
in my district, and is worthy of his parentage, goes one step
farther than I would go, but that may be because the conservative influence of twenty years has not had its effect upon him.
[Laughter.]   Until yesterday I considered myself on the out-
post of the free-trade Democracy, and therefore I can afford to
say that I am not satisfied with the Wilson bill. There are
things in it that I would have been glad had been omitted.

There are omissions from it that I am sorry were not supplied. I would like to have seen the bounty on sugar repealed. I would have given almost anything to have seen tinplate put upon the free list. I would have been glad to have seen no duty in the bill higher than 30 per cent. But, take it all in all, it is a step in the progressive advance by which such reformation has to be made. It is not for the advance guard—not even for the great body of the army—that we are to frame our legislation. The timid, the halting, the doubtful, the uncertain, are our brethren. The conservative is our colleague; those who feel a divided duty deserve our consideration. They represent constituencies. We depend upon voting. We cannot reverse the decisions of thirty-five years immediately.

For myself I am willing to keep, as I have kept in every speech that I have made upon this floor, my own personal record clear. I am for ultimate free trade. I am for the possession of the oceans by free ships, freed from all the navigation laws which now hamper and embarrass us.

I am for taking possession of the great, long sea coast and making it fruitful by annexing thereto the billows which unite and do not divide us from other countries. There is no extent to which men can go to which I am not willing to go with them. But, on the other hand, I am willing to lag side by side with my brethren who agree with me on general principles. We are a country of sections, and I am willing to let Louisiana, with her sugar cane, and the Northwest, with her attempt at sorghum and beet sugar, come and be heard, and to be tender with them, so that they may not feel that we have slaughtered them.

And when I look at what we have done in eight years— when I see a Democratic Senate at the other end of the Capitol, a Democratic House here, a Democratic President in the White House—when I stand on the very eve of the day when the election laws are to be wiped from our statute books—when I see sectional animosities obliterated and the lines which divided us wiped out—I am willing to be more conservative than I otherwise might be, as I recall that it is for one country composed of diverse sections that a national party, compact and consolidated, is to govern in the coming years. [Applause on the Democratic side.] And, therefore, I say to those Democratic friends of mine who do not agree with all the provisions of this bill, we can either heartily and cordially sustain it or frankly point out our objections, and thus by mutual concession and patriotism reach an agreement. For myself, it would

obtain my earnest advocacy if it had nothing else in it than free
raw wool.

Here Mr. Breckinridge discussed the general need of
free trade. He said in conclusion:

I hope to live to see the day when the continent will be
one for freedom, and in that day our children will look back
upon these discussions as we look back upon some of the old
discussions about the relations of the union of church and
state, or the question of slavery. We have free speech, free
thought, free locomotion, and, beyond that, we will have free
trade. We will recognize that the primal curse, "by the sweat
of thy face thou shalt eat thy bread," is the primary right of
mankind; that the right to labor, the right to work, the right
to support his family, carries with it the right to spend the
fruits of his labor wherever he wants to, for whatever he pleases,
according to his own will. This is freedom; that he who works
has the freedom to work for whom he pleases without burden,
to spend its recompense where he pleases, for what he pleases.
And this is the mission of the Democratic party. We are the
friends of the laboring men; aye, we are the artisans of toil,
in whose name we have taken possession of sovereignty, for
whose benefit we labor, whose freedom we will secure, and, when
the end shall come, in humble homes that name will be the
sweetest that can be uttered. [Loud applause on the Democratic side.]

Nelson Dingley [Me.] opposed the bill.

The free-trade theorists say that we should not undertake to
carry on industries in which foreign producers or manufacturers have an advantage over us, but should confine ourselves to
industries in which we have advantage over other countries.
This is the free-trade contention of the gentleman from West
Virginia [Mr. Wilson] and the contention of the majority report.

Now, if this free-trade contention referred simply to a natural advantage; if the argument of the majority report, insisting that we should not attempt to extend our industries and
business to "artificial channels," referred to disadvantages of
climate, soil, or other natural conditions, it would be accepted
as sound. No protectionist holds that the protective policy
should be applied to any industry which must be carried on

here under natural disadvantages, that is, where a larger amount of labor is permanently required to make or produce a given article here than is required elsewhere, except as there may be cases where national defence demands it.

What is meant by opponents of protection, however, is not this. It is that we should not carry on any industry here in which our higher wages of labor make the product cost more in money, although no more in labor or service than elsewhere where the laborer receives less pay—this, the gentleman from West Virginia [Mr. Wilson] tells us, would be an "artificial channel"—but should confine ourselves to "natural channels," or such crude industries, mainly agriculture, in which we have sufficient natural advantage to offset the difference of wages.

Indeed, the free-trade contention—and it is noticeable that nearly all the speeches for this bill on the other side have adopted free-trade arguments to their logical conclusion, and as such have been most enthusiastically applauded by nearly all our Democratic friends, thus showing that the Democratic party no longer disguises its free-trade policy—the free-trade contention is that where we find industries in which our higher wages of labor make the product cost more in money (although not more in labor or service) than they cost abroad because we pay higher wages for a certain amount of labor, we should drop such industries, notwithstanding they comprise nearly all our manufacturing industries, and import such goods instead of making them here, and turn the labor which has been employed in such manufacturing industries into agriculture or the production of crude materials in which we have natural advantages. This is the policy which has been again and again enthusiastically applauded on the Democratic side. And it is seriously contended by the free-trade theorist that this policy —which in fact would be going back where we were a hundred years ago—would give us the largest production of wealth, highest wages, and greatest consuming capacity. Perhaps the gentlemen who advocate this theory will be able to tell us what any of our farm products would be worth with such a multiplication of farmers and such an annihilation of nonagricultural consumers.

It is sufficient to say in reply that any economic theory which, put into practice, would prevent a diversification of industries, and especially the establishment of advanced manufactures, is fundamentally wrong. For nothing is clearer in the light of reason or in the teachings of experience than that people who so far multiply their pursuits as to give an opportunity for every variety of talent, and especially the highest skill, to do most effective work, take the lead in agriculture, manufacturing, and commerce. A nation with advanced industries, placed alongside the farm, produces far more per inhabitant than one which confines its industries to what free-traders call "natural channels." [Applause.]

On January 12 Sereno E. Payne [N. Y.] spoke in opposition to the bill.

I have studied this bill to see if I could find any theory upon which it was constructed. It is not a protective bill, although the committee have left some protective features in it. They have even seen fit to adopt a number of the rates contained in the McKinley bill. The title of the bill says that it is "to raise revenue," yet it proves to be a bill to reduce revenue by $76,000,000 a year.

As I have gone through its provisions, and examined its paragraphs, and studied its relations to the different industries of the country, I have come to the conclusion that the committee have gone back to the year 1880, and with their candidate for the presidency in that year [General Winfield S. Hancock] have agreed that "the tariff is a local issue." [Laughter.]

The committee have reduced the duty on hops from 15 to 18 cents. Now we shall be compelled to enter into competition with Canada, Germany, and England, and with any other country that raises hops; and why? To save 2 cents a barrel to the brewers of the country. It is time that the farmers of this country had a little consideration from the Democratic party as well as the brewers of the United States. [Applause.]

Mr. Chairman, the more we examine this bill the more we are convinced of the astuteness of that Canadian member of Parliament who stated that Canada got more out of the Wilson bill, without giving anything up in return, than she could have hoped to obtain by the most favorable reciprocity treaty.

The bill should read, for the encouragement of the Canadian farmer and the Canadian mechanic, the Algerian grape grower, the Bermuda onion grower, and the foreign mechanics the world over. That would be its most appropriate title.

The committee put salt on the free list. We paid $4 a barrel when we did not make enough salt to meet the demand in this country; but now it has gone down under a high rate of duty to 40 cents a barrel at the factory.

Every pound of salt shipped from Liverpool to the United

States and to Canada pays a profit to a single agent at New York City to-day. Give them free salt—what then? Why, they would cut down just enough below our prices to get into the country from Canada. But what gentleman is so credulous as to believe that a single individual consumer of the United States would get his salt a hundredth part of a cent lower than he gets it to-day. Then when they have got into our trade, when they have closed our factories (and when a salt factory is closed

"I PRESS THE BUTTON, THEY DO THE REST (ING)"
Cartoon by Victor Gillam in "Judge"

it deteriorates very fast and soon loses its usefulness) we shall have to pay tribute to this English subject in the city of New York for every pound of salt that comes into the United States from across the water.

I might speak of flax and hemp. I might speak of the peculiar consideration and the love that this committee have for the rags that fall from the paupers of foreign countries, that they should put rags and shoddy, unmanufactured, on the free list in this bill.

The committee has put lower duties on wire rods, wire, and wire cloth. If the manufacturers continue to make wire cloth in this country under this bill they must cut wages right in two in the middle.

There are some things about this bill that I cannot understand at all, unless the rates were put into one basket and the subjects into another, and one man drew out the rates and another the subjects, and the clerk wrote them down as they thus came out. [Laughter.]

The chairman of the Committee on Ways and Means wants to go out after the markets of the twelve hundred millions of people who buy only 10 per cent. of the consumption of the world. Better keep the market of those who, though they be but seventy millions of people, buy more than 30 per cent. of the consumption of the world. [Applause on the Republican side.]

With what would the native of Africa, whose sole possession is the necklace around his neck, pay for the railroad iron which the chairman is going to send to that market? [Laughter.] Oh, this *ignis fatuus* of a foreign market! Let us keep our own market, pay our own wages, keep our own consumers what they are, the best consumers in the world. Do not cut off the very life-blood of the prosperity of this great nation. [Applause on the Republican side.]

I want you gentlemen to amend this bill only as suits your own sweet wills. Put all the direct and war taxes upon it you choose; fix it even to suit the Ohio free-trader, who was so vociferously applauded by you, then when you have perfected it I shall stand ready to vote to strike out its enacting clause that it may remain as a monument to your folly.

I shall do this to save the present law, which gave us the three most prosperous years of our national life. I shall do this because this bill will encourage fraud and perjury; will drive the honest importer from the business; will put a direct, offensive, and inquisitorial tax upon our people; will give a gratuity to the sugar producer, without a farthing of benefit to the country; will foster the interests of sections at the expense of others; will impoverish our farmer, destroy his wool industry, leave him defenceless against the tobacco of Sumatra, give his market for barley to Canada, for hops to Germany; cripple by a reduction of their purchasing power the consumer of his vegetables, his poultry, his dairy products, his small fruits, ruin his home market, and because it will tend to reduce labor to the level of its foreign impoverished rival; will stop many a wheel, put out many a forge, bring poverty and want to American homes, sap the manhood of American citizens, and continue the blight of poverty and want, and hunger and cold, which has so recently overtaken the people of a country one year ago the busiest, the most prosperous, the most progressive, the happiest, and the most independent the world ever saw. [Loud and long-continued applause on the Republican side.]

Jerry Simpson [Kan.] followed Mr. Payne.

I believe that in the discussion of this question one very important factor has been excluded. I believe, since this is an agricultural country, with more than one-half the population depending on agriculture for a livelihood, that any law or system of laws which results in injury to agriculture must finally endanger every other branch of business, for all depend upon it.

I have not heard an argument from the Republican side on this question that has to me given proof that agricultural interests are benefited one particle by this system of protection.

The history of the last twenty years proves that the interest of agriculture has been constantly declining, until to-day the farmers of this country are producing nearly everything that the soil yields, that they cultivate, at a very low profit, and a great many at an actual loss. For Republican protection-tariff advocates to stand here and say this difficulty, this disaster to the laboring classes that now confronts us, and to the business interests of the country generally, has come upon us suddenly within the year is to ignore all the facts of the case.

There has been a good deal said about trusts in this discussion. Let us see what the effect of a protective tariff is. It was very cogently stated by Mr. Henry George, who says that out of a protective tariff, as naturally as grow toadstools out of a rotten log, grow the trusts and combines of your country.

When, in 1888, an enormous campaign contribution was levied upon the sugar trust it refused to pay it. Senator Plumb advised Chairman Foster to "put it over the fire and fry some of the fat out of it." This was done, and the McKinley bill reduced its protection from 1½ cents to one-half cent a pound. But plenty of fat was left. The protected sugar trust did collect from the people in the year 1892 its protection of half a cent per pound on 3,600,000,000 pounds of sugar, or $18,000,000 to "pay the difference in wages." The total wages it pays is 14 cents per 100 pounds, or $5,040,000, leaving $12,960,000, which it pockets from the money collected to pay its workmen the "difference in wages" after getting its labor practically free of cost.

The window-glass trust was protected in 1891 by a duty of $2.37½ on $2.20 worth of foreign glass 16 by 24. Wages paid, ten-pot furnace, per month, were in United States, $2,241. The duty levied on a month's product of a Belgium furnace was $2,937, or $796 more than the total wages paid in this country, collecting this money from the people. They never paid it to their laborers, but have put it into their own pockets.

The enormous amount collected from the people for this extraordinary privilege for the products they produce fell heavily upon the agricultural classes. They are the consumers of sugar and window glass and all of those things that the four hundred and fifty trusts that have been formed under your protective system produce, and that is what has brought the agricultural interests of this country to poverty and bankruptcy to-day, and it must follow that the other interests, as I stated before, must fall into it, and if they do not look to the upbuilding of those interests the whole fabric of your institutions must bring us to bankruptcy as sure as the sun will rise in the morning.

Mr. Chairman, I am not pleased with this bill. I like much better the bill of the gentleman from Ohio [Mr. Johnson]. But, inasmuch as the gentleman from Michigan [Mr. Burrows] says in his speech that this bill carries large reductions as compared with the McKinley system of robbery, and inasmuch as it puts one hundred and thirty-one more articles on the free list, therefore every man who has his article on the free list will be an enemy to the protection the other fellow gets, and must eventually come in the direction of free trade. I support and welcome the bill as a step in the direction of what may eventually follow. [Applause.]

On January 13 W. Bourke Cockran [N. Y.] supported the bill.

Gentlemen tell us that this bill will operate such a reduction of the revenue as will paralyze the Government. I deny it. I insist that this reduction in the tariff will increase the revenue of the Government. It will stimulate consumption, it will quicken trade, it will broaden commerce, it will not only increase the revenue by a larger yield of taxes, but it will increase the opportunities of the people to earn the money with which the taxes are to be defrayed. [Applause on the Democratic side.]

When we consider the objections to this measure we find that they are twofold. One objection is that it will increase business. Another objection is that it will decrease business. And, strange as it may seem, I have heard both propositions advanced by the same orator, and that, too, by a gentleman who is a leader of thought and an exponent of doctrine on the other side of the chamber. I refer to the gentleman from Maine [Mr. Dingley]. He took the ground that in order to raise sufficient revenue under the provisions of this bill we will be compelled to increase our imports $250,000,000; and he said that such a prospect was calculated to spread rejoicing among the foreigners and to fill the cottages and homes of this land with gloomy apprehension. He told us in the very next paragraph that between nations, as between individuals, all trade is an exchange of commodities; that money is used only to accomplish the movement or circulation of the goods from the hands of one man into the hands of the other; and, if that be so, must not this $250,000,000 worth of goods that we import be paid for by $250,000,000 of other goods that we export, and in the exportation of which we find our profits? [Applause on the Democratic side.]

MR. DINGLEY.—My answer is simply this, that experience has demonstrated in the past that, in a situation such as sketched by the gentleman, we paid for excessive importations, over and above our exportations, by sending gold abroad, and to that extent depleting it from this country.

MR. COCKRAN.—Let me ask the gentleman from Maine on what basis we could expect to carry on trade if his theory of prosperity be sound? If it be an injury to send abroad money, it must be a benefit to import it. If we imported $250,000,000 in money the gentleman manifestly thinks that we would be better off than if we imported $250,000,000 worth of goods.

Am I right in that? [Laughter.]

MR. DINGLEY.—I suppose the gentleman is aware that we very often purchase things and get into debt for them instead of paying for them. My proposition is simply this, that anything which leads to the importation of goods such as we should produce ourselves therefore deprives our laborers of the opportunity of making those goods, and inevitably tends to reduce the price for labor in this country, and tends to produce the evils of which I spoke in my speech.

MR. COCKRAN.—If I understand the theory of the gentleman from Maine [Mr. Dingley], it is that the importation of $250,000,000 worth of goods into this country, provided we manufactured similar goods ourselves, would be a startling event, pregnant with danger to the prosperity of this country. Yet my friend spoke of the importation of money as something that would indicate great commercial prosperity.

Now, Mr. Chairman, I venture to state that, as between an

importation of money and an importation of goods, the general prosperity of the people would be best subserved by the importation of goods. [Applause on the Democratic side.]

Suppose that instead of importing goods we imported gold; what would be the consequence? If you could maintain for any length of time large importations of gold you would soon bankrupt all the rest of the world and nobody would be left to trade with you. But, assuming for a moment that such a course of trade would not result in universal bankruptcy, what would be done with the gold after it had been imported? You know, my friend, it would not be left idle in the vaults; you are too good an economist for that. You know that the only use to which it could be put would be to exchange it against commodities. You would have to produce your commodities here. It would take time to produce them, the cost of production would be higher, amount of commodities would necessarily be smaller and the national wealth would be correspondingly lessened.

The true course is to bring in from abroad the goods that you can obtain best and cheapest in exchange for the goods that you can produce best and cheapest. If your natural position gives you an advantage in that trade, all the powers of earth cannot rob you of it unless you yourself close the doors of your ports in the teeth of your own prosperity, by a vicious system of protective legislation based upon all the errors that have ever afflicted political economy. [Prolonged applause on the Democratic side.]

Here Mr. Cockran pointed out that it was the military nations of Europe which had adopted protection.

One vice breeds another, one oppressive political institution is always buttressed and defended by other vicious institutions. Men instinctively adjust their economic systems to their political systems. As a sleeper on a cold night brings his knees in the direction of his chin, unconscious of the physical law which controls his action, so the Government, which prevents its most efficient laborers from engaging in industrial pursuits instinctively, unconsciously perhaps, but none the less surely, adopts a protective system, because it lessens production, reduces the demand for labor, and thus conceals from the people the worst features of a military system which forces into idleness a large part of the population and drives from the fields of industry the strongest productive forces in the country. And thus we see that an oppressive government adopts an oppressive commercial system as inevitably as a duck takes to water. [Laughter.]

What was it that caused the Corsican Napoleon to fall from the great eminence to which his military genius had raised him? It was not any decay in the strategic skill which he had displayed in the days when he commanded the army of Italy. His military reverses were not caused by the recklessness of his ambitions; they were the fruits of his economic mistakes. He wrote his abdication not at Fontainebleau in 1814, but at Berlin, when he penned the Berlin decrees by which he sought to command the course of trade and to limit the freedom of commercial intercourse throughout Europe. [Loud applause on the Democratic side.]

Mr. Chairman, let us dispose of this question in the interest of the American people, in the interest of freer trade, of freer production, of labor better paid because more widely employed. [Loud applause.]

In seeking to find the freest markets for our products, we seek the welfare of the whole human race, we seek to establish a commercial system which will make this land the fountain of civilization—this people the trustees of humanity—which will make the flag of freedom in the air above us the emblem of freedom on the earth beneath us—freedom in our fields, freedom in our mines, freedom on the seas, freedom through all the world, for all the children of men. [Loud and long-continued applause on the floor and in the galleries.]

William J. Bryan [Neb.] supported the bill.

The committee has recognized that it had to deal with a system vicious in principle and yet present with us, and it seemed wiser to make a journey toward an ultimate revenue tariff than to attempt the accomplishment of it by a single enactment. The bill makes many reductions of prohibitory duties, so that in such cases the revenue will be increased rather than diminished. On other articles it both reduces the rate of duty and the amount of revenue, believing that the tax is greater than the people should bear even for revenue on those particular articles. Generally speaking, the bill leaves the tariff lowest upon articles of necessity and highest upon articles of luxury. Many duties upon agricultural products which afforded neither revenue nor protection were reduced or abolished.

One very important feature of the bill is the addition to the free list of several articles classed as raw materials. Perhaps, technically speaking, there is nothing separated from realty and having value which can be called absolutely raw material, but commercially speaking those things are called raw material which lie at the basis of great manufacturing enterprises and which are only utilized after conversion into a finished product.

The average tariff left on woolen goods is a little over 39 per cent., which is a reduction of about 60 per cent. on that schedule.

Mr. Chairman, this bill brings to the farmer ten dollars for every dollar it takes from him. We have put wheat upon the free list because we are selling it in Liverpool in competition with the cheapest labor in the world, and if we can sell it there we can sell it here. But we put in a provision in regard to grain, limiting it to grain from any country which will admit ours free, in order to bring an influence to bear upon Canada to admit our grain products free.

JOHN A. PICKLER [S. D.].—I thought you were not in favor of reciprocity?

MR. BRYAN.—I am not in favor of the reciprocity which you had last year, but I am in favor of commercial freedom. [Applause.] And I am willing to say to Canada, ''We will treat your products as you treat ours. We will open our gates to you if you open your gates to us,'' and that is what we have provided for in that clause. It may possibly do some good, although it is not absolutely necessary, for Canada has, I am informed, a standing offer to admit our grains free whenever we remove the duty from Canadian grains. Trade between the two countries will be profitable to both. But, sir, if that clause is left out and wheat is admitted absolutely free, and corn free, and these other great products of agriculture free, it will not harm the farmers of the United States a single dollar.

Now, Mr. Chairman, there is another provision in this bill to which I shall very briefly invite your attention. The bill provides for a gradual repeal of the sugar bounty—one-fourth of one cent to be dropped each year. It also reduces the tariff on fine sugar one-half. I believe that this is the best solution possible at this time of the difficulties surrounding this schedule.

We had a condition to deal with—a condition brought about by Republican legislation—and we made the best of it. When I was called upon to choose between a tax upon sugar which would raise the price of it to every consumer and a bounty reduced gradually, I chose the latter. I preferred to let the bounty fall by degrees, and raise the needed revenue in a way that, instead of taxing the poor man as much as the rich man on the same number of pounds of sugar, would make wealth bear its share of the expenses of government. [Applause.] In other words, I would rather give free sugar to the people and make up the deficit by an income tax. [Prolonged applause.]

And now, in conclusion, let me repel a charge which has been made against this bill by our opponents. They have said that it is sectional; that it is drawn in the interest of the South. They have waved the bloody shirt and drafted into service the Confederate constitution. Let us see what section will profit most by the duties retained. The gentleman from Michigan [Mr. Burrows] complained because we left a high duty on rice, but he forgot to tell you that we left the duty 28 cents on the dollar lower than the duty fixed in the McKinley bill; he complained that we had left a high duty on Tennessee marble, but he forgot to tell you that we had reduced the duty on that same marble more than one-third.

Our opponents entirely fail to mention the generosity shown by Southern members toward Northern industries. Texas has more sheep than any Northern State, and yet her members are willing to give free wool to the manufacturers of Massachusetts. [Applause.]

When Michigan iron ore is placed on the free list, Alabama ore is placed there also; when Pennsylvania coal is placed on the free list, West Virginia coal is placed there also; when the rough lumber of Maine and Wisconsin is placed upon the free list, the rough lumber of North Carolina and Georgia is placed there also.

The same bill which gives free cotton ties to the South gives free binding twine to the North; the same bill which gives to the farmers of the South free cotton bagging for export gives to the farmers of the North free agricultural implements. There is one section in this country which gets the lion's share, but it is not the South. [Applause.] For every dollar that the Southern States receive in protection from this bill New England will receive five dollars. [Applause.] One State, Massachusetts, will reap more benefit from the tariff left in this bill than all the Southern States combined. The State of New York alone, and the State of Pennsylvania alone, will reap more benefit from the tariff left in this bill than all the Southern States together. Why, sir, the little State of Rhode Island has more money invested in the manufacture of cotton and woolen goods than all the States south of Mason and Dixon's line, yet they tell us that a bill which leaves 38 and 39 per cent. on these goods is a sectional bill drawn in behalf of the South.

Aye, sir, if this bill is sectional, it is not drawn to give special protection to the interests of the South; but the South is justified in voting for it. Why? Because, sir, you cannot aid the South and West by means of protection. You can lay burdens upon them and press them down, but you cannot build them up by means of import duties. The South and West can vote for this bill because, while it gives protection to the Northeastern States, it makes the tax less burdensome than it is now. History is repeating itself. A generation ago New England helped to free the black slaves of the South, and to-day the Southern people rejoice that it was accomplished. [Cheers and applause.] The time has come when the Southern people are helping to free the white slaves of the North; and in the fulness of time New England will rejoice in its accomplishment. [Great applause.]

On January 15 the question of wages arose.

MR. PAYNE said: What I want to do is to put the manufacturers of this country in condition such that they can pay higher wages; and one thing is certain, that the workingmen of this country, organized as they are, when the manufacturers shall have been enabled to pay higher wages, will compel them to do so. [Applause on the Republican side.]

MR. COCKRAN.—Now, Mr. Chairman, my colleague [Mr. Payne] has placed this question before the committee in a shape in which it can be disposed of in the briefest possible space. He tells us that the theory upon which this protective system is maintained is to stimulate the profits in the hands of the manufacturers, and then trust to the trades unions to get those profits out of the manufacturers. [Laughter on the Democratic side.] We believe in putting the profits in the first instance into the hands of the laborers. [Applause on the Democratic side.]

JOSEPH H. WALKER [Mass.].—How?

MR. COCKRAN.—By increasing the demand for their labor and increasing production in this country. [Derisive laughter on the Republican side and applause on the Democratic side.]

Why are the laborers hungry and the manufacturers comfortable? What basis of division is that which enables these employers to look forward to this winter with composure, which forces the men over whose fate you gentlemen shed your tears to wander in the streets hopeless, homeless, without food or shelter, while all around them the favored objects of your legislation are dwelling in comfort as a result of that legislation? [Prolonged applause on the Democratic side.]

CHARLES A. BOUTELLE [Me.].—Mr. Chairman, Jack Cade exhausted that style of argument more than five hundred years ago.

MR. COCKRAN [pounding on his desk].—Mr. Chairman, the gentleman is faulty in his history. Jack Cade lived four hundred years ago.

THOMAS B. REED [Me.].—Mr. Chairman, I am exceedingly sorry that, with all the répertoire of eloquence which the gentleman from New York [Mr. Cockran] has at his command, he should resort so frequently to that portion of it which is merely physical. [Laughter.]

The gentleman has indulged himself both to-day and on Saturday last in expressions of contempt for our industrial system, because under threat of changes business is paralyzed, and because the accumulated wealth of this country is too little to tide it over the difficulty. But unfortunately, throughout all the language which he has used on this subject, there went this continuous error; he made no distinction between wealth which is consumable and wealth which is intended to produce consumable wealth.

There is an immense amount of unconsumable wealth which is used in the production of other wealth existing in this country and in other countries; but, from the very nature of the case, the amount of consumable wealth that there is in any country at any time is exceedingly limited.

Now, let me come for a moment to this question of wages. The gentleman says that it depends upon supply and demand. I say that is an utterly exploded doctrine. Wages depend upon the amount of the market, and also upon the nature of the workingman himself. I anticipate what the gentleman is going to say in response to the suggestions of other gentlemen on his side, that what they need is a more extensive market; that what they need is to go forth to the rest of the universe and obtain a market; and the method they propose is to obtain a market somewhere else by giving up the market that we have here. [Applause on the Republican side.] But we on our side believe in enlarging the market in a different fashion. We do not mean to go to the ends of the earth and struggle with the cheaper labor of the whole world. What we mean to do is to elevate the market of this country by giving higher wages to the laborers, and thereby constituting a market as broad as our production. [Applause.]

In this country, with the laborer seeking to obtain higher wages and fewer hours of work and the demand of the public for lower prices, there is going on a tremendous struggle; and that is all the struggle that the inventive power of this country can sustain.

Now you propose, by bringing us in contact with a lower civilization without protection, to make the success of that struggle an absolute impossibility. You are crushing down the laboring man by your efforts; and you are thereby intensifying this struggle between the employer and his employees, which is liable to be fought out as long as selfishness reigns in this world. But, thank Heaven, the success, the good fortune, and the prosperity of the laboring man do not depend on these men who rend the heavens with their shouts of praise, but upon the laws of the Lord God Omnipotent. [Prolonged applause on the Republican side]. And among the laws of Omnipotence is the use of human brains by aid of law to provide the laborer with opportunities for work. [Renewed applause on the Republican side and in the galleries.]

MR. COCKRAN.—An opportunity to listen to my distinguished friend from Maine [Mr. Reed] is always a liberal education. The conclusion of his remarks explains the beginning of them, and adds a significant light to the examination which we can bestow upon them. He began by stating that much of the discussion on this side was physical; let me compliment him by saying that the conclusion of the protection argument is purely spiritual. [Laughter and applause on the Democratic side.]

In this way you will observe that the distinguished warrior who had entered the ring when his partisans were sore beset proves that his final reliance is on the Lord of Hosts rather than upon the reasoning power of the American people. [Laughter on the Democratic side.]

But I do not think, Mr. Chairman, that there ought to be any contest between the two. My judgment is that every conclusion which the American people have reached in their history upon any great question has sooner or later come into direct conjunction and harmony with the laws of God; and the American people are moving in that direction now by this bill which is before the House. [Great cheering on the Democratic side.]

Mr. Chairman, that the wages of labor depend upon the law of supply and demand is a proposition so evident that I never expected to have heard it denied on this floor by a gentleman to whom a great part of the intelligent thought of this country looks up for guidance. I had never supposed that the value of any material or element of wealth depended upon any other law than that of supply and demand. But I regard the statement of the gentleman from Maine on this subject as the crowning admission of the correctness of the position occupied by the majority. I am willing to leave this dispute on the issue which he has framed. If the laws of supply and demand do not control the price of labor, then you gentlemen of the minority are right. If the laws of supply and demand do control the price of labor, then according to your own statement we are right, and on that issue we challenge the verdict of the American people. [Applause on the Democratic side.]

On February 1 Mr. Reed replied to Mr. Cockran on the question of wages.

When I talk about wages I use the word in its broadest sense as the price and value of service whether of brain or muscle. When I speak of constant and continuous increase of wages, I do not mean the caprices of benevolence or of charity, or the fantasy of a mind longing for the impossible.

What is the rule and measure of wages? "Supply and demand" in no sense solves the problem. Only last week in this very city the builders and material men and the workers met together to see if in response to oversupply compared with demand concessions could be made. The material men were ready to yield, but the workmen, whose labor was the only perishable article involved, utterly refused. According to supply and demand they ought to have been hustling each other to see who could get into the job. Instead of that they are ready to struggle and to endure privations rather than give up what have become to them necessaries of life. Of course in time they will have to submit unless this bill is beaten, but there are limitations beyond which you cannot go. No nation can endure in peace any cut which goes into the quick. Necessities born of social life and advancing civilization are the real measure of wages.

This question of wages is all-important as bearing upon the question of consumption. All production depends upon consumption. Who are the consumers?

Unfortunately the gentlemen on the other side have persistently retained the old idea that the producers are one class and the consumers are another, and hence we hear on all hands such stupidities of speech as those which sum up the workers in each branch and compare them with the whole people. One hundred and fifty thousand workers in woolens—you ask what are they compared with 70,000,000 of consumers; 200,000 workers in steel, what are they compared with 70,000,000 of consumers; 200,000 workers in cotton, what are they compared with 70,-000,000 of consumers, and so on all through the long list, forgetting that all these people added together make the whole 70,000,000 themselves.

Where do our high wages come from? Just think a moment what wages are. They are the devourers of consumable wealth. In order to have more consumable wealth you must have an incentive for its creation. Wealth will never be made unless a consumer stands ready. More consumable wealth, therefore, depends upon a broadening market. This does not necessarily mean more purchasers, but purchasers with better purses, though for that matter in this country we have both.

Here let me meet one other question, and let me meet it fairly. We are charged with having claimed that the tariff alone will raise wages, and we are pointed triumphantly to the fact that the wages of France and Germany, protected by a tariff, are lower than England, free of all tariff, and to America with a tariff and still higher wages. We have never made such a claim in any such form. Free-traders have set up that claim for us in order to triumphantly knock it over. What we do say is that, where two nations have equal skill and equal appliances and a market of nearly equal size and one of them can hire labor at one-half less, nothing but a tariff can maintain the higher wages, and that we can prove.

If there be two bales of goods side by side made by the same kind of machinery and with the labor of the human being in both of the same degree of skill, and if the labor of one bale cost only half, for example, as much as the other, that other bale can never be sold until the extra cost of the costlier labor is squeezed out of it, provided there is an abundant supply of the product of the cheaper labor. If the bale with the cheaper labor of England in it meets the bale with the dearer labor of America in it, which will be bought at cost of production? I leave that problem just there. The sale of the English bale will be only limited by England's production.

Now, as to France and Germany. England had centuries of peace or distant war, while both France and Germany were the battlefields of Europe. Until Bismarck made Germany a nation she was not even big enough to enter successfully modern industrial warfare. To compare either of those nations in machinery or wealth to England, a hundred years in advance of them both by reason of her history before 1850 and her tributary provinces, is absolutely farcical.

We are the only rival that England fears, for we alone have in our borders the population and the wages, the raw material, and within ourselves the great market which insures to us the most improved machinery. Our constant power to increase our wages insures us also continuous progress. If you wish us to follow the example of England, I say yes, with all my heart, but her real example and nothing less. Let us keep protection, as she did, until no rival dares to invade our territory, and then we may take our chances for a future which by that time will not be unknown. [Applause.]

Charles F. Crisp [Ga.] arose amid prolonged applause by the Democratic side and in the galleries, and replied to Mr. Reed.

The gentleman from Maine, with a facility that is unequaled, when he encounters an argument which he is unable to answer, passes it by with some bright and witty saying and thereby invites and receives the applause of those who believe as he does. But the gentleman does not attempt, the gentleman has not to-day attempted, to reply to the real arguments that are made in favor of freer trade and greater liberty of commerce.

The gentleman points to the progress of the United States, he points to the rate of wages in the United States, he points to the aggregated wealth of the United States, and claims all this as due to protection. But he does not explain how we owe these blessings to protection. He says, we have protection in the United States, wages are high in the United States, therefore protection makes high wages.

When we ask the gentleman from Maine to give us a reason why a high protective tariff increases the rate of wages he fails to give it, but points to the glory, the prosperity, and the honor of our country. The gentleman belongs to that school who believe that scarcity is a blessing, and that abundance should be prohibited by law.

Assuming, if you please, for the purposes of the argument. what these gentlemen claim, that a protective tariff gives higher wages in protected industries, and still your proposition is wholly without foundation. The consumer and the producer the same! Why, Mr. Speaker, do you know the proportion the producers of protected manufactured products in this country bear to the producers of all other products? You do not pretend that your tariff raises the price of the farmer's wheat, or his cotton, or his corn, or his meats; yet in spite of this great class, which is as three to one or more against the other, you gravely say that the producer and the consumer are the same!

Will you tell me how your protective tariff benefits the man who raises cotton, or corn, or wheat, or meats? The producers of those great staples are forced to seek their market abroad. A hundred years of this fostering system have not yet built up a home market for more than one-third of the cotton produced in the United States. Our market is abroad. Will you tell me how this protective tariff benefits our agricultural producers?

Suppose a farmer in Minnesota has 5,000 bushels of wheat and a farmer in Georgia has 100 bales of cotton. That wheat at 80 cents a bushel is worth $4,000, and that cotton at 8 cents a pound is worth $4,000. Let those producers ship their staples abroad. The Minnesota wheat grower ships his wheat to Liverpool; whether he ships it there or not that is where the price of his wheat is fixed. The Georgia cotton raiser ships his cotton to Liverpool; whether he ships it there or not that is where the price of his cotton is fixed. The wheat and the cotton are sold in that free-trade market. The wheat is sold for $4,000; the cotton brings the same amount. The Minnesota farmer invests the $4,000 he has received for his wheat in clothing, crockeryware, iron, steel, dress goods, clothing—whatever he may need for his family in Minnesota. The Georgia cotton raiser invests the proceeds of his cotton in like kinds of goods. Each of those men ships his goods to this country and they reach the port of New York. When either undertakes to unload them he is met by the collector of customs, who says, "You cannot bring into this market those goods for which you have exchanged your products unless you pay to the United States a tariff fixed by the McKinley law—a tax of $2,000!"

The man will in vain refer the collector to the statement of the gentleman from Maine that the foreigner pays the tax. What is the result? The goods that cost $4,000 without the tariff cost him $6,000 with it.

Ah, but says the gentleman, he ought to buy his goods at home. Let him try it. Let him go into the home market; and, according to the statement of the gentleman from Maine, when he enters the home market he will buy the home products almost on equal terms, in competition with those same goods which are sent here from abroad, embracing the cost of raw material, plus labor and plus the present rate of the tariff. [Applause on the Democratic side.]

If he buys his goods abroad and pays the duty, it goes into the treasury of the United States and is called a tax; if he buys the goods at home and pays the increased price that is put upon them by the tariff, it goes into the pocket of the protected manufacturer and is called "protection." [Applause.] In either case the increased price is practically the same amount, and in both cases the consumer pays it.

Perhaps it is dangerous to enter a field where the gentleman from Maine invites one. The gentleman is so cunning of fence, so wily an adversary, that it may be dangerous to accept his challenge; yet I will venture. The gentleman says he hopes he will never hear again the old cry that we have free trade in labor, and then proceeds to say that the laborer who comes here from abroad does not bring his reduced rates of wages with him. Nobody ever contended that that was the purpose or effect of the foreign laborer coming here; but the argument which the gentleman from Maine derides has been made by gentlemen on the side of the question which I represent to show that, while the manufacturers are seeking and the Republican party is granting them a high tariff to protect them from competition, yet that party has never passed any law to protect the wage-earner from competition, but any man from abroad may come here and compete with him for the employment which the manufacturer has to give. [Applause on the Democratic side.]

Now, our friends on the other side criticized our bill because they said that it created a deficiency of $75,000,000. We have tried to relieve ourselves from that criticism. We have amended the bill. We have established a new subject or another matter of taxation. We recognize the justness of the statement of the other side, that we ought to show in our bill where we propose to raise the revenue. We recognize that. There will be a deficiency of $70,000,000 or $75,000,000 on the basis of last year's importations. We propose to raise $10,000,-000 by increase of the whisky tax; a little by the tax on playing cards, and a little on an increase of the tax on cigarettes; and we propose to raise $30,000,000 by a tax on the incomes of corporations and on the net incomes of individuals. [Loud applause on the Democratic side.] That makes, say, $45,000,000. And we propose to meet the other deficiency if there be any, in the good old Democratic way—by reduction of expenditures. [Loud applause.]

Mr. Wilson closed the debate.

I must apologize to my friends on the other side if I pass by their arguments for lack of time to refute them. But for this I should delight to take up, at least for a few moments, the beautiful and elaborate oration which my honored colleague from Michigan [Mr. Burrows] brings into this House every Congress like a cluster of wax flowers under a glass case [laughter and applause], with a pathetic but firm admonition that no member shall fling at it a pebble of interruption or interrogatory. [Laughter.]

The gentleman from Maine, Mr. Reed, has appeared this morning in a rôle somewhat different from that in which he usually addresses the House. He has laid aside his ordinary methods of debating great public questions and has given us a set oration. He has endeavored to take up the stock arguments of protection and sickly them over with a pale cast of philosophy. [Laughter.] But, after all, his main argument was that which is heard on every platform in the country, that, because we have had protection in the United States for the last thirty years we have drawn all our prosperity, our national greatness, our individual and social advancement from a law of Congress, and not from the character and enterprise of our people, the resources of our country, the freedom of our Government, and the blessing of Almighty God.

An argument which gentlemen upon this side are using to excuse themselves for hesitating, at least, to vote for this bill is that the income tax has been added to it. I need not say to them that I did not concur in the policy of attaching an income-tax bill to the tariff bill. I have had some doubt as to the expediency of a personal income tax at the present time, but when the committee decided otherwise I threw in my fortunes earnestly and loyally with them because I had never been hostile to the idea of an income tax. [Loud applause on the Democratic side.] It has been opposed here as class legislation; it is nothing of the kind, Mr. Speaker; it is simply an effort, an honest first effort, to balance the weight of taxation on the poor consumers of the country who have heretofore borne it all. [Loud applause.] Gentlemen who complain of it as class legislation forget that during the fifty years of its existence in England it has been the strongest force in preventing or allaying those class distinctions that have harassed the other governments of the Old World.

And now, but one word more: We are about to vote upon

this bill. If I knew that, when the roll is called, every Democratic name would respond in the spirit of that larger patriotism which I have tried to suggest, I should be proud and lighthearted to-day. Let me say to my brethren who are doubting as to what they shall do that this roll call will be entered, not only upon the journals of this House, it will be written in the history of this country, it will be entered in the annals of freedom throughout all time. [Applause.]

This is not a battle over percentages, over this or that tariff schedule—it is a battle for human freedom. [Applause.] As Mr. Burke truly said, every great battle for human freedom is waged around the question of taxation. You may think to-day that some peculiar feeling or view of your own will excuse you for not supporting this great movement; you may think to-day that some excuse which seems to cover you as a garment will be sufficient in the future; that some reason which seems strong and satisfactory to you, some desire to oblige a great interest behind you, may justify a negative vote when the roll is called, but the scorching gaze of a liberty-loving posterity will shrivel them away from you forever. [Applause.] The men who had the opportunity to sign the Declaration of Independence and refused or neglected because there was something in it which they did not like—thank God there were none such, but, if there had been, what would be their standing in history to-day? If men on the battlefield at Lexington or at Bunker Hill, from some ground of personal or local dissatisfaction, had thrown away their weapons, what think you would have been their feelings in all the remaining years of their lives when the Liberty Bell rang out on every recurring anniversary of American independence? [Applause.]

This is a roll of honor. This is a roll of freedom, and, in the name of honor and in the name of freedom, I summon every Democratic member of this House to inscribe his name upon it. [Loud and prolonged applause.]

Various amendments were passed changing, not to a great degree, rates of duties on certain articles of the bill. An internal revenue amendment whose most important provision was the imposition of an income tax [see page 406] was adopted. The leading Republicans did not vote on the measure.

By a partisan vote of 204 to 140 the bill was then passed, amid great cheering and applause on the Demo-

XII—21

cratic side.   Mr. Wilson was carried in triumph around
and out of the House on the shoulders of the Democratic
Representatives.

The Senate referred the bill to the Committee on Finance, the chairman of which, Daniel W. Voorhees [Ind.]
reported it with amendments on March 20.   Justin S.
Morrill [Vt.] announced that the Republican minority
were opposed to the income tax, the many changes from
specific to *ad valorem* duties and to the great bulk of the
provisions of the bill.

The debate on the bill lasted until July 3, when the
bill was amended in a number of material points, chiefly
by the activities of Calvin S. Brice [O.] and Arthur P.
Gorman [Md.], Democrats, and passed.

The amendments in general increased the duties of
the House bill.

The bill was passed by a vote of 39 to 34.

When the amended bill came back to the House Mr.
Wilson declared that the Senate had changed the principle of the bill, and so he advised the House to reject
the amendments.

On Mr. Wilson's motion a conference was appointed
between the two chambers.   The joint committee failed
to come to an agreement, and a second committee was
appointed, which also failed to agree.   Finally the House
accepted the Senate amendments (on August 13) by a
vote of 182 to 106.   Tom Johnson [O.] voted in the negative.   The Democratic Representatives resolved to mitigate their humiliation by subsequently voting to replace
on the free list, in separate bills, the articles which had
been stricken from it in the general bill.

Before the vote was taken Mr. Reed twitted the Democratic Representatives over their "back down."   Amid
cries of "Vote! Vote!" he said:

I think your feeling, gentlemen, is perfectly natural.   The
job that you have got to do is such that the sooner you get over
it the better you will feel.   [Laughter and cries of "Vote!"
"Vote!" on the Democratic side.]   But at the same time you
will have to listen to a plain statement of what you are doing,
and you will recognize it yourselves, and it is because you rec-

ognize it in advance that you are crying, "Vote!" "Vote!" "Vote!" Your class of people in the latter day will be crying, in similar fashion, for the mountains to fall on them. [Laughter.]

DIGGING HIS GRAVE

"Oh, what was I begun for, if I'm so soon to be done for?"

Cartoon by Victor Gillam in "Judge"

Mr. Wilson expressed his great disappointment at the situation.

I had hoped and believed, until there seemed no ground

scarcely for hope or belief, that in such a contest this House, backed by the American people and enthusiastically sustained by the Democratic party, would be able to achieve some honorable compromise between the two Houses which we could have accepted, not from a sense of duty, but with a sense of satisfaction and a feeling that we had responded to the mandates of the American people.

Mr. Speaker, we have simply realized in this great fight the fact so well stated by the great leader of the tariff reform fight in Great Britain—that when the people have gained a victory at the polls they must have a further stand-up and knockdown fight with their own representatives. And we have realized, if nothing else, the warning lesson of the intrenchment of the protective system in this country under thirty years of class legislation, until the mere matter of tariff schedules is a matter of insignificance, and the great question presents itself, is this to be a Government by a self-taxing people or a Government of taxation by trusts and monopolies? [Applause on the Democratic side.]

But whatever the measure of shortcoming of this bill in its present form—whatever be its demerits in mere schedules—this I do believe, that it is not as bad as the McKinley bill. [Loud applause on the Democratic side.]

This I do know, that in part of it it does afford some relief to the taxpayers of this country, and does clip the wings of the gigantic monopolies that are now oppressing them and blocking legislation. [Applause on the Democratic side; derisive cries on the Republican side.]

Immediately following the passage of this bill we propose to present and pass a bill putting sugar on the free list. [Applause on the Democratic side.] The question is now made as to whether this is a Government by the American people for the American people, or a Government of the sugar trust for the benefit of the sugar trust. And this House will show the people, I doubt not, what its position is on that question, and the Senate will show the people its position.

MR. REED.—Mr. Speaker, I am somewhat reluctant to address the House, because my feelings are divided between two emotions. One is an emotion of regret for the Democratic party and for its position, and the other is a feeling of equal regret for the country and its position, too. So far as the gentleman from West Virginia is concerned and his compatriots, there is not the slightest necessity of my commenting on the difference between this scene of sorrow and the triumphal procession which carried him out of this House. [Laughter and applause on the Republican side.] He is not so joyous now, having been carried out in another branch, and more effectually. [Renewed laughter.]

The gentleman from West Virginia and his compatriots appear before us now, not as the triumphal reformers, marching to glory at the sound of their own sweet voices. They are little babes in the wood, and it will be found pretty soon that they were left there by their "uncle" in the White House. [Great laughter and applause on the Republican side.]

Out of your own household has come your condemnation. Nay, out of your own mouths has your condemnation come. For we shall read that bold and uncompromising declaration of the chairman of the Committee on Ways and Means that we were to sit here until the end of our term to put down the sugar trust. What do we have instead? Why, we have a proposition to fire one of those pop-gun tariff bills for which the gentleman from Illinois [Mr. Springer] was deposed from the Committee on Ways and Means. [Laughter on the Republican side.] His successor, after filling the atmosphere with his outspread wings, finds his nest in some other bird's premises. [Laughter on the Republican side.] Why not resign if you were to adopt the action of the other person? I congratulate the gentleman from Illinois [Mr. Springer] upon his personal triumph. I wish I could congratulate the country upon something, and I will— upon the speedy departure of incompetency. [Applause upon the Republican side.]

Lafe Pence [Col.], a Populist, paid an earnest tribute to Mr. Wilson.

Mr. Speaker, I am not prepared to agree with the course of the majority here to-day, although it may be the best that my fellows and I can do. But we cannot hesitate to recognize the magnificent courage as well as ability of the men who have led this fight, above all the man who is standing here to-day with blindfold off, who is a great deal bigger than he was the other day when he stood here blindfolded. Mr. Speaker, the gentleman from West Virginia [Mr. Wilson] may not live to see the end of the fight for tariff reform. He may not live to stand again and sound the call to the clans for the roll of honor and every man to answer, but, if I live to be a hundred years old, when I remember him it will be as he stands to-day, accepting the inevitable. To him I address the words of Edwin Arnold:

Charge, charge once more
Then, and be dumb.
And let the victors, when they come,
When the forts of folly fall,
Find your body by the wall.

[Applause.]

The bill was presented to President Grover Cleveland on August 15. He refused to sign it, announcing the fact that he had not done so on August 28, 1894, at which date the bill went into effect even without his signature.

CHAPTER XV

THE TARIFF OF 1897

[THE DINGLEY BILL]

Nelson Dingley [Me.] Introduces a Tariff Bill in the House—Debate: in Favor, Mr. Dingley, Albert J. Hopkins [Ill.], Jonathan P. Dolliver [Ia.], Gen. Charles H. Grosvenor [O.], Joseph H. Walker [Mass.], John Dalzell [Pa.], Sereno E. Payne [N. Y.]; Opposed, Gen. Joseph Wheeler [Ala.], John C. Bell [Col.], Edward W. Carmack [Tenn.], John L. McLaurin [S. C.], James G. Maguire [Cal.], John Sharp Williams [Miss.], Benton McMillin [Tenn.], Champ Clark [Mo.], Jerry Simpson [Kan.], John M. Allen [Miss.]—Bill Is Passed—Nelson W. Aldrich [R. I.] Introduces the Bill in the Senate—Debate: in Favor, Sen. Aldrich, Richard F. Pettigrew [S. D.]; Opposed, Donelson Caffery [La.], Roger Q. Mills [Tex.], Benjamin R. Tillman [S. C.]—Bill Is Passed with Amendments—Conference Report; Debate in the House: in Favor, Mr. Dingley, Mr. Payne; Opposed, Joseph W. Bailey [Tex.], Mr. McMillin—Report Is Adopted by House and Senate—Bill Is Signed by the President.

PRESIDENT WILLIAM McKINLEY convened Congress in special session on March 15, 1897, to revise the tariff. On March 22 a bill to this end was introduced in the House by Nelson Dingley [Me.], chairman of the Committee on Ways and Means.

THE DINGLEY TARIFF BILL

HOUSE OF REPRESENTATIVES, MARCH 22-31, 1897

Mr. Dingley supported the measure.

In this revision the committee have endeavored to discard mere theories, and have addressed themselves to the framing of a practical remedy, at least in part, for the ills which have for so many months overshadowed the country.

It is a "condition and not a theory which confronts us." Our problem is to provide adequate revenue from duties on imports to carry on the Government, and in imposing duties to secure this result to so adjust them as to secure to our own people the production and manufacture of such articles as we can produce or make for ourselves without natural disadvantage, and thus provide more abundant opportunities for our labor. For rest assured that no economic policy will prove a success unless it shall in some manner contribute to opening up employment to the masses of our people at good wages. When this shall be accomplished, and thus the purchasing power of the masses is restored, then, and not until then, will prices cease to feel the depressing effect of underconsumption, and the prosperity of our people rise to the standard of 1892.

The great secret of the prosperity of the United States up to 1893, especially after the resumption of specie payments in 1879, was the fact that our people were all at work at good wages, and thus had large purchasing power. It was this large consuming and purchasing power that made our markets the best in the world, that maintained prices at fair rates—in short, that made this country the admiration and envy of the world.

When, by first the anticipated and then partially realized overthrow of protection, industries were arrested, machinery stopped, wages reduced, and employees discharged, through the transfer of the producing and making of part of what we had previously made to other lands, then the purchasing power of the masses was diminished and the demand for products decreased, and this gorged the markets, abnormally lowered prices, and prostrated industries and business.

Mr. Chairman, the past four years have been enlightening, especially to candid investigators of economic problems. We have been attending a kindergarten on a gigantic scale. The tuition has come high, but no people ever learned so much in so brief a time. [Laughter.] Hereafter theories, preached in however captivating language, will have to give way to the teachings of experience.

It has been the favorite assumption of some theorists that revenue and protection in the same tariff schedule are impossible. But we have had, in the past seven years, in the contracted working of the protected wool and woolens schedule of the tariff of 1894, a most striking demonstration otherwise.

By placing wool on the free list and reducing the duties on manufactures of wool, the treasury lost $21,000,000 of revenue, our farmers lost a market for the 80,000,000 pounds of wool which they raised in 1892 in excess of what they raised in 1896-97, as well as nearly 10 cents per pound in price, involving a loss to them of nearly $30,000,000 per annum already on this one farm product, and our manufacturers and their workingmen lost a market not only for the goods which increased foreign imports had supplanted, but also a market for goods which the farmers and masses of the people were able to purchase in 1893, but which they could not buy in 1896 because of a loss of employment and purchasing power.

Beyond this it has been demonstrated that by placing wool on the free list, to the injury of the farmer and manufacturer, we have not been thereby enabled to increase our exports of manufactures of wool (as was claimed would be the case), but we have greatly increased the use of shoddy by diminishing the purchasing power of the masses and thus compelling them to seek the cheapest cloths. In 1893 less than 300,000 pounds of shoddy and woolen rags were imported, but in 1896 the imports of these exceeded 11,000,000 pounds.

If it be claimed that this has reduced the cost of clothing to the people (rather a surprising position for men who have been bewailing the fall of prices), the reply is obvious that it has done so only in appearance, because in point of fact the masses, deprived of work and wages by what has given foreign manufacturers the making of so large a part of our goods, have found it harder to buy their clothing than they did before. The true test of real cheapness is always what any article costs in labor, not in dollars. Nothing is cheap that is thus made by degrading man. Nothing can be cheap in the last analysis when it is thus made by purchasing abroad what we can produce or make without natural disadvantage, when such purchase necessitates the idleness of many of our own workingmen.

This is the lesson taught by the bitter experience of the past four years.

Profiting by this experience, the Ways and Means Committee in framing the pending bill have taken wool from the free list, where it was so unjustly placed by the present tariff, and have restored it to the dutiable list at the same rates as it bore in the tariff of 1890 (11 cents per pound for class 1, clothing wool, and 32 per cent. on the great body of carpet wools) ; and have also restored the same compensatory duties on manufactures of wool as provided by that act, in order to place the manufacturer of wool on the same basis as to his material as his foreign competitor, as is always necessary in order to provide a market for our domestic wool. A few kinds of wools heretofore classed as carpet wools, which are used for clothing purposes, have been transferred to clothing wools. To this have been added in a partly specific form duties practically equivalent to the *ad valorem* duties imposed by both the tariff of 1890 and 1894 as a protection to the wool manufacture.

This, it is believed, will greatly aid the wool grower, stop the further depletion of our flocks, and presently regain what we have lost in the past four years, and ultimately result in the home production of nearly all the clothing wool that we require. It will also greatly encourage the wool manufacturing industry, which has suffered so severely under the tariff of 1894, by giving a partly specific duty on imported wool goods, and also by increasing the purchasing power of the farmers. At the same time it will ultimately increase the revenue from duties on wool and woolens not less than twenty-five millions per annum.

The duty on sugar has also been increased, both for purposes of revenue and also to encourage the production of sugar in the United States, and thereby give to our farmers a new and much-needed crop. We now pay foreign countries about $84,000,000 for imported sugar, notwithstanding the abnormally low price, and this sum will soon be increased to $100,000,000. The success which has attended the growing of sugar beets and the production of beet sugar in California and Nebraska in the past five years, not to mention the progress in the production of cane sugar in Louisiana, has made the problem of producing our own sugar no longer doubtful; and, now that we must have the increased revenue from sugar for the present, a favorable opportunity presents itself to give this boon to our agriculture.

There is little doubt that the increase of nearly three-fourths of 1 cent per pound in the duty will be sufficient to gradually develop beet-sugar production in this country, and that for the present it will increase the annual revenue twenty millions.

An increase has been made in the duty on flax and hemp, as well as jute and manufactures thereof, to practically the same as that borne by cotton goods. This will both increase the revenue for the time being and ultimately develop flax cultivation and linen manufacture here.

For the most part otherwise the increase of duties in the pending bill to the figures of the tariff of 1890 have been in the schedules or paragraphs covering luxuries like tobacco, liquors, silks, laces, etc., which, being articles of voluntary consumption, are always regarded as objects which will bear the highest duties. The exceptions are the earthenware and glass schedules and the agricultural schedule, on which the duties have been placed the same as in the act of 1890, because no other rates seemed to be protective.

The iron and steel schedule, except as to some advanced products, has not been changed from the present law, because this
schedule seemed to be one of the two of the present law which
are differentiated from most of the others and made in the main
protective. The duty on tin plate, the manufacture of which
was so successfully established under the tariff of 1890 by the
duty of 2 1-5 cents, has been increased from the 1 1-5 cents duty
of the present law to 1½ cents, which it is believed will prove
as protective as the higher rate of 1890, now that the industry
has been so successfully established.

The same is true of the cotton schedule, which has been left
as it was placed in the act of 1894 for the most part, with some
needed advances on fine goods.

In all the other schedules the rates proposed in the pending
bill are between the rates of the tariff of 1890 and the present
law.

There have been transferred from the free list of the tariff
of 1894 to the dutiable list of the proposed bill not only wool,
lumber, salt, burlaps, bags, cotton bagging, and cotton ties,
which should never have been made nondutiable, but also argols,
crude opium, asphaltum, chicle, paintings, and statuary, except
when imported for free exhibition by an established gallery or
institution; straw ornaments, etc., which under existing conditions ought to contribute something toward the much-needed
additional revenue.

Here Mr. Dingley explained why the committee had
placed paintings and statuary upon the dutiable list.
This was done, he said, to correct several abuses, such,
for instance, as the importation of valuable fans under
the guise of paintings.

The committee, he said, had found it also necessary
to modify the provisions relating to the free admission
of clothing and personal effects of tourists, serious
abuses having arisen under the existing law.

Mr. Dingley stated that the increase of revenue under
the bill was estimated at $113,000,000 a year.

On the question of reciprocity he said:

The report of the Committee on Ways and Means has set
forth the fact that the pending bill has not only restored the provisions of the tariff of 1890 as to reciprocity under which our
trade was so successfully enlarged, but has extended that policy.

Joseph Wheeler [Ala.], a member of the Committee on Ways and Means, replied to Mr. Dingley. He declared that the bill had been framed solely in the interests of the manufacturers of the country—indeed, that these interested parties had dictated the very phraseology of the instrument. He prophesied that the bill, if it passed, would fall short of the expectations of its promoters.

Albert J. Hopkins [Ill.], of the committee, supported the bill. Pointing to the failure of the Democratic predictions concerning the effect of the McKinley bill, he declared that the opposition would likewise be confuted by the results of the present measure, which largely was founded upon its Republican predecessor. The Wilson-Gorman bill, on the contrary, failed disastrously to fulfil the roseate promises of its advocates, as the present depressed condition of the Government and the country strikingly proved.

I cannot find a better illustration to show the utter inability of the Democratic party successfully to administer the affairs of the Government and the inadequacy of their industrial policy than to call the attention of the members of this House and of the country to the condition of the railroads of the United States during four years of Democratic administration. The Democrats claimed, among other things, that the railroads of the country would prosper under free trade, and that railroad employees would also be benefited, as they had prospered under the protective principles of the Republican party, and illustrated their position by saying that the products of the farm must be transported to the seaboards and that the imports from foreign countries here must be carried through the various States to the localities where the people could consume them, and that this industry would prosper better under the policy of free trade, as advocated by their party, than under the industrial system that has been made so prominent a part of the history of our party. Our contention then was, and always has been, that under a well-regulated and graduated tariff law every industry and every citizen in all of the various vocations of life would be benefited; that what brings prosperity to one interest brings it to all. This claim has been amply and adequately proven again and again.

Let me, sir, present to you some figures to show how the railroads and railroad employees have suffered during the four years last past.

The earnings of the railroads for the year ending June 30, 1895, under free trade, and Democratic administration, were $1,075,371,462, a decrease in the gross earnings in 1895 as compared with 1893 of $145,038,412.

But this, sir, does not represent the full force of the blow the railroad interests of the country have received from the Democratic party. The railroads of this country, on June 30, 1893, gave employment to 873,603 men. On June 30, 1895, only 785,034 found employment. An army of 88,568 railroad employees were thus turned out upon the highways to seek in vain for employment, and in many instances to be compelled to beg for bread for themselves and families. These men in 1893, according to the statistics which I have obtained from the Interstate Commerce reports, received in wages $51,285,300. The men who remained in the employ of the railroads suffered a reduction in their wages in 1895, as compared with what they had received in 1893, of $9,800,000, so that the loss to railroad labor that has been brought upon them by this policy of free trade aggregates the marvelous amount of $61,085,300. Is there a railroad employee in the country to-day that believes that his interests will be subserved by the restoration to power of this repudiated Democratic party, or that the policy of free trade will bring him and his family the comforts, to say nothing of the luxuries, of life? But, sir, what is true of this great branch of business of the country is equally true of all of the great manufacturing interests and agriculture as well.

Mr. Hopkins closed with a eulogy of the reciprocity feature of the bill.

John C. Bell [Col.] opposed the bill.

The Populist party believes that no tariff bill is fair, and that the system is unfair, unless you incorporate with it a graduated income tax which provides for the wealth of the country paying something for the advantages it receives. [Applause.] Our customs duties are amply sufficient to furnish a basis of such protection, and more than is necessary to preserve our wage scale if they could be equally distributed, and I take it that the war that is made upon the tariff is not a war upon the system itself, but is directed against the pernicious system of giving protection to one industry or to one community and making other industries and other communities go without protection.

Now, Mr. Chairman, let us look at this tariff question without losing ourselves in discussions of what the Democrats have done or what the Republicans have done. If we follow blindly in the footsteps of our friend from Illinois who has just taken his seat [Mr. Hopkins], we shall think that the population of this country, the births and the deaths, all stop when the Republican party goes out of power. [Laughter.] Let us look at the facts. The tariff question has been greatly obscured by the professional politician and the stump speaker calling a tariff on imports, when made into law by the Republican party, a "protective" tariff, and calling the same tariff, when enacted by the Democratic party, a "free-trade" tariff, or "a tariff for revenue, with incidental protection," which is the same thing under a different name. Then when the Democrats put an article on the free list the Republican party shouts "Democratic free trade!" while at the same time, when the Republican wants to put it on the free list, he has a little scheme which he calls "reciprocity," but which is simply free trade in its most cunning form, under another name, and by this device the Republicans sometimes even bribe other countries to join in free trade with us. [Laughter.]

Now, I wish to say this: With but few important and distinct exceptions, such as some raw materials and specific instead of *ad valorem* duty in part, and ignoring the income tax, there is no more difference between the Gorman-Wilson bill in principle and this bill than there is between tweedledee and tweedledum. And the changes are in the main against the struggling masses. Let us see about this. For the income tax, provided by the Wilson-Gorman bill in order to lighten the burden of the poor and require the rich to contribute to the protection of their own property, is substituted in this bill a tax on every pound of sugar and on every stick of lumber and every sack of salt—upon everything that is consumed.

The difficulty is not so much in the theory of our protective system as in its flagrant abuse and the influence of great aggregations of capital and favored industries. Protection is always asked in the interest of others. Now, observe how it is asked in behalf of the poor laboring man—just enough to cover the difference between the European scale of wages and our own. What hypocrisy! Who ever heard of the laboring man getting rich manufacturing? The statisticians clearly figured from the census of 1880 that about 6 per cent. on our dutiable list would cover the difference between the European wage schedule and ours. While the manufacturer then asked for the poor laborer his 6 per cent., he got for himself at the hands of Congress six times 6 per cent.

The great English statesman, John Bright, said in the debates in Parliament that the rich man paid only 1 per cent. of his income in protective tariffs, while the wage worker—the poor man—paid 20 per cent. of his wages. And that was probably the foundation of the principle of the income tax in Great Britain, to even up what the wage earner paid out of his income with that which was paid by the rich man out of his.

John Bright said that "wages in England had increased 40 per cent. since the system of free trade was introduced there in 1846." Adam Smith said that wages in the United States when we had free trade were 100 per cent. higher than in England at the same time and when England had the high protective-tariff system.

"Give the American workmen the home market" is a deceptive outcry that is showered incessantly upon the ears of every voter; but your laws give the American labor market to the lowest responsible bidder of the world, excluding the Chinese only.

As long as we have free trade in labor, the wage worker must be injured rather than benefited by a high tariff.

Now, Mr. Chairman, in conclusion, it is vain for us to protest against the passage of this bill as your cherished remedy; but we predict that until you legislate some for the consumer and laborer, who are powerless to protect themselves, the masses will continue to go into bankruptcy, and the army of the unemployed will continue its tramp in search of work. What the people want is the money of the Constitution, a free competition in our own country, and a fair chance in the markets of the world for all the people and for all of our industries.

E. W. Carmack [Tenn.] opposed the bill. He spoke chiefly on the delusion of the protectionists that the tariff increased home markets.

The farmer must sell his products in open and free competition. The price of every bushel of wheat and of every pound of cotton sold in this country is fixed by the price of the surplus in Liverpool and by the competition of the most degraded pauper labor on earth. No tariff law can prevent the competition of the Russian peasant, the Indian ryot, and the Egyptian fellah with the American producers of the field and farm. The farmer, while thus compelled to sell in open competition with all the world, must buy the necessaries of life in a market where protection laws exclude competition from abroad and trusts and combines have strangled competition at home. He is thus ground between the upper and the nether millstone of competition and monopoly, and crucified between the foreign pauper and the American thief. [Laughter and loud applause on the Democratic side.]

Is it possible, Mr. Chairman, for any sane man to even hope for the time when all our agricultural products will be bought and consumed at home? By what process is this to be accomplished? Gentlemen tell us that by "fostering American industries," by encouraging the building of mills and factories, we will increase the number of consumers of American farm products. But there is a limit beyond which we cannot pass in this matter of creating consumers by developing manufactures. The manufacturers themselves must find consumers for their products, and whenever they reach the point that they can find no more they have reached the limit of their own capacity to consume the products of others. I believe it is true that in nearly all the great branches of industry in this country there is a capacity to produce in six months more than the American people can consume in twelve months. Sir, American industry has already grown so great that it can grow no more until it breaks down the walls that confine it to one country and goes out upon the sea. [Applause.]

Sir, this country is not large enough, the wide world is none too large, to give ample scope for the genius and enterprise of American industry. The greatest protection to American labor is that which the American workingman has within himself—his superior skill and productiveness, his energy, his intelligence, his industrial prowess, which make him more than equal to any competitor the world can send against him. Mr. Blaine demonstrated a great truth when in his Report on the Cotton Goods Trade he showed that, while the American operatives received a higher wage rate, they turned out more goods for every dollar they received than any other workingmen on earth, and that, in fact, their labor was cheaper to their employers than the labor of European operatives. The same is true in practically every branch of trade and industry.

On March 23 John L. McLaurin [S. C.] opposed the bill, chiefly because of its discrimination in favor of manufacturers against farmers, especially the planters of the South.

Mr. Chairman, it is claimed that the manufacturer, by reason of his investment in buildings, machinery, etc., should be encouraged in his enterprise, and to a certain extent insured against loss. Just why this class should be selected for Government favor I am unable to conceive. The census shows that there are more farmers than manufacturers and operatives, with nearly three times as much invested in lands, buildings, etc. Why is the investment of one class more sacred than that of another? Why should one be favored by legislation and the other neglected?

Mr. Chairman, there is no such thing in commerce or exchange as a raw material. The very moment that the hand of labor touches it it ceases to be a raw material, and so far as this laborer's effort goes becomes a finished product. [Applause.] The rough and muscular arm of the miner who takes the iron ore from the bowels of the earth is as necessary to the manufacture of the delicate mainspring of my watch as the skillful hand which finally fashioned it. While the mainspring was the finished product of its maker, the iron ore was no less a finished product to the miner. Cotton and wool are classed as raw materials, while the fact is, they are indeed a finished product. I venture the assertion that the labor, time, and money expended in selecting, grading, and bringing to its almost perfect state the fiber and texture of our present wool and cotton have been more than has been expended in perfecting all the manufacturing machinery in this country. Then why, I ask, are the fostering arms of the Government thrown about the one while the other is made to shift for itself?

Again, is the cheapening of the manufactured article through free raw material or the lowering of wages really a benefit to the people? I contend it is not. The tyranny of money is at the bottom of cheap production. When the East had, through its protected industries, plundered the balance of the country of nearly all its stock of money, it instituted a series of congressional enactments which doubled the purchasing power of every dollar.

It is this monopoly of money and manufacture that we of the South especially meet face to face in all of our productive efforts. And it is this monopoly that would be broken to a certain extent if equal rights were extended to each and every industrial enterprise regardless of place or kind. It is this monopoly that has cheapened production at the expense of labor and raw material, and which will continue to exercise this power until we of the South awake from our present theoretical dreams and grapple with the stern realities that confront us. The census gives some facts that should not pass unheeded. While manufactured products increased from $5,249,000,000 to $9,054,-000,000, or 69 per cent., the product of raw material increased from $3,395,000,000 to $5,018,000,000, or 47 per cent. No one will deny that the raw material increased in volume as much as the manufactured product; in fact, the census confirms that proposition. Why, then, should it not increase equally or more in value? To me the reason is plain—agriculture was plundered by this monopoly of money and manufactures. As long as the country is to be controlled by a system of protective duties the application of the doctrine of free raw material will, in my opinion, result in agricultural disaster. The farmer who takes a hide to town and exchanges it for a hitching strap gets a fair idea of the benefits of selling free hides and buying protected leather. [Applause.] Viewed in any light, considered from any standpoint, the doctrine of free raw material cannot with profit to the producer obtain while the finished product remains protected by customs duties.

Jonathan P. Dolliver [Ia.] supported the bill. He denied that sectional influence had been heeded in the preparation of its schedules.

No man has asked, "Where is this industry or that?" The only question has been, "Is this an American industry now suffering or likely to suffer a damaging foreign competition?" and with impartial consideration we have tried to bring the law to the rescue of every interest, whether of farm or mine or factory, in every State.

The movement of our industries, I will say to my friend from South Carolina, is west and south. Iron and steel, cotton and woolens are going west and south, drawn by natural forces which in the long run will set the finished output of labor by the side of the great resources with which it deals. But that will not do any harm to anybody. If the new cotton loom goes south, as it has gone, and as it is going, into the very heart of the State of South Carolina, New England will not take alarm, for the old cotton loom, in the hands of the skill that turns the fiber into textures as fine as woven silk, will remain on the banks of the busy river where the protective tariff first established the cotton weavers' art in America. [Applause.] If the woolen mill follows the sheepfold into the interior, as it undoubtedly will, nobody will be harmed, for the training and experience of the old woolen factory will go on to that perfection which will one day tempt even the dudes of the United States into the experiment of wearing American clothes. [Laughter and applause.]

There is another thing about this bill that suits me and that I think will suit nearly everybody whose attention is called to it, and that is the effort we have made to convert the existing *ad valorem* rates into a specific statement of the duties levied. With an *ad valorem* rate no possible diligence can prevent inequalities almost as numerous as the imported cargoes, and business, instead of being a fair competition, becomes a mere contest of skill in the falsification of invoices. It is even worse than that; for, in the case of goods consigned and not sold directly to the trade, the invoice is useless and the mercantile community, especially of the interior ports, suffers a ruinous injury. These abuses adhere from necessity to any levy of duties on the basis of foreign values, and for that reason the *ad valorem* system has been condemned by nearly every secretary, without regard to party, from the beginning of the Government.

Again, I am in favor of this bill because its aim is in a practical way to increase the aggregate revenues of the United States. The transition of our affairs from the embarrassing affluence of Mr. Cleveland's first administration to the ragged edge of bankruptcy in the last presents an aspect almost comic and grotesque. The burden and misfortune of the years, it is true, are somewhat lightened by the American sense of humor which has been able to see and realize that the President's breathless proclamation against the surplus of 1887 has ever since appeared in Democratic newspapers and orations as a part of the general assets of the treasury. [Applause and laughter.]

Here Mr. Dolliver dwelt at length on the financial panic during Cleveland's administration.

James G. Maguire [Cal.] asked the speaker to account for the industrial depression between 1875 and 1878, "under the highest protective tariff that any country ever had up to that time—a depression which Mr. Carroll D. Wright, in his report, says was the severest depression we ever had before or since."

MR. DOLLIVER.—Well, Mr. Carroll D. Wright ought to be out in some parts of the country now. [Laughter.]

Mr. Maguire.—That is the retort which is always given to that question.

Mr. Dolliver.—I wish to finish my speech. I am not ambitious to compose a catechism; but I will say to my friend that, as I understand, the panic of 1873 was produced by the depreciation and disorder of the currency of the United States.

Mr. Maguire.—I admit that as a cause which operated for two years before the commencement of the panic in 1875.

Mr. Dolliver.—But that it disappeared and remained out of the sky of our politics from the day that the American dollar was of known and stable value throughout the world. [Applause on the Republican side.]

I say that, without regard to the character of the legislation proposed by the Congress, the mere election, the success of the threat at the polls, was enough to account for all that followed.

Mr. Chairman, there are no miracles in the everyday business world in which we live. It is a steady, arduous, difficult, and often discouraging movement. Congress can do something both for and against, but not everything either for or against, though vastly more against than for. If the American people ever get their prosperity back, it will come by their own individual enterprise and courage, not by edict and proclamation, but by the honest and careful settlement of conditions favorable to industry and investment. If William McKinley has been described as an advance agent, hastening to the seat of government in order to deliver prosperity to the people from the east portico of the Capitol in a few well-chosen words, the conception belongs to the world of dreams, and not to the earth on which we live. No man bears any such relation to the prosperity of a great people; but a man may stand, and I reverently believe that William McKinley does stand, as the chosen instrument in the hand of Providence to restore in the United States a public policy under which the American people have never yet failed, by their own hard work, to secure, out of the resources of their own country, a fair level of prosperity, a reasonable reward for their labor, and a reasonable dividend on their investments. [Continued applause on the Republican side.]

On March 24 John Sharp Williams [Miss.] opposed the bill. In replying to Mr. Dolliver he said:

The gentleman from Iowa, who has done as much as any man in this House to reproduce its old-time oratory, whose high-flown periods of eloquent diction wrestled with an acute sense of humor for the mastery, "yearned for the factory bells calling millions back to work." May I ask the gentleman from Iowa, and through him the country, why he desires, or why anyone should desire, to open the mills? The object in opening a mill is to manufacture something; the object in manufacturing something is to sell something; the object in selling something is to make a profit out of it. Of what use, then, is it to open the mills if the mills have, already manufactured in their warehouses, more goods than they can sell to the jobber, although they offer them at the cheapest prices which have ever prevailed in the history of the world, and when the jobbers have on their shelves under the same conditions more goods than they can sell to the retailer, and when the retailer has on his shelves under the same conditions more goods than he can sell to the consumer, and when the consumer is hungering and is shivering for want of the goods for which he yearns, but which he cannot buy?

Mr. Chairman, how can increased duties upon manufactured articles aid the capital or labor engaged in manufacturing, except by increasing prices, and how can increasing the price enable the consumer to buy more goods than he is able now to purchase at the lower price? And how can it be said that the trouble with American manufacturing consists in foreign competition, when that competition is less to-day than it ever was in the history of the Republic? How can it be said that the distress of the laboring man engaged in manufacturing is due to the fact of the "importation of foreign goods made by the pauper labor of Europe," when the real fact is that importations are to-day less, comparatively, than ever before, and are growing day by day less and less, notwithstanding increased opportunities to import? The startling fact stands out, like Banquo's ghost, not to be downed by any amount of sophistry, by any amount of eloquence, by any amount of humor, or by any amount of false statement, that the volume of foreign goods imported into the United States during the last fiscal year was $160,000,000 less than the value of the importations during the fiscal year 1893, which was itself a year of restricted importations. Look on that dagger-like fact! [Applause.]

The gentleman from Iowa was right about one thing, which he said in reply to the gentleman from South Carolina; this tariff issue is not a sectional issue. It is a class question. A protective tariff proceeds upon the assumption that the manufacturing class is born booted and spurred to ride, while the agriculturists walk; that the right exists to tax the capital and labor engaged in agriculture in order to give artificial, law-bred prosperity to the capital and labor engaged in manufacturing.

A tariff tax may legislate money into the pockets of an individual or class of individuals, but it must first legislate it out of the pockets of other individuals or other classes, for the simple reason that the money must be gotten from somewhere before it can be given anywhere. As a Democrat who believes in free trade, or the nearest possible approach to it, I rejoiced in the passage of the Wilson-Gorman bill. Not because the tariff features of it were Democratic—for, on the contrary, they were protective—but because the act contained the income tax, and I regarded the passage of the income tax in time of peace as the first step on the high road toward a system of raising revenue for the Government from the net accumulations of wealth rather than from the backs and bellies of the people. There was within it a germ from which something approaching free trade might have come by evolution. But

> Of all sad words of tongue or pen,
> The saddest are these: "It might have been!"

Since one Shiras[1], of the land of Pennsylvania, on the way to the goal—the Damascus—of plutocratic desire—a nullification of the income tax—saw suddenly a light or vision or something, even this germ has disappeared [laughter], and it would seem that we are condemned permanently to tariff taxation for Government revenues.

Benton McMillin [Tenn.] opposed the bill.

Mr. Chairman, after a careful and painstaking examination of this bill, I do not hesitate to declare it the most unconscionable effort at legislative robbery ever attempted upon a people. Neither the great fire of Chicago nor of Boston, nor the fearful flood that now devastates the Southland, could begin to compare with it as a calamity.

Mr. Chairman, this bill carries not only higher rates of duty than the present law, and higher rates than the McKinley bill, but higher than any law ever passed by an American Congress or groaned under by an American people. Sir, not only is the bill itself higher, but the different schedules average above those of the McKinley bill.

[1] See page 409.

My friends, I might go on illimitably with these things, but I have stated enough to let you see what are the unconscionable rates of duty proposed by this measure. This bill is not a tariff for revenue. It is not a tariff for revenue with incidental protection. It is not a tariff for protection with incidental revenue. It is intended to be a tariff for protection with accidental revenue. [Laughter and applause.]

Sir, in answer to the statement which has been made in this debate, that these deficiencies were created by the Wilson bill, I will incorporate in my remarks a statement showing that before Mr. Charles Foster retired from the office of Secretary of the Treasury he ordered new plates to be prepared, in order that the bonds, which were afterward issued in another Administration, should be issued.

CHARLES H. GROSVENOR [O.].—I hope the gentleman will not again put that old story in circulation. It was false in its origin, and it is false to-day.

MR. MCMILLIN.—I know it has been denied so often that a lot of gentlemen will go down to history as lineal descendants of Ananias if they do not take care, the only difference between them and Ananias being that Ananias told his story to get out of trouble and hold the plunder; they tell theirs in cold blood and for the sake of political advantage. [Applause on the Democratic side.]

Mr. Chairman, the principles of government adopted by our fathers are all-sufficient if their original purity and wisdom are retained. We have the most beautiful and yet the most delicate system of government ever devised for the happiness and prosperity of man. The powers of government are so distributed between the general Government and the States as to make despotism impossible without this distribution is disregarded. It has weathered the storms of a century, and under it the American people have flourished and progressed as no nation ever did in the history of our race.

I have hoped that by this wonderful contrivance we may escape the wreck that has followed the other republics of the world. But if the agencies of government are to be prostituted, if favoritism is to originate in the committee room and be promulgated from this hall, if every man's vocation is to be regulated here, if every man's business is to be dictated here, a Solomon with all his wisdom could not do the work, and we must fail as the other republics of the world have failed. But, my friends, I am a believer in the doctrine that right and correct principles of government will survive. May the merciful God guide the wise heads and patriotic hearts of the American people, that our flag shall float in triumph for all time and constitutional government be the everlasting inheritance of the American people. [Prolonged applause on the Democratic side.]

Joseph H. Walker [Mass.] supported the bill. He denied that the tariff was a tax.

Now, the fact is that what you are talking about as a tax is no tax at all. It is simply a devise for the equitable distribution of the wealth of the country. What was our experience during the war? Notwithstanding the immense taxes that were collected in this country, those taxes, being disbursed here, did not impoverish the country a farthing. The energy that was incited in our people, the immense impetus that was given to manufacturing, was such that we were richer after expending those immense sums than when the war began. The same thing, as Mr. McDuffie says, was shown in the case of England during her long wars.

Can you gentlemen on the other side learn nothing by experience? You talk about taxation. Not a single speech has been made on your side that has not practically declared, and often in direct terms, that taxation is legalized robbery. That is the whole burden of your speeches—that there ought to be no taxation, and that if the country would give you the power you would have no taxation. You denounce the collection of taxes of every name and nature; you call it "robbery," instead of what you know it is—simply the public expenditure by the Government for us of the money collected, because it can thus be done more economically than we could expend it individually for ourselves.

You know that a protective tariff is the same thing to a country that coal mines and waterfalls and other natural advantages are. You gentlemen on the other side are willing to walk over the surface of the earth, and not use these natural advantages, while you denounce the men who do use them and want conditions to increase their use.

On March 25 Champ Clark [Mo.] opposed the bill.

Mr. Chairman, as an American citizen, in sympathy with the great body of the people and with five persons whom it is my duty and pleasure to support, I am dead against this bill. It is a vicious, a monstrous, an unnecessary measure. [Applause.] As a Democratic politician, I will rejoice at its passage. You are delivering yourselves into our hands. This bill in the days to come will compel every merchant in the land, Democrat, Republican, or Populist, to make a Democratic stump speech every time he sells an article over the bargain counter. [Laughter.]

Here Mr. Clark discussed the question of agriculture.

Protect the farmer, do you? You undertake to protect the sheep farmer on his wool! You are helping the sheepmen with a vengeance by putting a tax of 35 per cent. on sheep dip!

Go to your people and tell them the truth. Say to them that the awfully bad Fifty-third Congress—and I will admit that it was not as good as it ought to have been; there were too many traitors in the camp—tell them that the Fifty-third Congress put agricultural implements on the free list [applause], while you have undertaken to benefit the farmer by putting upon all such implements a tariff duty of 45 per cent.—that is to say, a reaper which now costs the American farmer about $80 will, under this bill, cost him about $120. But it does not make any difference how much his reaper costs him, or his plow; he can look to Governor Dingley and the gentleman from New York [Mr. Payne], and the rest of the leaders on this floor, and thank his Maker that he has got catgut, whip gut, and worm gut free. [Laughter.] His harness will cost him 45 per cent. more under the Dingley bill than under the Wilson-Gorman bill, but he can console himself with the blessed thought that cocculus indicus is free. [Laughter.]

Now, I understand perfectly that it is a difficult thing to drive an idea into a Republican's head. But such arguments as a raise of 45 per cent. on everything a Republican farmer uses in his business will finally lead him to see the light and convert him from the error of his way. He cannot raise wheat, corn, oats, barley, and hay now at a profit. In what condition will he find himself when he gets no more for his products, for, tariff bill or no tariff bill, he must still sell his stuff in the open markets of the world in competition with pauper labor? [Applause.]

You want more revenue, do you? You have no business with it. [Applause.] There are two ways of making buckle and tongue meet. One is to cut down expenditures [applause]; the other is to increase the revenue. You Republicans over there never seem to dream of cutting down expenditures. One of the chief differences between Republicanism and Democracy is that Democracy means economy, and Republicanism means extravagance run riot. [Applause.]

Jerry Simpson [Kan.] opposed the bill. He replied particularly to Mr. Walker.

Mr. Chairman, I am a farmer. I farm the farms; I do not farm the farmer, like a good many other statesmen. [Laughter.] I have heard very much said during this discussion to the effect that this bill is in the interest of the farmer and the laboring man. These "cheap johns," ready-made, "hand-me-down" statesmen [laughter] talk about the "farmer" and "the laboring man" as though the farmer was not a laboring man. If the farmer's interests as a laborer are not greater than they are in any other direction, I do not know anything of the farmer or farming. If there are any people in this country who rise earlier in the morning, who work earlier and work later than the farmer, and the wife and the children of the farmer, I have not yet discovered them.

I want to know if these gentlemen who know nothing of the farmer or the farming interests of the country, and who talk so knowingly of them, know the facts that to-day there is a great agricultural interest; that all of the agricultural products we produce, or the great surplus of the farm, must find a market abroad, and that that surplus and the market abroad determine the price of the commodities produced in this country, so to speak; that no tariff that does not make adequate provision for this condition of affairs could be of any benefit to the great masses of the people of this country, and that, if they will scan the provisions of this bill closely, they will find no single provision in it to benefit the farmer; but, on the contrary, there has been a studied neglect so to do?

Now, the cattle industry of the country is a great one in connection with agriculture. We import into this country an enormous quantity of hides every year. I note that you have left hides on the free list. If you had put a reasonable tax upon hides in comparison with the other taxes in this bill, you would have put directly into the pockets of the agricultural class in this country not less than $30,000,000. Yet you put hides on the free list and a duty of $1.50 a ton on straw, which does not benefit the farmer at all.

Now, in principle and in practice, where my vote ever counts, I am a free-trader without any string to it. [Applause.]

I favor the raising of revenue in the way that every government ought to, by a system of direct taxation [applause], so that every man would know exactly what he was paying and what he was paying it for.

Now, the only reason that I voted for the Wilson bill in the Fifty-third Congress was because it had the income-tax provision. The Populists stood here for eight days refusing to vote to make a quorum, until they agreed to put that tax in the bill, and then we voted for it.

But, Mr. Chairman, there is another fund to draw from that would give us a more equitable system of taxation than any heretofore applied to the affairs of mankind, a system that would give us more than enough revenue and at the same time prevent the monopoly of land and open to man these natural opportunities and release to him the free gifts of God to all. I mean the single tax.

John Dalzell [Pa.] supported the bill. He particularly opposed the view that trusts were based upon the protective tariff.

Mr. Chairman, in our own country the trusts with which we are most familiar are not in the protected industries. For example, the Standard Oil Company deals in an unprotected article. So does the anthracite coal combination. So far as the sugar trust is concerned, it does not seem to make any difference to it whether there is a duty on sugar or not or what that duty is.

Not to further trespass upon the time of the committee, let me sum up what I have to say on this subject.

First. Trusts are unlawful at common law and under our statutes. They are therefore indefensible.

Second. They are not attributable to protective tariffs. They flourish in free-trade countries, and in our country they are most conspicuous in nonprotected enterprises.

Third. They grow as an abuse out of modern economic conditions which favor the conduct of business by the method of combination of work and capital rather than through the medium of individual enterprise.

So that, in a word, they err who use the existence of trusts as any argument against a protective tariff.

This tariff question, after all, is simply a question of labor. There is no wealth save that which comes from labor, and, if that proposition be correct, then the tariff is simply a question of labor, and, if it be true that it is a question of labor, then it is a question of wages.

Why, our friends on the other side of the House suggest that the skill of the American workman has naught to fear from the skill of the workman from the other side of the ocean, from Europe or from Asia. That may be true. But what the workman of America has to fear is the putting of American environment against the European or Asiatic environment, and subjecting him to the same conditions that in those environments prevail. The old theories as to wages have long since been exploded. The wage-fund theory, who believes in that now? The measure of wages, the standard of wages, is what will bring to the laborer the necessaries of life according to the environment in which he lives. American wages are such as are necessary to maintain an American in an American civilization, according to the requirements of American manhood. [Prolonged applause on the Republican side.]

Underlying American civilization is the principle of the political equality of individuals. So much granted; then it necessarily follows that upon the intelligence and worth of the individual rest the character and stability of the State. That which secures to the State good citizenship secures good government. And, if that be so, then the character of our civilization, the welfare of the body politic, and the future of the Republic depend upon the social condition and advancement of the individual. But the social condition and advancement of the individual depend upon his freedom from competition under unequal conditions with a civilization lower than his own. [Applause on the Republican side.]

Sereno E. Payne [N. Y.], of the Committee on Ways and Means, supported the bill. He discussed its various schedules, and closed with an appeal for an early vote on the measure.

Every day of delay means an enormous loss of revenue to the treasury; but it means more than that. It means another day of closed factories, of silent machinery. It means another day's loss of wage to thousands of workingmen, a loss never to be made good.

Will prosperity come with the dawning of the day following the passage of this bill? you mockingly ask. Will the remedy work an immediate and radical cure? Do you forget that the country is desperately ill; that it has been cursed by your inexcusable quackery almost beyond recovery; that business is ruined, confidence destroyed, credit gone, and labor paralyzed? We make no pretence of working miracles. It will take time, as well as this wise legislation, to bring full relief. We have been traveling the down grade for four years; we cannot get back in a day.

Pass this bill, and I believe that the blindest of you will see a change for the better. Slowly but surely it will come. You will not acknowledge it at first. I remember how some of your predecessors in 1891 would walk through a tin-plate mill and, witnessing the whole operation, come out into the sunlight and swear that tin plate could not be made in this country. Some of you will deny it when the full tide of prosperity is upon us. But your wails will not be heard. A busy people will pass you by, as you sit by the wayside croaking about an income tax, the wickedness of our courts, a tariff for revenue which brings deficiency and disaster, and the everlasting glories of Turkey's system of *ad valorems*. [Loud and prolonged applause on the Republican side.]

On March 31 John M. Allen [Miss.] spoke in opposition to the bill.

MR. CHAIRMAN.—Up to this time I have refrained from participation in this debate. The people of the United States all know my position on the subject of tariff taxation [laughter and applause], and I preferred to allow members of less prominence [laughter] to air their views rather than take the time of the committee myself. But the country does not seem to be satisfied with the character of the debate we have had [laughter], and I feel impelled to yield to the public demand and come from my modest retirement to the front in this discussion. [Laughter.]

Now, the first proposition made by the Democrats when the reading of this bill was commenced for amendment was to incorporate an amendment that would deprive trusts of the benefit of the protective features of the bill; and then began the most remarkable exhibition of parliamentary quibbling and dodging that was ever witnessed in a parliamentary body. [Applause on the Democratic side.]

It was contended and ruled that that was not the time, and that the place in the bill where such an amendment would be appropriate had not been reached. But the trouble is we will never reach the time or the place for the Republican party to commence smashing trusts; it owes too much to the trusts to do that. [Applause on the Democratic side.]

A word or two with my brilliant friend from Iowa [Mr. Dolliver]. You all heard him the other day, in concluding his great speech, say that this idea of McKinley's bringing prosperity was a mere dream. Did you all understand that this was an effort on his part to hedge against one of his brilliant predictions of a year ago? You see he is the man who first spoke of McKinley as the advance agent of prosperity. [Laughter.] He now finds that his advance agent is too far ahead of his show. He has seen the country go from bad to worse since McKinley's election. He sees that the banks continue to break; that the business depression gets worse, and that wheat and cotton and almost everything else not controlled by a trust are going down. There have been more than 4,000 failures in the United States in the last three months, with liabilities of more than $60,000,000, and in the number are included 74 banks. Cotton has gone down more than a cent a pound since the election, entailing a loss on the people of the South of fully $40,000,000.

No wonder Mr. Dolliver wants to hedge against his prophecy of McKinley and prosperity and have the people accept it as a mere dream. [Laughter.] I once saw a little boy caught in a story by his mother, and, when it was proven on him, he said, "Why, ma, can't you take a joke?" [Laughter.]

Since Mr. Dolliver has been found to be a more brilliant than reliable prophet, he says: "Can't you all take a dream?" [Laughter.]

Here Mr. Allen replied to the speakers who had dwelt upon the sectional animosities of the South. In conclusion he said:

The South has learned some hard lessons in the bitter school of experience. Our people are not tramps, but they are at work; they have learned to live at home; they decline your proffer to enter into a scheme of public plunder in order to secure a small division of the stolen goods. [Applause on the Democratic side.] We do not believe in your scheme of legislative robbery, and we will not go into it. All we ask of the North is that it will keep its tramps at home and keep its hands out of our pockets. [Applause.]

After a discussion of the separate schedules of the bill it was passed by the House on March 31 by a vote of

205 yeas to 122 nays. On April 1 the Senate referred the bill to the Committee on Finance. On May 4 Nelson W. Aldrich [R. I.], chairman of the committee, reported the measure with amendments. On May 25 Senator Aldrich explained and supported the bill as amended by the committee.

The Dingley-Aldrich Tariff Bill

Senate, May 25-July 7, 1897

The committee believe that in the reductions they have suggested from the rates imposed in the House bill they have not gone in any instance below the protective point, and if the bill should become a law in the form presented by them every American industry would be enabled to meet foreign competition on equal terms; that is, so far as this equality can be secured by tariff legislation. The rates suggested by the committee's amendments are considerably below those imposed by the House bill, and in most instances below those contained in the act of 1890.

In suggesting these reductions the members of the majority of the committee reaffirm and emphasize their position as friends of the protective policy. The ultimate purpose of this policy is to secure, as far as this is possible by wise and conservative legislation, the steady growth and development of all interests—agricultural, manufacturing, and commercial. The provisions of a tariff law affect all these interests in numberless ways, and unless there can be stability in tariff policy there can be no assurance of continuous prosperity.

Industrial conditions in this country, with very few exceptions, do not demand a return to the rates imposed by the act of 1890. The bitter contest which is going on among the leading nations of the world for industrial supremacy has brought about improvements in methods and economies in production to an extent which was not thought possible a few years ago. These new conditions must be taken into account in considering the rates to be imposed.

Without relinquishing one particle of our devotion to the cause of protection, we feel that we have a right to ask that the cause shall not be burdened by the imposition of duties which are unnecessary and excessive. In the readjustment of rates suggested the committee have tried in every instance to make them sufficiently protective to domestic interests without being prohibitive.

The speaker then discussed the schedules of the bill in detail.

The Senate at once applied themselves to the consideration of the measure, discussing the various amendments and voting upon them. At times general principles were discussed in connection with particular schedules. Thus, on June 8, Donelson Caffery [La.], in discussing the tariff upon cotton manufactures, said:

When a Democrat plants himself upon a tariff for revenue only, he comes as near to being a free-trader as the Constitution of the United States will permit; and that is the sort of a Democrat I am. Free trade has no terrors for me—not one particle —and I believe that, when the manufacturing interests of this country develop into larger and greater proportions than they now have, the enlightened self-interest of New England itself will take the initiative step in the direction of free trade in cotton and other manufactures. Under present conditions the tariff must rest upon imported articles. In placing a tariff upon imported articles it is essential, in order to follow out the creed of Democracy, announced in every convention, in every platform of the party, if not expressly, by necessary implication, that the tariff should be placed upon articles which produce most revenue with the least burden to the people.

When the Senator from Rhode Island got up and confessed the failure of protection, it occurred to me that he had a forecast of the doom to come of his protective theories. He had to borrow the Democratic principle for revenue in order to eke out a surplus necessary to uphold the credit of the nation; he had to go to the rejected article of sugar; he had to go to beer, and also tea—to place a tariff upon tea and beer, to be retained until that blessed time shall come when an overflowing treasury can dispense with them, confessing weakness, confessing the inability or incompetency of a tariff based upon protective principles to meet what the Republican party deems a public exigency.

On June 9 Roger Q. Mills [Tex.] dwelt at length on the injustice of various rates which the bill contained.

Mr. President, we have been listening for two months to the efforts to adjust and readjust, and unadjust and readjust again, the relative claims of the beneficiaries who are to share in the monumental trust fund that this measure is intended to raise.

Where is this money to come from? I look upon the rates of taxation in this bill with the profoundest astonishment, and ask you where this money is to come from? Commencing at the very beginning of this measure, I find that you have put a tax upon boracic acid of $126.89 on $100 worth of that product. Who is to pay it? What right have you to take the property of the taxpayers of this country and distribute it among the men who own boracic acid?

Here are some, and only some, of the rates of taxation imposed upon the necessaries of life:

The speaker here read a long list of articles, with their respective rates of duties as fixed by the Senate bill. Among them may be mentioned: Alcoholic compounds, 349.27 per cent.; sulphuric ether, 318.33 per cent.; window glass, 126.46 per cent.; cutlery, 111.05 per cent.; rice, 133.33 per cent.; salt, 114.23 per cent.; blankets, 125.95 per cent.; wool shawls, 171.15 per cent.; felts, 224.55 per cent.; carpets, from 80.22 to 164.17 per cent.

I want to fix the attention of the country, if possible, to this stupendous system of legislative rapine and robbery. Two billion two hundred and ninety-three million dollars annually goes to the beneficiaries of this fund, to the protected classes, contrary to the doctrine of liberty as written by Massachusetts, contrary to all the teachings that are written in Virginia, contrary to the teachings of our fathers from that day to this; and the attempt to bring this idol into camp and compel us to uncover our heads and bow down and say our prayers to this god of Dagon will not be accepted in the Democratic camp, no matter where it comes from. When you attempt to bring this Philistine idol into our temple and compel us to worship it, if it does not fall down like the statue of Dagon fell before the Ark of the Covenant, the American people will kick it down, and then kick the life out of it after it is down.

What is the reason for this harsh, oppressive, and destructive measure? Why is it that these enormous exactions are demanded? What cause exists for it? The revenues are increasing. The Government treasury is full to overflowing. We know of no such instances of taxation in any of the States or in any of the cities. Go to the great city of New York, the great city of Chicago, or any other great city, and you do not find the tax rate over 3 per cent.; and, if it does go beyond that, it almost raises a revolution. Why is it that the people resent a 3 per cent. tax in the States and submit to a tax of 300 per cent. by the national Government? Because the tax in the States is levied upon wealth and every man knows when he pays his tax that he is paying it upon his property, and there is a boundary beyond which no government can pass. But here this taxation is indirect.

Raising money by taxation to give to favorites is a scourge to the people and exhausts the strength of the Republic. It has already built up a tremendous power whose heavy hand is felt on legislation every day. It is felt everywhere. We see it at the ballot box. We see it in the executive and judicial departments of governments, and everywhere its repulsive features are scowling upon our institutions and threatening their overthrow.

Of what use was it for our fathers to warn us against perpetuities, monopolies, entailments, and primogenitures? Why did they tell us in the early constitutions that they were against the genius and spirit of a free people? And yet they have hung those signboards all along our path.

We are casting our pearls away faster than our enemies can gather them. We are turning dead ears to the voices that come to us from Massachusetts and Virginia that our Government is for free men, for the preservation of our natural rights, for the security of our happiness and well-being, and not for the profit of any one man, or family, or class of men. Our ship is driving upon the rocks, and, unless we seize the helm and change its course, the historian will emerge from the darkness to write the melancholy pages of the decline and fall of the great American Republic.

On June 14 Richard F. Pettigrew [S. D.] supported an amendment to the bill, which he had previously offered, abolishing duties on trust-controlled articles, and providing for legal proceedings to determine what articles were of this nature.

Mr. President, our civilization is founded upon the theory of evolution, upon the doctrine of the survival of the fittest, upon the law of competition, and is opposed to socialism. We say, as far as is consistent with the existence of protection under the law, let man, untrammeled and unrestrained, work out his destiny. The result of this theory in the past was feudalism, or the supremacy of brute strength and physical courage, and its resulting paternalism. But feudalism, by the operation of the law of competition and evolution, destroyed itself by the subjugation of the weaker by the stronger and the creation of monarchical forms of government in its place.

To-day, under the operation of this law of competition, we are drifting toward socialism on the one side and plutocracy on the other. It is for us to say whether we will stop the march of events in their course, and make this again a government of the people, by the people, and for the people, or allow the present to crystallize and thus continue to be what we now are—a government of the trusts, by the trusts, and for the trusts—a plutocracy of artificial persons, sustained by bribery.

When the Republican party came into being as the advocate of protection to American industry by the means of a tariff, it wisely based its advocacy of the doctrine of protection upon the theory on which our civilization rests—competition—and declared that the building of American factories to supply the protected article would create competition and thus lower the price of the article to the consumer. In every campaign we have told the people the story of nails—how they were 6 cents per pound, and we put a duty on them of 2 cents per pound, and American genius and energy produced the machinery, and competition reduced the price, and nails sold for 1 cent per pound, and the Republican doctrine of protection was triumphantly vindicated.

Last year the nail trust was organized, and the price of nails rose from 1 cent a pound to 3¾ cents a pound, and thus the Republican theory of protection was completely overthrown. The same story can be told of almost every manufactured article in this bill. How to remedy this defect so as to justify a tariff for protection in the future is the problem which every Republican is called upon to solve. The two questions are so intimately connected that they must go together. No tariff bill can be defended that does not protect the people against trusts.

But you urge in opposition to my amendment that but part of the manufacturers may be in the trust, and that this amendment punishes the innocent with the guilty. But there can be no innocent persons, for the amendment provides that in order to be a trust the effect must be to restrict the quantity of production or increase the price of the article. Thus those not in the combination are the recipients of the benefits, and the willing recipients, or they would have prevented the rise in price resulting from the trust. If the trust ceases to exist as to any article, the Secretary of the Treasury may commence proceedings to have that fact declared by the court, and the duty again collected.

If these remedies fail, we must resort, unless others are found, to the last remedy, that of public ownership.

This may take the form of public ownership of such natural sources of supply as anthracite coal mines and oil wells, or possibly the leasing of their operation to private companies; or it may take the form of public ownership and operation of all industries that have become practical monopolies. This remedy begins to loom up as a distant possibility, but is as yet too remote a contingency to come within the domain of practical politics. But of one thing we can rest assured, socialism is preferable to despotism, and the right of each citizen to enjoy the products of his toil must be maintained if we are to maintain our institutions.

These problems, Mr. President, are pertinent. We can no longer satisfy the American people by quarreling and by fighting a sham battle over schedules in a tariff bill. We have done that for the last several years, with first one party in power and then the other, until to-day the tariff issue has fled from our politics.

On June 15 Senator Pettigrew's amendment was tabled by a vote of 35 to 32.

On June 29 Benjamin R. Tillman [S. C.] proposed an amendment restricting immigration. Calling attention to the declaration of both parties in favor of such restriction, he said:

I am simply asking you, my Republican friends, and asking the Democrats, to vote here to give some value to American citizenship, and, as you stand here pretending that you value it, that you want to hold it up, that you want to maintain the price for it, that you do not want it to sink to the level of the pauper labor of Europe, it remains to be seen whether you will continue to allow the stream of a quarter of a million annually to pour into the American labor market, competing directly with our own people and with those foreigners who have preceded them for the work that is to be had, when there is no work here under the conditions that exist.

If you are honest protectionists and want to protect labor,

you cannot help but vote for this measure, or something akin to it. The mere pretence that you will restrict immigration to those who can only read and write is not sufficient, and will not go down with American laborers. It is not a question of being able to read and write; it is whether you can handle brick and mortar and whether you can go into a factory or not. Thousands and tens of thousands of these ignorant and degraded foreigners who have come to our shores and debauch our suffrage were the main instrumentality of carrying the last presidential election. I stood in the city of Chicago on the day of the election, and saw hundreds and thousands of them stand there waiting to be bought. These are the men who have brought this country to the verge of ruin, both from a business standpoint and from a political standpoint.

Senator Tillman's amendment was rejected by a vote of 3 to 48.

The amended bill passed the Senate on July 7 by a vote of 38 to 28. The House failing to concur in the amendments, a conference committee was ordered, which reported on July 19 a recommendation that a compromise be made on the amendments, and stated the advisable compromises in detail.

The Dingley-Aldrich Bill

House of Representatives, July 19, 1897

In presenting the report to the House Mr. Dingley, of the committee, spoke as follows:

The proposed tariff bill has been framed not only to secure adequate revenue, but also on protective lines with a view of encouraging American industries.

The object of the protective policy is to enlarge the opportunities for labor and to maintain a high standard of wages, and its yokefellow, a high standard of living for the masses. It rests on the assumption that that country is the most prosperous in which the standards of wages and of living are the highest. It assumes that the standard of living or purchasing power of the masses, which creates the demand for products and sets in motion the intricate machinery of production and distribution in modern civilized society, is dependent on the opportunities to use their labor at good wages, and that these opportunities widen and wages rise as diversified domestic industries multiply and the production of whatever we want which can be made or produced here without natural disadvantage goes on at home rather than abroad. An economic policy which tends to de-destroy home industries in which no more labor is required for production here than abroad, or to reduce wages under the plea that the products of such industries can be purchased at a lower price abroad simply because our labor is paid higher wages, is destructive to prosperity, for the reason that nothing is cheap which deprives our own people of opportunities for employment of their labor and reduces the wages paid to labor.

Now, Mr. Speaker, the majority of the committee who have framed this proposed tariff bill believe that any economic measure whose effect is to transfer to Europe or other countries the making of articles which can be produced here without natural disadvantage can never produce anything but ruin to any country. [Loud applause.] We believe that when the protective principle is applied of imposing duties equivalent to the difference of the cost of production and distribution arising from our higher wages of labor, as proposed in the pending bill, and thus increased opportunities are offered to American labor, giving the masses a purchasing power which they have lost under the conditions of the past four years—a purchasing power which enables them to buy more of the farmer, more of the merchant, more of the manufacturer, and more of every producer in the land—then confidence will begin to return, prices will begin to rise to a paying point, and prosperity begin to set in upon the land. [Loud applause on the Republican side.]

Joseph W. Bailey [Tex.] opposed the bill.

Assuming for the sake of argument that the industries of this country have suffered from foreign competition, let us inquire how the framers of this bill have undertaken to correct what they consider a great evil. They have written it in the very title of their bill that one of its purposes is to prevent foreign manufacturers from selling their goods in American markets.

Mr. Speaker, I lay it down as an elementary principle of political economy that no government can encourage the industries of its people by discouraging the exchange of their products. Exchange is the great inducement to production, and whatever interferes with the freedom of exchange must ultimately curtail production. In the nature of things no man would produce more than enough to satisfy his individual needs, unless he believed that he could find somebody to buy his surplus; and, if no purchaser for the surplus could be found or expected, each man would cease to labor when he had supplied his own wants. The right and the opportunity of buying and selling are the salutary and indispensable motives to produce, and it is the consummation of folly to teach the people of this country that their industries can be encouraged by abridging their right to exchange the products of their labor with the people of other countries.

Instead of employing our labor and materials in the production of commodities which can only be produced for the home market at a loss, it would be wiser to extend our commerce by exchanging what we can produce at a profit for articles which can be more cheaply produced in other countries, because profitable commerce is infinitely better than unprofitable manufacturing. [Applause.]

Remove your vexatious restrictions, and under the old motto of "Free trade and sailors' rights" we will fleck the waters of every sea with the white-winged messengers of our commerce and carry our flag into every region of the earth. [Applause.]

Here Mr. Bailey discussed the general principles of the Democratic party in relation to free raw materials.

It certainly was not regarded as late as 1885 as a departure from Democratic principles to resist the doctrine of free raw materials, because those who resisted it were Democrats then and have remained Democrats, while many of their former colleagues have abandoned our party. Of the four men who voted against free raw materials, Mr. Mills occupies a seat in the Senate as a Democrat, and Mr. McMillin is a distinguished member of this House.

MR. McMILLIN.—When do you say this occurred?

MR. BAILEY.—In the Forty-ninth Congress.

MR. McMILLIN.—And where do you say it occurred?

MR. BAILEY.—In a meeting of the Committee on Ways and Means.

MR. McMILLIN.—And that I voted against free wool?

MR. BAILEY.—That is what Mr. Morrison told me. And he told me more than that; he told me you and Mr. Mills both voted against the metal schedule.

MR. McMILLIN.—If the gentleman will permit me, I would

rather deal in modern than in ancient history, and as he has seen fit to attack my record here——

MR. BAILEY.—Oh, no; I am going to praise it.

MR. McMILLIN.—What excuse have you to give to this House for voting against striking out the wool and woolen schedule of this infernal bill and incorporating the wool and woolen schedule of the Wilson bill?

MR. BAILEY.—I offered an amendment to reduce the duty on both wool and woolen goods 33 1-3 per cent.

MR. McMILLIN.—Your amendment failed, and then you proposed to take the high rates which this bill carries rather than the low rates of the Wilson bill?

MR. BAILEY.—Yes, sir. And we may just as well understand each other right now. Never as long as I am in Congress will I vote to give the woolen manufacturer a 50 per cent. duty on his woolen goods and charge him nothing upon his wool. [Prolonged applause.]

And, since the gentleman has asked me a question, I ask him how can he justify voting for free wool in face of the Chicago platform, which he helped to adopt and defend?

MR. McMILLIN.—I say to my friend from Texas that the Chicago platform did not take the back track on the doctrine of a tariff for revenue only, as he has represented here to-night.

MR. BAILEY.—Not on the doctrine of a tariff for revenue only, but on the doctrine of free raw materials.

I state of my own knowledge that this very question was presented to the committee on platform and resolutions of the Chicago convention, and it deliberately omitted the commendation of free raw materials contained in the platform of 1892 and inserted what I have read here. Not only is that true, but it has been stated in the Senate by gentlemen who were members of the committee, and it is well known to all who took any interest in the question, that it was the deliberate judgment of the Chicago convention that it was unwise and undemocratic to give one class of people in this country what they buy free of taxation while levying a tax upon all the poor people throughout the land. [Applause.]

Whatever strength its advocacy of free raw materials may have brought to the Democratic party in the past, it can bring none now, and will not bring any in the future. There are not in all this broad land to-day one hundred men who could be induced to vote the Democratic ticket for the sake of free raw materials as long as the Democratic party holds to the free coinage of silver; while, on the other hand, there are thousands of brave and honest men throughout the Western States who, agreeing with us upon the great financial question, will embrace our tariff doctrine when we have thoroughly repudiated this Cleveland heresy [applause] and returned to the old and unchangeable creed of our party, which declares that Congress shall lay no tax except for revenue, but that revenue taxes shall be just alike to all classes and sections.

Mr. McMillin followed Mr. Bailey.

The Democratic doctrine on taxation is that taxes should be levied for the support of the Government alone; and that in the levy of such taxation the lowest rate that would yield the revenue necessary to run the Government should be adopted. And the doctrine that has been put into platform and hurled from stump and forum everywhere has been "a tariff for revenue only." By that sign we conquered in the past, and by that sign we shall conquer in the future, if we stand by our principles and do our duty. [Applause.]

Mr. Speaker, I regret exceedingly that my distinguished friend from Texas [Mr. Bailey] instead of pointing out the outrageous features of this bill should, in lieu thereof, see fit to parade my past record here. This bill would be a fruitful source for a two hours' speech to any man who ever lived, if the time were accorded, without fomenting strife among ourselves and attacking Democrats. But I should be recreant to my duty, I should be unjust to those who have been fighting by me in the past, if, being attacked, I did not tell the plain, unvarnished tale of what the Democratic party has done, and what has been my own action as a Democratic Representative.

First, any statement from any quarter that I have ever advocated a tariff on wool is inaccurate and wholly unjust to me. I have been consistent in this matter. I have all the time believed that cheap clothing for the people would be most surely attained by the method of taxation whereby wool is free. But if I had been in error I had others standing by to sustain me in that error, and he was one of them. I have favored and do favor a tariff for revenue only, because it is Democratic and right.

Sir, in this discussion it has been denied that "a tariff for revenue only" is Democratic doctrine. A tariff is either "for revenue only" or for something besides revenue. Democracy has always denied that any tax could be imposed except to obtain money to run the Government. It has opposed taxation for any other purpose; hence has favored always a tariff for revenue only as against a tariff for protection.

Here Mr. McMillin quoted the tariff planks in the Democratic platforms from 1876 to 1896. He continued:

It will also be noted that the platform of 1892 declared it a "fundamental principle of the Democratic party that the Federal Government has no constitutional power to impose and collect tariff duties except for purposes of revenue only."

Away with the charge that this is "heresy"!

But what are the facts with reference to the gentleman's [Mr. Bailey's] own record? Who are the heretics he denounces?

If past records are to be raked up, let us have the whole record. Let us come to the question upon which the gentleman lays so much stress. Let us come to the commodity which is the keystone in the arch of Republican protection—wool. There can be no high protective system maintained now without taxed wool. There was a proposition as far back as the Fifty-second Congress, first session (volume 123, *Congressional Record*, page 3057), to put wool on the free list. It had no other question in connection with it. There was no tax on the finished product in connection with it.

What was the position taken by my friend from Texas who criticizes the balance of us who voted for free wool then and all people who favor free wool now? If I was a "heretic" then I had "heretics" standing all around me; and as the gentleman himself voted on that occasion for free wool he is in no condition to criticize me now. [Applause on the Republican side.]

Mr. Speaker, what I favor is the Democratic party going to the battle again with its old flag untarnished, with its old mottoes upon it. We have conquered in that way in the past. We can conquer in that way again. You who predict the destruction of the Democratic party should remember that the Democratic party has refused at all times to act as corpse at any of the funerals which you have planned for its interment. [Applause on the Democratic side.]

Mr. Payne followed.

The House has been amused and interested by the discussions going on in the Democratic party; and each one of the parties to the discussion finds justification for its position in a Democratic platform. [Laughter and applause on the Republican

side.] They generally find justification for opposite positions
in every platform that the national convention sends out. [Re-
newed laughter.] If not, they do so every four years, anyhow.
In 1884 they declared distinctly for a protective tariff. They
wanted to reduce the tariff in such manner as not to lose a job
for a single laborer and to protect all in the United States alike.

But then, in 1892—and I commend this to my friend from
Texas [Mr. Bailey]—Grover Cleveland, I believe, was nominated. That was a foregone conclusion when the convention assembled, and his particular representative, his envoy extraordinary and ambassador plenipotentiary, who worked faithfully
for him, was one Henry Watterson, of Kentucky. He wrote the
platform, and for some reason or other excluded from that platform free raw material, for which Mr. Grover Cleveland was
so anxious! He would not allow it to go into the platform
when it was reported to the convention. Then one of the delegates from Ohio, a Mr. Neal, got the chairman's eye and moved
an amendment to the platform, wherein he commended the Democratic party in Congress for their efforts in behalf of free raw
material, and the convention by a vote of about two-thirds, as
I now recollect, adopted the new plan and seemed to be in favor
of my friend from Tennessee [Mr. McMillin] and his idea of
free raw material. [Laughter and applause.]

The gentleman from Texas says they went back on that in
1896. Well, they change so often I can hardly keep up with the
procession. [Laughter and applause on the Republican side.]
I would not be at all surprised if they did. But there is consolation for either of them in either horn of the dilemma. I
heard my friend from Texas, for an hour and a half, advocating
a tariff on raw material. I heard the illustrations he used,
which seemed familiar to me. I expected he would reach the cli-
max of his argument, finally, by giving us the illustration formerly used by the present Speaker of this House, telling us
that there is no raw material except the round earth without a
single hole even dug in it! [Laughter and applause on the Republican side.]

I wondered where my friend got his education, and then I
thought, Mr. Speaker, that in 1894 his party put wool on the
free list. Texas then had more sheep than any other State in
the Union. During the past three years the butcher has got
abroad among the sheep of Texas, and they are rapidly disappearing from the hills. So my friend has got his line of vision
out as far as some of the farms in his district, and has seen the
effect of free raw material on the sheep herds there, and gradu-

ally he has got his eyes opened, and he is advancing toward Republican doctrine. [Applause on the Republican side.]

Now, what we want is a tariff bill that will make the normal

THE CHIEF MOURNER

Victor Gillam in "Judge"

conditions right, and it is written in every line and syllable of the bill we are considering here. [Applause on the Republican side.] We want a bill that will bring sufficient revenue to show to every man that every obligation which he brings against the treasury shall be met, and promptly met, in the best money of the world. [Applause on the Republican side.] When you get that, you have inspired confidence in the treasury of the United States; and, when you get confidence there, you will have confidence among the citizens of the United States.

But, Mr. Speaker, I must not pursue this. I must not talk longer if we pass this bill by the midnight hour. Seventy millions of people are looking on you to-night, anxiously awaiting and demanding the passage of this bill. [Applause on the Republican side.] Every idle workingman, every suffering wife and child deprived of comfort because the husband's strong right arm has been deprived of the privilege of labor for decent wages, is looking anxiously to-night for the passage of this bill. Paralyzed business, paralyzed industries, all over the country want this bill to pass. Men come here from their homes, members of either party, and report the feeling of the people. No set of men, no clique, no party, dare stand in the way of the American people who are demanding the immediate passage of this bill. [Prolonged applause on the Republican side.]

The conference report was adopted in the House by a vote of 187 to 116. After considerable discussion it was adopted by the Senate on July 24, 1897, by a vote of 40 to 30. President McKinley approved the bill on the same day.

CHAPTER XVI

THE TARIFF OF 1909

[PAYNE-ALDRICH BILL, INCLUDING CORPORATION TAX]

Insufficiency of Revenues under Dingley Act—President William H. Taft in His Inaugural Address Urges Revision of the Tariff—Sereno E. Payne [N. Y.] Introduces a Tariff Bill in the House—Debate: in Favor, Mr. Payne, Richard Young [N. Y.], James R. Mann [Ill.], Charles F. Scott [Kan.], Joseph G. Cannon [Ill.], Francis W. Cushman [Wash.], Arthur L. Bates [Pa.], Nicholas Longworth [O.], Joseph H. Gaines [W. Va.], Samuel W. McCall [Mass.], John Dalzell [Pa.]; Opposed, James B. Perkins [N. Y.], Choice B. Randell [Tex.], William W. Rucker [Mo.], Champ Clark [Mo.], Oscar W. Underwood [Ala.], Morris Sheppard [Tex.], Ollie M. James [Ky.], William Sulzer [N. Y.], Arsène P. Pujo [La.]—Report of the Minority of the Committee on Ways and Means—Bill Is Amended and Passed—It Is Amended and Passed by Senate—Conference Committee Is Appointed—Debate in the House on Committee's Report: in Favor, Mr. Payne, Mr. Longworth; Opposed, Mr. Clark, Henry D. Clayton [Ala.], Swagar Sherley [Ky.], Mr. Underwood, Robert C. Wickliffe [La.]—House and Senate Agree to Conference Report—Bill Is Approved by the President.

UNDER the Dingley Act revenues decreased during 1908 to such an extent that all parties agreed that a revision of the tariff was imperative. It was estimated that the expenditures for the fiscal year ending June 30, 1909, would exceed the receipts by $150,000,000.

President William H. Taft, in his inaugural address (March 4, 1909) referred to the situation as follows:

A matter of most pressing importance is the revision of the tariff. In accordance with the promises of the platform upon which I was elected, I shall call Congress into extra session to meet on the 15th day of March, in order that consideration may be at once given a bill revising the Dingley Act. This should secure an adequate revenue and adjust the duties in such a manner as to afford to labor and to all industries in this country, whether of the farm, mine, or factory, protection by tariff equal to the difference between the cost of production abroad and the cost of production here, and have a provision which shall put into force, upon executive determination of certain facts, a higher or maximum tariff against those countries whose trade policy toward us equitably requires such discrimination. It is thought that there has been such a change in conditions since the enactment of the Dingley Act, drafted on a similarly protective principle, that the measure of the tariff above stated will permit the reduction of rates in certain schedules and will require the advancement of few, if any.

The proposal to revise the tariff made in such an authoritative way as to lead the business community to count upon it necessarily halts all those branches of business directly affected; and, as these are most important, it disturbs the whole business of the country. It is imperatively necessary, therefore, that a tariff bill will be drawn in good faith in accordance with promises made before the election by the party in power.

To secure the needed speed in the passage of the tariff bill, it would seem wise to attempt no other legislation at the extra session. I venture this as a suggestion only, for the course to be taken by Congress, upon the call of the Executive, is wholly within its discretion.

In the making of a tariff bill the prime motive is taxation and the securing thereby of a revenue. Should it be impossible to so arrange the duties as to secure an adequate income, I recommend a graduated inheritance tax as correct in principle and as certain and easy of collection.

On March 17 Sereno E. Payne [N. Y.] introduced in the House the expected bill, whose title was "a bill to provide revenue, equalize duties, and encourage the industries of the United States, and for other purposes." It was referred to the Committee on Ways and Means, of which Mr. Payne was chairman. It was reported back next day. It came up for discussion on March 22.

THE PAYNE TARIFF BILL

HOUSE OF REPRESENTATIVES, MARCH 22, 1909

Mr. Payne supported the measure.

The country is overwhelmingly in favor of a protective tariff.

It is an American policy. It seems to be acquiesced in by a great majority of the American people. It is true there are some looking for protection to industries who do not come out into the open, who declare themselves in favor of a tariff for revenue, disguising, or trying to disguise, their real belief in a tariff for protection. We have advanced some in the last twenty years in this regard, and now I do not believe that there is a man within the sound of my voice that would rise in his place and say that he is in favor of "tearing down every custom-house in the United States from turret to foundation stone."

Here Mr. Payne spoke in eulogy of the Dingley bill.

While it is true that this bill has not brought a surplus during every year of its existence, the expenditures have increased beyond the anticipation of any of the originators of the Dingley law. We did not dream then of the Spanish war. Much less did we imagine the increased expenditures that would come after that war had ceased, with great victory and honor to the national arms and the national flag, but it brought increased burdens and increased responsibilities. We jumped forward to a place as a world power without a peer in the world. Our relations with other countries were changed. We not only changed the map, but we changed our responsibility with the foreign nations, and with that change came the burdens; the burden of an increasing navy, which seems to be one of the most popular things we have among the citizens of the United States; an increased army, increased coast defences.

The grand result of the Dingley bill to-day is that, having paid all the expenses of the war and all the expenses incurred thereby, and having expended a large amount for the Panama Canal, there is a surplus of $25,000,000 for the entire period.

But time makes changes. It becomes necessary to have a revision of our revenue laws. There are two controlling reasons for this revision.

Since the time of the enactment of the Dingley bill other nations have been adopting the maximum and minimum tariff, with a lower tariff at protected rates and a maximum tariff much higher—even 100 per cent. over the minimum rates, scarcely ever below 40 per cent.—although some of the articles of these maximum and minimum tariff countries are at the same rates in both maximum and minimum schedules.

Then came the tug of war. Then came the hard part of the proposition. We saw our rivals for the trade of the world getting conventional rates that we could not get, partially because of our system that under the Constitution no change can be made in the tariff except Congress takes the initiative. We must pass legislation to enable the Executive to offer favorable trade agreements. It is with us here to originate it.

Furthermore, the time had come to hunt for more revenue in a tariff bill, and these two considerations hastened the consideration by the House and the country of a new tariff act. Hence it came about that the Republican platform in the last election pledged the party to the revision of the tariff. Already, before that, your Committee on Ways and Means had begun its work, anticipating the verdict of the country, even before the Chicago convention met, and that committee had set its clerks to work looking up information that would aid the committee in the passage of this bill.

Now, the question of revenues under this bill is a serious question, and yet is not so serious as it would appear at first blush. It is true we had a big deficit on the 1st day of July last for the previous year, but we had had a big depression in business. Importations had halted, revenues had been cut down, and when that continued during the fiscal year 1909 down to the present time, showing a deficiency of $87,000,000, it looked like a difficult task to provide sufficient revenue for the expenditures of the Government.

But this was only a surface view of the case because, with reviving industry, with prosperity, with putting money in the purses of the people that their demands may be supplied, revenues will increase from all the sources from which the Government derives revenue.

Mr. Chairman, I will take up some of the schedules in the bill. In the first place we have provided a minimum and maximum tariff. Our minimum tariff is a protective tariff, built on the lines of our party platform and sometimes a little more than the party platform, because it is impossible to hold the scales evenly, even with all the information available to your committee on all these schedules.

We provide that any country which gives us as fair trade relations as they give to any other country, which makes no discrimination against us which they do not make against the most favored nation under their conventions or tariffs, shall receive this minimum tariff provided for in sections 1 and 2. But if they do not, if they do not give us an equal chance in their markets with any other nation, we do not propose to allow them to come into our market at this minimum rate. Our market is the market of the world, for we are the greatest consumers, the greatest buyers of any nation on earth, consuming from one-third to one-half of the productions of the world over.

Now, Mr. Chairman, I am going to speak of some of the changes made in this bill. The committee have transferred some items from the free list to the dutiable list. The increases are few in number. They are not very serious, but every one of them was made for a reason, after examining the evidence that was before the committee.

Here Mr. Payne went into detailed discussion of the various changes. When he reached the question of women's gloves, upon which article he said the committee had recommended an advanced duty of $1.50, James B. Perkins [N. Y.] questioned him as follows:

The gentleman believes that this dollar and a half a dozen pairs will materially increase the price of women's gloves?

Mr. Payne.—Yes; in the first operation it would—that is, while we were having protection, increasing the price first as a benefit to the manufacturers, and then when competition comes in you get back to the old rates, just as we have on men's gloves, or below.

Mr. Perkins.—Then, as I understand, this duty is not intended as a means of increasing the revenue?

Mr. Payne.—Fortunately, both meet in this schedule. It is beautiful for revenue and magnificent for business.

Mr. Perkins.—Then I understand that, if we manufacture 90 per cent. of the women's gloves that are used, instead of what we are doing now, there will be no importation, and the revenue on gloves will certainly be less. You cannot both get the revenue and make the gloves without making the revenue less.

Mr. Payne.—Well, we need the revenue now, right off, next year. The year after that we will not need so much of it, and before this bill is repealed I hope we will not need any from this source.

Richard Young [N. Y.].—While the manufacture of gloves will be greater the importation of leather will be increased very much, and the revenue will not be so greatly changed as it would seem on the first statement of the case.

Mr. Payne.—That is true. I am glad that my colleague made that statement.

Choice B. Randell [Tex.].—I will ask the gentleman from

New York what the purpose of the majority of the committee was, in drafting this bill, in reducing the tariff on barley to 15 cents a bushel and on barley malt to 20 cents a hundred? Was not that in favor of the brewers, or was it intended for some other purpose?

MR. PAYNE.—Fifteen cents is perfectly high protection on barley. It is in proportion to the duty on wheat and oats.

WILLIAM W. RUCKER [Mo.].—Is this a reduction to protect the American farmer or the beer manufacturer?

MR. PAYNE.—You gentlemen, every man of you, has gone on the stump and said these duties were prohibitive; that they did not need any such duties, and they were put in and held out as a sop to the American farmer. Have you not done so?

MR. RUCKER.—I have so charged and I believe it now——

MR. PAYNE.—Why are you whining about it now?

MR. RUCKER.—I believe this talk of protection to the products of the American farmer is a fraud, a sham, and a pretence. [Applause on the Democratic side.]

MR. PAYNE.—I never saw the like of the agility with which you gentlemen can get on both sides of the rail at the same time.

MR. RUCKER.—Not on both sides, but we want to get you on the other side a little bit. [Applause on the Democratic side.]

MR. PAYNE.—Now, Mr. Chairman, they say there is a joker as to coffee. Coffee is placed on the free list; but there is a proviso as to coffee, and what is it? That whenever any country levies an export tax on coffee we will levy an import tax equal to the amount on the coffee exported.

Brazil is now levying an export duty of forty-seven one-hundredths of a cent upon every pound of coffee exported to the United States. We are paying that, and it is added to the price of the coffee, and we are paying that toward the support of the Brazilian Government. Some South American republics are putting on a larger export tax even than that. We propose to meet them on that ground and say to them that whatever the amount of their export tax we will put the same amount as an import tax. We will double it, and we will get half of it and they will get the other half.

CHAMP CLARK [Mo.].—Does not that mean in plain, everyday English that the American consumer of coffee will be paying both taxes?

MR. PAYNE.—Well, now, I will come to that before I get through.

Now, there are some countries that do not levy an export tax. They are rivals of Brazil. If they can get in here forty-seven one-hundredths of a cent a pound cheaper than Brazil can, then, unless Brazil cuts off her export tax, the exporters of coffee in Brazil will be paying on their coffee to get into this market forty-seven one-hundredths of a cent to the Government of Brazil and forty-seven one-hundredths of a cent to the Government of the United States, or ninety-four one-hundredths of a cent, while the other countries will have no export tax and will not have to pay any duty to the United States. That is all the joker there is in this paragraph—a plain business proposition. We propose, if we let coffee free into the United States, by proper legislation, to compel those countries to export it free into the United States. [Applause on the Republican side.]

Mr. Chairman, we have put iron ore on the free list after full consideration by the committee. I do not think I will go into that in detail, but I want to say that the evidence of Judge Gary, president of the United States Steel Company, was that in the production of pig iron 2 tons of our iron would go as far as 3 tons of the iron imported from across the sea; and that is true also of the Nova Scotia iron, they yielding about 40 per cent. and ours about 60 per cent. Of course while that is true, it follows that there would be no occasion or necessity of a duty of 40 cents a ton on iron ore.

MR. RANDELL.—Is it not a fact, as shown by the evidence before the committee, that the imported iron ore is used simply on the Atlantic coast, and that to take off the tariff will not decrease the price of iron products to the consumer, but will be giving the revenue to certain furnaces in New England on the Atlantic coast? Is it not a fact that that amounts to about half a million dollars a year?

MR. PAYNE.—If we collect $200,000 on iron ore some one must pay it. The gentleman's theory has ever been that it was the ultimate consumer that paid that duty.

MR. RANDELL.—Is not this a special case, and do not the facts show that this action could not reduce the price of iron because it affects only certain furnaces at certain points, and that in this particular case it is a gift of that much revenue to these furnaces, and taking that much from the treasury?

MR. PAYNE.—The gentleman was solicitous about the steel trust for some reason or other in the hearings, and there has been some fear in some quarters that the steel trust might ultimately drive the smaller concerns out of business. Some of the smaller concerns are located near the Atlantic sea coast—the Pennsylvania Steel Company at Sparrows Point; and perhaps this company is at more disadvantage than some of the others who are manufacturing iron and steel goods. If they can get their iron ore a little cheaper on account of the taking off of this duty, it would strengthen them and help them to keep on in the uneven race which they have with the great concern, the United States Steel Company.

MR. RANDELL.—But, Mr. Chairman, how can that happen when the tariff is taken off ore that belongs to the steel trust?

MR. PAYNE.—Well, if I have not made it plain to the gentleman, I despair, and will have to give it up.

Mr. Payne at this point postponed the conclusion of his speech until the morrow.

Champ Clark [Mo.] filed the report of the Committee on Ways and Means.

MINORITY REPORT

There are many changes—for the most part minor changes—of the Dingley rates, some up and some down. Most of the changes in a downward direction are reductions more apparent than real, the Payne rates being as prohibitive in their results in many cases as the Dingley rates.

The treatment of the farmer by this bill is along the same lines as have characterized Republican methods in the past. He gets practically no relief, and the laborer and producer have greater burdens imposed upon them. The cost of living for the average man is increased; the advantage of wealth and power is also increased.

As to the maximum and minimum tariff plan of the Payne bill, it is an open challenge to a trade war with every other nation on earth.

In this connection it may be well to ponder our relations with Cuba. Does any sane man suppose for one moment that the great commercial nations, our competitors for the world's trade, will concede that Cuba is one of our "dependencies"? It is a thing incredible. To ask that question is to answer it.

The bill is in many respects crude, indefinite, sectional, and prohibitive. It seems to us from our examination, which was necessarily hasty, that on the whole it increases the cost of living. Many increases of the sort might be mentioned. In numerous instances the protection exceeds the entire labor cost of production. This can not be defended on any ground whatsoever, even by a standpatter. In all, the reductions, both apparent and real, fall far short of the substantial relief which the people were led to expect.

We do not desire to delay the passage of the tariff bill, and do not propose to waste an hour; but, having had no opportunity whatsoever to modify or amend it before it was reported, we will insist on having full opportunity to amend and debate it paragraph by paragraph under the five-minute rule, as is right and proper. That much we demand. We will be satisfied with nothing less.

Mr. Payne continued his analysis of the bill on March 23. In explaining the action of the committee in putting hides on the free list he said:

People do not raise animals for hides. They raise them for their meat, and the meat is the principal item when they come to sell the cattle. Not only that, but it is the foundation for half a dozen industries; and every time you put a duty on what is called sometimes the "raw material"—and, as far as hides are concerned, they are raw material—you have got to go all up along the line of goods made from that raw material and increase the duty. That is well recognized. There is no use in keeping hides out of this country in order to sell the domestic hides. If you have got to send domestic hides abroad to be tanned, to be made into shoes, to be made into harness, to be made into carriage leather, you want a duty on the manufactured goods, you gentlemen who are clamoring for a duty on hides.

The removal of the duty will not hurt anyone in the United States except the middlemen and the packers. The latter have gone into the tanning business and are tanning their own hides.

Mr. Chairman, I come now to the miscellaneous sections of the bill. Section 5 provides for free trade between the Philippine Islands and the United States on all articles except sugar and tobacco, and on sugar up to an importation of 300,000 tons in one year and on tobacco up to 300,000 pounds of wrapper and 3,000,000 pounds of filler and 150,000,000 cigars, beyond which the usual rates will apply.

I trust that this long-delayed measure of justice to the Philippine Islands will no longer be delayed, and under the beneficent provisions of this bill they will be allowed to enter our markets up to the extent of the limit. As far as the limits are concerned, I would not have put them on, but a majority of the committee favored it.

It was a sort of compromise between the friends of the islands and the friends of the sugar beet and other outlying industries, and this section was adopted in the shape it is presented to the committee, and I hope it will meet with the approval of the House.

Section 6 provides that no part of this act shall abrogate or impair in any way the Cuban treaty for reciprocal trade, and the gentlemen of the minority are very much disturbed about this—a continuation of the Cuban treaty.

Now, the question is asked in the minority report whether any sane man supposed that the commercial countries of the world would stand for it to have us admit Cuban goods here at a discount of 20 per cent. of our duty and still allow us a minimum rate. If the gentlemen who asked that question had thought back for the last four or five years of the existence of the Cuban treaty, they would have found that nearly every nation of the earth did give us better trade relations and the same rate of duty that they gave to the most favored nations, although we were carrying out the Cuban treaty in full and to the letter, because these nations recognized what the minority of the committee do not, that when we give that concession to Cuba we get a concession from them of a reduction of 20 per cent. of her duty; and then the nations of the earth also recognize the relation which we have to Cuba as the guardian of her interests and of her people and our effort to uphold her government and try to make her an independent nation, that she may not have to come in under our flag.

Now I come to the inheritance tax, a proposition that has created a great deal of discussion throughout the country, as it did in the committee. We want some more revenue. We want about $20,000,000 worth of it in order to be sure to make ends meet under this bill. And the committee cast about for a proper subject for taxation. I think they considered everything in sight. Some suggestion was made about a tax on the net earnings of corporations. Now, no man will deny but that the corporations of the United States, during the last two years at least, have been in a pretty precarious condition in a great many instances. They pay taxes; they pay State taxes, municipal taxes, and all kinds of taxes; and, although we put a pretty good tax on their net revenue, we still would not get our $20,-000,000; so the committee did not think it was best to put that tax on.

Then the question of the income tax was presented to the committee. Well, I have pretty strong convictions about the constitutionality of an income tax.

MR. CLARK.—The income tax that was incorporated in the Wilson bill was only declared unconstitutional as to the income arising from land or rents of lands, was it not?

MR. PAYNE.—Also the income from municipal bonds.

JAMES R. MANN [Ill.].—And also the income from personal property.

MR. CLARK.—Is it not true the President of the United States has intimated very broadly that an income tax can be drawn that the Supreme Court as now constituted would declare constitutional?

MR. PAYNE.—Whether he did or not, I have a right to my opinion about the constitutional law as well as has the President of the United States, and I want to say to the gentleman that that Wilson income-tax law has never been repealed in a single line or letter, and, if there is a court now that will hold that it is constitutional, why, it will be the law of the land.

MR. CLARK.—My idea of the Attorney-General is that one of his duties is to supervise the enforcement of all the laws that are on the statute books.

MR. PAYNE.—Whether they are constitutional or not?

MR. CLARK.—Certainly.

MR. PAYNE.—And after the Supreme Court has decided that they are not constitutional?

MR. CLARK.—I know that the Supreme Court never decided, except in certain features of it, that the Wilson income act was unconstitutional.

MR. PAYNE.—I can never sign a recommendation of the gentleman from Missouri for Attorney-General.

Now, Mr. Chairman, to proceed with the discussion. Even if an income tax was constitutional, I would greatly prefer an inheritance tax. There is no denying that an income tax occasions perjury and fraud unlimited. The knowledge of a man's income is within his own breast largely and he can cheat and defraud, and if he is one of that class of beings that do not stop at perjury he can cover up a large portion of his income. There is a great incentive in the minds of some men to do that thing.

The objection that I have raised to an income tax on account of the perjury and fraud which it breeds can not apply to an inheritance tax, because every time an estate passes by the death of either a testator or an intestate the estate goes to the probate court in the State. Everything is done publicly.

There is a hearing in the probate court. Witnesses are sworn, affidavits are filed, inventories of the estate are filed, valuations of the estate are made. Everything is done in readiness for the collection of this tax, and there is no question of perjury and fraud to be raised. In that case and for that reason it is infinitely to be preferred to an income tax.

The objection is made that most of the States already have an inheritance tax, and that is true. I think 33 out of the 45 States are collecting such a tax. In some States the tax is almost as great as that imposed in this bill, and in some fully as great, and in some greater.

We have provided in this bill 1 per cent. from $10,000 up to $100,000, 2 per cent. from $100,000 to $500,000, and after that 3 per cent. That is, where it is a direct descent, but in case of collaterals in this bill we provide a tax of 5 per cent. on all legacies and inheritances exceeding $500.

I think that if these people have to pay both the State and the national tax they are not overburdened with taxation if this bill should become a law. What easier tax to pay than this? A man gets a legacy, a stranger perhaps to the testator, a clear gain to him; why should not he pay a part of that to the support of the Government?

It is a fair tax; it is a tax easily collected; and it is a tax that this class of people ought not to hesitate to contribute for the support of the Government and the protection of the law.

Gentlemen say that it interferes with the State. Well, the States have a wider range of taxation than the Federal Government; they can tax all property in the State.

MR. CLARK.—Let me ask the gentleman this: Suppose there are no minor heirs to an estate and the estate is settled out of court, does not come into the probate court at all, is there not just as much premium upon perjury in that case in this inheritance tax matter as there would be in the case of an income tax?

MR. PAYNE.—Well, not quite, because the estate is more visible than the income is, but there would be a chance for perjury and fraud in that case. But I want to call the attention of the gentleman to the fact that a very small percentage of estates are settled in that way, at least that is so in my own locality.

Now, Mr. Chairman, I am anxious to get at the consideration of this bill and pass it through the House. The country is waiting for the action of Congress. Trade is waiting. The wheels of industry are silent until our action upon this bill.

I believe it will open the ports of other countries. I believe it will give better trade relations the world over. I believe it will not stop the labor of a single hand. I believe it will start up industries throughout the United States. I believe that labor will be fully employed. I believe that good and blessing to the people of the United States will come from the passing of this bill, and my ambition and hope is that at the earliest possible moment the bill will go through the House and to the Senate, on its way to become a law. [Loud and long-continued applause on the Republican side.]

On March 24 Mr. Clark opposed the bill.

I desire to congratulate the distinguished chairman of the Ways and Means Committee [Mr. Payne]. He has now become a great historical personage. The history of the United States cannot be written now and leave out the name of Sereno E. Payne, of New York. [Applause.] He takes his place in the company of Henry Clay, Robert J. Walker, Justin S. Morrill, William McKinley, William L. Wilson, and Nelson Dingley, as father of a great tariff bill, which must be referred to as long as men discuss the tariff in the United States, which, judging the future by the past, will be until Gabriel blows his trumpet. [Laughter and applause.]

There is another thing on which I congratulate the chairman of the Committee on Ways and Means, that, by his nine and one-half hours' speech, he has knocked higher than a kite the idiotic theory of Doctor Osler.[1] [Laughter.]

It was a superb vindication of his physical and mental strength, and under the character of the speech he was making, explanatory and defensive, answering a good many questions from this side, and carrying on an extended debate with his political confrères on that side, I do not see how it could have been shorter; and, what is more, I am not dead sure but that it was the wisest thing he could have done from a political standpoint, because a good many Republican gentlemen, having fired their shots, will not want to make speeches on the bill.

For the benefit of all concerned, as this debate in all human probability will run in one shape and another for a good while, and as you all ought to be posted on both sides, I will give you my opinion about certain documents. There are four great documents on the subject of the tariff which are invaluable, and you can get them all now, as Professor Taussig has re-

[1] William Osler, M.D., a physician of international repute, was reported as declaring that a man was unfit for doing his best work after the age of forty.

printed them in a book, which is easy of access and which does not cost much.

The title of that book is "State Papers and Speeches on the Tariff." The four documents are Alexander Hamilton's great report on manufactures in 1790; Robert J. Walker's great tariff report on his bill in 1845; John Quincy Adams's great report in 1831; and Albert Gallatin's great free-trade memorial in 1832. Those are the documents that are invaluable. In addition there are four books which are almost invaluable—Professor Taussig's "History of the Tariff in the United States"; Professor Taussig's book, "State Papers and Speeches on the Tariff"; Franklin Pierce, on "The Tariff and the Trusts", and a book printed by Cicero W. Harris, with the strange title, "The Sectional Struggle." In addition to that I recommend to every man in this House to immediately lay hold of this book I have in my hands, "Imports and Duties," prepared by William W. Evans.

This is no time for an academic discussion of the tariff. Every tariff theory ever hatched in the brain of man has been discussed repeatedly in this country with thoroughness and splendid ability. Since John G. Carlisle made his first masterful tariff speech in the House, some thirty years ago, it is not much exaggeration to say that we have had a continuous tariff debate in this country.

There is no Democrat I know of who wants to consume one hour unnecessarily in the discussion of this bill—not one. [Applause.]

While the minority members of the committee have no desire whatever to waste one moment, we do desire a thorough consideration of the bill and a chance to amend it wherever we think it would be improved by amendment, and my judgment is that it could be greatly improved by amendment in many respects.

The tariff is a tax paid by the consumer. Nobody with any reputation for veracity or intelligence to lose will deny either of these two propositions. If he does deny them, he will be confounded by the evidence of high-protective advocates contained in the hearings before the Committee on Ways and Means, which hearings are made up almost exclusively of the evidence of such advocates. Most of the witnesses wanted an increase of the Dingley rates or wanted those held *in statu quo*. It seems from an examination of the hearings on the tariff bills of the past that the witnesses were usually the beneficiaries of the tariff, struggling to keep what they had and to secure any increase they could.

Most of the cross firing among witnesses was where one set of protected manufacturers fell afoul of another, growing out of two facts: (1) That the tariff pie was not evenly distributed and each one wanted the biggest piece. Not more than half a dozen of them suggested that things be evened up by reducing their own tariff, but almost everyone that saw anybody else more highly protected than himself wanted the leveling process to consist of raising his tariff to the maximum; (2) that what is one man's finished product is another man's raw material, which produced clashes among some of the protected classes. For instance, neither Richard Cobden, Sir Robert Peel, John Bright, Henry George, nor Tom Johnson could yell more lustily for free trade on raw materials than the New England Republican tariff reformers, while, on the other hand, neither Benjamin Disraeli, Horace Greeley, Henry C. Carey, "Pig Iron" Kelley, Joseph Chamberlain, nor the gentleman from Michigan [Joseph W. Fordney] could yell louder for a prohibitive tariff on their manufactured products.

The situation in which the Ways and Means Committee found itself was unprecedented. Both parties claimed in platforms, in the public press, and on the stump during the late canvass to be in favor of reducing the tariff rates of the Dingley bill. Of course the Republican platform was equivocal and might be construed to mean either revision up or revision down. Judge Taft in his speeches construed it to mean revision down; but nevertheless many benighted Republicans did not believe he was candid, for they boldly came before the committee after the election asserting that the platform declared in favor of raising the tariff rates, and that they were here to demand their pound of flesh.

Of course I am not the official adviser of the Republican party. It may be very unfortunate that I am not, but I am not. [Laughter.] I believe that the Republicans made two tactical mistakes about the tariff very lately.

Here are the Republican tactical mistakes. The chairman of the Ways and Means Committee let us scare him last year into making on the floor of this House in the last Congress the declaration that he did make—that he violated no confidence in saying that they were going to revise the tariff and that he was in favor of a maximum and a minimum.

The second mistake, tactically, that the Republicans made was putting those two propositions into their platform. They

THE WARRIOR'S RETURN

[Referring to Roosevelt's reputed "back-down" on tariff revision]

Cartoon by Joseph Keppler in "Puck"

put them in there because we had scared them out of their wits. The reason that I say that they made tactical mistakes is that I believe recent events show you could have beaten us anyhow at the general election. [Laughter.] I will tell you what would have done it: The immense and widespread popularity of Theodore Roosevelt. [Applause.] I never had any delusions about that man and about his influence. But he has gone. Some of you Republicans wish he would never come back. [Laughter and applause.] All that I regret is that he left at all [applause], because, if he had stayed here, you would have been in such a row in less than ninety days that you would not have known whether you were Republicans or Democrats. [Laughter.]

The historian of our times will record as Mr. Roosevelt's highest honor that he refused a third term when he had it in his grasp.

Mr. Chairman, the most easily understood portion of this bill is the authorization to issue $250,000,000 of 3 per cent. bonds during any one year, to run for one year. That process can be kept up perpetually, which means really a permanent increase of the bonded debt by $250,000,000. This in a time of profound peace. The framers of the Payne bill do not use the unpopular word "bond"; they use the more euphonious word "certificate." But they are precisely the same. This bond provision proves beyond doubt that the Republican managers do not believe this bill will produce sufficient revenues and are fixing to issue bonds to supply the deficiency.

The Republican members of the Ways and Means Committee offer a great boon to the American people in the sugar schedule by cutting the tariff on refined sugar from 1.95 cents per pound down to 1.90 cents, a cut down of five one-hundredths of 1 cent per pound. Why this remarkable tenderness for the sugar trust? It receives a rake-off of 26 cents on every hundred pounds of refined sugar.

The same old "joker" on petroleum is in the Payne bill— ostensibly on the free list, but in reality a protective tariff of between 150 and 250 per cent. I do not know whether we are going to get a chance to amend this bill or not. I hope we will; and, if we do, I will risk my head on the proposition that that countervailing duty on petroleum goes out. [Applause on the Democratic side.]

CHARLES F. SCOTT [Kan.].—Those of us who represent districts in which there are large independent petroleum-producing interests have received a great many letters and publications urging us to insist upon the countervailing duty on petroleum on the ground that the very life of the independent petroleum-producing interests depends upon it. The argument is that the Standard Oil Company is a refining industry; that it is a purchaser of raw petroleum; that it produces only about 20 per cent. of the petroleum it uses and buys 80 per cent.; that it would really be to the advantage of the Standard Oil Company to be able to buy raw petroleum and import it into this country without any duty. I should like the opinion of the gentleman from Missouri upon the soundness of that argument from the standpoint of the independent petroleum producer.

MR. CLARK.—I think it is all a humbug. Year by year the Standard Oil Company produces less and less crude oil. It develops very few fields. It has too much sense. It permits the gentleman from Kansas and myself and the rest of us to go out hunting for oil fields, boring holes in the ground at our own expense, and when we have discovered a rich field it comes in and takes possession of it at its own figure. [Applause on the Democratic side.]

If I could be convinced that the revenue tariff on crude petroleum would help the producers of crude petroleum—that is, if they would get the benefit of it, at the same time raising revenue for the Government, and the Standard Oil Company would not get the benefit—I would vote for it. [Applause.]

The Standard Oil Company compels the producer to take its price, and then it compels the consumer of oil to pay its price; and I give it without any fear whatever that the Standard Oil Company is the greatest marauder that the sun ever looked down upon in six thousand years. [Applause.]

MR. SCOTT.—Would that condition be changed by eliminating this countervailing duty?

MR. CLARK.—Why, certainly. If they put up the price of refined oil too high, somebody else would ship refined oil in here. [Applause.] A straight revenue tariff of 15, 20, or 25 per cent., whatever the wisdom of the Congress thought, on petroleum would be an honest performance. But this countervailing duty is simply a dodge. [Applause.]

Now, one other thing. Under this drawback provision, a man that manufactures stuff out of foreign material gets back 99 per cent. of the tariff he has paid on that stuff when it is shipped out. The biggest user of tin plate in the United States, or in the world, is the Standard Oil Company. It does not use American tin plate. It uses foreign tin plate to make its cans for the foreign trade, and then gets 99 per cent. of the tariff

on that tin plate returned. [Loud applause.] Now, here you
are in this bill giving it from 150 to 250 per cent. on oil, and
then giving to it tin plate practically free. [Renewed applause.] I will not stand for any such performance. Remember that, while Standard Oil gets in its foreign tin plate for
foreign export practically duty free, the rest of us have to pay
a stiff tariff on all the tin plate which we use.

Of course, everybody stands around and asks what I think
about zinc [a Missouri product]. I think the very same thing
about zinc that I do about every other article of common consumption in the United States. If it turns out on investigation
that a cent a pound is a good revenue tariff on zinc, I am going
to vote for it; and if it turns out that it is a prohibitive tariff,
or anywhere in the neighborhood of that, I am going to vote
against it. [Applause.] I am in favor of a revenue tariff, and
dead against a prohibitive tariff or anything approximating
thereto.

I want to announce a general principle, and that is that I
will not help any living human being oppress the great masses
of the people of this country. [Loud applause.] I do not care
a straw whether they come from Maine or from Missouri, all
public plunderers look alike to me. [Loud applause.]

We are all tariff reformers. A few days ago there was a
meeting at the White House, a conjunction, so the papers stated,
of four stellar bodies of the first magnitude. Perhaps I ought
to say one solar body and three stellar bodies—the President
of the United States, Senator Aldrich, the Secretary of the
Treasury, Mr. MacVeagh, and "my prophetic soul, my uncle,"
the Speaker of the House. [Laughter.] They met together as
tariff reformers, so the papers said, to discuss what should be
the Payne bill. When these four tariff reformers got together,
if the angels did not weep it is because they were so completely
dumfounded that they had completely lost all emotion whatsoever. [Laughter.]

Joseph G. Cannon [Ill.].—I do not recollect that the tariff
was referred to or anything else except the general condition
of the treasury, the desire for good administration, and so far
as possible an organization and an administration of that great
department that would tend to bring the expenditures of the
Government within the revenues. [Applause.]

Mr. Clark.—Mr. Chairman, I do not propose to talk about
all the schedules. But I cannot help remarking that the increase of 30 per cent. in the rates on hosiery is a cruel outrage
on men, women, and children, for no man in his senses will

claim that hosiery is a luxury in this day and in this climate. These remarks apply with equal force to the increase of 75 per cent. on women's, misses', and children's gloves. In this connection it is well to remember that the women had much to do with overthrowing the Republican party on account of the extortions in the McKinley bill. It is to be hoped that history will repeat itself in this instance.

Here Mr. Clark discussed the rates on woolen manufactures, which, he said, were practically the same as those in the Dingley tariff. He characterized the continuation of these duties as "the most monstrous feature of the bill." To support his statement he read an editorial from the *Kansas City Star,* on "Tuberculosis and the Tariff," in which it was urged that cheap wool clothing would do more to suppress the disease than all the means now employed for that purpose.

Mr. Clark continued:

Probably the worst "joker" in this bill is the one on lumber. Now, in plain language, the situation is this: If any province, State, or dependency of any foreign country shall place any tariff rate or restriction on the exportation of any forest product, then the old Dingley rates go into effect against all the forest products of that entire country. It happens to be a fact that Ontario has a restriction as to the exportation of forest products cut (by government permission) from her forest reserves. Being a province of Canada and a dependency of Great Britain, then, under the involved provisions of the Payne bill, all the forest products of Great Britain and her dependencies and provinces, on entering this country, have to pay the rates in the Dingley law, the very rates that are so odious to the users of lumber in this country at this time.

Now, Mr. Chairman, as far as conserving the forests is concerned, I am in favor of free lumber for that reason. [Applause.]

FRANCIS W. CUSHMAN [Wash.].—Is not Mr. Gifford Pinchot the greatest expert in this country on questions of forest conservation? He said:

If the tariff on lumber were to be removed, it would be done, I take it, for one or both of two purposes; either to reduce the price to the consumer, or to preserve our forests. In my judgment it would accomplish neither.

XII—25

That is his letter addressed to Hon. Sereno E. Payne, chairman of the Ways and Means Committee.

MR. CLARK.—No man in America did as much to build up the sentiment in favor of free lumber as that same man, Gifford Pinchot. [Applause.] But wait a minute. These smart lumber kings and their attorneys got hold of him down here and pumped into his head their ideas and he was converted. As a conservator of forests he seems to have fallen from grace. I do not charge any corrupt motives in the case. I believe he has been deceived.

Now, in conclusion, I want to give it as my deliberate opinion, with what study I have been able to devote to it, that this bill raises the Dingley rates. [Applause on the Democratic side.]

I do not believe that the American people voted to do that. I believe that when we get that maximum and minimum into operation that will place the tariff rates more than 20 per cent. higher than they are in the Dingley bill. I believe that the speech that the chairman quoted yesterday from President McKinley, at Buffalo, which may be taken as his farewell address to the American people, was the thing that set in operation this widespread movement for the reduction of the tariff. It is a revolution, and revolutions do not move backward. No matter what happens, the men who are in favor of a tariff revision downward this year will be in favor of tariff revision downward next year, especially if you make the tariff bill higher than it is now. Revolutions do not move backward; they move forward.

> Though beaten back in many a fray,
>   Yet freshening strength we'll borrow,
> And where the vanguard halts to-day
>   The rear will camp to-morrow.

[Loud and long-continued applause on the Democratic side.]

On March 25 Oscar W. Underwood [Ala.] opposed the bill. On the question of free raw material Arthur L. Bates [Pa.] questioned him as follows:

The gentleman is opposed to free raw material?

MR. UNDERWOOD.—I am.

MR. BATES.—The gentleman is in favor, therefore, of reducing the tariff rate on manufactured goods?

MR. UNDERWOOD.—I am in favor of putting everything on a revenue rate.

Mr. Bates.—Or, in the words the gentleman used a moment ago, reducing them to a competitive basis?

Mr. Underwood.—Undoubtedly. They could not be at a revenue rate without their being on a competitive basis.

Mr. Bates.—Precisely. Now, is the gentleman in favor of that, notwithstanding the fact that it would reduce the number of jobs for workmen in this country, or else reduce their wages? Is the gentleman in favor of reducing the wages of the American workman?

Mr. Underwood.—No; I am not in favor of reducing the wages of the American workman, and if the industries of this country are put on a healthy competitive basis, when hard times come, when panics come, the workman of this country will hold his job, and foreign goods will cease to come in; but, when you build this protective tariff wall so high that the American people have got to buy every commodity and all they desire in times of great prosperity and great development alone from American manufacturers, you expand conditions, develop your business to such an extent that when hard times come there is no place to retrench or dispose of your surplus production, and you have got to shut up your factories at home. But if you build up the great industries of the country, not with an unhealthy, hothouse growth, but along conservative lines, recognizing fair competition and only revenue rates of duty all the time, while you might not build your industries as rapidly as under a forcing process, yet you would not have the present unhealthy growth, and, when hard times and panics come and it is necessary to reduce production, the foreign goods would be driven out; in most cases American mills would continue in operation. [Applause on the Democratic side.]

Morris Sheppard [Tex.] opposed the bill. In referring to the Republican platform of 1908 he said:

The tariff declaration in the Republican platform gives the protected interests a deed to the treasury of the United States. The wildest socialist could not have invented a more dangerous and alluring fallacy. The Payne bill completes the delivery of the treasury to the trusts, and the American people, unable to resist the appeals and promises of Republican leadership, a leadership buttressed with the oratory of Beveridge and Hughes, the perverted logic of Elihu Root, the fulminations of Roosevelt, and the imposing proportions of Mr. Taft, having indorsed the atrocious transaction at the polls, are now witnessing the violation of their confidence in this new license for unlimited pillage. Amusing, indeed, were the ponderous assurances of Mr. Taft that the Republican party would revise the tariff downward. His volcanic predecessor realized the hopelessness of such a proposition and evaded it to the last. Is it possible that the complacent Mr. Taft may succeed where the bifocal whirlwind that recently swept from Washington to Oyster Bay failed utterly? [Laughter.] I say to you that there is more real power in one 5-cent cigar between the iron lips of Joseph G. Cannon, the stand-pat leader, than in the big sticks of a whole regiment of Roosevelts and Tafts. [Laughter and applause.]

On March 27 Nicholas Longworth [O.] supported the bill. In defending the Republican party in its relation to the tariff he said:

The President of the United States, in his inaugural address, said that, on account of the changes in conditions since the passage of the Dingley Act, a measure could be drawn on a principle equally protective which will permit the reduction of rates in certain schedules and require the advancement of few if any.

This bill illustrates the truth of that statement.

A number of gentlemen on that side have said that this bill in effect was not a reduction measure; that the reductions were insignificant in number. I propose to show that this claim is not founded on fact.

I do not see any better way to determine whether a tariff bill reduces duties than to take the number of duties it reduces, and the Payne bill has reduced five duties for every one that it has increased; and if you include the whole free list and include those articles transferred from the free list for dutiable purposes it reduces fifteen articles for every one that it increases. If that is not a genuine reduction I do not know how there can be one.

On March 29 Ollie M. James [Ky.] opposed the bill.

Mr. Chairman, we have heard a great deal said about the Republican platform and its provisions with reference to the question under consideration. The truth of it is that the last utterance of the Republican platform was the highest protective-tariff declaration ever written by any party. All the other Republican platforms heretofore have contented themselves by declaring for a protective tariff that would equalize the cost of production at home and abroad; but the Republican platform adopted at Chicago in 1908 goes a step farther in this pillaging of humanity and declares not only that the tariff shall be high enough to equal the difference in the cost of production at home and abroad, but in addition thereto that there shall be given to the manufacturer a "reasonable profit." Now what is a "reasonable profit"? Who shall decide how much it shall be? And what right have you to provide that a certain class of our people shall receive a "reasonable profit" from all the rest?

As the trusts gather about this bill, looking over its various items, seeing safely written upon its pages their continued license to steal, a broad smile spreads over their faces, as they throw their hands up and exclaim, "Thank God, there is loot enough in it for us all!" [Laughter and continued applause on the Democratic side.]

On March 31 William Sulzer [N. Y.] opposed the bill as class and sectional legislation, and as injurious to our foreign trade. On the latter point he quoted President McKinley's last speech. He continued:

Sir, there is not a line in the Payne bill to restore the American merchant marine; and increase our revenue by taxing the carrying capacity of foreign-built ships in our deep-sea trade; and it is a matter of much regret that the few Republicans in Congress who control its affairs and dictate legislation favor a ship-subsidy bill, which is another phase of protection, but no remedy at all, only a mere temporary makeshift to rob the many for the benefit of the few by taking money out of the pockets of the taxpayers generally and giving it to a few favored individuals.

Sir, I am in favor of immediate action by Congress for the resumption of the shipping policy which prevailed under the first five Presidents of the Republic, and which brought forth and maintained the best merchant marine on the ocean without the cost of a cent to the American people. We do not need to take a dollar out of the treasury of the United States to revive our shipbuilding industries or restore our merchant marine. All we need to do is to repeal the restrictive laws against our deep-sea shipping now on our statute books, put in their place laws similar to the navigation laws that were enacted by the early statesmen of the country—laws that built up our merchant marine in those historic days—laws that placed our flag on the high seas and gave us nine-tenths of our entire over-seas carrying trade, and we would do it if it were not for the greed and the selfishness of the shipping trust. [Applause on the Democratic side.]

On April 1 Joseph H. Gaines [W. Va.] supported the bill. He spoke chiefly on the question of trusts. In conclusion he said:

I do not hesitate to say that, so far as I am concerned, being as hostile to what are known as "trusts" in all their unlawful operations as any other gentleman on this floor, I yet would not send the business of the country out of the country, even if it were under the control of a trust; and it might just as well be repeated here, that it may be known to as many persons as possible, that this country is the least trust-ridden country in the world. The other countries of the world have trusts more than we have. They may not have such big ones; they cannot have anything of any kind as big in a small country as in a country the size of this; but it ought to be known—and our Republican speakers have made very little of this fact in the great debates they have held with our Democratic friends—it ought to be known that, whereas our Government does whatever it can to destroy trusts or prevent their formation, almost all the other commercial countries of the world foster and aid the formation of manufacturing and selling combinations.

Arsène P. Pujo [La.] opposed the bill, particularly its provision for an inheritance tax.

I am not entirely persuaded that the inheritance tax, as provided for in the measure, will stand judicial scrutiny. While, of course, an inheritance tax has always been construed not as a tax upon property, but as a tax upon the right of succession, yet strong argument could be urged that it is as much a tax upon real estate, constituting the principal asset of the inheritance, as it was held in the income-tax cases that a tax upon rents was a direct tax, and could only be levied by apportionment among the several States. Conceding for a moment the constitutionality of this measure, the policy of its adoption is of doubtful wisdom.

The effect of the adoption of this measure would be the imposition of a double tax upon the right of inheritance by bequest or by the operation of law.

The measure under discussion provides for a tax upon all inheritances exceeding $500. It is my firm belief that a large per cent. of the tax contemplated under this provision would be collected from people of moderate means, whose estates would not exceed $5,000 or $10,000, and I do not believe that it is a wise policy to impose taxes which would be borne principally by one class of people. However, it seems these days that the function of government is to devise new methods of taking away from the people that which they have worked for instead of making their burdens as light as possible.

Samuel W. McCall [Mass.] supported the bill.

I believe of this bill, as a whole, when we consider the necessities for revenue and the general conditions of the country, that it contains the best set of tariff schedules ever submitted to the House of Representatives by a Committee on Ways and Means. While it recognizes the principle of protection to American industries, and recognizes it as a national and not as a sectional policy, it is leveled against the idea that it is an important function of tariff taxation to increase the fortunes, already great, of those gentlemen who have secured control of some of the great natural resources of the country, or that it is a function of a tariff law to put duties so high that producers in this country by a combination to destroy competition may use them for the purpose of extorting excessive profits from the people.

On April 5 John Dalzell [Pa.] submitted, from the Committee on Rules, a resolution that general debate on the bill should close and certain specified amendments (as to duties on lumber, hides, barley, and petroleum) be acted upon. The resolution was adopted by a vote of 195 to 178.

The bill was amended upon the designated points generally by an increase in duties, and was passed on April 9 by a vote of 217 to 161.

The Senate referred the bill to the Committee on Finance, which, through its chairman, Nelson W. Aldrich [R. I.], reported it with amendments on April 19. It was debated at great length until July 8, when it was passed by a vote of 45 to 34. A conference was appointed, which reported on July 30. Mr. Payne spoke upon the report on July 31.

Mr. Speaker, in presenting this conference report, I do it with confidence that it will be accepted by this House and that it will be accepted by the country at large as meeting the full requirements of the Republican platform, as meeting the pledges made by our candidate, now the President of the United States [applause on the Republican side], and at the same time will not stop a single wheel of industry, will close no factory, and will deprive no man of labor at a decent, fair wage. [Applause on the Republican side.]

The Senate did not agree with the House as to its provisions in the bill. Exercising their prerogatives under the Constitution, and in accordance with the usual practice, they made many amendments. Many of them were substantial. Great was the divergence of thought and great the disagreement as to the provisions of the bill. Your conferees have had no easy task in the past three weeks in striving to maintain the mandate of the House as put forth in the bill which passed the House. We have made concessions. We have exacted concessions from the Senate, and the concessions on both sides are embodied in this report. I am frank to say that many of the concessions which we made to the Senate improved the original bill, and, on the other hand, some of the concessions which we were obliged to make did not improve the original bill. But I think upon the whole the result is one upon which we may congratulate ourselves on having framed a bill which, if it becomes a law, will reflect credit upon the Congress which enacted it. [Applause on the Republican side.]

Here Mr. Payne discussed in detail various schedules of the conference report, comparing the duties with those imposed in the House bill. The most important changes were as follows:

The *ad valorem* duty on cotton was increased from 40.87 per cent. to 44.07.

The duty on paper was advanced from $2 a ton to $3.75.

The reciprocity provision concerning bituminous coal was omitted, and the duty reduced from 67 cents a ton to 45 cents.

Iron ore was taken from the list and subjected to a duty of 15 cents a ton.

The duty on belting leather and sole leather was reduced from 20 per cent. to 5 per cent., on shoes from 25 per cent. to 10 per cent., on harnesses from 40 per cent. to 20 per cent.

The duty on rough lumber was increased from $1 to $1.25, on shingles from 20 cents a thousand to 50 cents.

Mr. Payne continued:

I want to speak about a few things in the internal revenue. The House put a provision increasing the tax on cigarettes equal to the tax that was put upon cigarettes in the Spanish war revenue bill. The Senate added another provision taxing manufactured tobacco equal to the tax in the war revenue bill, or about equivalent to it, and the House accepted that provision. The House did not have much difficulty in reaching an agreement upon it. That provision altogether will bring in revenue estimated at $9,300,000, and that is quite an addition to the revenues.

Now, Mr. Speaker, the Senate put a tax on corporations of 2 per cent. on the net earnings. It is not for me here to give a history of that legislation in the Senate or why it was brought about, but it was brought about as an amendment to an income tax. I have no use for an income tax, and what use I have for a corporation tax is the fact that you can sometimes get rid of an unconstitutional income tax appended to a bill. It came before the conference committee. It came to the Republican side of that committee as an administration measure proposed by the President of the United States, and we accepted it. We did reduce the tax from 2 to 1 per cent., made some minor amendments, and reported it with confidence to the House. We may have preferred our inheritance tax to that proposition, but under tne circumstances we were more than justified in accepting this provision in the bill, which I hope in its workings will yet prove popular with the people of the United States.

Now it has been asked why the corporation tax as it went to the Senate excluded holding companies. There is no reason in the world why a corporation that owns stock in another company should pay a double tax upon those holdings. It is not equitable, it is not right, and it ought not to be exacted. [Applause.]

When it comes to the breaking up or absorption of a company in order to get rid of competition by another company, I will go the full length in preventing it; but I am not in favor of using the taxing power for that purpose, and, of course, a tax of 1 per cent. would not accomplish any purpose in that respect. It would be an additional burden upon the innocent stockholder who had stock in either corporation.

A word more as to the revenue. These rates increase the revenue from customs less than $4,000,000. The corporation tax is estimated to produce $26,000,000; tobacco, nine and one-third million dollars—about $40,000,000 of increase of revenue —revenue enough, when this bill gets into full working order, to supply the necessary demands of the Government; not to build the Panama Canal. We will leave that to another generation. We have provided for bonds that will establish the policy of the Government in that respect. The Dingley law during all its period of existence has provided ample revenue, and there is no doubt this law will do the same for another twelve years. Let us pass it, gentlemen on this side of the House. The duty is ours; the time has arrived. Vote against it if you want to drive your party into chaos; vote against it if you want eternal agitation about the tariff. Go on and vote against it if you choose, but do not do that on the idea that you are going back to the Dingley bill or the Dingley rates.

That is a delusion; you will not get it, but you will get agitation instead. There would come in another bill one of these days, and in the meantime the wheels of industry will stop, enterprise will be paralyzed; the country will stand still or will move backward, and you will curse the day when you failed to go with the great majority of your party, almost all of them, your President having lent his approval to this bill, if you fail to stand in the hour of the country's need and of your party's need and vote against this bill. Let us pass it when the hour of 8 o'clock arrives, and give courage and joy and happiness to the people of the United States. Let us start the remaining idle wheels of industry; let us put every man who wants to work at work; let us build up the happy homes in the United States as they will be, and they will bring the great pæans of their applause for your patriotism and statesmanship in meeting this emergency. [Loud and long-continued applause on the Republican side.]

Mr. Clark rose and was recognized amid prolonged applause on the Democratic side.

Mr. Speaker, this conference report has been heralded and headlined in the newspapers as a tremendous victory for President Taft over the forces of evil in the Republican party, represented by Senator Aldrich and other distinguished Republican statesmen. We are told that congratulations are pouring in upon him from every side.

Well, a man must have a very curiously constituted mind to conclude that the result of this conference is in any reasonable sense a redemption of Republican pledges before the last election to revise the Dingley rates down. [Applause on the Democratic side.]

I want to do President Taft justice. I am his personal friend, and have been since I first set eyes upon him. His laudable desire for the square deal and his love of fame would naturally and inevitably cause him to wish that his pledges be redeemed in such a way that he could look the American people proudly in the face; but he has been grossly misled as to the nature of this report. Those downward revisionists who are congratulating the President uproariously are most assuredly thankful for small favors. No man will begrudge him any glory justly his due; but when we reflect upon the fact that, even according to his most enthusiastic eulogists, he insisted at a late day on lowering the rates on only half a dozen items, or thereabouts, when the rates should have been lowered on hundreds of items, and that the conference report still reeks with largesse for the few and extortion from the many, his glory will experience a greater diminution than have the rates of the Dingley law.

Here the speaker presented a table comparing the Dingley duties with those of the conference report. It showed a total increase over Dingley duties, $5,649,002, or 1.71 per cent. increase. These estimates were based on the imports of 1907.

Mr. Clark continued:

These estimates do not take into consideration a whole lot of things which were taken from the free list in the Dingley bill and put on the tariff list in this conference report, and when they enter into the calculation it will run the average increase of the conference report above the rates in the Dingley bill by about 2 per cent.

The very best that the Republican arithmetician of the Republican conferees [Major Lord] can figure out as a great vic-

tory for the President and a great victory for the downward revisionists of the Republican party is that after all of this hullabaloo, after all of the time, delay, sweat, and toil on this bill,
beginning on the 10th day of last November and coming down
to the present day, you have made the infinitesimal reduction
of ninety-seven one-hundredths of 1 per cent. [Applause on
the Democratic side.]   As a genuine tariff reformer, who has
stood by his guns in season and out of season, in sunshine and
in storm, I say that that is the most pitiful conclusion of a
great movement that is recorded in the history of mankind.
[Applause on the Democratic side.]

A classical scholar like my friend from Pennsylvania [Mr.
Olmsted] must think of the old Latin sentence, *"Parturiunt
montes; ridiculus mus nascetur,"* which, with tense changed,
may be freely translated, The mountains were in labor and a
ridiculous mouse was produced.   [Laughter and applause on
the Democratic side.]

Here Mr. Clark discussed the duty on lumber.

There is a great hullabaloo in the newspapers about the
tariff on rough lumber having been reduced to $1.25.   Is it re-
duced to $1.25?   No.   If rough lumber is worth $10 a thousand, when this bill goes into effect in March next the rate will
be $1.25 per thousand and 25 per cent. *ad valorem*, which
would make it $3.75 per thousand.   So that instead of getting
cheap lumber, which we have been clamoring for for a great
many years, some on both sides of the House, we are to get very
high-priced lumber, and I protest against it in the name of
everyone who has to build a house between the two oceans.
[Applause on the Democratic side.]

The lumber feature is a sample of the rest, 25 per cent. *ad
valorem* increase above the conference rates on all the rest,
and I say that, with that feature staring me in the face, as a
proposition to reduce the tariff downward this bill is the most
stupendous fake in the history of mankind.   [Applause on the
Democratic side.]   It is a colossal bunko game.   The people
asked for bread and you are giving them a stone.

Here Mr. Clark declared that the bill would create a deficiency in the Treasury.   He said in conclusion:

The final verdict on this bill is not made up by the syco-
phants and enthusiasts who sound praises into the ears of Presi-

dent Taft at this time, but the verdict on the merits of this
bill will be made up piecemeal every time the head of a family,
every time the woman of the house, buys a bill of goods in any
store. [Applause on the Democratic side.]

Mr. Longworth supported the bill. He dwelt particularly on the corporation-tax feature. He denied that
this provision had been evolved for the purpose of defeating the income tax in the Senate, declaring that it had
been planned by President Taft even before his inauguration.

Three definite propositions have been considered since the
beginning of this extra session—an inheritance tax, such as
was contained in this bill as it passed the House; a tax upon
the receipts of corporations, such as was contained in the bill
as it passed the Senate; and a proposition which contained
these two; and, in addition, a tax on individual incomes, which
was presented in the Senate and was known as the Bailey-Cummins amendment. It is true that the inheritance-tax feature
of this amendment is not precisely the same as that which
passed the House, but it is, nevertheless, a tax on inheritances.
It is true, also, that the corporation tax of this amendment is
not the same as the corporation tax as it passed the Senate, but
it is a tax upon the net income of all corporations, and in principle they are practically identical. While the Bailey-Cummins amendment is generally referred to as an income tax
solely, it is, in fact, in addition to this, an inheritance tax and
a corporation tax measure.

Generally speaking, the Bailey-Cummins amendment is an
almost exact reproduction of the income tax adopted in the
Wilson bill. Hardly any change has been made in it, except
that the exemption has been increased from two to five thousand dollars. I gathered in the debate here the other day that
some gentlemen on the other side would prefer that the exemption should be increased even above this point. The gentleman from Alabama [Henry D. Clayton], in reply to a question
I addressed him, said that he would exempt incomes of $7,500.
Evidently the gentleman from Alabama, if he had the drafting
of an income-tax law, would see to it that those who voted for
it should not be included in its provisions. [Laughter.]

MR. CLAYTON.—I would exempt all the poor men and all the
men with small incomes, so that I might get their support, in
order in that way to make the multimillionaires, who now pay

no taxes, contribute something to the support of the Government. [Applause on the Democratic side.]

MR. LONGWORTH.—Oh, the gentleman advocates a class system of taxation.

MR. CLAYTON.—It is not a class system. Does not the gentleman admit that every corporation whose net income does not exceed $5,000 is exempt?

MR. LONGWORTH.—Most assuredly.

MR. CLAYTON.—Is not that the same principle that would exempt the individual in an income tax? What is the difference in principle? I should like to have the gentleman elucidate it.

MR. LONGWORTH.—The difference between investigating the personal affairs of an individual and the affairs of a corporation, which I think should be made public.

SWAGAR SHERLEY [Ky.].—If the gentleman is warranted in saying that the corporation tax is superior to an income tax, how is the gentleman warranted in not taxing bondholders in place of stockholders?

MR. LONGWORTH.—It was seriously considered in drafting this measure, as I understand it, whether constitutionally the bonds could be gotten at, but it was deemed that it would make the measure unconstitutional, and for that reason it was not put in.

Mr. Speaker, that this measure discriminates between corporations and individuals is, to my mind, not a fault, but a virtue. I have heard over and over again this argument: Suppose A is a corporation engaged in doing business upon one corner of a street. B is a partnership doing a business precisely the same, both as to character and volume, on the other corner of the street. Is it fair that establishment A should pay a tax to the Government upon its net earnings, and that establishment B should go free? My answer is, "Yes." By virtue of having incorporated his business, A has certain advantages which B, managing his affairs as a partnership, has not. Among other things, his liabilities are limited, and he has the right of perpetual succession. He has paid something for the privilege of becoming a corporation and of enjoying these advantages, and hence has shown that he deems them to be of value. The members of the partnership have not asked from the Government any privileges that they are not entitled to as individuals, and it seems to me that they have the right to consider that their profits are their own private affair.

As to the constitutionality of this tax I shall have but little to say, because I take it to be beyond argument. If anyone holds any doubt upon this question, I would recommend the reading of the speech recently made in the Senate by the junior Senator from New York [Mr. Root], in which he goes thoroughly into the question of the constitutionality of this legislation. His speech is a masterpiece of clearness and force, and leaves practically nothing to be said upon the subject.

But there is a feature of this measure which, to my mind, is of special importance, and that is the feature of publicity. This measure compels the corporations to state in general terms what their gross earnings have been, what has been charged off to repairs, renewals, maintenance, and overhead charges, and what remains which can reasonably be considered their net profit from the business every year. To my mind, it will be of immense advantage to the stockholders of corporations throughout the country. I venture to say that the vast majority of all the stockholders have no real idea of what their legitimate profits have actually been.

I have heard again and again urged against this measure the old argument that it will cut into the savings of the widows and orphans. This is the argument we always hear when any legislation is contemplated which affects a corporation. I believe this measure is for the direct benefit of the widows and orphans and all stockholders, to whose interest it is that the affairs of the corporations of which they are part owners shall be wisely and intelligently administered.

The junior Senator from New York, in his speech, called attention to another feature of this measure which I think is of the greatest importance, and that is the difficulty of making a well-considered protective tariff with the almost inconceivably meager information that we really have concerning the affairs of corporations which the tariff really affects.

I thoroughly believe that publicity in the affairs of corporations will be a benefit, not only to the public at large, not only for the benefit of the small stockholders, but for the benefit of the corporations themselves. I believe that a reasonable publicity will cause millions of the public's money to come out of hiding and seek investment in corporate stock, and that floods of money will come to this country from foreign investors.

I believe that this measure is in line with the great progressive measures which have been enacted by the Republican party in the past eight years for the supervision and regulation by the Government of corporate wealth, the question which, to my mind, together with the question of the conservation of our national resources, overshadows all others in importance. I believe that in evolving and advocating the passage of this law the President of the United States has redeemed in the fullest measure his pledge that he would, during his administration, proceed along the paths blocked out by his predecessor; that he would use every effort to bring to his policies their fullest fruition. [Applause.]

Mr. Underwood, at the close of a speech, more or less statistical, against the bill, discussed the feature of the corporation tax.

I know there is a sentiment among some people that is antagonistic to corporations; that in some quarters the antagonism to corporate interests is intense; but the American people are just and cannot be misled by an appeal to prejudice, so I am surprised that a great political party should, under the cloak of that sentiment, attempt to put a tax on the people of the United States that is not intended primarily to raise revenue, but has for its ultimate goal the purpose of invading the rights of the States in their control of domestic corporations. [Applause on the Democratic side.]

The Democratic party, recognizing that every man should pay in proportion to what he has, proposed to exempt him on his consumed earnings, the money that the ordinary man spends in his living expenses, because he is already paying his taxes to the full amount of his living expenses, and proposed to adopt an income tax to make him pay taxes on his unconsumed wealth that the Government is protecting for him. Now that was fair, that was just. It was so just that when the Democrats in the United States Senate proposed such an amendment to this bill the Republican ranks could not stand the fire, and they broke to our standard. [Applause on the Democratic side.] They came to our proposition, that to put an income tax on the unconsumed wealth of this country was equality in taxation, and therefore just.

To defeat that proposition, to prevent that righteous verdict from being found, the President of the United States and the Republican leaders in Congress proposed this tax on the incomes of corporations—incomes that go to the poor as well as the rich; income that is consumed in living expenses as well as that which is unconsumed and hoarded.

ROBERT C. WICKLIFFE [La.].—Suppose a holding corporation has a net income of $5,000 derived from business, and in addition to that it owns four-fifths of the stock in a dozen other corporations, no one of which other corporations has a net income exceeding $5,000; then this holding company would receive $53,000 net income if the income of each of these twelve corporations was $5,000; and yet under the provisions of this corporation-tax law as now written it would not pay one cent of taxation on that net income. Is not that correct?

MR. UNDERWOOD.—The gentleman is absolutely correct, and his illustration is a good one to show the inequalities of this proposition.

Now, here is the proposition when you analyze it. The great corporations in this country that are violating the law of the land should be regulated by the Government, but there is no prejudice in the minds of the people against the little domestic corporations in the States that are doing a legitimate business. Their charters are granted by the States. If the people of the States think these corporations are performing an unrighteous act, they have the power to revoke their charters or to regulate them; but when you reach out, as in my opinion this law is intended to do, and first make these little corporations pay a small tax, then say they must take out a federal charter when they pay that tax, and then put an additional tax on all State corporations that have not taken out a federal charter, your State control has gone to the winds; you have destroyed your control at home and you have built up the vastest power in the Federal Government that the mind of man can conceive of. [Applause on the Democratic side.]

As to the question of the justice of the taxation, you can readily see that the great millionaire who has got hundreds of millions of dollars invested in bonds, hundreds of millions in real estate in some great city which is protected by the Government, pays no tax under this corporation-tax law he would pay under an income tax. And yet the small merchant or a dozen little fellows off in a State who have ten or twenty thousand each invested in some little corporation, the income from which they are spending in living expenses, every dollar that they are getting out of those corporations, paying taxes on it when they buy their clothes, when they buy their cigars, when they spend their money—and yet must have an additional tax placed on them because, forsooth, they have joined together under the State law for a legitimate purpose. For what purpose? Not for the purpose of raising more revenue for the Government, but to give the national Government control of domestic corporations, and that it might be used as a weapon to defeat an hon-

XII—26

est income tax that would equalize the burdens of taxation on all the people. [Great applause on the Democratic side.]

The House agreed to the conference report by a vote of 195 to 183. The Senate agreed to the report on August 5 by a vote of 70 to 0. President Taft approved the bill on August 5, 1909.

CHAPTER XVII

The Income Tax

Origin of the Tax—Acts of 1861, 1870 and 1894—Act of 1861: in Favor, Representative Jacob H. Ela [N. Y.]; Opposed, Representative Dennis McCarthy [N. Y.]—Act of 1870: in Favor, Senator John Sherman [O.]; Opposed, Senator Roscoe Conkling [N. Y.]—Act of 1894: in Favor, Representative Benton McMillin [Tenn.], Representative Uriel S. Hall [Mo.]; Opposed, Representative W. Bourke Cockran [N. Y.]—Proposed Single Tax Substitute for Income Tax (1894): in Favor, James G. Maguire [Cal.], Tom L. Johnson [O.]—Income Tax (1894) Is Declared Unconstitutional by Supreme Court—Nelson W. Aldrich [R. I.] Reports in the Senate from the Committee on Finance a Joint Resolution Proposing the Submission to the States of a Constitutional Amendment Providing for an Income Tax—Debate: Speakers of Varying Views, Anselm J. McLaurin [Miss.], Norris Brown [Neb.], William J. Stone [Mo.], Joseph W. Bailey [Tex.], Joseph M. Dixon [Mont.], Weldon B. Heyburn [Ida.], Hernando D. Money [Miss.], Porter J. McCumber [N. D.], Albert J. Beveridge [Ind.]—Senate Passes Joint Resolution—Debate in the House on the Resolution: in Favor, Sereno E. Payne [N. Y.], Champ Clark [Mo.], Ollie M. James [Ky.], Gen. J. Warren Keifer [O.], Adam Byrd [Miss.], Richmond P. Hobson [Ala.]; Opposed, Samuel W. McCall [Mass.], Ebenezer J. Hill [Ct.]—Robert L. Henry [Tex.] Offers an Amendment to Joint Resolution to the Effect That Proposed Constitutional Amendment Be Submitted to the Conventions of the States Instead of the Legislatures—His Amendment Is Ruled Out of Order—Bill Is Passed by House, and Becomes Effective Without the Signature of the President.

SHORTLY after the outbreak of the Civil War, while the vexing question of raising revenue to supply a deficiency of $20,000,000 was before Congress, James R. Simmons [R. I.] advocated in the Senate "a moderate tax on all incomes exceeding $1,000." This tax, he declared, was well adapted to the purpose of providing the necessary money without public distress. It was heartily endorsed in both Houses as a fair and equitable measure.

Accordingly, on August 5, 1861, a provision was inserted in an internal revenue bill by which a general tax of three per cent. was laid on annual incomes, $800 being exempted from taxation in each case. Foreign residents, however, paid five per cent. upon incomes, and all owners, whether at home or abroad, of Government securities paid only one and one-half per cent. upon the interest from these.

Act of 1870.

When, in June, 1870, a bill to reduce internal revenue came before the House Dennis McCarthy [N. Y.] moved to strike out the income tax clause.

This tax is unequal, perjury-provoking, and crime-encouraging, because it is at war with the right of a person to keep private and regulate his business affairs and financial matters. The people demand that it shall not be renewed, but left to die a natural death and pass away into the future as pass away all the evils growing out of the Civil War.

Jacob H. Ela [N. Y.] opposed the motion.

I believe the income tax as at present paid is one of the most just taxes laid, and affects no person who has not received a net income above the amount required for the reasonable support of a family, while most other national taxes, except those from succession and legacies, come from people who are struggling to get the means of support.

Mr. McCarthy's motion was defeated by a vote of 60 to 124.

On June 3 various amendments proposed were voted upon. The minimum amount of income was fixed at $2,000. It was also agreed that the statements of incomes be kept secret from all but the Internal Revenue Department. Substitutes for the measure, namely, a tax on Government bonds, and a tax on corporations, to be deducted from interest and dividends before payment, were voted down.

When the bill came before the Senate, Roscoe Conkling [N. Y.] opposed the income tax feature.

This tax breeds more jealousy, more discontent, more invidious and odious discrimination, and more demoralization, I undertake to say, than any other tax enforced by law.

John Sherman [O.] replied to Mr. Conkling.

The Senator says this tax is unequal, that rogues escape
and honest men pay. Is not that so with all taxes in all the

THE FINANCIAL INQUISITION

Grand Inquisitor, U. S. GRANT. *Associate Inquisitors*, G. S. BOUTWELL, F. E. SPINNER, JOHN SHERMAN.
Executioner, C. DELANO.

Associate Sherman: "Well, well, Uncle Sam does stand a good deal
of pressure. Executioner, keep piling the weights on"

From the collection in the New York Public Library

States? Was there ever a tax that was fairly assessed and honestly collected in all respects?

But, sir, there never was so just a tax levied as the income
tax. Why? The income tax is simply an assessment upon a
man according to his ability to pay.

The Senate greatly modified the income tax provision, limiting the operation of the tax to two years, and
reducing the rate to two and one-half per cent.

The house refusing to concur in all the Senate amendments, a conference committee was appointed. The committee in their report advised virtually the adoption of
the Senate amendments in regard to the income tax.
Both Houses concurred in the report, and the bill was
signed by President Ulysses S. Grant on July 14, 1870.

Act of 1894.

On January 29, 1894, Benton McMillin [Tenn.], from
the Committee on Ways and Means, offered in the House
an amendment to the Wilson tariff bill, laying a two per
cent. tax on incomes over $4,000 a year. In supporting
his amendment he presented the following arguments:

1. An income tax would remove part of the great
burden resting upon the consumer and place it upon accumulated wealth.

2. It was not unjust to tax wealth for the support of
a government from which it receives protection.

3. The argument that an income tax is productive
of perjury was not pertinent—to carry out this reasoning would be to advocate removing from our statute
books every law that is enacted against crime.

4. A method was proposed by which the income tax
was made less inquisitorial than customs and internal
revenue taxes.

5. The amendment was so constructed that the income tax could not operate as a tax upon thrift. Each
citizen was exempted from taxation to the extent of
$4,000, and every income exceeding that amount was
taxed at a uniform rate.

6. The adoption of an income tax would remove
much of the discontent among the laboring classes.

Other speakers advanced various arguments in favor
of an income tax. Uriel S. Hall [Mo.] said that one of
its best features was the constant change in the amount
of revenue collected under it.

Without an income tax the only method at your command
for producing the proper flexibility of revenue to meet the flex-
ible demands of the Government, without disturbing the busi-

ness interests of the country, is to change your tariff schedule every two years.

Another argument presented by Mr. Hall was that the income tax would reach a certain class of men living outside of the cities who had their property invested in choses in action, which were not taxable under the laws of most of the States.

W. Bourke Cockran [N. Y.] spoke against the amendment. It was opposed, he said, to the principles of the Democratic party.

This is not a tax upon the men who have enjoyed any special benefit from the Government; it is a tax upon the men who have made the best use of the benefits which are common to all. The vast majority of the persons affected by this tax have never received any special benefit from the Government, but have been injured by the inequality of tariff laws.

Sir, I protest against this betrayal of our ancient principles. I protest against this treason to our faith, to our platform, to our traditions, to our heroes. I protest against partial laws, whether they be intended to favor the few or the many. I demand for all men the same equality before the law which they enjoy in the sight of God.

On January 31 James G. Maguire [Cal.] proposed as a substitute for the income tax that a direct tax of $31,-311,125 be annually laid on the land values, exclusive of improvements (the single tax), in the United States, and apportioned to the States and Territories and District of Columbia, these values to be assessed at the full market rates.

The immediate purpose of my amendment is to provide a method better than the general income tax for $31,000,000 to meet a portion of the deficiency expected to arise under the Wilson tariff bill. The income tax, proposed by the gentleman from Tennessee [Mr. McMillin], can nearly all be shifted from the immediate payers to the shoulders of the poor, or comparatively poor, who consume the products of the industries out of which the incomes arise, or who borrow the money upon which incomes, in the form of interest, are paid.

The vote was taken at once on Mr. Maguire's amendment to Mr. McMillin's amendment—yeas 6, nays 180.

Tom L. Johnson [O.] said:

Mr. Chairman, I desire to put on record the names of the gentlemen who have had the foresight and the patriotism to vote for this single-tax amendment. They are the gentleman from California, Mr. Maguire (the mover of the amendment); the gentleman from New York, Charles Tracey; the gentleman from New York, John DeWitt Warner; the gentleman from Ohio, Michael D. Harter; the gentleman from Kansas, Jerry Simpson, and myself.

Mr. McMillin's amendment was then passed, amid loud applause on the Democratic side, by a vote of 175 to 56. Mr. Cockran voted in the negative.

The passage of the Wilson bill by the House carried with it this amendment. The income tax feature was upheld by the Senate, though strenuously opposed by David B. Hill [N. Y.] and others.

Income Tax Decision of the Supreme Court

On March 7, 1895, a suit [the Pollock case] was begun in the Supreme Court to test the constitutionality of the Income Tax law. On April 7 the Court decided:

(1) That taxes on the rent or income of real estate are direct taxes.

(2) That so much of the Act of 1894 as attempts to impose a tax upon the rent or income of real estate without apportionment (among the several States according to their population) is invalid.

These questions were decided by a vote of 6 to 2. The Court further decided that the tax upon income derived from municipal bonds was invalid. This tax, they declared, was a tax on the power of the States and their instrumentalities to borrow money, and was therefore unconstitutional. On this point the vote was unanimous.

On the other features of the law of 1894 the Court was evenly divided, and hence no opinion was expressed.

William D. Guthrie [Cal.], who had argued against the law before the Court, became impressed with the idea that, upon a rehearing, a majority of the Court could be induced to declare the entire act invalid. This led to an application for a rehearing, which was granted. The Court convened again to consider the case on May 7, 1895.

On May 11, by a majority of 1, the Court declared the Income Tax law constitutional. Chief-Justice Fuller began at once to prepare the opinion of the minority. Later, however, Justice Shiras, who, ever since the first hearing on the case had seemed in doubt on many points, changed his vote, thus turning a minority into a majority, and deciding adversely the fate of the entire Income Tax law. The final vote of the Court was as follows: Against the law—Chief-Justice Melville W. Fuller [Dem.], Justices Stephen J. Field [Dem.], Horace Gray [Rep.], David J. Brewer [Rep.], and George Shiras, Jr. [Rep.]. Dissenting—Justice John M. Harlan [Rep.], Henry B. Brown [Rep.], Howell E. Jackson [Dem.], and Edward D. White [Dem.].

The decision of the majority was taken on the ground that the taxes on income from real estate, as well as those on bonds, stocks, and investments of all kinds, were direct taxes not apportioned among the several States, and were therefore repugnant to the Constitution. And these taxes, they said, "formed a vital part of the whole scheme." If they were stricken out,

This would leave the burden of the income tax to be borne by professions, trades, employments, and vocations, and in this way what was intended as a tax on capital would remain in substance a tax on occupations and labor. We cannot believe that such was the intention of Congress.

Justice Harlan delivered the principal dissenting opinion. He argued that the main feature of the income tax, *viz.:* the tax on income derived from rents, was not a direct tax. He also declared:

The judgment just rendered defeats the purpose of Congress by taking out of the revenue not less than thirty and possibly fifty million dollars. We know that taxation would not have been reduced to the extent it was by the Wilson act, but for the belief that if the country had the benefit of revenue derived from a tax on incomes it could be safely done. If all the income tax sections of the Wilson act must fall because some of them are invalid, does not the judgment this day rendered furnish ground for the contention that the entire Wilson act falls when the court strikes from it all of the income tax provisions, without which the act would never have been passed?

This dissenting opinion of Justice Harlan was considered remarkable, not only for its arguments, but for its *delivery*. Said the New York *Herald:*

He began in a low and distinct tone, but it soon became evident that there was a good deal of feeling in his words. He raised his voice and gesticulated with considerable violence to the members of the bar in front of him. It is doubtful if ever before in the history of the Supreme Court there has been witnessed a scene as remarkable as this, or if ever before a justice has gone to such lengths in criticizing and denouncing the action of a majority of a tribunal of which he was a member. Some of Justice Harlan's phrases almost caused consternation among the members of the bar who sat before him. His impassioned denunciation of the decision, and some of the criticisms he made on the reasoning of the justices who prepared it, indicated that his opinions had a strong leaning toward advanced socialism.

As we have seen in the debate on the Payne-Aldrich revenue bill, [see page 376ss], a strong desire arose in Congress in April, 1909, to embody in the general tariff bill an income tax provision that could not be construed by the Supreme Court as unconstitutional. This method, however, was finally discarded as impracticable—it was urged that, no matter how the provision might be formulated, the tax would be declared unconstitutional.

The logic of the situation, therefore, was that Congress, to be consistent, should place the constitutionality of the admittedly desirable tax beyond question. This could be done only by proposing an amendment to the Constitution, especially declaring that an income tax might be levied by the national legislature.

Consistency further required that the party in power introduce the proposition. Therefore, and with further appositeness, Nelson W. Aldrich [R. I.], the Republican leader in the Senate on the tariff bill, on June 28, 1909, while the tariff bill was still under discussion, reported from the Committee on Finance a joint resolution proposing the submission to the States of the following amendment to the Constitution:

Article XVI. The Congress shall have power to lay and collect taxes on incomes, from whatever source derived, without apportionment among the several States and without regard to any census or enumeration.

The resolution was based on one which had been offered on April 27 by Norris Brown [Neb.] and referred to the committee.

The resolution came up for discussion on July 3.

THE INCOME TAX [CONSTITUTIONAL AMENDMENT]

SENATE, JULY 3, 1909

ANSELM J. McLAURIN [Miss.].—Mr. President, I do not believe that there is any necessity for any constitutional amendment to authorize the Congress of the United States to enact an income tax. Whatever may be the intention in bringing forward the proposed amendment, I think the effect will be to defer the enactment of any law providing for an income tax. I think the effect of it will be that there will be probably more than a fourth of the States of the Union which will refuse to ratify the action of Congress when this proposed amendment to the Constitution is presented to the States for ratification, and then I think that will be presented to the Supreme Court of the United States as an argument why an income tax should be held to be unconstitutional. I think it would be urged as a very plausible argument before the Supreme Court of the United States that the people are not in favor of an income tax and do not believe that an income tax would be constitutional.

I cannot conceive that there can be any necessity for any constitutional amendment. If I understood the vote yesterday, the proponent of this proposed constitutional amendment voted against the income tax.

SENATOR BROWN.—I voted for an income tax.

SENATOR McLAURIN.—The Senator from Nebraska, as I heard it, voted to substitute the corporation tax for the income tax.

SENATOR BROWN.—I did. A corporation tax is a tax on incomes, which the court has sustained. I voted for that which the court sustained and rejected that which the court rejected.

SENATOR McLAURIN.—I do not see that the Congress of the United States should be called upon to zigzag around the inconsistent rulings of the Supreme Court of the United States. Without intending any reflection upon that tribunal, it is composed of men just exactly as the Congress of the United States is composed of men. I believe there are just as good lawyers in the House of Representatives and in the Senate of the United States as there are on the Supreme Bench.

SENATOR BROWN.—That is true; but they are not on the bench.

SENATOR McLAURIN.—I know that the members of the Senate and the members of the House are not on the Supreme Bench, but that does not necessitate nor argue for the abnegation of the right of the Senators and Representatives in Congress to pass their judgment upon a constitutional question. It is for us to pass that which we consider to be a constitutional law, and it is for the Supreme Court to undo it or not, as it sees proper.

On July 5 William J. Stone [Mo.] supported the Brown resolution.

I wish to read a declaration contained in the Democratic national platform which was promulgated at Denver in 1908. It is as follows:

We favor an income tax as part of our revenue system, and we urge the submission of a constitutional amendment specifically authorizing Congress to levy and collect a tax upon individual and corporate incomes, to the end that wealth may bear its proportionate share of the burdens of the Federal Government.

That declaration, clear and explicit, is alone sufficient to determine my attitude with regard to the resolution to be voted upon to-day. I am gratified to note this one more example, in addition to those I have heretofore pointed out, of Republicans following in the wake of Democratic leadership and along lines blazed by our Democratic pioneers. The President has taken his stand on the Denver platform, and a Republican Senator has culled one of its declarations and formulated it into the legislative proposition now before the Senate.

Mr. President, fear has been expressed that more than one-fourth of the States will withhold their consent to the amendment and reject it, and then it is apprehended that an argument will be based on that circumstance to induce the Supreme Court to adhere to the doctrine announced in the Pollock case if ever the constitutionality of an income tax is again before that tribunal.

Mr. President, I cannot persuade myself that more than one-fourth of our American States will reject this proposed amendment to the Constitution. But if 12 States should by bare majorities in each reject the proposition, and 33 States should agree to it, as they would by large majorities, it would still be manifest that the great body of the people favored the amendment. If the Supreme Court should be called upon to review the Pollock case, and should be inclined to return to its earlier and, I think, sounder rulings, namely, that an income tax was within the Constitution, I can see no good reason why the court would hesitate to adopt that course even if this amendment should fail of ratification.

Joseph W. Bailey [Tex.] offered an amendment to the Brown resolution.

I move to strike out the word "legislatures," in line 5, and to substitute the word "conventions"; and in line 9, after the word "incomes," I move to add the words "and may grade the same."

Mr. President, of course the Senate will at once understand that the purpose of the first amendment is to submit the ratification of this proposed amendment to conventions called in each State for that purpose, rather than to the legislatures. Legislatures are elected with reference to many questions. Legislatures may be chosen upon local issues. The members may change their opinions, as members of the Senate have done upon this very question, between the time they are chosen to the legislature and the time when they are required to vote.

The second amendment, Mr. President, gives distinct and specific authority to graduate an income tax, and I think that necessary only as a matter of abundant caution. I would not, perhaps, have thought it necessary at all, except for the statement of Judge Brewer, in the case of Knowlton vs. Moore, where he dissents from the opinion of the court sustaining the validity of the inheritance-tax law upon the ground that Congress had no power to grade it.

SENATOR McLAURIN.—There are many Senators who believe that it is not necessary to have any amendment to the Constitution.

The mischief in reference to an income tax in every discussion of it before the court has grown out of six words, three of them in clause 3 of section 2 of Article I of the Constitution, and three of them in clause 2 of section 9 of Article I of the Constitution. In the first place it says:

Representatives and direct taxes shall be apportioned among the several States—

The words "and direct taxes'" in that instance, and in the next—

No capitation or other direct tax shall be laid.

The words "or other direct" are the words that make the mischief in this clause 4 of section 9. With these six words stricken out of the Constitution in the places where they occur, as I have indicated, there could be no trouble about the levying and collecting of an income tax.

Senator McLaurin therefore proposed as a substitute for the Brown resolution to strike out of the Constitution the words indicated.

Joseph M. Dixon [Mont.] opposed the submission of the Amendment to State conventions.

In many of the States the expense of holding elections for delegates to a constitutional convention will be so large that the question of expense will be used as an argument against it. I think in my State it will cost the State $100,000 to hold its constitutional convention and the election for the choosing of delegates.

I am convinced this will complicate matters. On the other hand, if the joint resolution passes both the Senate and House, as it will undoubtedly, the governor of each State in the Union will certify to the next general assembly of the States the fact that the joint resolution has passed both Houses of Congress, and it will be brought directly and forcibly to the attention of the people in every State.

I for one believe that this amendment will carry in nearly every State of the Union. Suppose, as it has been intimated, that influences should be used in a State with the members of the legislature against it and that legislature returns and goes home without adopting the amendment, it makes it the burning live issue in that State. The joint resolution of Congress does not become *functus officio* because one legislature of a State at that time has not adopted it. It will rest on the legislatures that will assemble in the future, and whenever three-fourths have finally ratified it, whether it be one, two, three, five, or ten years, it then becomes a part of the fundamental law of the United States. I am thoroughly convinced that the convention method will complicate more than it will help.

WELDON B. HEYBURN [Ida.].—Does the Senator contend that it might be submitted to an indefinite number of subsequent legislatures, or would the action, either positive or negative, of the legislature to which it was first submitted exhaust the right?

SENATOR DIXON.—I presume if the legislative action were positive or negative it would be exhausted in that State.

SENATOR HEYBURN.—Then, if the legislature to which it was submitted failed to act that would be the equivalent of a rejection of the amendment.

SENATOR DIXON.—No; if the legislature failed to act, I do not think for a moment it would be.

SENATOR BROWN.—Unless some good controlling reason is presented why we should change our method of amending the Constitution, I do not think we can justify our vote against following the usual method. The legislature is an existing institution in every State. A convention would have to be arranged for. The legislatures, by virtue of the several State constitutions, meet every two years in most of the States. We do not have to wait for somebody to call a convention. The legislature is already called. We do not have to worry about the expense of the legislature, because the expense is already incurred.

In addition to all these objections, Mr. President, there is one other which ought to cause Senators in this body to vote against the proposed amendment for ratification by conventions. I know the fight that has been made in a large majority of the States of this country for a primary law. There has been a fight of the people in a majority of the States of the Union to get away from legislators who are nominated in conventions, and in many States they are now nominated at a primary. Members of Congress who used to be nominated in conventions are now nominated at a primary. The members of the several legislatures of the States that have primary laws do not have conventions. They have no law for electing delegates to any convention at a primary.

Now, then, Mr. President, as to the other amendment offered by the Senator from Texas, where he asks that the words "and the right to grade" be put in, I think already the language of the joint resolution gives Congress the power to grade the income. The power to lay a tax includes the power to grade. Of that no doubt can reasonably exist, in my judgment.

HERNANDO D. MONEY [Miss.].—The difficulty that presents itself to my mind is to secure the 12 States which everybody admits are quite likely to defeat any amendment of this sort to the Constitution. The method presented by the Senator from Texas is probably the best, but the same influences that will control the votes of the legislature will prevent the legislature from calling a convention.

We had great difficulty in passing the last two amendments to the Constitution, which seemed to be so very necessary in our system of political economy as to fix the status of several million freedmen. I am one of those who do not believe that either the fourteenth or fifteenth amendment was ever validly made a part of the Constitution.

Mr. President, I do not believe that this amendment to the Constitution will ever be a part of it. I am willing to vote for it, and I should like to see it adopted, if possible; but I am quite sure that those influences which have prevented a vote on the income-tax amendment in this Senate will also prevent a vote in at least twelve of the legislatures of this Union. We can feel quite sure that an act of such far-reaching importance, that touches the pockets of very many rich people, is not very likely to become a part of the organic law of our Republic or of our confederation.

SENATOR BAILEY.—Mr. President, if, instead of submitting this amendment to the legislatures, that may act and react, and go forward and recede, we submit it to a convention in every State, then every member of that convention will be selected solely with reference to this single question; he will be compelled to stand in the presence of the people whose suffrage he seeks and declare, upon his honor as a man and as a citizen, whether or not he favors this amendment. This procedure will be as nearly as possible a submission of the question to a direct vote of the people.

Now, a number of Senators have suggested to me that the

question of expense might be an important one, and therefore I desire to say that, if the amendment I propose should be adopted and we should refer this joint resolution to conventions, instead of to the legislatures, I shall follow it with a resolution providing, out of the general treasury, for the expense of holding the conventions in every State.

PORTER J. McCUMBER [N. D.].—If the legislature were composed of men who would naturally be against the amendment, would it not be more convenient and more easy for them to avoid the calling of a convention than it would to meet the matter directly?

SENATOR BAILEY.—If I were a member of the Texas legislature, and this amendment were submitted for ratification by the legislature, and I were opposed to it, I should vote against it; and they might bring Gatling guns and train them on the capitol, but I would still vote against it if I were honestly opposed to it. But, sir, if the amendment were submitted to the ratification or disposition of a convention, I should feel in honor bound, both as a member of the legislature and as a citizen, to afford to the people of Texas an opportunity to pass in a lawful and an orderly way upon the question.

So I do not hesitate to say that there is a vast difference between a legislator who might vote against the ratification of the amendment if submitted to the legislature and one who would vote against submitting it to a convention in pursuance of the resolution of Congress.

SENATOR HEYBURN.—As I read Article V of the Constitution, which is the article providing for amendments, a State legislature has nothing to do with the question whether or not an amendment shall be submitted to a convention. Congress is to say whether it shall be passed upon by the legislature or by a convention, and the legislature cannot refer it to a convention. Congress is clothed with the authority to adopt that course if it sees fit.

ALBERT J. BEVERIDGE [Ind.].—How could the convention be called if the legislature did not call it?

SENATOR HEYBURN.—The governor would call the convention if the act of Congress authorized him to do it.

SENATOR BAILEY.—The trouble with that is that it would be necessary to provide for the manner in which members should be elected, and the governor could hardly do that.

SENATOR BROWN.—That would require a session of the legislature.

SENATOR HEYBURN.—I merely gave out the suggestion be-

XII—27

cause it seemed naturally to grow out of the language of Article V.

SENATOR BROWN.—Under the proposal of the Senator from Texas to refer the matter to a convention, we not only have the legislature still in the way, but we have the convention in the way. In other words, you have to have a legislature that is friendly enough to the proposition to pass a law that will be fair enough to allow the people to select delegates to a convention; and then you have to wait until the adjournment of the legislature, and until a convention is called, before you get any action either for or against the amendment. Will some Senator tell me the need of that postponement? In the West we can trust to the legislatures of the States.

Senator Bailey's first amendment was rejected by a vote of 30 yeas to 46 nays, and he withdrew his second amendment. Senator McLaurin's amendment was rejected. The joint resolution was passed by a vote of 77 to 0 on July 5, 1909.

The House referred the resolution to the Committee on Ways and Means, which reported it back on July 12.

THE INCOME TAX [CONSTITUTIONAL AMENDMENT]

HOUSE OF REPRESENTATIVES, JULY 12, 1909

SERENO E. PAYNE [N. Y.].—I am utterly opposed to the general policy of an income tax. I believe with Gladstone that it tends to make a nation of liars; I believe it is the most easily concealed of any tax that can be laid, the most difficult of enforcement, and the hardest to collect; that it is, in a word, a tax upon the income of the honest men and an exemption, to a greater or less extent, of the income of the rascals; and so I am opposed to any income tax whatever in time of peace. But if this nation should ever be under the stress of a great war, exhausting her resources, and the question of war now being a question as to which nation has the longest pocketbook, the greatest material resource in a great degree, I do not wish to be left, I do not wish this nation to be left, without an opportunity to avail itself of every resource to provide an income adequate to the carrying on of that war.

I hope that if the Constitution is amended in this way the

time will not come when the American people will ever want to enact an income tax except in time of war.

Samuel W. McCall [Mass.] opposed the income tax amendment. It abrogated, he said, one of the fundamental principles of the Constitution—the principle that direct taxes should be apportioned among the States according to population.

He continued:

While gentlemen say that they desire this power for time of war, we see to-day in time of peace an attempt to exercise the power to its utmost extent. Why not, then, limit it expressly to time of war? Why not, for the just protection and the equal rights of the people of New York and of the other great States of this Union, five of which probably will pay nine-tenths of an income tax, although they will have only one-ninth of the representation in the Senate—why not preserve the limitation upon the power of the central Government? Why drag every government power to Washington so that a vast centralized government may devour the States and the liberty of the individual as well?

Mr. Speaker, believing that this amendment, with no compensation whatever, does away with an important part of the great compromise of the Constitution, and that it is not limited to the emergency for which it is said to be intended, I shall vote against it. The amendment has not carefully been considered by a committee of this House or by anybody else in the United States that I know of, unless possibly by Mr. William J. Bryan. [Applause.]

CHAMP CLARK [Mo.].—The income tax is a Democratic proposition. We put it in the tariff bill of 1894. A very large majority of us have been in favor of it ever since. We wrote it in our platform of 1896 and have advocated it ever since. We proposed it as part of the war-tariff bill of 1898, and Republicans voted it down with practical unanimity. We are in favor of it now; and we welcome the conversion of the Republican party to another Democratic principle. [Loud applause on the Democratic side.] Better late than never. One by one the roses fall, and one by one you adopt the planks of our platform. [Renewed applause.] The whirligig of time brings its own revenges. What was denounced by Republicans in 1896 as anarchy is advocated by them to-day as sound political gospel. My own judgment is that the wit of man never devised a fairer or juster tax than a graduated income tax.

It is monstrous to say—I do not care what the gentleman from Massachusetts or anybody else says—it is monstrous to say that the accumulated wealth of this country shall not bear its just proportion of the public burdens. [Loud general applause.] The decision on the income-tax law of 1894, when the peculiar circumstances under which it was rendered are considered, is one of the great blots on the judicial system of this country. Everybody knows that we had two income-tax laws prior to the act of 1894. They were held to be constitutional. I believe firmly that if we had been engaged in a war with a first-class power in 1898, instead of in a war with Spain, Congress would "incontinently," as the gentleman from Massachusetts [Mr. McCall] says, have reënacted the income-tax law of 1894 and that the Supreme Court of the United States would have held it to be constitutional. [Applause.] Nobody had any doubt of that then, and nobody has any doubt of that now. The vast majority of the American people have always believed the income-tax law of 1894 constitutional.

We would much prefer making an income tax part of the tariff bill than to vote for this joint resolution submitting an income-tax constitutional amendment for ratification to the States; but, as it has been demonstrated that we cannot secure the passage of an income tax through this Congress, we will do the best thing possible under the circumstances and vote for this joint resolution, hoping for the best.

The gentleman from Massachusetts [Mr. McCall] talks about the sacredness of the Constitution. I am glad to hear a Republican say something in that behalf. [Laughter on the Democratic side.] Of course the Constitution is sacred, but the fathers of the Republic acted according to their lights and according to the circumstances under which they lived.

We must act according to our own lights and the circumstances under which we live. At the time when those clauses that the gentleman from Massachusetts talks about were put into the Constitution population was about equally distributed, and wealth was also; but times change and men change with them, and things change, too.

The Constitution provides that you cannot levy a direct tax, except by making it a head tax. That is the plain English of it. No Congress is ever going to order a direct tax under that section of the Constitution except, perhaps, in the stress of a great war with a great power, because it is palpably unjust.

Arkansas has one-sixth as many people as New York has, and would under that provision of the Constitution pay one-sixth as much direct tax as New York would, but New York has thirty times as much property value as the State of Arkansas has.

The relative situation of people and of States having largely changed, there is no reason why we should longer adhere to that part of the Constitution relative to a head tax and population. Consequently, while Democrats revere the Constitution, they are in favor of amending it so that the swollen fortunes of the land can be justly taxed.

EBENEZER J. HILL [Conn.].—Mr. President and gentlemen of the House of Representatives, I shall vote against this amendment for the following reasons: In the first place, I do not believe that this extra session of Congress was called to completely change and revolutionize the taxation system of the United States. I think that a question of such magnitude should be submitted to the people and discussed in a campaign preparatory to the presentation of so important a matter as an amendment to the Constitution of the United States. This proposition was found in the Democratic platform and not in the Republican platform on which the presidential campaign of 1908 was won. My understanding is that Congress was called together for the sole purpose of revising the Dingley tariff law on the basis of the difference in the cost of production at home and abroad.

Stop a moment and consider what we are doing in voting to give this Government the power to lay an income tax in time of peace. I know of no better measure of the way in which this burden would fall on the various States in the Union than to judge of it by the inheritance tax laid to meet the expenses of the Spanish-American war.

Of the entire amount collected from the inheritance tax in the whole Union six States paid three-fourths of it.

All told, 35 States paid $31,000 less than the little States of Connecticut and Rhode Island, and yet you come and ask me in time of peace and to pay the ordinary current expenses of this Government to vote now for a constitutional amendment which will enable these 35 States to impose a far greater tax upon my people. But it is claimed that the property in the Eastern States escapes taxation. That is not true. In the State of Connecticut more than 80 per cent. of all the expenses of our State government is now paid by corporations, and during the past ten years no State tax has been laid upon our people, but the whole amount has been met by corporation, inheritance, and other forms of direct taxation imposed by the State. Every corporation in the State is taxed; every legacy under the inheritance-tax law, which we have, pays its fair share.

Is it fair now, after two hundred years of expenditure on our part, that you should come and ask us to vote to tax ourselves in time of peace for a duplication of these things in all of the new and undeveloped States of the Union? It is not because our people desire to avoid taxation, and, as I have shown you, the accumulation of wealth in these Eastern States does not escape a fair and just charge upon it. We are ready to vote for an income tax to meet any emergencies which may arise in this Union and to stand by the Government in time of war; but do not ask us, at least without consultation with our people at home, to put this burden on them in addition to one already severe because of local expenditures, made necessary by our geographical position, but cheerfully assumed for the general good. [Applause.]

OLLIE M. JAMES [Ky.].—Mr. Speaker, I desire to say that the argument of the gentleman from Connecticut [Mr. Hill] does not appear to me to be one that will stand analysis. He tells us that Connecticut, which has been taxing all the rest of the people of the United States under the protective-tariff system until it has grown so rich, if this taxation upon incomes is placed upon her wealth, would pay more than 30 other States in the Union. Yet the gentleman is so patriotic that he is willing to state that when the poor man is willing to give his blood or his life when the Republic is in peril, when the battle is on, that not until then is he willing that his people shall make any contribution to sustain the Government out of the abundant fortunes they have piled up under the system of the protective tariff.

Here Mr. James dwelt at length on the constitutionality of a tax upon wealth. He quoted the dissenting opinions upon the income tax case of Justice Harlan and Justice Brown, and the arguments for constitutionality given by William J. Bryan in his speech in Madison Square Garden, New York City, in 1896. Of Mr. Bryan's stand on this question Mr. James said in conclusion:

Here we behold, Mr. Speaker, this patriot throwing down the gage of battle in the very citadel of wealth. He was maligned and slandered then, but what a glorious victory he is having upon this question! What a marvelous vindication he is receiving now! The whole nation upon tiptoe now approving his stand on the question of an income tax! And, sir, when those who have maligned him have been forgotten, this man who bore three times with honor and with courage the standard loved by millions of his countrymen, battling for equality of taxation, equality of opportunity, striving for the righteousness a republic owes to its people, obedience to law by the great and small, that the tax gatherer should visit alike the cabin and the palace, the hut, and the mansion, I say, sir, that, when the flunkeys and the adulators shall no longer find favor in their fawning nor pay for their abuse, the principles advocated by William J. Bryan, the lover of men and of the rights of men, will live in the Constitution and shine in the statute laws of the land.

To my mind the income tax is the most equitable of all systems of taxation. It is the ideal way to support the Government. Let those who prosper little pay little, for they are least indebted to the Government; let those who prosper more pay more; let those who prosper most pay most; let those who prosper greatly pay greatly, for certainly they have been most blessed and are therefore most indebted to the Government. What man is so ungrateful to his country that he is unwilling to pay a small tax upon his income above $5,000 to help sustain and perpetuate the Government under which he enjoys such success? Many bills have made such provision, but to meet defeat at the hands of the Republican party, which has always opposed taxing wealth in any degree.

Who is prepared to defend as just a system of taxation that requires a hod carrier, who for eight long hours each day wends his way to the dizzy heights of a lofty building with his load of mortar or brick, to pay as much to support this great Republic as John D. Rockefeller, whose fortune is so great that it staggers the imagination to contemplate it and whose property is in every city and State in the Republic and upon every sea protected by our flag. [Applause on the Democratic side.]

How men can defend a system of taxation in a republic which requires of the poor all of its taxes and exempts the rich absolutely I am totally unable to see. In the everyday walks of life we expect more for church, for charity, for the uplifting of society, and education from those who are most prosperous, most wealthy, most able to give.

I have heard it urged by some gentlemen upon the Republican side that the passage of an income-tax law would undermine and at last destroy the protective-tariff system. This, Mr. Speaker, is equivalent to saying that in order to give a few monopolists and manufacturers the right to reach into the pockets of all the people, you have kept the tax gatherer from reaching into the pockets of the few, the fortunate few, the intrenched few, the successful few; but you have driven the tax gatherer to the same pockets which monopolies pillaged under the protective tariff for taxes to sustain the Government. The protective-tariff system is vicious enough in itself without adding to it the iniquity of saying that in order to perpetuate it you must place the taxing burden of the Government upon the masses of the people, who must also bear the heavy burden the protective-tariff system inflicts upon them.

Mr. Speaker, this battle for an income tax will go on. This is the people's Government and the right will prevail. During all these years the mighty rich—an army of millionaires—have been exempted from taxation, but the people are now aroused. There are two lines of battle drawn for this great contest. Under which flag will you stand—the flag of democracy or the flag of plutocracy?

We shall win, for—

> Still, Truth proclaims this motto
> In letters of living light:
> No question is ever settled
> Until it is settled right.

[Applause on the Democratic side.]

And I would scorn, Mr. Speaker, a government whose taxing power provides that Lazarus must divide his crumbs with the tax gatherer, but that Dives shall not give of his riches. [Great applause on the Democratic side.]

J. WARREN KEIFER [O.].—If there ever is any necessity for an income tax, of course it is when the nation is at war. I want to say, Mr. Speaker, with the utmost kindness, that so far as history shows the Democratic party has not been in favor of an income tax in time of a great war, and it might well be that it should stand converted now. In the Civil War, in the most trying period of it to the Union, when the question of an income tax was voted upon on this floor, every Democrat present and voting voted against it and denounced it as unconstitutional. [Applause on the Republican side.]

Not a single Republican, as the *Congressional Record* shows, voted against it.

In the Senate of the United States at that time every Democrat voted against an income tax save Mr. McDougal, of California—one only in both Houses. Now I congratulate the Democratic party after these many years on a conversion to the income tax so that it may be levied in time of war.

Now, Mr. Speaker, there is something said about the necessity of an income tax to reach the idle rich; but, if we had only the idle rich, I think I would rather like the program; but there are in this country thousands and tens of thousands of enterprising spirits who have gone forth with energy, industry, and by displaying economy have acquired fortunes, and they are the persons who are to be reached by an income tax; and I am willing that they shall be reached when the trying times come.

While it may be true that those who by their ability and providence amass an estate are secure, an income must bear a proportionately great share of the government taxes; it should not be imposed upon them merely as a punishment.

ADAM M. BYRD [Miss.].—Mr. Speaker, I am afraid that the unanimous passage of this measure through the Senate and the favor with which it is being received in this House by your party are too hopeful of good to be accepted with a full measure of confidence. I am afraid that this is a case of ''Greeks bearing gifts.'' It was introduced in the Senate for the avowed purpose of defeating the Bailey-Cummins income-tax bill, and I am apprehensive that after it shall have been rushed through this House and goes to the States for ratification all the power and influence that can be marshaled against it by sordid wealth and Republican chicanery will be used to compass its defeat. It is necessary to debauch the legislatures of only 12 States to secure its rejection, and the same evil influences that have corrupted and carried so many elections have already started a crusade against its adoption by the States.

We were warned by the gentleman from Connecticut [Mr. Hill], in his speech a few moments ago, what opposition might be expected from New England. He boldly contends that it is unjust to tax the wealth of those favored States for the support of the common country, stating that that section, because of its great prosperity, was now compelled to contribute more than its part of the internal-revenue tax. The inconsistency of such an argument is only excelled by the seeming avarice that prompted it. New England, that has bled the country of its wealth for quite half a century; that has her millionaires by the thousands—made so by virtue of the infamous policy of protection—should be the last section of the Union to reject this righteous measure. With her millions invested in manufactures, protected by the tax of from 50 to more than 100 per cent., it would be the height of political ingratitude for any statesmen from that section, whether Democrat or Republican, to act otherwise than to urge a speedy ratification of this amendment.

RICHMOND P. HOBSON [Ala.].—I believe that this measure is a wise movement in the direction of substituting direct taxation for indirect taxation. A prime advantage of the direct method is that the people know when they are being taxed. To-day I am sure that the great masses of the American people have not the slightest idea how many times in the day they are being taxed for all the comforts, conveniences, and necessities of life. If the people were fully informed they would not submit to such tariff schedules as have been in effect for many years and such as are now carried by the present bill.

Another prime advantage of a direct tax is that it enables a people to know *how much* they are being taxed, and only when they have such knowledge can they prevent abuse of the taxing power.

To-day I do not believe our people have the slightest idea of the amount of taxation that is levied upon them. One, 2, 3 per cent. is considered a sore burden, yet to-day our people are taxed 10, 20, even 30 per cent., and do not know it.

Still a third prime advantage of a direct tax is that we know *where* the tax goes. In the present juncture the bulk of the taxation of the American people does not go to the Government of the American people. I will illustrate: There are about 200,000 tons of pig iron imported into the United States in a year. The indirect tariff tax causes the Government to get the impost duty from 200,000 tons. The country consumes about 25,000,000 tons, the price of all of which is raised to the extent of the tariff. The net result is that the pig-iron tariff gives the tax on 200,000 tons to the Government and the tax on 24,800,000 tons to certain favored individuals, practically giving over to individuals the sovereign right of taxation that can only reside justly in the Government itself. When the people are taxed, they ought to know who gets the tax, and they would know under a system of direct taxation.

A fourth prime advantage of direct taxation is that it would be more adjustable to the legitimate needs of the Government, and it would tend to a more economical and efficient administration of the Government.

Robert L. Henry [Tex.] offered an amendment to the joint resolution to provide that the proposed constitutional amendment be submitted to the conventions of the States instead of the legislatures. The Speaker [Joseph G. Cannon] ruled the amendment out of order as violating the agreement between the party leaders of the House that debate be limited and a vote be reached at a specified time. This ruling was sustained by the House.

The bill then (on July 12, 1909) passed by a vote of 318 to 14. Having received a two-thirds majority in both Chambers it became effective without the signature of the President.

The constitutional amendment (Article XVI) was declared ratified by more than the necessary three-fourths of the States on February 25, 1913.

CHAPTER XVIII

RECIPROCITY WITH CANADA

The Treaty of 1854; It Provides for Free Trade with Canada on Natural
Products—It Is Repealed by Congress in 1866; Debate in the House,
in Favor of Repeal, Justin S. Morrill [Vt.], Frederick A. Pike [Me.];
opposed, Elijah Ward [N. Y.]—Reciprocity Provisions Are Embodied in Various Tariff Bills—President William H. Taft Nego-
tiates a Reciprocity Treaty in 1911—Samuel W. McCall [Mass.] Intro-
duces in the House from the Committee on Ways and Means a Bill ''To
Promote Reciprocal Trade Relations with the Dominion of Canada''—
Report of the Minority of the Committee—Robert F. Broussard [La.]
Presents Separate Report in Opposition to the Bill—Debate on the Bill:
in Favor, Ebenezer J. Hill [Conn.], Oscar W. Underwood [Ala.], Champ
Clark [Mo.], Mr. McCall, Isaac R. Sherwood [O.]; Opposed, Eben W.
Martin [S. D.], George W. Norris [Neb.], J. Hampton Moore [Pa.],
George W. Prince [Ill.], Andrew J. Volstead [Minn.], John Dalzell
[Pa.], Gen. J. Warren Keifer [O.]—Bill Is Amended and Passed by
House—It Fails to Come to a Vote in the Senate—The President Calls
a Special Session of Congress—Mr. Underwood Reintroduces the Bill
in the House and also a ''Farmer's Free List Bill''—Debate on the
General Reciprocity Measure: in Favor, Paul Howland [O.], Mr. Hill,
Mr. McCall, Mr. Underwood; Opposed, Asher C. Hinds [Me.], Joseph
W. Fordney [Mich.], Mr. Dalzell—Bill Is Passed by House—It Is
Passed by Senate and Approved by the President—''Farmer's Free-List
Bill'' Is Passed by House and Senate—It Is Vetoed by the President—
House Sustains Veto—Treaty for Reciprocity Is Rejected by Canada—
Canadian Debate on Reciprocity: in Favor, W. S. Fielding, Ralph
Smith, Sydney Fisher: Opposed, Z. A. Lash, T. Chase Casgrain, Prof.
Stephen Leacock, Clifford Sifton.

A S early as 1848 a bill proposing reciprocity with
Canada passed the House of Representatives. It
was defeated in the Senate, however, because
of the uncertainty then prevailing as to Canada's attitude toward American shipping on the St. Lawrence.

In 1853 Congress passed a resolution authorizing the
President to arrange reciprocity by means of a treaty.
On June 5 of the following year a treaty was signed by
representatives of the two governments, and was subse-

quently validated by the national legislatures. It became a law by the signature of President Franklin Pierce on August 5.

This treaty provided for free interchange of natural products, settled the question of fisheries, and fixed the rights of navigation on the St. Lawrence.

In May, 1864, a joint resolution was introduced in the House of Representatives from the Committee on Commerce, authorizing President Lincoln to give notice for terminating the treaty, and negotiating a new one "based on the true principles of reciprocity."

Justin S. Morrill [Vt.] moved as an amendment to the bill that the Government simply give notice of the termination of the treaty.

Frederick A. Pike [Me.] supported the amendment. He was opposed to the renewal of the treaty on any terms. He said the old treaty operated adversely to our fishing interests, brought the balance of trade in favor of Canada, and caused a serious loss of revenue. He said:

Of course, if the treaty has failed in the respects I have mentioned, it must be regarded as a business failure. If our total exports have lessened since it went into operation, and particularly if our export of manufactured articles has diminished, and if in the meantime our commerce has not been benefited by additional employment, if the large fishing interest is anxious to put an end to this arrangement because of the detriment it receives from it, and if the revenue suffers greatly by its continuance, then I say as a commercial arrangement it has not answered the expectations which gave it existence, and it should be abrogated.

Elijah Ward [N. Y.] spoke in favor of a continuation of the treaty. He quoted statistics to show that, during the operation of the treaty, the excess of our exports to the Canadian provinces ($171,628,779) over imports therefrom ($144,183,096) was $26,445,683.

He continued:

It is argued that the treaty has deprived us of revenue. During the last year the imports and exports between the

United States and Canada of articles free under the treaty
were nearly equal. If we levy duties on their productions
they may do the same on ours. This principle is a two-edged
sword. Or they may admit our products free of duty as
they did before the treaty, and thus be the carriers of a considerable portion of our produce as well as of their own.
When a revenue was paid to our Government on Canadian
productions the provincial railroads and means of communication were imperfect and its population was comparatively
scanty. By renewing the duties we shall drive away the trade
and render our people less able to pay taxes. The utmost
amount of revenue the Government can derive from duties on
colonial productions is inconsiderable compared with the loss
of commerce we shall sustain, and the consequent loss of employment to the laborer and profit to the merchant or capitalist.

By a vote of 77 yeas to 72 nays the bill was postponed
until the next session.

During the next session Congress repealed the existing treaty, the House voting against it on December 13,
1863, by a vote of 85 yeas to 57 nays, and the Senate voting against it on January 12, 1865, by 33 yeas to 8 nays.
The treaty expired during 1866.

Following the repeal of the treaty no legislation on
the question of reciprocity with Canada was enacted
until 1890, when, as we have seen in the debate on the
McKinley tariff bill, certain provisions for reciprocity
on a limited number of articles were adopted. Similar
provisions were incorporated in the Dingley bill (1897)
and the Payne-Aldrich bill (1909).

President William H. Taft in his second annual message, December 6, 1910, referred to the question of reciprocity with Canada as follows:

The policy of broader and closer trade relations with the
Dominion of Canada, which was initiated in the adjustment
of the maximum and minimum provisions of the tariff act of
August, 1909, has proved mutually beneficial. It justifies further efforts for the readjustment of the commercial relations
of the two countries so that their commerce may follow the
channels natural to contiguous countries and be commensurate
with the steady expansion of trade and industry on both sides

of the boundary line. The reciprocation on the part of the Dominion Government of the sentiment which was expressed by this Government was followed in October by the suggestion that it would be glad to have the negotiations, which had been temporarily suspended during the summer, resumed. In accordance with this suggestion the Secretary of State, by my direction, dispatched two representatives of the Department of State as special commissioners to Ottawa to confer with representatives of the Dominion Government. They were authorized to take such steps for formulating a reciprocal trade agreement as might be necessary and to receive and consider any propositions which the Dominion Government might care to submit.

Pursuant to the instructions issued, conferences were held by these commissioners with officials of the Dominion Government at Ottawa in the early part of November.

The negotiations were conducted on both sides in a spirit of mutual accommodation. The discussion of the common commercial interests of the two countries had for its object a satisfactory basis for a trade arrangement which offers the prospect of a freer interchange for the products of the United States and of Canada. The conferences were adjourned to be resumed in Washington in January, when it is hoped that the aspiration of both Governments for a mutually advantageous measure of reciprocity will be realized.

On January 26, 1911, the President sent a special message to Congress, in which he noted the success of the negotiations.

On the 7th of the present month two cabinet ministers[1] came to Washington as representatives of the Dominion Government, and the conferences were continued between them and the Secretary of State[2]. The result of the negotiations was that on the 21st instant a reciprocal trade agreement was reached, the text of which is herewith transmitted with accompanying correspondence and other data.

In accordance with the plans of the administration Samuel W. McCall [Mass.], on January 28, introduced in the House a bill "to promote reciprocal trade relations with the Dominion of Canada. It was referred to the Committee on Ways and Means.

[1] See speech of W. S. Fielding, one of the Canadian negotiators of the treaty, on p. 457.
[2] Philander C. Knox.

Early in February the bill was reported back with amendments. The report of the minority of the committee was filed by John Dalzell [Pa.]. It said in part:

The minority of the Committee on Ways and Means regret that the bill has been prosecuted by its advocates with such undue and precipitate haste that many of its features remain obscure and without explanation.

Up to the time when the President's message informed Congress that he had entered into a trade agreement with Canada, the House of Representatives—where all "bills raising revenue" must originate under the Constitution—knew nothing about it. It is safe to say that no member of Congress had been consulted as to it or its terms.

By the terms of the bill four general classes of products are affected:

First. Leading food and agricultural products, rough lumber, some raw materials, and printing paper. These are put on the free list.

Second. Secondary food products, such as fresh and canned meats, flours, and partly manufactured food preparations, upon which rates are reduced and made identical.

Third. Manufactured commodities, such as motor vehicles, cutlery, sanitary fixtures, and miscellaneous articles, on which rates are mutually reduced.

Fourth. A small list of articles on which special rates are given by each country. Canada reduces the duty on coal and cement, and the United States reduces the duty on iron ore and aluminum products.

The bill revises our tariff law in part, involves millions of the national revenue, involves also our commercial relations with other nations, and comes to us to be voted on after a week's deliberation.

We protest against its passage for the following, among other, reasons:

(1) It renews a trade agreement with Canada similar to one that heretofore existed from 1854 to 1866, and the operation of which proved disastrous to the United States.

As a business proposition it is wholly indefensible. Advantages under it will accrue to Canada without any corresponding advantages to the United States. It is uncalled for by any great body of our people.

(2) It is un-Republican. It proposes reciprocity in com-

peting products, which is absolutely inconsistent with the policy
of protection. It is an abandonment of the protective policy.
It is in violation of the history, the traditions, and the platforms of the Republican party.

(3) It is class legislation of the most obnoxious character.
It selects from out all the classes of our community the farmer
and deprives him of the protection accorded to all other classes.
It compels him to produce in a free-trade market and to buy
in a protected market. It is in the interest of the foreigner
and against the American. The same undue haste that has
characterized the treatment of this bill here seems to have
prevailed also in the Canadian Parliament.

A new definition is sought to be given to the term protection. It is said not to apply as between parties whose production is substantially similar, and then it is asserted that
Canadian production and American are substantially the same.
The assertion is not borne out by the facts. The average of
Canadian wages is below that of American wages. The value
of Canadian lands is below the value of American lands. The
Canadian gets his raw material from abroad at a lower import
duty than does the American. He prefers others to us at
the custom house. The Canadian manufacturer of metals is
paid a bounty. An exhaustive investigation by the Mann committee into the pulp and paper question demonstrated that by
reason of lower wage rates Canadians can make paper $2 a
ton cheaper than we can. The same conditions that relate to
wage rates in paper manufacture prevail all along the line.

Robert F. Broussard [La.] filed a separate report.

As a Democrat I wish to add to the report that I agree with
almost everything urged except that the statement that the bill
is un-Republican is not nearly so accurate as the further statement that it is also un-Democratic and absolutely un-American.

The bill came up for discussion on February 13.

THE COMMERCIAL TREATY WITH CANADA
HOUSE OF REPRESENTATIVES, FEBRUARY 13 AND 14, 1911

Ebenezer J. Hill [Conn.] supported the bill.

Mr. Chairman and gentlemen of the House of Representatives, a protective-tariff policy presupposes reciprocity and

XII—28

trade agreements. A free-trade policy has nothing to give in return for concessions, and hence nothing to gain from them.

Since the Republican party was organized and while it has been in power there never has been a time but that reciprocal agreements with other countries have been in operation, and President Taft stands to-day in full harmony with Lincoln, Grant, McKinley, Roosevelt, and all of his illustrious predecessors with regard to that principle.

Under reciprocity trade between Hawaii and this country flourished to the great advantage of both, until by the logic of events the islands became a part of this nation.

Under reciprocity our trade with Cuba has more than doubled.

Under free trade with Porto Rico, which met with a storm of denunciation when first proposed, but which William McKinley declared to be our "plain duty," our trade with that island has increased nearly fifteenfold.

Under reciprocal relations with the Philippine Islands, a territory containing a larger population than the Dominion of Canada, our mutual trade has grown in less than a single year 70 per cent.

In every one of these cases the proposition to enter upon such trade relations was met with prophecies of dire disaster to some existing industry in our own country.

In every case the prophecy has failed of fulfillment, and the new policy has resulted in mutual advantage to both parties.

A new proposition confronts us now—a reciprocal trade agreement in some of the natural products of two contiguous countries with a like character of population, with a climate and soil very similar to that of each other, and with forms of government differing in few essential features, affecting the productive and consuming power of either people. Indeed, both parties to this proposed agreement are under the protective-tariff system, and from my point of view both are likely to continue that policy in the future, the United States striving to apply the policy on the fixed principle of the difference in the cost of production at home and abroad as the true measure of its protection, and Canada supplementing its protective rate with direct aid from the Government in many of its industries.

I stand for this treaty as a whole, without any qualification and without any amendment, for, if I am rightly informed, it must be so considered and it must stand or fall as a single proposition, except with reference to the paper and pulp schedule, upon which no final conclusions were reached by the negotiators. If I could have my way, there are some things in it which I would change, and I have no criticism to make upon anyone who feels that the particular industries in which he is interested have not been cared for as he thinks they should have been. That feeling is but natural and is not confined to the United States, for I find by the perusal of the Canadian papers that the ratification of these proposals is looked upon by some citizens of Canada as absolutely destructive, not only to their agriculture, their fisheries, and their manufacturing, but also to the investments made by domestic and foreign capital in their railway systems and public improvements generally. So that we do not have in this country a monopoly of the timid ones, who look upon any change in the commercial relations of the two countries as a change for the worse, no matter how small or comparatively unimportant it may be.

This measure is a straightforward business arrangement for the reciprocal exchange of such articles as the representatives of both Governments believed, after most careful consideration, could be made with safety to each other and for the mutual advantage of both, and that would result in largely increased business transactions in other articles not directly affected or named in the agreement.

On February 14 Oscar W. Underwood [Ala.] spoke in favor of the bill.

Our Republican friends who wrote the Payne-Aldrich bill were so insistent that we should have a high tariff in this country and that no President, whoever he might be, should make any concessions from the high rates of taxation that they fixed that the President himself, under the law that he signed, has been driven to make a compact with Canada outside of the law to accomplish what was claimed could be accomplished when the law was originally written.

Now, the President, without warrant of law, has entered into an agreement with the Canadian Government—for what purpose? For the purpose of reducing taxes for the benefit of the American people. That is what this proposition is. It is not in the language that I would have written it, it is not in the language that many of you on this side of the House would have written it, but I want to say to you this, there is not one single item in this bill that does not reduce the taxes levied on the American people under the Payne law. The members of this House on this side of the Chamber, both in this Chamber and before the American people last fall, repudiated the Payne-Aldrich law. They denounced it as unjust taxation. The opportunity has come to us to-day to reduce these taxes and reduce them on some of the necessities of life.

Champ Clark [Mo.], the Speaker, followed.

I am for this bill because I hope to see the day when the American flag will float over every square foot of the British North American possessions clear to the North Pole. They are people of our blood. They speak our language. Their institutions are much like ours. They are trained in the difficult art of self-government. My judgment is that if the treaty of 1854 had never been abrogated the chances of a consolidation of these two countries would have been much greater than they are now.

I am in favor of universal peace, and I am in favor of this reciprocity treaty because it helps along the cause of universal peace. [Applause.]

EBEN W. MARTIN [S. D.].—Will the gentleman favor the abrogation of our tariff law entirely so far as Canada is concerned, and making free trade with Canada on all products?

MR. CLARK.—By taking Canada in to become a part of the United States; yes.

MR. MARTIN.—No; I mean commercially. Would the gentleman support a policy of complete free trade with Canada on all products?

MR. CLARK.—I would support a Democratic tariff bill, prepared by the Ways and Means Committee, brought into a Democratic House, and passed by that Democratic House. [Applause on the Democratic side.]

GEORGE W. NORRIS. [Neb.].—I want to ask the gentleman something along the line of universal peace. As I understand it, the gentleman favors this bill, for at least one reason, that it will have a tendency in the end to bring Canada into the Union.

MR. CLARK.—Yes; I have no doubt about that.

MR. NORRIS.—Will that have a tendency to preserve peace with Great Britain?

MR. CLARK.—Why, certainly it will. I do not have any doubt whatever that the day is not far distant when Great Britain will joyfully see all of her North American possessions become a part of this Republic. That is the way things are tending now.

MR. NORRIS.—Was the gentleman correctly quoted in the newspapers this morning, where it was stated that in his speech last night he said he was in favor of reciprocity with the entire world?

MR. CLARK.—Yes.

J. HAMPTON MOORE [Pa.].—Would these reciprocal treaties with European countries contemplate the raising of revenue sufficient to run this Government?

MR. CLARK.—Oh, if we did not get enough money in that way, we would collect it by a graduated income tax, and that would bring in enough. [Applause.]

Mr. Speaker, I would levy a revenue tax on lead and zinc, iron and coal, and cobalt, and everything that comes into the United States, except on the necessaries of life. Nothing on earth would induce me to help report a tariff bill which puts a tariff on salt. I would not do it, because free salt is a hereditary Missouri doctrine. Thomas Hart Benton worked for 28 years to get salt on the free list. And Theodore Roosevelt, who is somewhat of a Republican at least [laughter]—and it is hard to tell who is a Republican just now [laughter]——

GEORGE W. PRINCE [Ill.].—The Speaker is a Republican.

MR. CLARK.—I rather think the Speaker is. [Applause.]

Mr. Speaker, I am in favor of this bill because it enlarges our markets, because it brings us into closer relation with our neighbors, and because it increases the prospects of the consolidation of these two great countries in the days to come. [Prolonged applause on the Democratic side.]

Andrew J. Volstead [Minn.] opposed the bill. Reciprocity with Canada, he said, was entirely hostile to the agricultural interests.

The naked proposition is that this treaty has been entered into for the purpose of lowering the price of farm products, and that it will accomplish that purpose no one at all familiar with the situation can doubt. It is undisguised, selfish, class legislation in behalf of the cities as against the producers of food.

This treaty puts practically every farm product of the North on the free list, as Canada is the only country that can successfully compete. No pretence is made that the farmers are to get anything in return except some slight reduction in the duty on lumber. The treaty does not open to the Northern farmer a market for a single bushel of grain or any other of his products, but it compels him to compete with Canada for his own market. We might consent to this if there were a corresponding reduction in manufactured products, but extreme care has been taken that no manufacturer shall suffer. As an illustration it might be noted that the American miller may buy his wheat in Canada, but the American farmer who has got to sell in competition with the Canadian farmer can not buy his flour in Canada without paying a tariff duty of fifty cents per barrel.

Mr. Dalzell, at the conclusion of a long speech in opposition to the bill, said:

Is it not an astounding proposition that we shall legislate away our advantages in the interest of the Canadians? Yet that will be the result of the passage of the bill reported by the Committee on Ways and Means. No concealment is made of the fact that we propose to give away $5,000,000 a year revenue in return for two millions and a half of Canadian revenue. In other words, we propose to trade a good American dollar for a Canadian half dollar. We propose to throw open the markets, the splendid markets, of 90,000,000 of prosperous people to the meager markets of less than 9,000,000. [Applause on the Republican side.] Why, the proposition is so astounding that it staggers belief.

Mr. Chairman, this measure is an unwise business measure. It is un-Republican; it violates the principles of the Republican party; it abandons protection and espouses free trade. It is a violation of the pledge of every Republican platform for the last 50 years of our history. [Applause.] This measure is obnoxious class legislation, it sacrifices the farmer, the bone and sinew of the Republic, and destroys his interests. And now I fain would appeal to party loyalty, but I know it is of no use. The Republican protectionist, when this vote is taken, marches to his doom. He can not resist a united Democratic party and such Republicans as hear from somewhere else an appeal louder than the appeal of party loyalty. United, together they will march to victory under Democratic leadership under the folds of the Democratic free-trade flag. I decline to follow. I shall stand where I have always stood, and go down with my party. [Applause.]

Samuel W. McCall [Mass.] supported his measure. At the conclusion of a speech more or less statistical he said:

Mr. Chairman, I hope this bill will pass as it was reported, and pass by a decisive majority. I believe that the President of the United States has risen above the narrow interests of localities and that he has comprehended the whole country, that he has not been swayed by the clamor of special interests, but that he has had the wisdom and the courage to negotiate an agreement in the interest of the masses of the people, and I trust that this House will rally behind him and share with him in the glory of having secured the establishment of a policy of enlightened statesmanship, of high patriotism, and of single-minded justice. [Applause.]

General J. Warren Keifer [O.] opposed the bill.

Mr. Speaker, I wish to give, without going into great detail, some of the reasons for my opposition to the so-called Canadian reciprocity agreement.

The bill purports to provide for reciprocity in tariff or import duties between the United States and Canada, though, by all known principles, it provides for no reciprocity at all.

The bill seems to fix, by its first section, certain uniform rates of import duties on the principal products of agriculture of the two countries, leaving Canada to maintain present and to establish further preferential rates with Great Britain and other foreign countries. No general trade relations, reciprocal or not, are proposed save as to farm products. Uniform rates on commodities produced in each of the two countries do not produce reciprocity.

Reciprocity in international trade requires an equivalent interchange of things under equal conditions, though not of the same kind. There is no such thing as reciprocity in an even exchange of the same kind of articles or commodities, as such exchange accomplishes nothing, and an exchange of such articles or commodities on an uneven basis means a cheat or a fraud on one or the other party.

Reciprocity imports an equivalent exchange of diverse articles produced in different countries. To secure something for one country without a corresponding equivalent moving to the other is the opposite of reciprocity. A trade arrangement that does not secure a market abroad for American goods, or which only admits Canadian goods free into the United States to compete in the market with its goods, is far from reciprocity.

The bill does not, by providing the same duties on certain articles and free trade for certain other articles in both countries, establish reciprocity, but it only provides for putting the articles in trade competition in the markets. When an article of one country is found to be of less value than in the other country, it will go there for sale, but not for reciprocal exchange. This does not constitute reciprocity—only competition in selling in the country where naturally the higher price would be paid, and the country with the cheaper lands, and usually paying the lowest wages for labor, soils, etc., being equal, can undersell the other, and bring down the proper market price all around to the American farm producer. A trade agreement that does not secure a market abroad for American-produced articles only opens the door for foreign-produced articles commonly produced in both countries to come into the United States for sale, and this is the opposite of reciprocity—discriminates against our own country and works injustice upon our people.

Tested by these principles, the arrangement or bill provides for no possible or real reciprocity.

Isaac R. Sherwood [O.] supported the bill.

Less than 30 days ago the President was vigorously working the White House power plant for a high-priced tariff commission, made up of five members, for a long term of service, the president of the commission to draw $7,500 per year and the other four members $7,000 each per year. And the President really forced such a bill through the House. This bill provides that the commission shall travel, not only in the United States but in foreign countries, to ascertain the cost of labor at home and abroad, in order to make a thoroughly scientific tariff. And now, all of a sudden, the President sends to the House of Representatives a new compact, evidently prepared in secret (and surely in a hurry), providing for absolute free trade in all agricultural products of the farm and garden produced on "cheap Canadian lands by cheap Canadian labor." (Quotation from a prophet of protection.)

Is it any wonder that the "Old Guard" of "protection to American industry" refuse to be comforted? What they said to-day on the floor of the House, that President Taft has flopped to the economic ideas of the Democrats, is not a circumstance compared with what they are saying in private conversation.

There is a couplet in Milton's "Paradise Lost" that fittingly depicts the present plight of our shifty Chief Executive, as the stand-y protectionists think he should feel. I quote a couplet from Milton:

> Which way I fly is hell; myself am hell;
> And in the lowest deep a lower deep,
> Still threat'ning to devour me.

In conclusion Mr. Sherwood discussed the subject of the annexation of Canada.

Quite recently I had a conversation with an ex-member of the Canadian Parliament on the question of annexation. He said that 25 years ago there was a powerful element in Ontario and the other provinces in favor of annexation, but now the Canadians were almost universally opposed to annexation. He called my attention to the recent statement of the Canadian Premier, Laurier, that during the past two years over 80,000 United States farmers from North Dakota, Montana, Iowa, and other Western States had sold their farms and moved across the border into Canada in order to better their condition.

Why have we been losing the most thrifty and most valuable citizens of the Western States, who, from choice, have left the protection of our flag and renounced citizenship in a Republic to become citizens in the Canadian provinces under the protection of a British flag? Why have these valuable citizens left their homes and firesides in a mild climate to settle in the frozen north? Here comes the startling thought: Why should any United States farmer care to repudiate the flag of his country for the flag of Great Britain, or why are the Canadians opposed to annexation to the United States?

Is it because we have parted with the simple Republic of the fathers and are now tending rapidly to a military oligarchy, with the military spirit dominant and a present military establishment more costly than the Empire of Great Britain? Is it because of the corruption of American politics? Is it because of the present unrest of our industrial classes? Is it because there is an economic and financial system in the United States controlled by not more than 5 per cent. of our people, who either own or control all the railroads, steamship lines, iron mines, steel mines, oil refineries, tank lines, copper mines, and copper industry, the woolen industry, and the cotton industry? Is it because the average Canadian, looking across the border line, sees in this country no fair opportunity or a poor man's chance, outside the controlling influences of monopoly?

I have never heard or read an explanation of the hostility in Canada to annexation, and can but guess. I am not a political diagnostician.

An amendment of the bill relating to the paper and pulp schedule was adopted, and the bill was then passed by a vote of 221 to 92.

On February 15 the Senate referred the bill to the Committee on Finance, which reported it back on the 24th without amendment. The bill failed to come to a vote, however, in this session.

On April 4 the President called a special session of Congress to consider again the question of putting the reciprocity agreement in operation.

The House bill to carry the treaty into effect was this time introduced by Mr. Underwood. He, on the same day (April 12), introduced a bill "to place on the free list agricultural implements, cotton bagging, cotton ties, leather, boots and shoes, fence wire, meats, cereals, flour, bread, timber, lumber, sewing machines, salt, and other articles." This was known as the "Farmers' Free-List Bill."

Both bills were referred to the Committee on Ways and Means. The general reciprocity bill was reported back the next day. It came up for discussion on April 15.

THE COMMERCIAL TREATY WITH CANADA

HOUSE OF REPRESENTATIVES, APRIL 15, 1911

Asher C. Hinds [Me.] opposed the bill.

The manner in which this bill distributes its supposed benefits and its undoubted hardships violates mankind's fundamental idea of justice and equity. Since the dawn of time, through all mythologies and religions, man has expressed his inborn idea that to those who have the suffering and self-denial should come the bliss of the better world, the peace of the Elysian fields, the joy of the golden streets. That is real reciprocity.

But this bill introduces into that ancient, instinctive idea of equity a new principle; that one class of citizens is to have the sacrifices, while another class enjoys the rewards. The dairymen of New York and Ohio are to tread the earthly pathway of self-denial, and in reward the makers of barbed-wire fencing are to roam the Elysian fields [laughter]; the wheat farmers of the Dakotas are to keep the long vigil of unrestricted competition, and in return the automobile makers of Detroit are to speed over the streets of gold; the fishermen of Gloucester who keep watch and watch with death on the banks of Newfoundland are to surrender their market, and in return the Connecticut clock makers are to set up their timepieces in the realms of bliss, where a thousand years are but as a day; the potato farmer of Maine or Michigan is to have the troubles of Lazarus, but the maker of harvesting machines is to rest his head on the bosom of Abraham. [Laughter and applause.] One class sows that another may reap, and you call it reciprocity.

On April 18 Paul Howland [O.] spoke in favor of the bill. On the subject of Canadian opposition to reciprocity he said:

Mr. Chairman, it might be interesting, after all the eulogies which have been paid and all the tears that have been shed in behalf of protected interests in this country, to read a brief extract from the debate in the House of Commons at Ottawa on this subject.

Mr. Lemieux, on February 21, 1911, said:

We are told by my honorable friend (Mr. Sproul) that it is a one-sided agreement, but we also have one of the highest protectionists on this continent, Mr. Joe Cannon—Uncle Joe—prominent in American public life, who objects to this agreement because it is one-sided. It is, indeed, strange to find protectionists on both sides of the line agreeing that it is a one-sided agreement to the prejudice of each.

[Laughter.]

On April 19 Joseph W. Fordney [Mich.] spoke in opposition to the bill.

Mr. Chairman, I want to call the attention of the gentleman from Massachusetts [Mr. McCall] and the gentleman from Connecticut [Mr. Hill] to one thing. They are very earnest in their efforts to bring about the adoption of Canadian reciprocity.

They are both protectionists. Just whether they can see beyond the limits of the State of Connecticut and the State of Massachusetts at this time I am not going to say. [Laughter.]

EBENEZER J. HILL [Conn.].—Mr. Chairman——

MR. FORDNEY.—Just one moment. Let me say to you, you wanted free trade in leather, and you voted for protection on shoes. I have repeatedly said, and I repeat now, that any step toward a reduction of our duties was only a step toward free trade. You are in favor of Canadian reciprocity, and here comes a full-born child of free trade, a bill that puts shoes on the free list and leather on the free list, and I do wish it also put other things produced in New England on the free list. [Applause and laughter.] I am going to ask you if you are going to vote for that bill. I am going to introduce a bill, and I give notice now, and no better protectionist has ever lived than is found in me—and I hope my Democratic friends will support the bill—to put ships on the free list, so that American goods may be carried between two American ports by any foreign ship, and then we shall see how New England will like that.

MR. HILL.—Mr. Chairman, I challenge the gentleman to vote with me in accordance with the principles laid down in the Republican national platform, that the true measure of protection is the difference in the cost of production at home and abroad, and, if he does it once, it will be the first time he ever did it in his life. [Laughter and applause.]

MR. FORDNEY.—Mr. Chairman, I happened to be a member of the committee on resolutions at the last Republican national convention——

MR. HILL.—Then the gentleman ought to be bound by the declaration.

MR. FORDNEY.—Are you?

MR. HILL.—I am. On manufactures from New England and lumber from Michigan, and on wheat also and every other product that we have in the United States.

MR. FORDNEY.—Oh, now, do not get excited, because you are in error. That platform says that the Republican party proposes to give protection to American industry by a tariff wall sufficiently high to offset the difference in the cost of production here and abroad, and to add thereto a fair profit. Where is there any protection for a profit in the free trade for which you vote?

MR. HILL.—I will ask the gentleman whether the figures on the other side do not also include a fair profit for them?

Mr. Fordney.—Suppose the cost there was identical with the cost here?

Mr. Hill.—Then I would have no duty. [Applause on the Democratic side.]

Mr. Fordney.—Wait a minute. Where is your profit? Figure it out if you can.

Mr. Hill.—Where is their profit? [Applause on the Democratic side.]

Mr. Fordney.—Let them keep their own market and we will keep ours. [Applause on the Republican side.]

Mr. Hill.—We would with the addition of from $3 to $5 a ton in our favor across the ocean.

Mr. Fordney.—Mr. Chairman, I want to say that I am an admirer of our President, William H. Taft. He will be the Republican candidate for reëlection, if he lives until that time. [Applause on the Republican side.] I am frank to say, gentlemen, that I disagree with his views on Canadian reciprocity. I am exercising my judgment as my conscience dictates as to what is right and best for the American people; and upon that platform I am going to stand.

On April 21 Samuel W. McCall [Mass.] supported the bill. He said in conclusion:

The President is recognizing the laws of nature. The fact that that country buys from us nearly twice as much as she does from all the other nations of the world shows most powerfully how the ties of nature are drawing us commercially together. It is not wise to try to float upstream. We should permit the laws of nature to work without obstruction, and they will work, for the benefit of both countries. The size of our planet is dwindling every year. The discovery of all of the lands of the world, the wonderful inventions of the last century, the railroad and the telephone and the telegraph make this world to-day as small, compared with the world of the time of Columbus, as one of Jupiter's satellites is as compared with Jupiter. We are rapidly growing smaller, and here is this great neighbor of ours that is industrially a part of the United States. I say it is wise for us to recognize that fact and to pass this bill. It does not go far enough, but it takes a long step in the right direction.

Mr. Dalzell spoke in opposition to the measure. In discussing the question of its constitutionality he said:

It is a bill to validate a reciprocal trade agreement made by the President with certain Canadian officials so as to make changes in our revenue law. The Constitution provides "all bills for raising revenue shall originate in the House of Representatives."

Should the pending bill be passed by a majority of the votes of both Houses, you will have as the result only the unauthorized legislative indorsement of an unauthorized executive act, and I apprehend that the constitutional powers of the House and the constitutional power of the Executive are not beyond the power of judicial definition. [Applause on the Republican side.]

In this measure, whereby you are asked—to use the language of the President—to put *"the agreement in the form of a statute,"* the President and the Canadian commissioners have selected the objects of taxation and also the rates of tax, and you cannot dot an "i" or cross a "t."

In all its history the House of Representatives never before knew so humiliating a day as this, called upon, as it is, to renounce its constitutional prerogative and register an executive decree.

Here Mr. Dalzell discussed at length the general arguments of protectionists against the bill. In conclusion he said:

If neighborhood and kinship of race and language and history furnish reasons why trade barriers should be removed, they furnish equally good reasons why political barriers should be removed and the two peoples consolidated under one flag. And, disavow much as we may any intention in that direction, if we adopt this measure the force of events will ultimately assert itself to that end. This bill itself in its new section proposes another step toward bringing together the two peoples under one flag, and that flag will bear the Stars and Stripes.

In the absence of any good reason why this bill should pass there are many and potent reasons why it should not.

It is unnecessary, not responsive to the popular demand, disturbing of the business interests of the country.

But, more than that, it is unfair to the farmer, whose interests in particular it attacks.

The gentleman from North Carolina [Mr. Kitchin], who honored me with so much of his attentions, portrayed me as shedding tears for the farmer while I had in mind the manufacturer.

The gentleman from North Carolina in part was right. I had both the farmer and the manufacturer in mind. When you direct my attention to the subject of a tariff I always have in mind the great city, dear to my heart, whose interests it is my highest ambition to serve. I recall its pillar of cloud by day, its pillar of fire by night, the roar of its machinery, its myriad workingmen in the receipt of the highest wages paid any workingmen in any place on earth [applause], a city which is a shining exemplar of the beneficent results of the system of protection. And when I have in mind the fact that if the farmer be robbed of his protection my great city will be robbed of its protection I refuse to participate in the robbery. [Applause on the Republican side.]

The Republican party as the party of protection is on trial here to-day. You and I, my Republican brethren, are on trial. As we respond, so shall we and our party, the party of McKinley, be dealt with in the great forum of the American electorate. Sometimes it is swayed by popular clamor, sometimes by the shadow of a great name, but in the end its deliberate judgment is true to righteousness; its last verdict invariably loyal to the loyal. [Applause on the Republican side.]

Mr. Underwood closed the debate. In the conclusion of a speech mainly statistical he said:

This treaty with Canada will prevent, to a large extent, speculators and manipulators from cornering markets and at times forcing exorbitant prices upon the people of the country. [Applause on the Democratic side.] That may not be a good reason from the standpoint of you gentlemen who believe in protecting profits, but it is certainly a good reason from the standpoint of men on the Democratic side of the House who are opposed to any proposition that leads to monopoly or oppression. [Applause on the Democratic side.]

The bill was passed without amendment by a vote of 267 to 89.

The Senate, on April 24, referred the bill to the Committee on Finance, which reported it back on June 13. The bill was finally passed on July 22 by a vote of 53 to 27. President Taft approved the act on the same day.

The "Farmers' Free-List Bill" was passed by the House on May 8 by the following vote: Yeas, 236; nays, 109. The Senate, on May 9, referred it to the Committee

on Finance, which reported it back adversely on June 22.
It was debated until August 1, when it was amended and
passed by a vote of 48 to 30. The House finally concurred in the Senate amendments with certain additional
amendments. These were agreed to by the Senate on
August 17. The bill, however, was vetoed by President
Taft on the following day. In explaining to Congress
the reasons for his disapproval he said:

I withhold my approval from this bill for the reasons, first,
because it should not be considered until the Tariff Board shall
make report upon the schedules it affects; second, because the
bill is so loosely drawn as to involve the Government in endless
litigation and to leave the commercial community in disastrous
doubt; third, because it places the finished product on the free
list, but retains on the dutiable list the raw material and the
machinery with which such finished product is made, and thus
puts at a needless disadvantage our American manufacturers;
and, fourth, that while purporting, by putting agricultural implements, meat, and flour on the free list, to reduce their price
to the consumers, it does not do so, but only gives to Canada
valuable concessions which might be used by the Executive to
expand reciprocity with that country in accordance with the
direction of Congress.

The House failed to pass the bill over the President's
veto by a vote of 226 to 127, less than two-thirds thus
voting in the affirmative.

Meanwhile, on April 28, President Taft had delivered
an address in New York City in defence of the reciprocity treaty. In this address, which aroused unfavor-
able comment throughout both Canada and the United
States, he said:

I have said that this was a critical time in the solution of
the question of reciprocity. It is critical because unless it is
now decided favorably to reciprocity it is exceedingly probable
that no such opportunity will ever again come to the United
States. The forces which are at work in England and Canada
to separate her by a Chinese wall from the United States and
to make her part of an imperial commercial band, reaching from
England around the world to England again, by a system of
preferential tariffs, will derive an impetus from the rejection
of this treaty, and if we would have reciprocity, with all the

advantages that I have described and that I earnestly and sincerely believe will follow its adoption, we must take it now or give it up forever.

The London *Standard* referred to the speech as follows:

It is not too much to say that President Taft's address has completely altered the situation with regard to Canadian reciprocity. If Mr. Taft had desired to urge patriotic Canadians to oppose the agreement to the full extent of their powers, he could hardly have spoken otherwise.

The same opinion was expressed by many Canadian newspapers, not merely the partisan Conservative organs, but independent journals. The Conservative papers and orators went further, and charged President Taft with deliberately planning, through reciprocity, to annex Canada to the United States. They also used, with great effect against the measure, the outspoken declaration of Speaker Clark in favor of annexation.

The question of reciprocity became the vital issue in the Canadian parliamentary elections of August. The Liberals, under the leadership of Sir Wilfred Laurier, the Prime Minister, supported the commercial treaty as a financial proposition that must operate finally to the advantage of Canada through the opening of more extensive markets for the products of field and mine, while the Conservatives, under the guidance of Richard Borden, were opposed to all forms of reciprocal trade with the United States, asserting that the adoption of a commercial past would divert the lines of trade from east and west to north and south, undermine the British influence, and result inevitably in bringing up the question of annexation.

The result of the elections on August 21 brought to naught all legislation on the subject of reciprocity. The return to the Dominion Parliament of 137 Conservatives to 84 Liberals, thus bringing the Conservatives into power for the first time in fifteen years, indicated that the elections were in effect a popular rejection of reciprocity by Canada.

XII—29

RECIPROCITY WITH THE UNITED STATES

CANADIAN DEBATE, MARCH 20 AND 25, 1911

The speeches of two public meetings held in Montreal, in March, 1911, form a debate that is typical of a number of discussions which took place in Canada on the ratification of the reciprocity treaty with the United States.

On March 20 Z. A. Lash, King's counsel, of Toronto; T. Chase Casgrain, Esq., and Professor Stephen Leacock of Montreal, and Clifford Sifton, a former Minister of the Interior in Laurier's Cabinet, spoke in Windsor Hall against ratification.

Mr. Lash called the proposition a "preposterous" one, and characterized the issue it presented as "the most important in the history of Canada." The agreement, he said, was made in Washington without the knowledge of its nature being communicated to the people of Canada. Of the Canadian negotiators he said:

They told us both parties, Liberal and Conservatives, were committed to reciprocity. Gentlemen, I deny that statement. I deny that the Conservatives in 1911 were committed to the principle of reciprocity with the United States. I shall demonstrate that twenty years ago Canada was opposed to such reciprocity, and that this is still the case. As I go along I shall show the difference between Canada twenty years ago and Canada to-day.

We have heard that the treaty of 1854 was beneficial to Canada. Canada in 1854 consisted of only the present provinces of Quebec and Ontario. Our efforts to create a nation began with the British North American Act of 1867, when these two provinces and Nova Scotia and New Brunswick were united into the Dominion of Canada. One clause of this act acknowledged the principle which has run through all our legislation, all our public policy, from that day to this, namely section 154, which declared that the building of the Intercolonial Railway is necessary to the union of the provinces—that east-and-west transportation is essential to the consolidation of British North America.

When British Columbia was admitted into the union in

1871 it was decided that the Canadian Pacific Railway should be built for this purpose. Prior to 1871 the Canadian Pacific Railway was being constructed by the Government in sections, on the plan of utilizing water stretches wherever possible. But when, in 1878, the Conservative party obtained power, it was decided to build the road right through, on the principle of section 154 of the consolidation act.

Accordingly in 1881 the Canadian Pacific Railway was started as a transcontinental road, and finished some six or seven years afterward. This was the beginning of the nation which we feel sure Canada is well on her way to become.

When we introduced protection we found that it was just the policy to aid this national aspiration. The Opposition went to the country upon this issue, advocating unrestricted reciprocity, and the country would have none of it, determining that we should go on in our own way.

In 1896 the present Government came into power. What did they do? Did they claim that the national policy was bad for Canada, and that we should not have protection for our own industries? On the contrary, they began to improve this policy, and in 1897 reappealed the clause relating to reciprocity with the United States. They began the construction of the Canadian Northern Railway, and committed the country to the expenditure of hundreds of millions of dollars in furthering the principle of section 154 of the consolidation act. On this the whole country was then agreed; there was no dissent to making Canada a nation by having that railway run from east to west, every inch on Canadian soil, and to-day, gentlemen, the purpose and principle remain the same: the trade of Canada must not be deviated to other channels—Canada must not lose the trade which by national right belongs to Canada. [Cheers.]

As a member of Sir Wilfrid Laurier's party in 1896, I was proud to hear him state in patriotic language that the policy of his Administration would be this national policy. Reciprocity with the United States had then been repealed. I say, therefore, that the Liberal Government in 1911 is inconsistent in reviving it; it should be considered a dead letter. [Cheers.]

Here the speaker illustrated the antagonism between reciprocity and the national policy by exhibiting a map showing J. J. Hill's railway system.

Do you see all these spurs, these feeders, running up from the main line to the Canadian border? They are all there ready to go *over* the border, if this agreement goes into force, like a lot of snakes with their mouths open, waiting to devour our trade.

Why do we oppose this agreement—we Liberals, as well as the Conservatives? Because we are Canadians first and party men afterward. [Cheers.] It is not because the price of eggs or butter may be diminished. It is not because some parts of the country and some individuals may make a little money at the expense of other sections and persons, but because the whole principle of confederation is menaced. Our traffic should be with each other, and not with the people to the south of us—it should be across the seas to Great Britain and her colonies, if we are to hold our present proud position as the most important link in the world-encircling chain of British federation. [Applause.]

The speaker closed by quoting from speeches in Congress and editorials in newspapers of the United States advocating reciprocity as a step toward the annexation of Canada.

T. Chase Casgrain developed the closing theme of Mr. Lash. One-third of the population of western Canada, he said, was composed of immigrants from the United States. He had heard that in many places there the Stars and Stripes floated in place of the Union Jack; the good old British songs were forbidden in the schools; and the Fourth of July was celebrated in place of the King's birthday. (A voice: Shame!) These influences must be counteracted and the national ideal must be preserved.

What will be the result of this new policy inaugurated by Sir Wilfrid Laurier? We know what we now enjoy. Under the present system Canada has already become the most prosperous country in the world. Why not leave well enough alone? Why take a leap in the dark?

Our opponents answer that this attitude is that of the Chinese. If to be devoted to the interests of our country is Chinese, if to believe that its welfare is bound up in continuing our historic policy is Chinese, if to be firmly convinced that ours is the most prosperous nation in the world is Chinese, then all that I can say is that I am a Chinese with a pigtail. [Applause.]

Mr. Casgrain went on to make a local point by arguing that reciprocity in national products would be inevitably followed by reciprocity in manufactures to the ruination of rising industrial cities like Montreal. He also appealed to the racial feeling of the French Canadians, who formed a large part of his audience, by pointing them to the results of annexation to the United States which occurred in Louisiana. Let them take a lesson, he said, from the history of this old French province, which had now become Americanized, and where no French people had any rights.

Professor Leacock declared that the Government had acted in autocratic fashion in making the treaty with the United States, and it should be repudiated.

Shall two old gentlemen in a hurry sneak down to fat entertainments at Washington, and come back to us fellow citizens with a paper in their hands, and say: *"La chose est faite"*—the thing is done? Is this the way our democracy is to be conducted?

The professor then played upon the patriotism of his auditors, opposing to the admitted commercial advantages of the treaty the danger to national integrity lurking therein.

There is no gain in the treaty compared to the sacrifices. Shall the maritime provinces be sold for Boston novelties? We defy the Government to come before the country on this question. The very farmers, the Prince Edward Islanders, who hope to pocket two cents more a bushel for their potatoes by the treaty, would have uneasy consciences over its ratification.

I do not wish to speak any evil of the American Republic. The Americans are a great people, but fifty years ago we settled the question as to what our lot was to be with respect to them. We have decided once and for all that the British flag was good enough for us. [Cheers.]

We took this country when nobody wanted it; when it was *quelques arpents de neige*.[1] We made it our home, and, now that we have found that it is one of the greatest and noblest heritages, our sturdy American President [Mr. Taft] looks

[1] "Certain roods of snow."

over the wall, hoisted up with the block and tackle of his compatriots, and says: ''Lo, there is a fair land,'' and, turning
back to those who lifted him, remarks: ''We have made a mistake; this place is well worth having. Hither to me, my trusts,
and let us begin our onslaught upon the Dominion of Canada.
Come hither, all ye of the Minneapolis Millers' Association, and
my stalwarts of the paper trust, look what lies beyond the wall!''

And whom have we at Ottawa to look out for our interests?
Come down to us, Mr. Fielding, and tell us how we may sell
our potatoes and wheat, and with them the institutions which
we so dearly prize.

Mr. Sifton, the last speaker, was greeted with great
enthusiasm, and his speech was punctuated with applause
and cheering. He said that he and Mr. Lash and other
Liberals who opposed reciprocity, were consistent with
their party's policy—it was the Laurier Administration
that was inconsistent.

The fiscal policy of the Liberal party was partially settled
in 1897, when our tariff was fixed substantially as it is now.

In 1898 there was an attempt to secure reciprocal trade relations with the United States. Sir Wilfrid Laurier and his associates spent a considerable time in Washington, but returned
without having made any agreement.

In 1900 a general election was held in which the fiscal policy
of the government was discussed from one end of Canada to the
other, and the Liberal Government was retained in power by
large majorities in almost every section of the country.

In 1904 and 1908 the fiscal policy of the Government was
again discussed, and was similarly approved.

*At no one of these three general elections was there a syllable breathed in favor of reciprocity with the United States
by any member or spokesman of the Government.*

Mr. Sifton then analyzed the tariff of 1897, and
showed that under it the farmers were benefited, their
products having risen greatly in price, and their purchases by a little.

So there is no ground for the suggestion that our manufacturing population is exploiting the farming population; on the
contrary it appears the farmers are getting the better of it.

The question now is, Was the principle of reciprocity abandoned during all these years from 1897 to the present?

Sir Wilfrid Laurier says in Parliament that it was not abandoned—at least, that he was not conscious that it was abandoned. He says that it was held, not in abandonment, but in abeyance. [Laughter.]

When Mr. Laurier came back from Washington in 1898, after his abortive attempt to secure reciprocity, he gave out the following public statement:

If we know the hearts and minds of our people at present, I think I am not making too wide a statement when I say that the general feeling in Canada is not in favor of reciprocity. There was a time when Canadians would have given many things to obtain the American market. There was a time when the market of the great cities of the Union was the only market we had, but these days are past and over. We are not dependent on the American market now.

The speaker said that Mr. Laurier had repeated the substance of this declaration at various times from 1898 to 1909, giving, in the latter year, as justification for the Government's enormous expenditure on the Grand Trunk Pacific, the absolute necessity of rendering the Canadians independent of the Americans. Mr. Sifton therefore claimed that reciprocity had been definitely abandoned by Mr. Laurier's Administration, and was not "held in abeyance."

He then compared the industrial condition of Canada with that of the United States.

During the last twelve years we have had, with perhaps one exception, no break in our prosperity. There was in 1907 a falling off in our business to a certain extent, but it was not serious enough to be termed hard times.

On the other side of the line they have had at least three serious business depressions in the same period, that in 1907 amounting to a long-continued and widely extended panic, which was followed by great suffering, especially among the poorer classes, who were deprived of opportunities to labor.

The result of our tying ourselves up to the people to the south of us will be that we will go on enjoying our present prosperity until the next panic, when we will have the honor and the pleasure of joining them in their financial embarrassment.

The advocates of reciprocity say to us that it will give the Canadian farmers ninety millions of Americans to whom they can sell their products. In answer, we say that these ninety millions produce more agricultural products themselves than we do. For instance, in 1909 the United States exported over $400,-000,000 of food products, the chief items being $216,000,000 breadstuffs and $156,000,000 animal products, both of which products are exported by us.

In this export the United States is our stiffest competitor. I do not think that any business man would succeed for long who let a rival run his factory.

One of the effects of reciprocity is that it puts a premium on bad farming by encouraging shipping raw products of Canada to a foreign country, there to be worked up at a profit, and sent back to us at an advanced price. Now there is no country in the world that ever made a practice of continuously shipping raw products of the farm to other countries, and at the same time succeeded in retaining its own country in a condition of agricultural prosperity.

Mr. Sifton then spoke of the manufacture of paper, which under the fiscal policy of the province of Quebec was developing there to the great advantage of the laboring people, and claimed that this industry would be ruined by reciprocity.

The newspaper association of the United States wants to get our pulp wood. The publishers do not want paper so much as pulp. Now it has been shown in the debates at Quebec that the province gets ten times as much benefit from the manufacture of paper as from the export of the raw material. We are satisfied to let the American publishers get cheap paper, but we want the mills to be located here. [Applause.]

Mr. Sifton then dilated upon the power of the great flour mills of the American Northwest and of the Chicago meat-packers, and claimed that it would be impossible for the small Canadian enterprises in these lines to maintain their existence against the competition which reciprocity would afford. Of the packing business he said:

The meat trust may think for diplomatic reasons it is advisable to let a meat establishment live in Canada for a little while, but so far as living in competition with them is concerned we have not the slightest chance.

Of the railways he said:

The Canadian roads spend about fifty per cent. of cost of labor and materials in Canada. We are going to cut this off. By this treaty, which will carry trade north and south, we are going to take off a large slice of the earnings of our railways, and give it to the railroads of a foreign country.

Mr. Sifton next remarked upon the danger of entering upon a policy the continuance of which depended upon the will of an independent second party. The United States might abandon reciprocity.

Then we will have to go back to where we were twenty years ago, and start off all over again to build up our trade.

The President of the United States tells us that we are "at the parting of the ways." Let the people of Canada decide which way they will take, that toward dependenec or that toward independence. Let them record their franchise on this question, and do their duty by burying this proposition so deeply that no government in Canada will ever again make the mistake which our friends in the present government have done. [Tremendous applause.]

On March 25 a meeting in favor of reciprocity was held in the same hall. The speakers were W. S. Fielding, Minister of Finance, and one of the two negotiators of the treaty at Washington; Ralph Smith, M. P. for Nanaimo, B. C., and Sydney Fisher, Minister of Agriculture.

Mr. Fielding began the discussion. He first denied *in toto* the statement of Mr. Casgrain that he, Mr. Fielding, a member of the Canadian Government, was an advocate of annexation to the United States. Reciprocity between the two countries was simply a commercial affair that would be to the advantage of every section of the nation, and so bind its parts together. Montreal, for example, was interested in building up western Canada and so making a market for the manufactures and importations of the eastern metropolis. How would reci-

procity make the west more prosperous? The miners of
British Columbia were in favor of the measure since they
would have a new market for their coke, this being admitted free of duty into the United States. The prairie
provinces of Alberta and Saskatchewan, it was admitted,
were solidly in favor of reciprocity for the benefits to the
farmers it was expected to confer.

Mr. Fielding then replied to the criticism that the
Government had received no mandate for making the
reciprocity treaty.

Sir, we have a mandate. [Cheers.] We have the mandate
of fifty years of Canadian history. There is a dividing line;
there is a point at which the history must begin. That point
has been chosen by one of the opponents of reciprocity, and I
will take him at his choice. You have all read, I am sure, the
letter of an enterprising citizen of Montreal, and one whom we
all respect as an enterprising citizen, Sir William Van Horne.
[Cheers.] Sir William Van Horne said:

"The other day, Mr. Fielding in a cable dispatch to the Canadian High
Commissioner in London, said that for fifty years the people of Canada,
in both political parties, had wished for reciprocity. That was true—"

[Cheers.]
But you must let me finish that sentence.

"That was true," said Sir William, "in the sixties and the seventies,
but it has not been true since."

[Cheers.]
I am glad there are some to applaud because I want to hold
them responsible for Sir William Van Horne's words.
Against that statement of Sir William I read the following
clause from the Statutes of Canada in the year 1880:

Here Mr. Fielding read a standing offer to abolish the
duty on virtually all important agricultural, animal, and
sea products imported from the United States when that
country abolished duties on similar Canadian products.

In 1886 the Statutes of Canada were revised, and that standing offer was crystallized into a permanent law. Yet Sir William
says that nobody wanted reciprocity in the eighties. Which tes-

timony will you receive, my good friends—Sir William's or that of the law books of the Dominion of Canada.

In 1888 Sir Charles Tupper went to Washington in behalf of the Canadian Government to seek reciprocity. So anxious was he for the agreement that he offered, as an extra inducement, free fishing privileges in Canada. But he was turned down. At this time we have formed a treaty without this concession on our part. [Cheers.]

Sir William Van Horne says that nobody wanted reciprocity in the nineties. Well, in a speech from the throne at the opening of Parliament, April 3, 1894, I read as follows:

My advisers, availing themselves of opportunities which were presented in the closing months of last year, caused the Administration of the United States to be reminded of the willingness of the Government of Canada to join in making efforts for the extension and development of the trade between the Republic and the Dominion, as well as for the friendly adjustment of those matters of international character which remained unsettled. I am pleased to say that these representations have resulted in the assurance that in October next the Government of the United States will be prepared to consider the best means of arriving at a practical solution of these important questions.

That was the last speech Sir John Macdonald ever put in the mouth of the Governor-General. Not many weeks later he passed away, and others took his place. Again we find that the Conservative Government lived up to its traditions on that question, for they also declared that they were anxious for reciprocity. In the tariff act of 1894, the last tariff act of the Conservative Government, they put on the Statute Book another standing offer, not so broad as the previous one, but of very much the same kind.

And so we have this conclusively proved that, not in the ancient history of Canada, but down to the last day upon which the Conservative party ruled this Dominion, they were and proclaimed themselves to be advocates of reciprocity. In the elections of 1891 Sir John Macdonald criticized and assailed the wider policy of his opponents, but the Conservative party at that time declared everywhere that they were the champions of reciprocity, and in that campaign the chief Conservative organ, the Toronto *Mail and Empire,* made the statement that there had been ten offers of reciprocity to the United States, and nine of them had been made by the Conservative Government.

Well, the Conservative Government passed away and the Liberal Government came into power. [Cheers.] The Liberal party had, at its convention in 1893, declared in the most positive terms that one plank in the platform of the Liberal party was that they wanted reciprocity. Here are the words of the resolution passed at the Liberal convention in 1893:

That a fair and liberal reciprocity treaty would develop the great natural resources of Canada, would enormously increase trade and commerce between the two countries, would tend to encourage friendly relations between the two peoples, would remove many causes which have in the past provoked irritation and trouble to the Governments of both countries, and would promote those kindly relations between the Empire and the Republic which afford the best guaranty for peace and prosperity.

That was the Liberal policy on reciprocity. But it has been said in a meeting held last week in this hall that the Liberal party had abandoned reciprocity in the tariff of 1897. Well, sir, the Liberal party at that date did not adopt the policy of the standing offer, because they did not think that was the best way, but in the very speech which, as Minister of Finance, I had the honor to make in bringing down the tariff of 1897, I said:

The Ottawa platform pledged the Liberal party to use all honorable efforts to bring about better trade relations with the United States. We have already taken the first step in that direction by commissioning two ministers of this government to visit Washington and make known the fact —if it is necessary to make it known—that Canada is willing to negotiate with our American neighbors for a fair and reasonable reciprocity treaty.

Was that abandoning reciprocity? [Cries of No.] Then I went on to say:

If our American friends wish to make a treaty with us we are willing to meet them and treat on fair and equitable terms. If it shall not please them to do that, we shall in one way regret the fact, but shall nevertheless go on our way rejoicing and find other markets to build up the prosperity of Canada independent of the American people.

Now, I have shown you that, through all these years when our good friend Sir William Van Horne said nobody in Canada wanted reciprocity with the United States, every public man of prominence on both sides of politics was declaring that he desired it. [Cheers.] Our American friends did not meet our advances in the spirit in which we thought they were entitled to be received, and there grew up in Canada a feeling, first of regret and afterward perhaps of resentment, at what we regarded as unfair treatment. Then we ceased to look to Washington for reciprocity. It was not because reciprocity had ceased to be desirable, but because we saw no indication that we would get it. The economic facts did not change, and if reciprocity was a desirable thing in 1897 it was equally desirable in the year 1898 and so on for the intervening years.

A VOICE.—No.

MR. FIELDING.—What change had happened? Does my friend over there think that since 1897 the conditions in Canada changed so much that we did not need reciprocity?

THE VOICE.—Hear, hear.

MR. FIELDING.—Then, what he means to say is that reciprocity was needed desperately when the Tories were in power, but when the bright sun of prosperity came under Liberal rule Canada did not need reciprocity. [Cheers.]

Then we are told that this reciprocity agreement came as a great shock to the country; it was a bolt from the blue; everybody was astonished. Well, let us again see what the facts are. Just one year ago there were some negotiations at Washington. It would occupy too much time to explain just how the difficulty of that time arose, but we had some negotiations with the United States and we turned a very uncomfortable corner and brought happiness to the great mass of business people in Canada, who had been very much alarmed. At that time, arising out of these negotiations, the President of the United States through his Secretary of State declared that it was his desire that we should enter into negotiations for reciprocal trade arrangements. The government of Canada replied that they were glad to find the Americans in a better frame of mind, and that we would be very happy to discuss the question with them. Now, mark, if that was all wrong, if we did not need reciprocity, if that was a disloyal proceeding, why did not our good friends of the Conservative party meet us right there and say: "No, you must not do it, we do not want reciprocity." What happened? The arrangement we have had made at Washington—not for reciprocity, but that which has been called the foundation of these later proceedings—was adopted by a unanimous vote in the House of Commons. To-day there are men who will come on the platform and tell you that it was a bad arrangement. What a great pity it is that we cannot be as wise in advance as we are when we look behind!

At the opening of Parliament in November, 1910, a passage was inserted in the speech from the throne stating that we were carrying on these negotiations and that we hoped they might result in success. Was anybody shocked then? No. That was the time to be alarmed if there was any cause for alarm, but instead of that we found that members of the House on the Conservative side were disposed to say that it would be a very good thing if we could make a satisfactory statement, but that they did not think we could succeed. [Cheers and laughter.] But we did succeed, and that was the "shock" to our Conservative friends.

Mr. Fielding then turned to the anti-reciprocity argument of the danger of interfering with the present prosperity of Canada.

Very ugly things are said just now about reciprocity. But the worst is not so bad as what Sir Charles Tupper said about the tariff policy of the Laurier Government when it was first introduced. If after a few years the Conservatives can forget all the ugly things they said, and can now come before a public meeting, and say: "We take it all back, the tariff policy of the government is lovely, and the country is prospering splendidly"; don't you think I have the right to expect that in about five or six years hence there will be a meeting in this hall and some good Conservative will tell you about the blessings of reciprocity and say that everything is lovely?

Now, this reciprocity agreement is chiefly confined to natural products, to the very things that were in the standing offer of the Conservative party for some years. If the public men of Canada, Liberal and Tory alike, for fifty years have not been fools, reciprocity in natural products is a good thing for this country. [Cheers.]

But what about the manufactures? This agreement should show to every intelligent manufacturer who reads it that manufacturing interests were carefully guarded. [Applause.] It is on public record—Mr. Taft, President of the United States, stated it in a speech a week ago—that his instructions to his commissioners were to offer Canada free trade in manufactures. I have no doubt he gave these instructions, but they never made a formal proposal of that character. They never were permitted to get near enough for that purpose. [Cheers.] We told them frankly at the beginning that in the matter of natural products we could meet them on even terms, but we said: "When it comes to manufactures we have to be more careful; we frankly admit that with your greater capital and your specialized organizations you are more than the equals of us in your manufacturing power, and we are not prepared to make a treaty with you including any wide range of manufactured goods.'' [Cheers.]

But it is said there are some manufactures on the list. Take up the whole list of free manufactures that you find in that agreement and you will discover that they are already in every case, or nearly so, free in Canada, and the only change made is that we are getting them free into the United States. How can that hurt us?—surely we are no worse off.

The manufacturers are not hurt; they are more frightened than hurt. [Applause.] I give it to you as my opinion,, worth much or worth little, that, if by the forces of the manufacturers this agreement be destroyed, there will grow up in the Western country a feeling that will be dangerous to the manufacturing interests of Canada and dangerous to the welfare of this Dominion. [Applause.]

It is urged very strongly that if we give free trade in agricultural products we cannot help giving free trade in manufactures. Now, to begin with, if that argument is used by a Conservative, it is a severe arraignment of the national policy, because the national policy, in the same act which established high protective duties, gives a standing offer of reciprocity in natural products. It is reasonable to suppose that when you put the farmer's products on the free list you do not sacrifice him, you satisfy him. He is asking you to have free trade in natural products, because, although there may be some little disadvantage locally, he knows he gets compensation in the larger markets of the United States. But that is not so with the manufacturer. With the great power and capital and specialized organization of the Americans they can, as a rule, beat us in manufacture. And if we were to have free trade in manufactures we would undoubtedly close up many of the factories of Canada. Well, we want factories in Canada. [Cheers.] We have guarded them in the past. [Cheers.] You manufacturers were told by the Conservatives in 1897 that if you trusted your fate to the Liberal Government dreadful things would happen. Did they happen? To-day you are teeming with prosperity as you see. Trust us again. [Cheers.]

Just a few words more and I will close.

Annexation! Is it not a scandal and a shame that our opponents should talk annexation? I read the other day a headline in the Montreal *Star* to a cable from England——

A VOICE.—Sorry you had nothing better to do.

MR. FIELDING.—It was a scare headline and it caught my
eye. [Laughter.] It read: "Annexation hurts our issues,"
referring to the issues of securities in London. Now, if annexation hurts our issues who is responsible for it? The friends of
reciprocity are not talking of annexation. [Hear, hear!] It is
the opponents of reciprocity who are waving the flag—Heaven
help us that the flag should be used for such a miserable purpose. [Cheers.] We are told that if we trade with the Americans we shall cease to be loyal; we are told that if we buy
and sell with them we shall impair our loyalty. That's it, is it
not?

SEVERAL VOICES.—That's it.

MR. FIELDING.—There comes back to my mind a memorable
scene of my childhood days. It is the summer of 1860, nearly
fifty-one years ago. All British America is astir with interest
for the coming of the future King. The young Prince of Wales
lands at Halifax. A procession is formed, and passes down
through the streets. The housetops and windows are filled with
loyal people, who with flag and wreath and loyal motto welcome
the prince, while cheering thousands hail him as he passes along.
Why do I recall this scene to-night? It is because that splendid demonstration of loyalty and devotion to the throne and person of our sovereign occurred in the very midst of the period of
the old reciprocity treaty. [Cheers.] We had bought from the
Americans and we had sold to the Americans. We had traveled to and fro and met them in all the walks of commercial
and social life. But it never occurred to anybody to say that we
ceased to be loyal. The scene in my native city of Halifax was
repeated throughout every province of this country. And then
something else of interest happened. Friendly trade relations
with the United States had brought about friendly relations in
other respects. The young prince was asked to cross the border
and visit the American people. He accepted the invitation and
traveled through a large section of the American nation and
received everywhere from the people the utmost respect. The
prince returned to the Motherland to tell the story of the happiness, contentment, prosperity, and loyalty of the Queen's subjects in British America, and of their happy and friendly relations with the people of the great republic. History will repeat
itself. There is a young prince to-day in training for his duties as our future King. He will come out to Canada one of
these days, as his grandfather, Edward the Peacemaker, came.
I trust he will come in the midst of the new period of reciprocity, and then he will be able to testify as his grandfather

did: That the people of this country, trading though they are with the Americans, buying and selling and dealing with them, are nevertheless more devoted than ever to the throne and person of our gracious sovereign. [Cheers.]

Ralph Smith opposed the doctrine of Mr. Sifton that lumber should not be sent out of the country.

If we should not send lumber out of the country, then we should not send coal out of the country, and if we should not send coal and lumber out of the country we should not send fish out of the country. I am simply driving my friend, Mr. Sifton, to the logical conclusion of his argument; if it was reasonable to build a wall around Canada and say, "Canada for Canadians," if that is his policy, then we will deteriorate as a nation. Why, there is no man that has goods to sell to-day in Canada that would not be glad to sell them to the United States or to any other foreign country if he could get a better price.

Now, I come to the coke industry. What is free coke going to do? What is the position of that industry now? It has been demonstrated within the last two years that the deposits of bituminous coal in British Columbia are the largest in the world. The deposits of coal in Alberta and British Columbia, in point of quality and quantity, are not equaled by those of any other nation on the earth. Are you not going to permit us to send our coal to the Yankee, if he wants it? We cannot live if you do not. British Columbia was exporting coal fifty years ago. Where did she send it? She sent it to San Francisco, and, if we could not have got it into the United States even against a high duty, there would have been no British Columbia in the Confederation in 1870 to pay the majority of the taxes for the Canadian people in 1911.

Now, what does that mean to British Columbia? The State of Washington has absolutely no coal that can be manufactured into coke. As a result of taking the duty of one dollar a ton off coke, all the great foundries and smelters in the Western States are going to use our product and then we will practically have a monopoly of the great markets of the American West for British Columbia coke manufactured out of British Columbia coal by British Columbia labor at good wages.

Let me look for a minute at this agreement with reference to its effect upon the consumer. The consumer represents the great interest of this country. The argument has been put up by a few people—How are you going to increase the price to the

XII—30

farmer, and reduce the cost to the consumer? You must remember that in Canada we have a great agricultural country, that we have millions of acres of the richest land in the world. The opponents of this measure say that if the United States take our natural products it is going to create a strong demand for these commodities and the result will be that these natural products will be dear. That is the argument. But you must remember that simultaneously with the finding of the market for our agricultural products in the United States you will have the greatest development of agricultural production in this Dominion that has ever taken place. The very fact that you have millions of acres of land, the very fact that you create a market in the United States, and consequently create an extraordinary demand, will bring about an enormously increased investment of capital in agricultural land and an enormously increased production of agricultural commodities which will operate in favor of the consumers of this country. British Columbia consumes thirty millions worth of agricultural products a year and she produces only fourteen and a half millions a year. If the working men of British Columbia, who are engaged in or enter into these industries can get their food supplies at less cost, they will be able to buy more articles from the merchants and manufacturers in Montreal.

Mr. Smith then discussed the question of annexation. He denied that an increase of commerce with the United States would tend toward political incorporation into that country. Pointing to the cumulative growth in recent years of the business transacted between Canada and the United States, even without a reciprocity treaty, he asked if it had made the Canadians less loyal to their country than when the trade with their southern neighbors was meager.

I need not say, ladies and gentlemen, that the independence of this country and our connection with Britain do not depend, as history proves, upon any principle of trade. If they did, we would have been annexed years ago. How is it that we did three hundred and fifty million dollars' worth of business with the Americans without anybody ever suggesting that we were going to have annexation, and how is it that because we prefer to get another million dollars' worth of trade we are going headlong to the devil of annexation? There is nothing in the argument. The only American of importance that I ever heard say with any emphasis that we were likely to be annexed to the United States, was Champ Clark. I beg the pardon of my friend, Mr. Foster, and of my friend Mr. Borden when I say that Champ Clark has as much right to say that as they have, and as little basis for saying it. Gentlemen, I will never think that an increase of friendliness with Uncle Sam will interfere with my respect for the old parent, John Bull, for one minute. It is a slander on the loyalty and independence of this country. Mr. Gladstone once said: "Liberalism consists in trust in the people, qualified by prudence; Toryism consists in distrust in the people qualified by fear." That statement was made thirty years ago, and it is absolutely true to-day. Who are the fearful men in this country? [Cries of "The Tories."]

MR. SMITH.—Why, the Tories, of course. Who are the men who are willing to trust the people? [Cries of "We are" and "the Liberals."]

MR. SMITH.—The Liberals, of course. Ladies and gentlemen, any trade arrangement between the United States and Canada is a mere incident in the great Anglo-Saxon movement. The democracy of England have three times said: We will not permit you to tax the food supplies of this country. The democracy of Germany have risen almost to rebellion because of the cost of living and the small increase in wages. The democracy of the United States have scared the Republican President, the protectionist Republican President, to look after the interests of the people, as against the trusts of that country. Will statesmen in Canada read the writing on the wall? Mr. Taft was pretty nearly too late, but it did not take him long to get into line when the democracy spoke. The democracy of this country insist that no special privileges shall be given to the trusts that terrorize and interfere with the rights and liberties of the citizens, and one of the best things that Mr. Fielding did was to make free the food of the people of this country. He has left the protection to the manufacturers, and they will profit by the larger production of food products.

Mr. Fisher declared that the interests of Canada had been fully guaranteed in the reciprocity agreement.

It has been commonly said throughout Canada that if the Americans wanted reciprocal dealings with us they should bring down their tariff to our tariff.

By the agreement the American duty on every article in it is brought down to the exact equivalent of the Canadian tariff. [Cheers.]

Again, this agreement has been brought about, not by a pilgrimage from Canada to Washington, but by a pilgrimage from Washington to Ottawa. We have been told that the Liberal party had deserted the reciprocity plank in their platform. We are told that since 1898, when Sir Wilfrid Laurier sent two of his ministers to Washington to obtain a reciprocity agreement, and the Americans turned the cold shoulder upon that offer, Sir Wilfrid has said: No more pilgrimages to Washington to secure reciprocity. That dictum of the leader of the Canadian people has been absolutely fulfilled. [Cheers.]

We left the American people to change their opinion of their own free will; we left them to come to Ottawa and ask us to resume the negotiations which in 1898 they had broken off somewhat abruptly. And, ladies and gentlemen, the result is that to-day we have reciprocity on Canada's conditions; reciprocity absolutely such as Canada has been wanting, absolutely such as Canada has been willing for all along. [Cheers.] And we have that reciprocity as the result of a request from Washington, and of friendly overtures which were made by the American Government to us.

Let me say a word in regard to the condition of affairs when that overture was made. The President of the United States, impressed by the agitation against the high cost of living in the United States, impressed with the necessity of overcoming in that country the mistake which was made when the Payne-Aldrich tariff, which was not received with favor by the people of the United States, was passed, felt it was necessary to do something to open to the people of that country the hope of lessening the cost of living, and he turned to reciprocity with this country.

We have heard much about annexation. It has been held up to us as a bugaboo to frighten the people. This is a line of argument which is very characteristic of our friends, but I want to say in solemn earnestness, and as a warning to the men who have so recklessly and unwarrantably raised this question before the people of Canada that to-day there is no annexation sentiment in Canada. Why? Because we have a prosperous and contented people, and we know that revolution cannot raise its head where the people are well off and contented. Annexation would be revolution.

I would say, however, that, if the Canadian people are to be divided, into one class in the East, selfishly looking to their own interests, and one class in the West, and these men in the West are to be deprived of the opportunity to sell where they can sell best, they may insist on having it by annexation. I tell you that the men who are raising this cry here to-day, in the lightness of their heart, and the ignorance of their thought, are playing with fire; that, if it were once kindled, might destroy the fabric of this great and glorious Dominion, that we have been laying the foundation of and carrying on to its highest development. They talk about it being disloyal to trade with the Americans. They say that the farmer who sells a cow across the line is doing what he ought not to do in the interest of the empire, they say that a farmer who sells a tub of butter, a chicken, or an egg on the other side of the line is guilty of disloyalty to the empire. What do they do? I have a little list of some of the things in which we trade with the United States. I will give some of them. We bought one and a half million dollars' worth of automobiles from the United States. I have no doubt that the members of the Anti-Reciprocity League bought some of them.

The people of Canada bought sixteen million dollars' worth of coal from the United States. Why? It is disloyal to trade with the United States. You can buy coal in Nova Scotia, you can buy coal in British Columbia, and you can buy coal in Alberta. Why do these disloyal anti-Imperialists, and, according to this argument, annexationists, buy sixteen million dollars' worth of coal?

There are cotton factories here in Canada. Now, what do you think these people do? Do in the interest of their industry, do in the interest of their trade, do because it is the most profitable thing for them, so that they may pay larger and larger dividends on their highly protected product? What did they do? They went to the United States and bought nine million dollars' worth of raw cotton.

A VOICE.—We do not grow cotton.

MR. FISHER.—No, we do not grow cotton, but this, say the opponents of reciprocity, is an imperial question, and Egypt and India, parts of the empire, grow cotton. My friend down there is no doubt one of the Anti-Reciprocity Imperialists. He, however, cannot include the whole empire in his view. When it comes to a question of buying cotton he has no fear of annexation, and makes his purchases in the United States.

But there are other things. Of drugs and dyes we bought seven million dollars' worth from the United States, and of electrical appliances three million dollars' worth. We have a large number of electrical establishments in Canada. How is it, then, that people go and buy three million dollars' worth of electrical apparatus from our hated rivals on the other side of the line? They are disloyal not only to the empire, but even to Canada.

Of furs we purchased three million dollars' worth, of rubber five million dollars' worth, and of hats one and a quarter million dollars' worth. I do not know whether these were men's hats or ladies' hats, but I would like to implore the Anti-Reciprocity League and the ladies never to buy their hats in future from the United States. Of leather hides we purchased three million dollars' worth, and of copper three million dollars' worth. We produce copper in Canada; we have some of the best copper mines in the world.

A Voice.—Owned by the Yankees.

Mr. Fisher.—Very likely, but still employing Canadian labor and producing Canadian wealth. We have been able to attract American capital over to Canada, and I hope to annex a very large portion of it, which, I suppose, is just as disloyal as it is to sell them an ox or a horse.

I said a few minutes ago what might happen if the question as between the East and the West were raised. It has been the glory of the Liberal party, led by Sir Wilfrid Laurier, so to regulate our policy and our administration as to bind not only different nationalities and creeds together, but to bind the different sections of this country from one ocean to the other in one great harmonious whole. When Mr. Fielding first amended the tariff of Canada fourteen years ago, we were told, even before we came into power, what folly it was for us to say that we could reduce the duties and raise the revenue. Mr. Fielding introduced in his tariff of 1897 reduced duties on a large number of individual items, and put a large number of items, chiefly the needs of the farmers and laboring classes, on the free list. When he had done that in a large measure, he introduced British preference and he cut a lot of the duties down on articles in which we trade with the Motherland, first by 12½ per cent. and then by 25 per cent. and then by 33 per cent. and produced a constantly growing and larger revenue. We have gone on from that day to this always carrying out the principal of the Liberal party in tariff adjustment, lowering the incidence of taxation upon the consuming classes, and at the same time so doing it by a proper, skillful, and scientific adjustment of the duties on individual items of the tariff on manufactured articles and raw material, that the industrial classes have prospered, advanced, and progressed in a way that was never dreamed of before in the history of the country.

To-day we are taking another step in the same direction. We are reducing the scale of duties upon a larger number of things that are imported into and exported from Canada. For the first time in the history of this country we have a say, a voice, in the arrangement of the American tariff. It is a tribute to this country that we have reached that stage of progress and advancement in which our great American neighbors find that we are a people to be reckoned with, and they come to us and ask us to barter and to treat in the adjustment of their own tariff, as we are doing in the adjustment of our own. Is this an occasion for Canadians to feel humility? Is this an occasion for Canadians to feel lack of confidence in their country and in their nation? No, this is one of the greatest tributes Canada has ever received at the hands of a foreign land.

In doing that we are accepting the right hand of fellowship which was held out to us a year ago, and I believe that we were not only wise, but that we were right in doing that instead of inviting the big stick of the maximum, non-intercourse item of the Payne-Aldrich tariff.

What is the condition to-day of international affairs the world over? We see overtures being made by one nation and another in favor of closer relations, amity, and friendship. Our great American neighbor has made a proposal to the head of the British Empire for a general treaty of arbitration, a step in favor of peace and good-will upon earth such as has never been known before in the history of the world. We have seen the foreign office in England, in the words of that great statesman, Sir Edward Grey, welcoming this overture from the American nation. We have heard the universal pæan, the cry of admiration, that has gone up from the friends of peace the world over, that the two great Anglo-Saxon nations are in favor of universal peace. Seeing them join hands, are you men who are trying to decry this reciprocity arrangement prepared to invite Canada to block this advance step toward an *entente* between America and the British Empire?

I appeal to you people here in the great city of Montreal, the great commercial center which has been built up and developed in its industrial production and its commercial interests by the tariff policy of Mr. Fielding and the Liberal Government to believe that in the future, as in the past, we will guard your interests while we are doing what is necessary in the interest of the other parts of the Dominion and of every class in the Dominion. That has been the keynote of the Liberal policy—the lowering of the tariff, and the maintenance of industry. We can do this as we did it in 1897. We reduced the duties to a moderate level, while at the same time maintaining and increasing the revenue. To-day we are giving an increased market to the farmers of Canada, moderating the exclusive tariff of the United States against our products, and at the same time safeguarding the industrial and commercial interests of the country. You people are afraid; you believe that we cannot do what the Tories have failed to do. We have shown you that we were able to do it in the past, we know that we can do it in the future, and it is our determination, with the backing and support of the people of Canada to carry this as a crown to the glorious work that Sir Wilfrid Laurier has done not only for Canada but for the empire and the world.